BINDING

Vol. V

The binding design on this volume is an authorized facsimile of the original art binding on the official Polish copy of the Versailles Peace Treaty, which was signed by President Pilsudski and Premier Paderewski and deposited in the Archives of the new Government of Poland.

THE GREAT EVENTS

OF

THE GREAT WAR

A COMPREHENSIVE AND READABLE SOURCE RECORD OF THE
WORLD'S GREAT WAR, EMPHASIZING THE MORE IMPORTANT
EVENTS, AND PRESENTING THESE AS COMPLETE NARRATIVES
IN THE ACTUAL WORDS OF THE CHIEF OFFICIALS AND MOST
EMINENT LEADERS

NON-PARTISAN   NON-SECTIONAL   NON-SECTARIAN

PRESENTING DOCUMENTS FROM GOVERNMENT ARCHIVES AND
OTHER AUTHORITATIVE SOURCES, WITH OUTLINE NARRATIVES,
INDICES, CHRONOLOGIES, AND COURSES OF READING ON SOCIO-
LOGICAL MOVEMENTS AND INDIVIDUAL NATIONAL ACTIVITIES

EDITOR-IN-CHIEF

CHARLES F. HORNE, Ph.D.

DIRECTING EDITOR

WALTER F. AUSTIN, LL.M.

With a staff of specialists

VOLUME V

National Alumni

CONTENTS

VOLUME V—1917

AMERICA ROUSED AT LAST

CONTENTS

CONTENTS

ILLUSTRATIONS

VOLUME V

1917
AMERICA ROUSED AT LAST

AN OUTLINE NARRATIVE OF

HOW RUSSIA FELL, AND WESTERN EUROPE HELD THE LINE UNTIL AMERICA CAME

BY CHARLES F. HORNE

NOT since the opening months of the Great War had there been such varied ups and downs, such wide alternations of confidence and despair, as swept men's minds during the changeful year of 1917. The terrible misery born of the War, the desolation which it was spreading over the whole of Europe, had gradually raised up against Civilization another foe, a survival from the forgotten days of beasthood, an ancient rival more horrible than the specter of German domination. This second hideous monster, which now began to display its growing strength, was Anarchy. Everywhere the ignorant masses were losing faith in a civilization which brought them only starvation and this seemingly endless slaughter. What wonder if they listened to each trickster, each dreamer, each madman who promised them an easy and immediate escape from the welter of blood in which the ancient civilization seemed perishing!

Germany, now in desperate case, sought to take advantage of the growth of this senseless monster, reborn of ignorance and despair. Could he not be lured into dealing his drunken blows in aid of Germany's battle? Germany thought herself the nation least likely to suffer from mob violence; her trained and obedient army could always crush a mob. And was not Autocracy the natural antithesis to result from mankind's revulsion against Anarchy? So the German Government began playing at the dangerous game of feeding fat a devil-thing in hope of using it. By cunning propaganda the Germans encouraged anarchy everywhere among their foes; until the new monster had made the desolation of the universe double what it was before. Civilization stumbled as near to destruction from the one beast as from the other; and in the end Germany also had to suffer from this second monster she had bred.

In 1917, however, Anarchy seemed to work wholly in her service. It caused the two great Ally disasters of the year; first, the complete disappearance of the mighty Russian army and collapse of the Russian front; and second, the temporary crumbling of an Italian army, which almost wrought similar disaster in the West.

At the opening of the year Germany had no hope of such an ally. Her position seemed to her leaders desperate. For their people they still kept up their boast of many victories; but for themselves they knew that another year like 1916 meant their complete defeat. If the Allies had the will to continue such destructive fighting as that of Verdun, the Somme, the Isonzo and the long battling on the Russian front, then the Allies could afford the awful sacrifice of life and the stupendous expenditure of ammunition as Germany could not. Nowhere could she break through the encircling ring; and not for long could she persuade her deluded people to continue in the hopeless death-fight.

THE RENEWED SUBMARINE WARFARE

Therefore at the beginning of 1917 Germany, or her leaders, resolved to make an effort in a new direction—the submarine. In the previous year she had abandoned her submarine destruction of neutral ships partly because of the American ultimatum demanding it, partly because her stock of submarines had been sadly depleted by the British navy. But now she had built new and much more powerful U-boats. She had tested the strength of these, and she had good reason to hope that by turning them loose to destroy every ship in European waters, she might really starve Britain, as the British blockade was seeking to starve Germany.[1]

No question of the righteousness of such destruction of

[1] See § I, "Germany Defies the Neutral Nations," by Bernstorff, etc.

neutral people bothered the German leaders. We have told our story of this deadly War to little purpose if the reader has not fully realized that German Kultur was wholly committed to the Nietzschian doctrine that there is no right but German might, that the superman seeks success by whatsoever means, and that honor and truth and mercy and the equal rights of other men are but words to juggle with in outplaying an opponent. Not only did the German leaders act upon this basis, but they took it for granted that all other men did the same. In studying an opponent they always asked, "Just what is the falsity in his words, and what the private profit which will direct his action?" So now, their only doubt about their renewed submarine attack was, how would the neutrals take it. Would the United States Government really stand by its ultimatum of 1916, and go to war for a mere principle? Germany thought not.

She saw that American merchants and manufacturers were growing wealthy on the profits of the War. She knew that President Wilson had just been reëlected by the American laboring masses on the slogan "He kept us out of War!" Surely he would strive to continue in popularity by continuing to avoid the fight. Moreover, the German leaders looked also to the other alternative. Even if these comfortable and prosperous Americans should be so angered as to plunge foolishly into the war, surely they were not to be dreaded. Few of them would care really to fight in person; and their government, being a Democracy, would not force them to enlist. Theirs would be but an amateur war-making. The utter and universal sacrifice to which Europe had been bowed perforce, these Americans could not be expected to assume voluntarily, merely of their own judgment and desire. Britain was the arch-enemy, the mighty pillar of strength on which the rest of Europe now leaned; and submarine destruction might bring Britain to her knees long before America's Democracy could be roused to any forceful action.

So, falsely reasoning upon American selfishness and narrowness and stupidity, Germany on January 3, 1917, proclaimed her new U-boat campaign of universal destruction. At the same time she planned to make her year on land one of merely defensive fighting. She would save her war-worn soldiers all she could, so that they might still be strong, and might triumphantly enforce her will, when Britain should be exhausted and ready to abandon the European continent to Germany.

Thus the first great military movement of the year was the remarkable "Hindenburg retreat." During the winter the German armies of the west under Hindenburg's command deliberately planned to evacuate a considerable section of the French territory which they had held for over two years. This was in the Somme region where both British and French had been so vigorously attacking them. There the long trench lines wound in and out with many angles, just as the last assault had left them. By a general withdrawal a much stronger line could be made, and a much shorter one, requiring not nearly so many troops to defend it.

Gradually therefore, Hindenburg, or really his able chief-of-staff, Ludendorff, directed the withdrawal of all his stores and almost all his men to the great "Hindenburg Line" of strong defenses; and when late in February the British launched attacks against the old trench line they found it but lightly held. They soon realized the truth, and then step by step and often at bitter cost from the machine guns which lay in wait for them, they pressed on, until by mid-March they found before them the new and sterner defenses.[1]

In this retreat, the Germans had turned the land they left into an utter desert. Part of this desolation had a military excuse. It was intended to make the French and British occupation more difficult and to leave the foe only an utterly unsheltered region from which to attack the Hindenburg line. In part, however, the destruction was openly malevolent; that is, it was planned so as to ruin France through all the years of peace that might come afterward. This destruction without military value was held by France as one of her severest indictments against German crimi-

[1] See § II, "The Hindenburg Retreat in France," by Rosner, etc.

nality, the wrong for which she most demanded recompense after the War.

The very successful Hindenburg retreat was celebrated by the Germans as a triumph. They knew that both France and Britain had been grimly determined to keep up the terrible "Somme fighting" of the preceding fall, that huge preparations had been made and that, as soon as the spring weather permitted, a tremendous assault was to have been begun against them. Now, they had made all these preparations of no value. The Allies, however, were not wholly disconcerted. The new Hindenburg line had been built from the city of Arras on the north to St. Quentin on the south. The Britons now began an attack at Arras, while the French launched one to the south of St. Quentin along the Aisne River.

Neither of these huge but perhaps somewhat too hastily arranged attacks met with any large success. The Britons began the Arras battle with a successful assault on "Vimy Ridge," in which the Canadian regiments won widespread fame.[1] Moreover such was the concentration of the long prepared British bombardment of Vimy Ridge, that the whole summit was literally obliterated. No earlier year had seen such a deluge of great shells. It necessitated another innovation in military tactics. No trench could be permanently held against a foe who could thus annihilate it. The old deep trenches were supplanted by widespread systems of slighter defenses, meant to be costly in the taking rather than to be permanently held. Beyond Vimy the British attack died down with enormous bloodshed on both sides, but little further progress.

In June the Britons made another valiant and spectacular effort. South of their old battle ground of Ypres lay a long hill known as Messines Ridge.[2] The Germans had held it for two years, and from its summit their guns "strafed" all the Ypres sector savagely. For over a year British engineers patiently mined an underground way to reach beneath the ridge. They stored tons and tons of explosives in their

[1] See § IX, "Canada Storms Vimy Ridge," by Gibbs, etc.
[2] See § XIII, "The Man-made Earthquake," by Haig, etc.

deep-dug galleries, and at last, on June 7th, they blew up the mine. Never elsewhere has man created such an earthquake. The ground rocked for leagues. The whole top of the ridge was blown off. British troops easily seized possession of the shattered hills held only by the fragments of the dead defenders. Yet even then the indomitable Germans charged up the eastern slopes in an effort to regain the still quivering ground. They were driven back, and Britain held Messines Ridge. The German casualties for that single day exceeded thirty thousand. But beyond Messines the British could not gain.

The French attack along the Aisne was an even more costly hurricane of slaughter.[1] General Nivelle, the successor of Joffre, believed that he could really break the German line, that previous efforts had failed because they had not been pushed to the bitter end. He, therefore, on April 16th launched his tremendous attack. The Germans had expected it, were fully prepared, and repulsed the assailants with terrific losses. Still Nivelle persisted, and France suffered here her chief disaster of the war. Even the long enduring poilus protested at last. There were impressive scenes of despairing mutiny, carefully hidden until after the War. Nivelle was hastily replaced by another general, Pétain; but only after months of effort did Pétain succeed in bringing his forces back to their high efficiency.

THE FIRST RUSSIAN REVOLUTION

While Germany was thus making good her policy of defense upon the western front, events happened both in the east and in America which totally changed her plans of war. In the east came the Russian Revolution. This took place really in three stages. First came the revolution of March, in which Democracy overthrew Autocracy. Then came the revolution of July, in which Socialism supplanted Democracy; and then the revolution of November, in which Anarchy triumphed over Socialism.

As only the first of these preceded America's entry into the War, let us for the moment look only to that earliest revo-

[1] See § IX, "Great British-French Attack," by Ludendorff, etc.

lution in March. It sprang from Russia's utter loss of faith in the Czar's weak government. The by no means strong-minded Czar was himself devoted to Russia; but he was ruled almost wholly by his German Czarina, and she was ruled by the monk Rasputin. There is no need to regard the Czarina as a traitress to Russia, though her people almost universally did so. But of Rasputin there is small doubt that he was directly in the enemy employ; and through obeying him, the Czarina did much to ruin Russia.

As each new rascality in the government was brought to light, the people protested, and the Czar obligingly changed his ministers. But each new Prime Minister was named really through Rasputin, and each was as worthless as the other. To Boris Sturmer the betrayer of Rumania, there succeeded a courtier general, active only in the palace; and then, in January, 1917, came Prince Golitzin, a leader of the "reactionaries" or staunch adherents of absolutism against every suggestion of representative government.

Golitzin's appointment was caused by the slaying of Rasputin. A number of Russian patriots of highest rank had determined that in his death lay the only hope of Russia, and they killed him on the last night of 1916. At this the Czar and Czarina were infuriated, and resolved on the severest measures. Hence Golitzin was made premier, and there was more or less deliberate incitement of the people, so that any who revolted might be seized and punished. The Duma or Russian parliament, a purely advisory body, met in February; but its advice did not please the angry court, and on March 11th the Czar ordered the Duma to dissolve. The Duma refused, and instead took command of what it now deemed an absolutely necessary revolution.[1]

For some days there had been bread riots in the streets; and the soldiers when ordered to fire on the mob refused. Disobedience by the army means the downfall of autocracy. Soldiers and civilians now united in attacking and destroying the hated police. The angry masses welcomed most gladly the proffered leadership of the Duma. A temporary government was quickly formed; and on March 15th the

[1] See § V, "Russia Proclaims a Republic," by the Czar, etc.

Czar was notified that he was deposed. He accepted quietly; indeed, he could do no otherwise, with his army already in revolt and his police slain or scattered.

The labor leaders and the Duma now united in forming a more permanent government. They named as Prime Minister Prince Lvoff, the leader of the upper class patriots, business men and nobles who had aided in the revolution. His Minister of Foreign Affairs was Professor Paul Milyukof, leader of the Democracy in the Duma; and his Minister of Justice was the Socialistic lawyer orator Kerensky, who had sprung into power by his oratorical influence over the soldiers and laborers. It was a "coalition" government; and its first step was to assure the Allies that now at last Russia was to be a Power indeed, and would give her whole strength to the War.

AMERICA ENTERS

This first Russian Revolution had unquestionably an enormous influence in America. The people of the United States had held back from the War not from any overmastering desire to profit by the world's suffering, and certainly not from any fear of Germany. Impossible as it was for the German Government to believe, they had been controlled by a principle. The fundamental fact about a Democracy is that it really believes in equal opportunity for all men, and has no desire for subjugating others. Hence for a Democracy, war can never come as a policy, but only as a cruel and terrible necessity.

Indeed, the contrast of Democracy's more peaceful and profitable methods of expansion was illustrated strikingly just at this time. For years the United States had been negotiating for Denmark's island possessions in the West Indies. The Danish Government was eager to sell, and the United States to buy; but beforehand the latter insisted on consulting the wishes of the islanders themselves. They voted to join the United States; and on March 31st, at the very moment when war with Germany was hanging in the balance, the islands were formally transferred to the American flag. The islanders quietly continued the prosperous self-government they had enjoyed for years. That is Democracy's way.[1]

The American people had ever been resolutely devoted to maintaining such self-government among themselves. If in all the years that came after 1914, the American masses had but once clearly seen the Great War for what it truly was, the final issue between Democracy and Tyranny, they would have entered it at once, without questioning the cost. But always the issue had been beclouded by the fact that Russia, the most populous and most ignorant of European autocracies, fought upon the Allies' side. Now, that Russia too proclaimed herself a Democracy, men saw clearly the meaning of Germany's domineering attitude towards neutrals. She meant to rule or ruin.

Her submarine note of January 31st called forth a general protest from all neutrals. The protest of the United States was, however, the most decisive in tone; because with the United States the position reverted at once to the ultimatum of the previous year, in which she had declared for war if the submarine murders were continued. Now she broke off diplomatic relations with Germany. Such action is a direct threat of war; and the German leaders, while professing a great desire to please and satisfy aggrieved America, knew secretly that they meant to persist in their U-boat war. So they planned to involve America in trouble at home, hoping thus to keep her out of Europe. Their secret agents in America redoubled their efforts, promoting dissatisfaction and even active destruction of every kind. Thus Germany really anticipated the coming events, and made treacherous war while still parleying for peace.

She could have found no course more sure to harden the American spirit against her. Her largest effort of the kind was an attempt by Zimmermann, her newly appointed Minister of Foreign Affairs, to rouse Mexico and Japan to war against the United States.[2] The note urging this

---

[1] See § VI, "The United States Extends Its Territory," by De Booy, etc.

[2] See § III, "The Zimmermann War Scheme Exposed," by Zimmermann, Wolff, etc.

was intercepted by the U. S. Secret Service, and was promptly made public to the American people. It was the last word necessary to overcome their earnest pacifism. Obviously Germany meant to strike them, whether they struck back or no. At once on top of this came the news of Russia's Revolution. Her conversion to Democracy cleared the last confusion from the decision. There was no genuine American who still protested against answering force with force. On April 2nd the President proclaimed the necessity of war; and on April 6th Congress in solemn session and with practical unanimity voted the declaration of the war "which has thus been thrust upon the United States." [1]

In that Congress there sat for the first time a woman member, and she voted against the war, weeping as she did so. But she too declared that she saw the necessity of this war and that she meant her vote only to voice the anguished protest of her sex against all war with its horrors and its agony. Indeed the Great War has this distinction in American history, that the American people have entered no other among all their wars with such unanimity as they displayed in this. Even the Revolution of 1776 had been opposed by many devoted British Loyalists. In the Civil War, a large party in the North had wished to let the Southerners withdraw in peace. But now even the German-Americans admitted sadly that their fatherland had transgressed beyond endurance. The great majority of them made decisive choice, and showed their loyalty to America by devoted service throughout the War.

As for the vast body of native Americans, the Government's only trouble was to select the best among the mass of volunteers eager to serve it without pay and in any capacity whatsoever. Thousands of men accustomed to large affairs laid aside every former interest to place themselves wholly at the disposal of the Government. Everywhere, voluntarily, the people bound themselves together for food conservation and the saving of supplies of every kind. There was no need for armed authority; Washington had only to suggest

[1] See § VII, "The United States Enters the War," by Wilson, Taft, etc.

a wish, and the nation answered. Every woman aided the Red Cross, and every man contributed to the Y. M. C. A. or similar organizations. Never had America known such a whirl of patriotic energy and self-sacrifice.

A nation so moved was sure from the start to upset German calculations. The United States had no intention of playing at war as an amateur, dabbling on the edge of this awful maelstrom of disaster into which she had been so unwillingly drawn. Six weeks after declaring war, she astounded the whole world by establishing universal conscription.[1] Britain, the other great home of individual freedom, had endured the War for nearly three years before she accepted this subordination of the right of the individual to the necessity of the State. America with the hard experiences of European Democracy before her as a warning, leaped to the inevitable decision at once. It assured her of an army of ten million men, and was a symbol and a warning to Europe of what America meant to do.

At the same time, the United States Government entered into immediate and most cordial harmony with her European allies. Commissions from all of them hurried to Washington, and the chief question asked of these envoys was not, what will you do for America, but what can she do for each of you. What will it be most helpful for you to have America do at once?

Britain said, "Help us against the submarines." For indeed the new German onslaught was proving cruelly effective. In its first month, February, over two hundred ships were sunk. In April the loss rose to almost a hundred ships a week; 800,000 tons of shipping were destroyed in that one month, with grim loss of life to neutrals as well as to belligerents. Of the total losses more than half had fallen upon Britain. If the destruction continued at that rate, or if it increased, she was beaten. America answered this appeal by sending a fleet of her "destroyers" immediately to British waters. They reached there on May 4th, and entered at once into service. Thus they struck the first actual blow for the

[1] See § XI, "Conscription in the United States," by Gompers, etc.

United States in the War.[1] Britain gave them a delighted
reception, and named their coming, what indeed it was, "The
Return of the *Mayflower.*" The descendants of those old-
time colonists who had left England in resentment to build
a New England, now returned in strangely altered ships for
the healing of all old wounds and the sealing of a new comradeship and world-purpose.

With the coming of the American destroyers, though only
to a small extent because of them, the tragic effectiveness of
the U-boat campaign grew less. The first dash of the new
U-boats was over, and British attacks were rapidly reduc-
ing their number. Soon both Britons and Americans devised
new ways of snaring the hidden submarines. Wireless elec-
trical devices located them, and nets and depth bombs annihilated them. That April month of destruction proved the
climax of their power, which gradually thereafter dwindled
into feebleness. One more turning point of the War was
passed; one more of Germany's confident hopes had failed
her.

In similar fashion, the French envoys had said secretly
to the United States Government, "Send us troops at once.
Our spring attack has broken down badly (as indeed it had
upon the *Chemin des Dames*) ; our people will fight to the
end, but they fight in despair. They need the joy of the actual presence of your soldiers, the stimulus, the promise it
will mean of more to come. Though you can send but a
few, send them at once before it is too late." That was the
startling message of France; and to that also America responded. General Pershing was selected as the commander
abroad, and he reached France with his staff on June 15th.
Some twenty thousand soldiers followed him at once. Their
transport ships risked the as yet untested danger of the U-
boats. They ran the dread gauntlet without a mishap; and
on June 26th the first United States regiments landed in
France "to pay the debt of Lafayette."

On July 4th there were in Paris and in London such cele-
brations of America's national holiday as the world had
never dreamed of. The actual help which America had given

[1] See § X, "The United States' First Stroke of War," Daniels, etc.

in the War was as yet but a trifle; but the splendid readiness with which that help was being given, the tremendous energy with which she was developing her immeasurable and unexpected power for warfare, these raised her at once to leadership in the War, where before she had been but an outsider. The orders given to every official serving the United States were, "Organize and prepare everything as though the War were going to last for unlimited years." If it stopped sooner, so much the better; but even though Europe should sink exhausted, America meant to fight on to victory. That was the spirit German "frightfulness" had at last aroused.[1]

On that rejoicing July 4th in Europe, it seemed as though the War was practically at an end. If Germany had been staggering before under the blows of Britain, France, Italy and Russia, what hope had she now with this new unsuspected military colossus preparing so gigantically for the attack. True, America had been wholly unprepared before she entered the War, criminally unprepared some patriots thought; and true, her utmost preparation now could bring little real fruition for yet another year. But what of that? If Germany still refused to see the inevitable end, Europe could surely fight a waiting fight until America made good her mighty promise.

GERMANY DENOUNCED BY THE WORLD

There were other causes for rejoicing also. The vigorous action of the United States had profoundly stirred the rest of the neutral world. Almost with one voice, other nations echoed the verdict of the United States Government as the verdict of Democracy. They declared that Germany was indeed a criminal among nations, that as the final champion of tyranny and conquest she must be curbed or else destroyed, so that other peoples might live and be free.[2] On the very day following the United States declaration of war, Cuba and Panama declared war also. These two states of course were in close alliance with the United States; but their

[1] See § XXIV, "The Vast Reorganizing of America," by Houston, Pershing, etc.

[2] See § VIII, "The World Union Against Germany," by Menocal, etc.

action was expressive of the sentiment of Latin America. Brazil and Argentine, the two largest South American countries, both announced a breaking of diplomatic relations with Germany on April 10th. Several of the others followed. Before the year was over Brazil declared actual war, as did most of the Central American states. Even from far-off Asia came the echo. Siam joined the war against Germany in July, and China joined in August. Even little Liberia, in Africa, declared war. Never before had there been such a world-wide unanimity of sentiment and action against a single state.

Moreover, now that Democracy was at last and wholly in control of the Allies' councils, the European powers took a step they had not previously ventured. King Constantine of Greece, who had long held Greece against them in an unfriendly and menacing neutrality, was deposed by them. The Greek revolutionists, who held eastern Greece under Venizelos, were allowed to assert their power, and they eagerly took control of the nation. Under their hands Greece too, on July 2nd, declared war on Germany, and on her own immediate foe, Bulgaria.[1]

RUSSIA DISAPPEARS FROM THE WAR

At the very moment when the Allied triumph seemed thus assured on every side, the breakdown came. The new monster, Anarchy, plunged blindly into the struggle. Russia, not through exhaustion, but through ignorance and a blind pacifism and lack of realization of the consequences, abandoned the struggle just as it seeemed won. Her armies refused to fight. They vanished. There was no longer an "eastern front" for Germany to defend; and transferring all her forces to the west, she was soon ready to strike there with double force. Instantly the whole face of the War changed like a kaleidoscope. The new problem was, could this now stronger Germany overwhelm the war-worn French and British and Italians before America was fully ready. In the apt epigram of the day, the War resolved itself into a race between Hindenburg and Uncle Sam.

[1] See § XIV, "Greece Enters the War," by Gauvain, etc.

Of course the completeness of this tragic change did not become manifest in a moment. All that the western world realized in July was that the Russian democratic leaders were having increasing difficulty in controlling the masses of ignorant soldiers and laboring-men with whom the mastery of Russia now really lay. First, Prime-minister Lvoff was compelled to resign, and then the long-honored patriot Milyukof. All power seemed concentrating in the hands of Kerensky, the Socialist. This in itself was not alarming to the West; for Kerensky was passionately enthusiastic for the War, and the Democratic war minister, Guchkov, had so ably reorganized affairs that never had Russia's army been so well supplied and apparently ready for battle.

The real danger lay beneath. Months before, as soon as the Czar was overthrown, every patriot, every ignorant fanatic, and every rascal, all who had ever been exiled from Russia, sought to return there. Germany, eager to encourage disunion in Russia's councils, had gladly aided the most extravagant and anarchistic of such agitators to reënter Russia. She had even paid the way of the most dangerous of them all, Nicolai Lenine, the founder of Bolshevism. The more extravagant these agitators were in their golden promises of future happiness, and the more recklessly they distorted facts and logic, the more influential they became with the ignorant Russian workmen and soldiers. Under pressure of such forces and of his own socialistic theories, Kerensky abolished the death penalty and the law of obedience in the army. Soldiers were encouraged to form "councils" of their own and these shared authority with their former officers.[1]

In still more open trickery, Germany issued orders to her troops along the eastern front to "fraternize" with the Russian troops. They were to make pretended friendships and assure their dupes that the German soldiers only desired peace, and that if Russia would stop fighting, Germany would do the same. Soon the entire Russian peasantry more than half believed that the millennium had come, that they had only to stop fighting and go home, and all the rest of the

[1] See § XV, "Russia's Military Breakdown," by Kerensky, etc.

world would do the same. Then they would be allowed to till their farms in peace forever.

From this came about the tragic military downfall in July. Already the soldiers were clamorous for peace; but Kerensky had roused them to the folly of their dream, and they agreed to make one more general attack. Brusiloff, the most brilliant of the former generals, was placed in command. Once more, as in earlier years, he hurled his troops upon the weary Austrians, broke their line, and seemed sweeping all before him. But, alas, he found that many of his own troops, when ordered to attack, called a soldiers' council instead. The result was obvious. While they talked, the moment for attack went by; or more often they decided not to attack. Meanwhile their comrades who had shown more valor or more obedience, were left unsupported, and the line was broken. Then the idle debators were themselves surrounded by the attacking foe and made prisoners, or they escaped by panic flight. The officers and veterans of the older army, who tried to stand firm in battle, were slain, often by their own fleeing men.

Kerensky, rushing to the front, tried to restore order. He even reëstablished the death penalty for those who disobeyed their officers. But the change came too late. The mutineers had learned the taste of blood. Their arguing councils now ruled everywhere. Some of their generals they deposed; others they slew. In mad humor they voted that the former officers should do the coarsest work as privates; privates they made officers. Never was there more absurd confusion of the real meaning and necessity of military rankings. A former ensign, Kyrilenko, was declared commander-in-chief of this rioting army, which was no longer dangerous to any one but its own hapless countryfolk.

Germans and Austrians had now only to push forward and take what territory they pleased. They swept the disordered Russian mob out of Galicia and began advancing into Russian territory hitherto uninvaded. On September 3rd, they seized the great seaport city of Riga, which previously had for two whole years defied their utmost forces. Korniloff, the last of the old generals to remain in command, attempted to restore order by seizing the governing power himself with his Cossack followers. But Kerensky overthrew him (Sept. 15th) and became dictator.

Then in November came the final disaster.[1] The Petrograd mob had long been swinging beyond Kerensky's moderate ideas. The workmen of the capital and the sailors in control of the fleet at its great nearby naval base of Cronstadt, were coming more and more under the control of the Bolshevist leader, Lenine. At length, on November 7th, the workmen ordered Kerensky to turn over his authority to Lenine. He refused, and there was some brief fighting. A band of women soldiers and another of young students who still remained faithful to the dreams of Socialism, tried to uphold Kerensky. But against these last idealists the sailors turned the great guns of the Cronstadt fleet, and the women and boys were overthrown. Many of them died hideously in the mad saturnalia which now replaced all government in Russia.

The theory of Bolshevism was a strangely inverted "absolutism," a tyranny more complete and far more hideous than German Autocracy had ever planned. Lenine stood for the rule of the laborers over all other classes, since the laborers were the most numerous. All property was to belong to the State; and the former wealthy and upper classes were all to become laborers. Yes, they were even to be forced to serve in all the lowest forms of labor, or else be slain. There was to be no aristocracy even of intelligence; Ignorance was to be the only lord. As to the further consequence of this, that the rule of Ignorance would plunge both public and private business blindly from disaster to disaster until all property was destroyed; that the ignorant ruling mob having no impulse toward industry would idle until starvation was inevitable; and that even the peasants would soon stop planting their farms for a government which took away all the produce and gave them no return; all this Lenine did not see. Or else with a fanatic's madness he was indifferent to its menace. Actual experience was to teach its horrors to

---

[1] See § XIX, "Bolshevism Triumphs in Russia," by Lenine, etc.

such Russians as survived the teaching, through the hideous years of Lenine's control.

His first step in the midst of the slaughter of "treacherous aristocrats" was to seek a peace with Germany.[1] He also declared that in all the provinces of Russia the masses of the people might determine their own form of government. Germany thereon promptly consented to an armistice, and commissioners met at Brest-Litovsk, the headquarters of the invading German army in Russia. Here the German commissioners asserted that all the Russian provinces which the Germans had seized would now prefer a German government; and hence under the Bolshevist doctrine, Russia must yield all these provinces, and must also grant independence to Finland and to the Ukraine, a new state which was to be created from the richest provinces of southern Russia. This was what the Germans now explained they had always meant when they talked to the Russians of a "peace with no annexations."

Even the Bolshevist Russians protested against seeing their country thus despoiled of all her fairest provinces. But they had now no army that would fight, and no means of resistance. The year closed therefore with the Bolshevists presenting the sorry spectacle of having ruined Russia, of having placed her utterly helpless under the German heel, and now of trying to preserve her by force of argument from the eagerly grasping militarists at Brest-Litovsk.

From this sorry spectacle of ignorance in its drunken, murderous, hopeless devastation, let us turn to see what effect Russia's downfall was having elsewhere in the world.

THE ITALIAN DISASTER AND RALLY

The Italian armies in July began a brilliant attack along the Isonzo River front. They hoped to coöperate with the Brusiloff attack in Russia; and later when a Russian recovery still seemed possible, Italy still hoped that her attack might give Russia time to rally. Before this vigorous assault the Austrians yielded slowly, until on August 24th

[1] See § XXII, "Bolshevist Russia Accepts an Armistice," by Trotsky, etc.

the Italians achieved one of the most striking victories of the War by storming Monte Santo.[1]   This was a high mountain summit so fortified that Austria had believed it impregnable.   Italian engineers diverted the entire course of the Isonzo River in order that their troops might reach the mountain.   With its fall the Austrian resistance became more desperate, the Italian advance slowed up—and then came the third great dramatic event of the year, the second disaster to offset America's entry.   On October 21st, the Italian front suddenly gave way, just as the Russian had done.[2]

Here too, as in Russia, it was Anarchy that struck the terrible blow at Democracy's cause.   German secret propagandists, triumphant at their success in reaching the Russian masses and destroying their resistance, attempted the same device in Italy.   Austrian and German soldiers fraternized with the Italians along the front and assured them that an Italian retreat would not be followed by Austrian invasion but by an equal peace, "without annexations." Meanwhile anarchistic agitators among the Italians told them the War was merely waged by capitalists for capital.   Forged newspapers, prepared by the Germans in imitation of Italian sheets, told of Italians back in the home cities being shot down by French and British troops for demanding bread.

Then when the moment seemed fully ripe, a German army of 100,000 men joined the Austrians, and at Caporetto struck suddenly at the Italian line.   They went through it like paper.   Whole regiments of Italians threw away their weapons and ran.   Others marched off home, singing that there was to be no more fighting.   Within a week the Teutons had captured two hundred thousand prisoners.   Italy seemed about to perish as Russia was perishing, or to fall as Serbia and Rumania had fallen.

Fortunately the insidious Teuton propaganda had seriously affected only one great Italian army out of four which guarded the frontier.   The other forces, compelled to retreat by the utter breakdown of the Caporetto army, fought splendidly, though at cruel disadvantage.   Every river, as

[1] See § XVII, "The Italian Attack on the Isonzo," by Trevelyan.
[2] See § XVIII, "Italy's Military Breakdown," by Cadorna, etc.

they fell back from the frontier, was made the basis of a new defense. Each defeat brought them nearer to Venice, whose capture seemed inevitable.

In this crisis French and British troops were rushed to Italy's aid; and a new Italian commander, General Diaz, superseded the aged General Cadorna. The retreating armies reached the Piave River, which had stronger defenses than the positions previously lost. Even the Piave, however, was only intended as a temporary holding place while permanent lines were being built yet further back. But those permanent lines were never needed. The infuriated loyal Italians held fast upon the Piave (November 18th). Even the foolish traitors, who had believed the Teuton promises of not advancing, now saw how they had been deceived, and came pouring back to Italy's defense. Never was a seemingly inevitable disaster more brilliantly retrieved. Venice was saved; and Italy, except for her tremendous loss of the deceived and captured soldiers at Caporetto, was as strong as ever.[1]

AUTUMN ON THE WESTERN FRONT

So much for the triumphs of the new foe, Anarchy. The weight of the War fell now mainly upon Britain. Her soldiers stood valiantly against the increasing numbers of Germans on the western front. France, as we have seen, fought all year along the *Chemin des Dames*. One likes to pause here also to record the most brilliant aërial feat of the War. Gradually the necessities of warfare had trained men in the handling of air machines until we may fairly speak of the last years of the War as the "Dawn of the Air Age." Huge airplanes began to carry from ten to twenty men; and squadrons of aviators fought battles with other squadrons in the air. Looking for the one chief air victory of the War, one must ascribe it to Guynemer (gē (g as in get) nā mare′), the most celebrated of French "aces." On May 25, 1917, he fought four aërial combats in a single day, and destroyed each of the four opposing battle-machines.[2]

[1] See § XX, "Italy's Great Rally on the Piave," by Buchan, etc.
[2] See § XII, "Triumphs of the Air Age," by Deschanel, etc.

The hardest fighting of the fall of 1917 was undergone by the Britons. At this time their army in France had reached the maximum strength of which the whole British Empire was capable. Canada and Australia vied with Britain itself in sending to the field every man who was fit for service. Not long could this tremendous maximum of strength have been maintained. France, as we have seen, already felt her powers waning. She who had been ready first and had borne the full brunt of the first fighting, had now to call on the great British army, as later the Britons were to call upon that of America. But for the moment, with Russia down and America unready, this was Britain's day.

On July 31st the British started the third great battle of Ypres or, as this one was more commonly known, the battle of Flanders.[1] Taking advantage of their possession of Messines Ridge, which they had won in June, the British attacked eastward from Ypres, and gradually regained the ground they had lost in the Ypres battles of the earlier years. All through a rainy August and a bleak and muddy autumn, the battle continued well into November. French forces repeatedly joined the Britons and made some of their most successful attacks. The Canadians again distinguished themselves at Passchendaele. The Germans on their side threw into the great battle almost all the forces they were withdrawing from the Russian front. Like the colossal battles of the previous year, the Flanders fight brought no decided change in the battle line. It only devoured endless human lives in its awful maw, and held the new German forces from striking a blow elsewhere.

One other effort Britain made in that dreary autumn. In the region of the Arras battle, the old ground laid waste in the Hindenburg retreat, the British general, Byng, started a sudden surprise attack on November 19th, directing it against the city of Cambrai. This Cambrai attack, unlike all the others for years past, was not heralded by a tremendous storm of artillery. Such storms, ever increasing in violence, destroyed the enemy's first lines; but they also

[1] See § XVI, "In Flanders' Fields," by Haig, etc.

warned him to hurry forward his reserves. This time Byng secretly assembled some five hundred "tanks" and hurled these suddenly against the enemy line without any artillery warning. The line broke; the British infantry went through after the tanks; a great victory seemed really near. But the Britons were slow in following up their advantage. Before the end of November the Germans struck back in huge counter-attacks which broke the unready British lines and regained most of what had been lost.[1]

In this retreat from Cambrai came the first real fighting of United States troops in the War. A regiment of U. S. engineers had been employed in the necessary rebuilding work behind the British advance. The breaking of the British lines left the engineers suddenly facing the foe. They seized weapons as they could from the falling Britons, and held the line so well that their valor won special mention in the report of the British Commander-in-Chief. So both France and America had their share in the great British attack of 1917.

BRITISH VICTORIES IN ASIA

One other section of the vast world warfare brought cheer to the Allies in 1917. In Asiatic Turkey, Britain more than retrieved the 1916 disaster of Kut. She launched two vigorous campaigns against the Turks. The first under General Maude, fought over the same old ground as in 1916. Maude forced his way up the Euphrates river valley, recaptured Kut, and then fought onward up the river to Bagdad. He captured that ancient center of the Mohammedan empire on March 11th, and scattered the Turkish forces in flight beyond it.[2] All Asia was amazed and deeply awed. The evil impression made by the surrender of Kut the year before was completely obliterated. These Britons were then indeed invincible; if you destroyed one army they merely sent another larger one, and the end was sure to be the same! Only Russia's downfall enabled Turkey to send such reenforcements to the Bagdad front as blocked the British

[1] See § XXI, "The Surprise Attack at Cambrai," by Doyle, etc.
[2] See § IV, "The Fall of Bagdad," by General Maude, etc.

further advance and so saved Turkey from a complete breakdown.

The second and similar British campaign was launched from Egypt against Palestine. The Britons succeeded where the Turks in the first year of the War had failed. They brought an army successfully across the ancient Sinai desert. In the spring, they only reached the southern edge of Palestine. In the summer, heat prevented their advance. But in October, under General Allenby, they fought their way north along the coast. In December they stormed position after position around Jerusalem; and on December 10th they entered the Holy City itself in solemn procession.[1] That was a world event indeed, profoundly significant in its symbolism. And Asia understood that symbol. Never again was the city of Christ and the city of David to be under Mohammedan control. The Turks' misrule had thrown away their religion's proudest heritage. The day of the Turk was gone forever.

That was the closing gleam of sunshine for the Allies, which ended the tumultuously changing year of 1917. Germany saw that her eastern partners were breaking down. Bulgaria was well-nigh as exhausted as Turkey. The new Austro-Hungarian emperor, Charles, was working secretly for the peace which alone could save his heritage and his exhausted peoples. Germany had, and she knew she had, but the one more chance. Could her strengthened armies, carefully conserved through 1917, break the western front in 1918 before the Americans were ready? The War had really narrowed itself to that one question, the issue of the race between Hindenburg and Uncle Sam.

[1] See § XXIII, "The Conquest of Jerusalem," by Gen. Allenby, etc.

GERMANY DEFIES THE NEUTRAL NATIONS

THE RENEWAL OF UNLIMITED DESTRUCTION BY U-BOATS

JANUARY 31ST

COUNT VON BERNSTORFF   VON BETHMANN-HOLLWEG
PRESIDENT WILSON
COUNT ROMANONES   LAURO MULLER

The first event of 1917 to rouse the warring nations from their
dreary winter's misery and endurance was the reopening of Germany's
U-boat warfare upon neutrals. Time has removed most of the uncertainty and perplexity in which this movement was at first enwrapped.
Americans simply could not believe that the German Government meant
so to juggle with words in dealing with them, or would so scornfully
ignore their declared opinion of their rights. It was as if a strong
and thoughtful man who had tried with much self-restraint to aid and
guide his neighbors should suddenly find that the biggest among them
had always regarded him as a simpleton to be played with, and as a
child to be ignored or buffeted aside in serious affairs. That is what
had happened. In the United States "diplomatic triumph" of 1916, Germany had at American insistence abandoned her attacks on neutral
ships. The United States Government had been patient but quietly insistent; and this pacific method had seemed effective. Germany could
be reasoned with successfully: the piratic assault was stopped.

Now, suddenly, not only did this evil thing recur, but it occurred in
a manner most amazing and insulting to American ideas. In the first
place the sudden notice of the renewal of the warfare was conveyed to
the United States by Ambassador Bernstorff in a typical German
Government note, wheedling, yet with a covert sneer, deliberately
ignoring the essential facts and substituting shallow pretense, in-
solently false from end to end. That note, here reproduced, did indeed
treat Americans as simpletons. A sharper insolence was to follow. On
that same day the German Chancellor explained to Germany his reasons
for resuming the U-boat attacks. In that explanation, also given here,
he scarcely even referred to the United States. He expected to have
to face some general verbal complaint from the neutrals, but nothing
more. The fact that the United States had last year declared she
would break diplomatic relations, a step almost tantamount to war,
if the U-boat attacks continued, this fact was apparently, to the Chancellor, unimportant. America learned that his real reason for stopping the U-boat warfare had been that his U-boats were so small, so
few and had been so badly battered by British ships that he had accepted gladly the most high-sounding excuse at hand for abandoning
an exhausted effort. Now Germany had built many new and better

U-boats. She had always meant to use them as soon as she could do so effectively. It was long before Americans could realize how completely Germans had ignored the possibility of their deliberately making—or being able to make—any serious trouble in the matter.

Without waiting, however, to digest this insult to their vanity, the American people had reverted at once to the stern central issue which both ambassador and chancellor neglected. The renewal of the U-boat attacks brought America back to the moment when she had declared what she would do if these attacks continued. That patient, restrained and determined word of warning America meant to keep, however Germany might juggle with German words. On February 3rd President Wilson formally severed diplomatic relations with Germany. He dismissed Ambassador Bernstorff, summoned home Ambassador Gerard, and on the same day appeared before a joint session of Congress to announce and explain what he had done. He received a practically unanimous support from the Congress and from the people.

President Wilson's address is given here; and every American should feel pride in contrasting its high, strict, restrained truth with the evasions and shallow platitudes of the German statesmen. There was a cry ran through the country at the time saying that Germany had broken her pledged word. But the President is careful not to make that charge; for Germany had in a strictly literal sense evaded that particular falsity. In 1916 the United States Government had demanded, "You stop!" And she had answered, "I have stopped, but under certain conditions I might feel justified in recommencing." The response had been, "We don't agree with your conditions and suppositions, but as long as you have stopped and stay stopped, no more is necessary." There the matter had rested.

In addition to the German and American viewpoints, we give here also the response of some of the other neutrals to Germany's general notice of January 31st. The reader may thus convince himself that the United States was not alone in regarding the U-boat war on neutrals as a form of murder, and an intolerable offense. Among neutrals, the Spanish Government was notably pro-German throughout the War; hence the response of its Prime Minister, Count Romanones, was among the mildest in tone, and is here presented for that reason. The first protest of Brazil, through its Foreign Minister, Señor Lauro Muller, and also that of Chile, are given to show the tone of South America's response. No other neutral had previously gone so far as the United States in presenting an ultimatum, yet several of them now followed her example, by threatening to sever, and later in their just anger severing, diplomatic relations with Germany.

C. F. H.

BY AMBASSADOR VON BERNSTORFF

WASHINGTON, D. C., January 31, 1917.

Mr. Secretary of State:

YOUR Excellency was good enough to transmit to the Imperial Government a copy of the message which the President of the United States of America addressed to the

Senate on the 22nd inst. The Imperial Government has given it the earnest consideration which the President's statements deserve, inspired, as they are, by a deep sentiment of responsibility.

It is highly gratifying to the Imperial Government to ascertain that the main tendencies of this important statement correspond largely to the desires and principles professed by Germany. These principles especially include self-government and equality of rights for all nations. Germany would be sincerely glad if, in recognition of this principle, countries like Ireland and India, which do not enjoy the benefits of political independence, should now obtain their freedom.[1]

The German people also repudiate all alliances which serve to force the countries into a competition for might and to involve them in a net of selfish intrigues. On the other hand, Germany will gladly coöperate in all efforts to prevent future wars.

The freedom of the seas, being a preliminary condition of the free existence of nations and the peaceful intercourse between them, as well as the open door for the commerce of all nations, has always formed part of the leading principles of Germany's political program. All the more the Imperial Government regrets that the attitude of her enemies, who are so entirely opposed to peace, makes it impossible for the world at present to bring about the realization of these lofty ideals.

Germany and her allies were ready to enter now into a

[1] These opening paragraphs have of course no real bearing on the purpose of the writer. They merely tend to make light of it by including it in a group of other matters. The sentence about Ireland and India can only be read as a sneer. It implies indirectly that the writer's real opinion is that America cares nothing about the freedom of other peoples, since she is not protesting against the British Empire. It ignores the obvious difference between the necessity of some sort of rule over the chaos of India, and the cruel and wholly unnecessary German domination over the people of Alsace and other European lands. Of course Germany had not the faintest intention of surrendering these. She had repeatedly proclaimed this. Hence the writer is really merely saying, "Since you choose to babble altruistic falsehoods, I will do the same. We both know we are lying." Bernstorff's only mistake was that America was in earnest.

discussion of peace, and had set down as basis the guarantee of existence, honor, and free development of their peoples. Their aims, as has been expressly stated in the note of December 12, 1916, were not directed toward the destruction or annihilation of their enemies and were, according to their conviction, perfectly compatible with the rights of the other nations.[2] As to Belgium, for which such warm and cordial sympathy is felt in the United States, the Chancellor had declared only a few weeks previously that its annexation had never formed part of Germany's intentions. The peace to be signed with Belgium was to provide for such conditions in that country, with which Germany desires to maintain friendly neighborly relations, that Belgium should not be used again by Germany's enemies for the purpose of instigating continuous hostile intrigues.[3] Such precautionary measures are all the more necessary, as Germany's enemies have repeatedly stated, not only in speeches delivered by their leading men, but also in the statutes of the Economical Conference in Paris, that it is their intention not to treat Germany as an equal, even after peace has been restored, but to continue their hostile attitude, and especially to wage a systematical economic war against her.

The attempt of the four allied powers to bring about peace has failed, owing to the lust of conquest of their enemies, who desired to dictate the conditions of peace. Under

[2] Here we have the usual German one-sidedness, so consistent that it really appears like a lack of intelligence rather than an obstinate persistence in falsehood. The German peace terms had implied that Serbia was to remain in Bulgarian and Austrian hands, that Germany was to take what she pleased from Russia and possibly from France, and was to give up nothing herself. Instead, by assuming practical control of Belgium she was to be placed in a position where her next attack would be fatal to both France and England. Bernstorff then declares that, "according to Germany's conviction" this robbery is "perfectly compatible with the rights of other nations." In other words, this is to be an "equal" peace in which Germany and her allies take everything they want.

As for the German Chancellor's declaration about Belgium, he made a new one, repudiating the last one, whenever he wished.

[3] Bernstorff here repeats in the usual German fashion the utterly disproven charges that Belgium had conspired against Germany. Until the German Government has formally withdrawn these charges, the German official word is absolutely valueless.

the pretense of following the principle of nationality, our enemies have disclosed their real aims in this way, viz., to dismember and dishonor Germany, Austria-Hungary, Turkey and Bulgaria. To the wish of reconciliation they oppose the will of destruction. They desire a fight to the bitter end.

A new situation has thus been created which forces Germany to new decisions. Since two years and a half England is using her naval power for a criminal attempt to force Germany into submission by starvation. In brutal contempt of international law, the group of powers led by England not only curtail the legitimate trade of their opponents, but they also, by ruthless pressure, compel neutral countries either to altogether forego every trade not agreeable to the Entente Powers, or to limit it according to their arbitrary decrees.

The American Government knows the steps which have been taken to cause England and her allies to return to the rules of international law and to respect the freedom of the seas. The English Government, however, insists upon continuing its war of starvation, which does not at all affect the military power of its opponents, but compels women and children, the sick and the aged, to suffer for their country pains and privations which endanger the vitality of the nation. Thus British tyranny mercilessly increases the sufferings of the world, indifferent to the laws of humanity, indifferent to the protests of the neutrals whom they severely harm, indifferent even to the silent longing for peace among England's own allies. Each day of the terrible struggle causes new destruction, new sufferings. Each day shortening the war will, on both sides, preserve the lives of thousands of brave soldiers and be a benefit to mankind.

The Imperial Government could not justify before its own conscience, before the German people, and before history the neglect of any means destined to bring about the end of the war. Like the President of the United States, the Imperial Government had hoped to reach this goal by negotiations. Since the attempts to come to an understanding with the Entente Powers have been answered by the latter with the announcement of an intensified continuation of the war, the Imperial Government—in order to serve the welfare of mankind in a higher sense and not to wrong its own people—is now compelled to continue the fight for existence, again forced upon it, with the full employment of all the weapons which are at its disposal.

Sincerely trusting that the people and the Government of the United States will understand the motives for this decision and its necessity, the Imperial Government hopes that the United States may view the new situation from the lofty heights of impartiality, and assist, on their part, to prevent further misery and unavoidable sacrifice of human life.

Inclosing two memoranda regarding the details of the contemplated military measures at sea, I remain, etc.,

MEMORANDA INCLOSED IN THE BERNSTORFF NOTE

From February 1, 1917, sea traffic will be stopped with every available weapon and without further notice in the following blockade zones around Great Britain, France, Italy and in the Eastern Mediterranean:[4]

In the North: The zone is confined by a line at a distance of twenty sea miles along the Dutch coast to Terschelling Lightship, the meridian of longitude from Terschelling Lightship to Udsire; a line from there across the point 62 degrees north, o degrees longitude, to 62 degrees north, 5 degrees west; further to a point three sea miles south of the southern point of the Faroe Islands; from there across a point 62 degrees north, 10 degrees west, to 61 degrees north, 15 degrees west; then 57 degrees north, 20 degrees west, to 47 degrees north, 20 degrees west; further, to 43 degrees north, 15 degrees west; then along the parallel of latitude 43 degrees north to twenty sea miles from Cape Finisterre, and at a distance of twenty sea miles along the north coast of Spain to the French boundary.

In the South—The Mediterranean: For neutral ships,

[4] Briefly summarized, the two following paragraphs describe a complete enclosure or blockade of Britain and adjacent isles, France, Belgium, Italy and their North African possessions, except for one small space on the French Mediterranean coast near the Spanish border.

remains open the sea west of the line Pt. Des Espiquettes to 38 degrees 20 minutes north and 6 degrees east; also north and west of a zone sixty sea miles wide along the North African coast, beginning at 2 degrees longitude west. For the connection of this sea zone with Greece there is provided a zone of a width of twenty sea miles north and east of the following line: 38 degrees north and 6 degrees east to 38 degrees north and 10 degrees west, to 37 degrees north and 11 degrees 30 minutes east, to 34 degrees north and 22 degrees 30 minutes east. From there leads a zone twenty sea miles wide, west of 22 degrees 30 minutes eastern longitude, into Greek territorial waters.

Neutral ships navigating these blockade zones do so at their own risk. Although care has been taken that neutral ships which are on their way toward ports of the blockade zones on February 1, 1917, and have come in the vicinity of the latter, will be spared during a sufficiently long period, it is strongly advised to warn them with all available means in order to cause their return.

Neutral ships which•on February 1st are in ports of the blockade zones can with the same safety leave them.

The instructions given to the commanders of German submarines provide for a sufficiently long period during which the safety of passengers on unarmed enemy passenger ships is guaranteed.

Americans en route to the blockade zone on enemy freight steamers are not endangered, as the enemy shipping firms can prevent such ships in time from entering the zone.

Sailing of regular American passenger steamers may continue undisturbed after February 1, 1917, if

(A) The port of destination is Falmouth.

(B) Sailing to or coming from that port course is taken via the Scilly Islands and a point 50 degrees north, 20 degrees west.

(C) The steamers are marked in the following way, which must not be allowed to other vessels in American ports: On ship's hull and superstructure three vertical stripes one meter wide, each to be painted alternately white and red. Each mast should show a large flag checkered white and red, and the stern the American national flag. Care should be taken that, during dark, national flag and painted marks are easily recognizable from a distance, and that the boats are well lighted throughout.

(D) One steamer a week sails in each direction with arrival at Falmouth on Sunday and departure from Falmouth on Wednesday.

(E) United States Government guarantees that no contraband (according to German contraband list) is carried by those steamers. [For the second Bernstorff memorandum see President Wilson's address, which follows.]

BY CHANCELLOR VON BETHMANN-HOLLWEG

Address to the German Legislative Leaders on January 31st

On December 12th last year I explained before the Reichstag the reasons which led to our peace offer. The reply of our opponents clearly and precisely said that they decline peace negotiations with us, and that they want to hear only of a peace which they dictate. By this the whole question of the guilt for the continuation of the war is decided. The guilt falls alone on our opponents.[5] Just as definite stands our task.

The enemy's conditions we cannot discuss. They could only be accepted by a totally defeated people. It therefore means fight. President Wilson's message to Congress shows his sincere wish to restore peace to the world. Many of his maxims agree with our aims, namely, the freedom of the seas, the abolition of the system of balance of power, which is always bound to lead to new difficulties, equal rights for all nations, and the open door to trade.

But what are the peace conditions of the Entente? Germany's defensive force is to be destroyed, we are to lose Alsace-Lorraine and the eastern provinces of the Ostmarken, the Danube monarchy is to be dissolved, Bulgaria is again to be cheated of her national unity, and Turkey is to be

_____

[5] This is a typical German Government argument. The Chancellor's peace offer had been just as much a "dictation" as that of his opponents. He had offered to discuss only such terms as presupposed that Germany had won and was to keep most of her spoils. Since the Allies had refused thus to surrender, the "guilt" is theirs.

pushed out of Europe and smashed in Asia.   The destructive designs of our opponents cannot be expressed more strongly. We have been challenged to fight to the end.   We accept the challenge.   We stake everything, and we shall be victorious.

By this development of the situation the decision concerning submarine warfare has been forced into its last acute stage.   The question of the U-boat war, as the gentlemen of the Reichstag will remember, has occupied us three times in this committee, namely, in March, May and September last year.   On each occasion, in an exhaustive statement, I expounded points for and against in this question.   I emphasized on each occasion that I was speaking *pro tempore,* and not as a supporter in principle or an opponent in principle of the unrestricted employment of the U-boats, but in consideration of the military, political and economic situation as a whole.

I always proceeded from the standpoint as to whether an unrestricted U-boat war would bring us nearer to a victorious peace or not.   Every means, I said in March, that is calculated to shorten the war is the humanest policy to follow.   When the most ruthless methods are considered as the best calculated to lead us to a victory and to a swift victory, I said at that time, then they must be employed.

This moment has now arrived.   Last autumn the time was not yet ripe, but to-day the moment has come when, with the greatest prospect of success, we can undertake this enterprise.   We must, therefore, not wait any longer.   Where has there been a change?

In the first place, the most important fact of all is that the number of our submarines has very considerably increased as compared with last spring, and thereby a firm basis has been created for success.   The second co-decisive reason is the bad wheat harvest of the world.   This fact now already confronts England, France and Italy with serious difficulties.   We firmly hope to bring these difficulties by means of an unrestricted U-boat war to the point of unbearableness.

The coal question, too, is a vital question in war.   Already it is critical, as you know, in Italy and France. Our submarines will render it still more critical. To this must be added, especially as regards England, the supply of ore for the production of munitions in the widest sense, and of timber for coal mines. Our enemy's difficulties are rendered still further acute by the increased lack of enemy cargo space. In this respect time and the U-boat and cruiser warfare have prepared the ground for a decisive blow. The Entente suffers in all its members owing to lack of cargo space. It makes itself felt in Italy and France not less than in England. If we may now venture to estimate the positive advantages of an unrestricted U-boat war at a very much higher value than last spring, the dangers which arise for us from the U-boat war have correspondingly decreased since that time.

A few days ago Marshal von Hindenburg described to me the situation as follows: "Our front stands firm on all sides. We have everywhere the requisite reserves. The spirit of the troops is good and confident. The military situation, as a whole, permits us to accept all consequences which an unrestricted U-boat war may bring about, and as this U-boat war in all circumstances is the means to injure our enemies most grievously, it must be begun."

The Admiralty Staff and the High Seas Fleet entertain the firm conviction—a conviction which has its practical support in the experience gained in the U-boat cruiser warfare—that Great Britain will be brought to peace by arms. Our allies agree with our views. Austria-Hungary adheres to our procedure also in practice. Just as we lay a blockaded area around Great Britain and the west coast of France, within which we will try to prevent all shipping traffic to enemy countries, Austria-Hungary declares a blockaded area around Italy. To all neutral countries a free path for mutual intercourse is left outside the blockaded area. To America we offer, as we did in 1915, safe passenger traffic under definite conditions, even with Great Britain.

No one among us will close his eyes to the seriousness of the step which we are taking. That our existence is at stake every one has known since August, 1914, and this has been brutally emphasized by the rejection of our peace offer. When in 1914 we had to seize and have recourse to the sword against the Russian general mobilization, we did so with the deepest sense of responsibility toward our people, and conscious of the resolute strength which says, "We must, and, therefore, we can."

Endless streams of blood have since been shed, but they have not washed away the "must" and the "can." In now deciding to employ the best and sharpest weapon, we are guided solely by a sober consideration of all the circumstances that come into question, and by a firm determination to help our people out of the distress and disgrace which our enemies contemplate for them. Success lies in a higher Hand, but, as regards all that human strength can do to enforce success for the Fatherland, you may be assured, gentlemen, that nothing has been neglected. Everything in this respect will be done.

BY PRESIDENT WILSON
Address to Congress on February 3rd

The Imperial German Government on the 31st day of January announced to this Government and to the Governments of the other neutral nations that on and after the 1st day of February, the present month, it would adopt a policy with regard to the use of submarines against all shipping seeking to pass through certain designated areas of the high seas, to which it is clearly my duty to call your attention.

Let me remind the Congress that on the 18th of April last, in view of the sinking on the 24th of March of the cross-channel steamship *Sussex* by a German submarine without summons or warning, and the consequent loss of lives of several citizens of the United States who were passengers aboard her, this Government addressed a note to the Imperial German Government, in which it made the following declaration:

"If it is still the purpose of the Imperial German Government to prosecute relentless and indiscriminate warfare against vessels of commerce by the use of submarines without regard to what the Government of the United States must consider the sacred and indisputable rules of international law and the universally recognized dictates of humanity, the Government of the United States is at last forced to the conclusion that there is but one course it can pursue. Unless the Imperial Government should now immediately declare and effect an abandonment of its present methods of submarine warfare against passenger and freight carrying vessels, the Government of the United States can have no choice but to sever diplomatic relations with the German Empire altogether."

In reply to this declaration the Imperial German Government gave this Government the following assurance:

"The German Government is prepared to do its utmost to confine the operations of war for the rest of its duration to the fighting forces of the belligerents, thereby also insuring the freedom of the seas, a principle upon which the German Government believes now, as before, to be in agreement with the Government of the United States.

"The German Government, guided by this idea, notifies the Government of the United States that the German naval forces have received the following orders: In accordance with the general principles of visit and search and destruction of merchant vessels recognized by international law, such vessels, both within and without the area declared a naval war zone, shall not be sunk without warning and without saving human lives, unless these ships attempt to escape or offer resistance.

"But," it added, "neutrals cannot expect that Germany, forced to fight for her existence, shall, for the sake of neutral interest, restrict the use of an effective weapon if her enemy is permitted to continue to apply at will methods of warfare violating the rules of international law. Such a demand would be incompatible with the character of neutrality, and the German Government is convinced that the Government of the United States does not think of making such a demand, knowing that the Government of the United States has repeatedly declared that it is determined to restore the principle of the freedom of the seas, from whatever quarter it has been violated."

To this the Government of the United States replied on the 8th of May, accepting, of course, the assurance given, but adding:

"The Government of the United States feels it necessary to state that it takes it for granted that the Imperial German Government does not intend to imply that the maintenance of its newly announced policy is in any way contingent upon the course or result of diplomatic negotiations between the Government of the United States and any other belligerent Government, notwithstanding the fact that certain passages in the Imperial Government's note of the 4th inst. might appear to be susceptible of that construction. In order, however, to avoid any misunderstanding, the Government of the United States notifies the Imperial Government that it cannot for a moment entertain, much less discuss, a suggestion that respect by German naval authorities for the rights of citizens of the United States upon the high seas should in any way or in the slightest degree be made contingent upon the conduct of any other Government, affecting the rights of neutrals and noncombatants. Responsibility in such matters is single, not joint, absolute, not relative."

To this note of the 8th of May the Imperial German Government made no reply.

On the 31st of January, the Wednesday of the present week, the German Ambassador handed to the Secretary of State, along with a formal note, a memorandum which contained the following statement:

"The Imperial Government therefore does not doubt that the Government of the United States will understand the situation thus forced upon Germany by the Entente Allies' brutal methods of war and by their determination to destroy the Central Powers, and that the Government of the United States will further realize that the now openly disclosed intention of the Entente Allies gives back to Germany the freedom of action which she reserved in her note addressed to the Government of the United States on May 4, 1916.

"Under these circumstances, Germany will meet the illegal measures of her enemies by forcibly preventing, after February 1, 1917, in a zone around Great Britain, France, Italy and in the Eastern Mediterranean, all navigation, that of neutrals included, from and to England and from and to France, etc. All ships met within the zone will be sunk."

I think that you will agree with me that, in view of this declaration, which suddenly and without prior intimation of any kind deliberately withdraws the solemn assurance given in the Imperial Government's note of the 4th of May, 1916, this Government has no alternative consistent with the dignity and honor of the United States but to take the course which, in its note of the 18th of April, 1916, it announced that it would take in the event that the German Government did not declare and effect an abandonment of the methods of submarine warfare which it was then employing and to which it now purposes again to resort.

I have therefore directed the Secretary of State to announce to his Excellency the German Ambassador that all diplomatic relations between the United States and the German Empire are severed and that the American Ambassador to Berlin will immediately be withdrawn; and, in accordance with this decision, to hand to his Excellency his passports.

Notwithstanding this unexpected action of the German Government, this sudden and deplorable renunciation of its assurances, given this Government at one of the most critical moments of tension in the relations of the two Governments, I refuse to believe that it is the intention of the German authorities to do in fact what they have warned us they will feel at liberty to do. I cannot bring myself to believe that they will indeed pay no regard to the ancient friendship between their people and our own or to the solemn obligations which have been exchanged between them, and destroy American ships, and take the lives of American citizens in the willful prosecution of the ruthless naval program they have announced their intention to adopt. Only actual overt acts on their part can make me believe it even now.

If this inveterate confidence on my part in the sobriety and prudent foresight of their purpose should unhappily

prove unfounded: if American ships and American lives
should in fact be sacrificed by their naval commanders in
heedless contravention of the just and reasonable understandings of international law and the obvious dictates of
humanity, I shall take the liberty of coming again before
the Congress to ask that authority be given me to use any
means that may be necessary for the protection of our sea-
men and our people in the prosecution of their peaceful and
legitimate errands on the high seas.   I can do nothing less.
I take it for granted that all neutral Governments will take
the same course.

We do not desire any hostile conflict with the Imperial
German Government.   We are the sincere friends of the
German people, and earnestly desire to remain at peace
with the Government which speaks for them.   We shall not
believe that they are hostile to us unless and until we are
obliged to believe it; and we purpose nothing more than the
reasonable defense of the undoubted rights of our people.
We wish to serve no selfish ends.   We seek merely to stand
true alike in thought and in action to the immemorial principles of our people, which I have sought to express in my
address to the Senate only two weeks ago—seek merely to
vindicate our right to liberty and justice and an unmolested
life.   These are the bases of peace, not war.   God grant
that we may not be challenged to defend them by acts of
willful injustice on the part of the Government of Germany!

BY COUNT ROMANONES

Spain's Official Protest of February 6th to the German Ambassador

His Majesty's Government has attentively examined the
note which your Serene Highness was good enough to re-
mit to me January 31st, in which is set forth the German
Government's resolute intention to interrupt as from the
following day all sea traffic, without further notice, and
by no matter what arms, around Great Britain, France,
Italy and in the Eastern Mediterranean.

I must say that the note caused a very painful impression on the Spanish Government.   The attitude of strict
neutrality which Spain adopted from the beginning and has

maintained with loyalty and unshakable firmness gives her the right to expect that the lives of her subjects engaged in sea trade should not be placed in such grave peril. It also gives her the right to expect that that trade should not be troubled nor diminished by such an increase in the extent of the zones in which the Imperial Government insists that, in order to attain its ends, it must use all weapons and suppress all limitations which it has hitherto imposed upon its methods of naval warfare.

Even before the Imperial Government had set aside these restrictions his Majesty's Government had protested, holding them insufficient to comply with the prescriptions of national maritime law. But *the methods of war announced by Germany are being carried to such an unexpected and unprecedented extreme that the Spanish Government, considering its rights and the requirements of its neutrality,* must with still more reason protest calmly but firmly to the Imperial Government, and must make at the same time the necessary reserves, imposed by the legitimate presumption of ineluctable responsibility, which the Imperial Government assumes, principally in view of the loss of life which its attitude may cause.

His Majesty's Government bases its protest on the fact that the decision to close completely the road to certain seas by substituting for the indisputable right of capture in certain cases a pretended right of destruction in all cases is outside the legal principles of international life. Above all and beyond all it considers that *the extension, in the form announced, of this pretended right of destruction to the lives of noncombatants and the subjects of neutral nations such as Spain, is contrary to the principles observed by all nations even in moments of the greatest violence.*

If the German Government, as it says, expects that the Spanish people and Government will not close their ears to the reasons which have caused its decision, and hopes that they will coöperate to avoid further calamities and sacrifices of human life, it will also understand that the Spanish Government, while disposed to lend at the proper time its initiative and support to everything that could contribute to the advent of a peace, more and more wished for, cannot admit the legality of exceptional methods in warfare. These methods, indeed, notwithstanding Spain's right as a neutral and her scrupulous fulfillment of the duties incumbent on her as such, make more difficult and even stop altogether her sea trade, compromising her economic life and threatening with grave dangers the lives of her subjects.

His Majesty's Government, supported more firmly than ever by the justice of its position, does not doubt that the Imperial Government, inspired by the sentiments of friendship which unite the two countries, will find, notwithstanding the severe exigencies of this terrible war, means of giving satisfaction to Spain's claims. These claims are based on the inexorable duty which binds a Government to protect the lives of its subjects and maintain the integrity of its sovereignty so that the course of national existence be not interrupted. For the reasons set out his Majesty's Government feels itself fully sustained in its position by reason and law.

BY LAURO MULLER

Brazil's Official Protest of February 6th to the German Government

I have transmitted to my Government by telegraph your letter of February 3rd, in which your Excellency informed me of the resolution of the German Imperial Government to blockade Great Britain, its islands, the littoral of France and Italy, and the Eastern Mediterranean by submarines which would commence operations on February 1st. Your letter stated that the submarines would prevent all maritime traffic in the zones above mentioned, abandoning all restrictions observed up to the present in the employment of means for sea fighting, and would use every military resource capable of the destruction of ships.

The letter of your Excellency said further that the German Government, having confidence that the Government of Brazil would appreciate the reasons for the methods of war which Germany was forced to take on account of the actual circumstances, hoped that Brazilian ships would be warned of the danger they ran if they navigated the interdicted zones, the same as passengers or merchandise on board any other ship of commerce, neutral or otherwise.

I have just been directed to inform your Excellency that the Federal Government has the greatest desire not to see modified the actual situation, as long as the war lasts, a situation in which Brazil has imposed upon itself the rigorous observance of the laws of neutrality since the commencement of hostilities between nations with whom she has had friendly relations.   My Government has always observed this neutrality while reserving to itself the right, which belongs to it and which it has always been accustomed to exercise, of action in those cases where Brazilian interests are at stake.   The unexpected communication we have just received announcing a blockade of wide extent of countries with which Brazil is continually in economic relations by foreign and Brazilian shipping *has produced a justified and profound impression through the imminent menace which it contains of the unjust sacrifice of lives, the destruction of property, and the wholesale disturbance of commercial transactions.*

In such circumstances, and while observing always and invariably the same principles, the Brazilian Government, after having examined the tenor of the German note, declares that *it cannot accept as effective the blockade which has just been suddenly decreed by the Imperial Government.* Because of the means employed to realize this blockade, the extent of the interdicted zones, the absence of all restrictions, including the failure of warning for even neutral menaced ships, and the announced intention of using every military means of destruction of no matter what character, such a blockade would neither be regular nor effective and would be contrary to the principles of law and the conventional rules established for military operations of this nature.

For these reasons the Brazilian Government, in spite of its sincere and keen desire to avoid any disagreement with the nations at war, with whom it is on friendly terms, believes it to be its duty to protest against this blockade and consequently to leave entirely with the Imperial German Government the responsibility for all acts which will involve

Brazilian citizens, merchandise, or ships and which are proven to have been committed *in disregard of the recognized principles of international law* and of the conventions signed by Brazil and Germany.

CHILE'S OFFICIAL PROTEST OF FEBRUARY 7TH

The Chilean Government has taken cognizance of the note sent to it by his Majesty the German Emperor, in which Chile is informed that Germany has fixed the limits of a blockade area around the coasts of England, France and Italy, and in the Eastern Mediterranean.   It has been informed also that within said limits Germany will resort to hostile acts against whatever ship is encountered, even if it belongs to a neutral power.

Such a measure, in the opinion of the Chilean Government, amounts to a restriction of the rights of neutrals, to which restriction Chile cannot agree because it is contrary to the principles that have been long established in favor of neutral nations.

The acceptance by Chile of the measures adopted by Germany would, moreover, divert her from the line of strict neutrality which has been followed during the European conflict.

Chile consequently reserves liberty of action to protect all of her rights in the event of any hostile acts against her ships.

THE HINDENBURG RETREAT IN FRANCE

UTTER DEVASTATION OF THE ABANDONED REGION

FEBRUARY 24TH-MARCH 18TH

KARL ROSNER   GEORG QUERL   MARSHAL HAIG
OFFICIAL FRENCH AND AMERICAN REPORTS

Of military events, the first striking one in 1917 was the skillfully but wickedly conducted Hindenburg retreat. We must view it from two standpoints. First, as a military maneuver, it was well planned and ably conducted. It was an aftermath of the terrible Somme battle of the preceding fall. That had cost the Germans heavily and left them in many portions of their line in positions but poorly defensible. Now, having resolved to spend this year on the defensive while their submarines fought for them, they selected a strong line some distance in their rear, spent the winter in making it stronger, and then toward the close of February began to retreat secretly to this new "Hindenburg Line." The country which they abandoned they deliberately desolated, so that it should furnish to their enemies neither shelter nor supplies. Thus the French and British, if they advanced, would have to confront the solid Hindenburg Line from new defenses, hastily constructed and with every ounce of material transported over perhaps twenty miles of this man-made desert, without roads or bridges or even a single field that had not been pitted with huge craters by the great guns of either side.

So quietly was the withdrawal conducted that the Allies did not suspect it until it had been in progress almost a month. From March 12th to the 20th, they pressed eagerly after the last squads of the retreating foe. These made the Ally advance as costly as possible with the deadly machine-gun fire; and the toll of lives increased with terrible rapidity as the Allies found their triumphant advance blocked sharply when they reached the Hindenburg Line.

Consider now, the other side of this maneuver, the human, or rather the unhuman, side of it. To destroy for military purposes has long been recognized as the harsh business of war; but to destroy without military need is a pagan, not a Christian deed. To destroy solely through a far-reaching economic selfishness, that is, to ruin a land's resources so that it shall lie stricken and unproductive through the generations of peace to follow, so that its hapless habitants must remain forever impoverished and can never again compete against the destroyer in the markets of the world, such destruction stands outside conceivable deeds for any nation that claims a human brotherhood.

Did Germany attempt such a destruction in this retreat? Her leaders have since denied it; but read the evidence that follows. Read the descriptions by the two noted German eye-witnesses, Rosner and

20

Querl. They represented two chief German newspapers, and theirs were the reports on which the German public fed and triumphed. Read the French Government official report made after close investigation and backed by masses of affidavits. Read the report of the United States ambassadors who visited the scene, Penfield, who was just returning from Austria, and William Sharp, Ambassador to France.

Perhaps the most obvious evidence lies in the fact that had not the Allies achieved their final victory and enforced the reconstruction of these districts upon Germany, then the economic destruction would have attained its end. Had Germany not been completely defeated, she would have won—as still it is conceivable that she may win—in the years of peace to follow. Without this German enforced labor of rebuilding, France and Belgium would have become like Serbia, Rumania, Poland, western Russia and northern Italy. They would have been commercially non-existent.

C. F. H.

BY KARL ROSNER

TO their hunger war, the Entente forces intended to add a new offensive of which the hell of Verdun and the bloody horror of the Somme were to be only foretastes. Once more they wanted to try it; they felt it must succeed. Therefore they armed themselves anew. They set up new divisions after divisions, new batteries after batteries; heaped up ammunition on ammunition all winter. America and Japan kept sending over their iron-freighted giant ships. Our foes gathered together all possible war material for their colossal army. They had the whole world in its service to be strong for the decisive struggle.

Our enemies did more. For months past they had built and built. A thick network of railroads and roads was constructed from deep in their country to their positions. At one word of command fresh material from the depots in the hinterland and fresh masses of troops could pour through a thousand arteries to the fire front. And they supplemented these lines of approach by a system of tracks paralleling their lines.

The idea was to give their front an almost unlimited inner mobility. For example, the troop masses that yesterday stood on the English left wing were to be able suddenly to appear to-day in the center or south of the Somme and be thrown into battle there to our consternation. A network of communications at their back was to make it possible for them at any time in this second Somme battle, which was finally to break our wall in the spring, to rapidly shift their forces and with completely surprising power to change the point of attack according to the conditions of battle. And not only the troops but artillery ammunition depots and war material depots were through this system of railways to receive unprecedented mobility.

The working strength of millions of men in France, England, and overseas has for months had only one creative goal —to build the foundation for the crushing blow—and the thought that the enemy might be able to avert this fate probably never occurred to them. The German highest leadership, which had no intention of leaving the initiative to the foe, thought otherwise, however.

The aim of our leadership was to create a wholly new situation and thereby be spared the colossal bloodshed which an offensive against the enemy's Somme positions would have entailed. Our leadership found the way to render null and void all the preparations of our enemies, and which in front of the new rearward positions at the same time gave us a free, wide-open battleground.

Our retreat from the old positions on the Ancre and the Somme has frustrated the whole of the planned great French and English spring offensive against our center. The enemy, advancing behind us, finds a zone which has been prepared by us as a battle glacis in front of our new positions.

Every German who knows the character and sensibilities of our highest leaders knows that it was no easy decision for them to make the terrain, which for two and a half years we had carefully spared, now ruthlessly serviceable for military purposes. But here there were greater things at stake than considerations for part of a country which had refused us peace. Here the guiding principle for our military decisions could only be that which would bring us the greatest advantages, and for the enemy the most frightful disadvantage.

Therefore, in the course of the last month great strips of France were converted by us into a dead land, which, ten, twelve to fifteen kilometers broad, stretches in front of the whole length of our new positions and offers a ghastly wall of emptiness for every enemy who designs to get at them. No village, no hamlet, remains standing in this glacis—no street remains traversable; no bridge, no railway tracks, no railroad embankment, remains. Where once were woods, only stumps are left. The wells have been blown up; wires and cables destroyed. Like a vast band, a kingdom of death stretches before our new positions. And this is the terrain over which the enemy must now attack us.

No cellar that might serve his troops for shelter remains from which he might build. All our own material was long ago removed, and all local sources from which they might be obtained have been annihilated. The giant trees lining the chaussées have been felled and lie across the roads, and the meadows were plowed up in the early rain; cannon that would attempt to pass here would be swallowed up.

To be sure, this had to entail hardship for the once beautiful country and for its inhabitants. The men who are leading us through the last phase of the war to victory have done everything humanly possible to soften the lot of the inhabitants. Many of them, including all men and youths capable of working, were sent to the rear, for no man capable of carrying arms was to be allowed to swell the line of enemy forces.

On the other hand, such women, children and old men as desired to return to France were brought to a number of villages, including Noyon and Roye, lying beyond the devastated area, which were spared by us as much as possible.

In my visit, I entered at Ham upon the Empire of Death —a Death which lays the shriveled hands of destruction upon all the works of men and all the bloom of Nature. We are in that broad zone of devastation which stretches from the Scarpe to the Aisne.

A year back and earlier I was so often in this country —and I do not know it again. The war has set its mark upon it. Old giant trees once stood here on either side of the road—they are no more. There were houses by the road and farms. There is nothing left of all that, and nothing of the bloom and prosperity of the countryside. As far as the eye can see, the land is bare and desert, a uniform, forbidding, open field of fire, through which the ribbon of road we are following runs as a last remnant of extinct civilization. And even the road will only give passage for a few days longer across the desert. At the crossways it is mined.

Troops meet us on the march and wagons piled high with the men's kit and properties. They have packed up at the front and have left those who will succeed them in the abandoned places nothing, nothing whatever, not a tub, not a bench. And what they could not take with them they have burnt or smashed. They have blown up behind them the shelter in which they had lodged; they have filled up or made undrinkable the wells that gave them water; they have destroyed the lighting and set the barracks on fire.

We push on further into the undulating distance caught in the paralysis of death, and its horror knows no end. Here there once stood villages on either hand, estates, châteaux—all gone. Burnt-out ruins with a spark glowing here and there are the only vestige left of the past that has been swept away—and in the air a sharp, pungent smoke from green wood, beds, dung-heaps, still smoldering. Occasionally, in the distance, the fires still flicker on into the light of day—yellow flames, which now and then veil themselves completely in murky smoke, and then shoot up again, hungry yet almost colorless in the bright light. Any piece of wall that still stands after the burning, is blown up or battered down by engineers. The enemy, when they come, shall not find here so much as a miserable half-burnt wall to shelter them from the wind. Even the cellars have been blown up. But all this is not the work of a few days; it was carried out systematically for weeks and months on end—it had to take months, if it was to pass unnoticed by the enemy. A zone of burning villages would have shown the enemy airmen in a flash what was afoot. No, one village was burnt somewhere one day, and the next day, if the weather was hazy and there was low visibility, two more somewhere else went up in smoke and flames. For the final days nothing was left but what was needed up to the last moment for the accommodation of the troops. And now the sorry remnant goes to ruin, that this stern work of destruction may be complete.

BY GEORG QUERL

It looked like a house-moving of humble folk—mattresses and chairs, with an occasional sewing-machine or hen-coop, and then a fine array of dismantled doors and windows and anything else that seemed worth carrying away from the houses that a few hours later were to go up in smoke and flames. And they sawed away tree trunks —fine, sound, solid wood.

And the desert, a pitiful desert leagues wide, bare of trees and undergrowth and houses! They sawed and hacked; trees fell and bushes sank; it was days and days before they had cleared the ground. In this war zone there was to be no shelter, no cover. The enemy's mouth must stay dry, his eyes turn in vain to the wells—they are buried in rubble. No four walls for him to settle down into; all leveled and burnt out, the villages turned into dumps of rubbish, churches and church towers laid out in ruins athwart the roads.

Smoldering fires and smoke and stench; a rumble spreading from village to village—the mine charges are still doing their final work, which leaves nothing more to do.

It is not so easy to scatter a whole village into brickdust. There are hundreds of villages out there which were under fire for weeks on end, yet still showed a wall or two and an occasional roof. But when our engineers get to work on a village, our engineers! Then it goes into the air as if a mighty earthquake had caught it, it crumbles and breaks up and falls, and the last pitiful houses are knocked out by the *coup de grâce*. And what a rubbish-heap there lies spread—bricks and clay and stones and timbers licked by the flames. Poor devil of a war zone, seek your habitation elsewhere! Old-time farms with massive walls, vaulting, and any amount of resisting power—their walls were drilled scientifically, and the charges fired. Then the whole

farm crumpled up, just as it was intended to do—half over
the road which it was its business to bury, and the other
half into the cracking cellars.

Rubble, nothing but rubble, all this ancient village history, all these future prospects of modern peasant life. The
fine broad yard sinks away with the cottage; the cottage
burns quietly to ashes, and the remains of its clay walls
yield to the first serious stroke of the battering-ram. The
great farm buildings put up a defense—only to fly into
the air, rain down again, and mingle themselves with their
neighbors' misery in a field of ruins which once bore a name
and paid a rent.

Let them see it over there! Let them see it over there!
This fearful naked war should be reflected in all the shop
windows of the Boulevards. We have put distance between
us and our enemies. It is a desert full of wretchedness.

Farewell, comrades of the Somme! The earth which
drank your blood is upheaved and torn asunder. It is made
unfruitful, it is turned into a desert, and your graves are
made free from the dwellings of men. Those who tread it,
your desert, will be greeted by our shells.

Till the last moment the exploding platoons remained
in the towns and villages to finish the work of destruction,
and then fight their way back the best they could. The
general system of retreat was something marvelous. Every
detachment knew exactly which way to turn. Every column
had its way prescribed, and, despite this gigantic movement
of man, beast and truck, there were no blockades, no congestion anywhere, all arriving exactly at the prescribed hour.
Messengers rode about to notify the different commands of
the time to start, while at the same time gigantic motor
cars distributed enormous quantities of explosives to the
pioneer platoons.

Wherever possible, without attracting the special attention of the natives or the Allies, houses were burned
down days before the evacuation. Walls that would not
fall were exploded when the Allies were in the heat of an
artillery fight, suggesting the tremendous effect of their fire.
These preparations took many days, but toward the end

heavy fogs in the mornings and cloudy atmosphere in the afternoons permitted the burning of villages without concealment. And to think, the Allies never had the slightest idea of what was going on! They never interfered with the German plans of destruction, and never thought of shelling the German lines of communication, while endless columns marched over them. The last I saw was German machine-gun platoons disappearing among the ruins and German patrols taking what little part was left to await the Allies. Slowly, with enormous losses, the hostile hordes are now feeling their way through the dangers lurking all about them.

The country behind the allied trenches had been covered with a great network of railways and roads for heavy mortars which would enable them to move divisions and army corps with lightning speed and so concentrate unexpectedly on any weak spot of the German line they might discover while shamming a general attack along the whole front. Day after day German flyers watched the mountains of ammunition and provisions pile up at the British base, to which well-metaled white roads reached out from the trenches like tentacles of some ghastly monster to suck in the whole world for slaughter and destruction. Billions of dollars' worth of material, iron, wood, and cement, and the labor of a vast army was sunk in this ground between the British trenches and the base. All these gigantic preparations were conducted with truly English naïveté, for any other nation would have told itself that flyers watching them day by day would have long ago supplied the German General Staff with very exact data of what was going on.

Then all of a sudden mysterious movements began on the German side. Soldiers, taking with them their kits and all other belongings, left the trenches and dugouts. The mountains of munitions grew rapidly less by the efforts of many hundreds of huge mortar carriers, of wagons drawn by eight horses, streaming incessantly, day and night, over the groundless roads which nobody now thought of repairing any more.

Whole villages disappeared over night, their inhabitants

being concentrated in a few singled-out towns and places where they were comparatively safe and from where they might easily reach their own people when the time would come. Of bush and trees, nothing was left standing that might serve the Allies as cover. Even the belongings were removed from the houses before the latter were leveled to the ground. Night after night the artillery rolled back in an endless chain, followed by regiment after regiment of silent gray war lords.

Small troops armed with machine guns remained behind, however, and kept up a sham of trench war. So well did they succeed in deceiving the British that they often drew the British heavy guns to furious bombardments of what was already a deserted strip of land. Behind their new positions, ten to fifteen kilometers back, the Germans chuckled when they read in the British reports of the explosions of German munition magazines caused by the never-failing British gunfire. They knew only too well that another village had been leveled, another bridge blown up by the astute German pioneers.

When finally the British hesitatingly felt their way into what were once the German lines, they discovered between the Oise and Arras a lifeless chaos which baffled all their zealous preparation of many months for the deadly blow that would now fall on the air.

BY FIELD-MARSHAL HAIG

It had been ascertained [March 12th] that the enemy was preparing a new defensive system known as the Hindenburg Line, which, branching off from his original defenses near Arras, ran southeastward for twelve miles to Queant and thence passed west of Cambrai toward St. Quentin. Various "switches" branching off from this line were also under construction. The enemy's immediate concern appeared to be to escape from the salient between Arras and Le Transloy, which would become increasingly difficult and dangerous to hold as our advance on the Ancre drove ever more deeply into his defenses. It was also evident, however, from the preparations he was making, that he contemplated an eventual evacuation of the greater salient between Arras and the Aisne Valley, northwest of Rheims.

Constant watch had accordingly been kept along the whole front south of Arras, in order that instant information might be obtained of any such development. On March 14th patrols found portions of the German front line empty in the neighborhood of St. Pierre Vaast Wood. Acting on the reports of these patrols, during that night and the following day our troops occupied the whole of the enemy's trenches on the western edge of the wood. Little opposition was met, and by March 16th we held the western half of Moislains Wood, the whole of St. Pierre Vaast Wood, with the exception of its northeastern corner, and the enemy's front trenches as far as the northern outskirts of Sailly-Saillisel.

Meanwhile, on the evening of March 15th, further information had been obtained which led me to believe that the enemy's forces on our front south of the Somme had been reduced, and that his line was being held by rearguard detachments supported by machine guns, whose withdrawal might also be expected at any moment. The corps commanders concerned were immediately directed to confirm the situation by patrols. Orders were thereafter given for a general advance, to be commenced on the morning of March 17th, along our whole front from the Roye Road to south of Arras.

Except at certain selected localities, where he had left detachments of infantry and machine guns to cover his retreat, such as Chaulnes, Vaux Wood and Bapaume, the enemy offered little serious opposition to our advance on this front, and where he did so his resistance was rapidly overcome. Before nightfall on March 17th Chaulnes and Bapaume had been captured, and advanced bodies of our troops had pushed deeply into the enemy's positions at all points from Damery to Monchy-au-Bois. On our right our allies made rapid progress also and entered Roye.

On March 18th and subsequent days our advance continued, in coöperation with the French. In the course of this advance the whole intricate system of German defenses in this area, consisting of many miles of powerful, well-wired trenches which had been constructed with immense labor and worked on till the last moment, were abandoned by the enemy and passed into the possession of our troops.

At 7 a. m. on March 18th our troops entered Péronne and occupied Mont St. Quentin, north of the town. To the south our advanced troops established themselves during the day along the western bank of the Somme from Péronne to just north of Epenancourt. By 10 p. m. on the same day Brie Bridge had been repaired by our engineers sufficiently for the passage of infantry in single file, and our troops crossed to the east bank of the river, in spite of some opposition. Further south French and British cavalry entered Nesle.

North of Péronne equal progress was made, and by the evening of March 18th our troops had entered the German trench system known as the Beugny-Ypres line, beyond which lay open country as far as the Hindenburg Line. On the same day the left of our advance was extended to Beaurains, which was captured after slight hostile resistance.

OFFICIAL REPORT OF THE FRENCH INVESTIGATING COM-
MISSION HEADED BY GEORGES PAYELLE, PRESIDENT
OF THE COURT OF AUDITS

Monsieur le Président,

We have just been over a part of the regions of the Oise, the Aisne and the Somme, which, after lying for over thirty months under German domination, have recently been delivered from its crushing and abominable yoke.

Every detail in the spectacle of devastation that met our eyes reveals a method so implacable and so strikingly uniform that it is impossible not to recognize the execution of a rigorously marked-out plan. The enslavement of citizens, the carrying off of women and young girls, the pillage of homes, the annihilation of towns and villages, the ruin of industries by the destruction of factories, the desolation of rural districts by the shattering of agricultural implements, the burning of farms and the cutting down of trees, were all inaugurated at the same moment and with the same ferocity, to create poverty, inspire terror and generate despair.

In the majority of the places we visited, the enemy, at the beginning of his occupation, does not seem to have indulged in sanguinary excesses comparable in numbers to those which marked his furious course through Champagne and Lorraine. Nevertheless, in several places we were informed of murders and serious assaults upon the person.

Though murders do not appear to have been numerous in the districts we have visited so far, the occupation was certainly of a most rigorous nature. Requisitions were continual everywhere. The communes had to contribute to the maintenance of the troops quartered in their territory, and were compelled to pay enormous subsidies. To provide these when their pecuniary resources were exhausted, they were forced to form unions among themselves for the purpose of issuing paper-money in the form of warrants. Mayors who declined to come into this scheme were arrested and sent to Germany. The enemy gave these notes forced currency and put them into circulation himself. The inhabitants were subjected to vexations of every kind, and daily witnessed the theft of the few provisions they possessed and of the household objects most necessary to them. In the shops, officers and soldiers took as if by right all that they coveted. Thus at Ham, in M. Gronier's ironmongery shop, an officer of high rank, said to have been the Grand Duke of Hesse, came to choose various articles, in payment for which he merely promised to send a warrant, which was never delivered.

Every moment our unfortunate fellow citizens had to endure fresh restrictions on their rights and fresh attacks upon their dignity—orders to be within doors by 7 o'clock in the evening, and not to go out before 8 o'clock in the morning; prohibitions upon the burning of lights in houses during the night, injunctions to doff hats to officers in salutation; compulsory labor in the fields—all enforced by terms of imprisonment and by fines, to which the inhabitants were continually exposed by the slightest infraction of the innumerable regulations. But nothing equals the abominations that occurred in certain communes, such as Fréniches, where, one day in May, 1915, all the young girls of the village were summoned to the house appropriated to the German military doctor and were subjected to the most brutal and revolting examination, in spite of their screams of protestation.

In February, 1917, that is to say, at the moment when the Germans were beginning to prepare for their retreat, they committed the savage depredations which are now known to the entire world, and which revolt the universal conscience of mankind.

There had already been deportations of a large number of inhabitants, whom the invader, quite without mercy in breaking up families, had sent to work in Germany or in the north of France. This measure was now generalized, and has affected the entire able-bodied portion of the population of both sexes from sixteen to sixty years old, the only exceptions being women with young children. It was applied in all the communes with the same rigor, and produced the most heartrending scenes. Among the 600 persons carried off from Ham there were four patients from the hospital. At Noyon, a week after sending off the first batch, on February 17th, the Germans selected fifty young girls who had been expelled from the region of St. Quentin and interned in the town. They were all sent to the north, in spite of the tears and entreaties of their parents, whose anguish was terrible.

Here, as in many other places, doctors, chemists and priests were among the first to be marked out for exile, and as nothing had been left in the pharmacy at the hospital, or in the operating-theater, which had been disgracefully pillaged, the numerous invalids and sick persons brought from the neighboring districts were unable, in spite of the efforts of charity, to obtain the care and succor of which they stood the more urgently in need because they were exhausted by cold, privation and sorrow. All these unfortunate creatures had arrived in a miserable state, and seven or eight of them died every day. They were persons who had been dragged from their beds, and who had not been

given time to carry away anything. Among them there
were paralyzed and dying people, several nonogenarians,
and even one woman of 102 years old. Many had been
carried off under the most atrocious circumstances. Mme.
Deprez, the owner of the Château of Gibercourt, one of
the victims of these pitiless orders, was suffering from a
serious affection of the heart, and was obliged to keep her
bed. An officer insisted upon her getting up and dressing
in his presence, although she begged him to retire. She
died twelve days later. Mme. Bègue, a woman of Flavy-
le-Martel, who was also suffering from cardiac disease, had
asked to be allowed to take with her her two young children, aged seven and four respectively, who were clinging
to the wheels of the vehicle. This favor was refused, and
the poor little creatures were left in the road. Another
woman of the same commune was ill in bed when she was
told that the Germans were about to carry off her husband.
She got up at once, and, in spite of the opposition of an
officer, succeeded in throwing herself into the prisoner's
arms. He had to leave without embracing his child. The
young woman was expelled from Noyon and brought to the
hospital, where she abandoned herself to the most violent
despair. On the day of her arrival she threw herself, together with her little girl, under the wheels of a motor car.
Fortunately the nuns succeeded in rescuing her in time.

All these deportations afforded an army which has turned
war into brigandage special facilities for appropriating at
its leisure all that had escaped its earlier depredations. "Our
compatriots were scarcely four kilometers on their road,"
we were told by M. Dacheux, a municipal councilor who was
acting as mayor at Guiscard, "when vans arrived at their
doors to carry everything off." At Ham, the head of the
Kommandantur took good care not to return a very valuable old table which he had borrowed from the Mairie, and
General von Fleck removed all the furniture from M. Bernot's house, where he had been quartered. The operation
was carried out so thoroughly that at the end of his stay the
General, who had nothing left to sit on, was obliged to ask
the municipality for a few chairs.

At Noyon, throughout the period of occupation, there was continual robbery. Many houses were sacked and the interiors defiled in a disgraceful manner. The bells of the cathedral and the pipes of the great organ were removed by order of the commanding officer. Safes belonging to private persons were broken open by revolver shots fired into the mechanism of the lock. On February 26th and 27th two soldiers, accompanied by two officers, came and opened the safes of the Société Générale by means of a blow-pipe, and carried off the contents. The same operation was carried out at Chéneau and Barbier's Bank and at Brière's Bank. The ledgers of each establishment were seized at the same time as the valuables. When M. Brière expressed astonishment that even his archives should be taken from him, and pointed out that they could be of no use to any one but himself, the officer whom he had addressed, and who gave himself out to be the emissary of the Berlin Treasury, merely replied: "My orders were to empty the safes, and I am emptying them."

At Sempigny, one of the few places where the houses are still standing, it is possible to form some idea of the scenes of plunder which occurred everywhere. From March 1st, the date on which such of the able-bodied inhabitants as still remained were expelled, until the departure of the invading troops, this unhappy village was incessantly pillaged. It looks as if a horde of violent maniacs had passed through it, and in truth the Germans displayed a sort of frenzy in destroying everything they could not carry off, shattering beds and wardrobes with pick-axes or mallets, pulverizing crockery and mirrors, breaking up agricultural implements and gardening tools, scattering corn and seed, stealing all the furniture of the High Altar in the Church, defiling drawers and cupboards with filth, and leaving excrements even in the kitchen utensils. Most of these exploits were performed by the 338th Infantry Regiment.

One asks oneself with stupefaction how the army of a nation which claims to be civilized could have been guilty of such deeds; but it is still more astounding to find that its soldiers even violated the resting-places of the dead. In the cemetery of Carlepont, the door of the chapel over the vault of the Swiss family Graffenried-Villars was carried off. Nothing but the copper fittings were left. A stone of the vault was prized up, and bones are visible through the aperture. The tomb of the Caillé family was also desecrated. The stone which covered it is broken, and human remains are exposed. At Candor, two witnesses surprised some Germans in the act of breaking open the tombs of the Trefcon and Censier families, and examining the interior of the Mazier vault, the lid of which they had worked off. The church to which the cemetery belongs had been shamefully pillaged; the silver figures of Christ on the Crucifixes had been torn off, and Mme. Collery herself removed the ornaments with which the soldiers had derisively decked the statue of a saint. At Roiglise there is a gaping hole in the pavement of the Derreulx Chapel which exposes the compartments of the vault. A coffin can be seen in one and some bones in another. All this damage is undoubtedly due to criminal enterprises, for there is no trace of bombardment either in or about the tombs.

After they had been pillaged, houses, châteaux and farms were destroyed by means of explosives, or were set on fire or demolished with pick-axes. At Margny-aux-Cerises, the operation was performed with the help of a powerful battering-ram. Annois, Flavy-le-Martel, Jussy, Frières-Faillouel and Villequier-Aumont no longer exist. Chauny, a manufacturing town of nearly 11,000 inhabitants, is nothing but a heap of ruins, save for the suburb of Le Brouage.

After the expulsion of the able-bodied inhabitants, the rest of the population, consisting of 1,990 persons, were herded into this suburb together with about 3,000 men and women from the thirteen communes of the district, on February 23, 1917. On March 3rd an order was issued from the *Kommandantur* ordering all these people to assemble the next day at 6 o'clock in the morning in one of the streets. Sick and infirm persons were not exempted, and some of them had to be carried to the place of assembly, which was over a kilometer long. There was a general call over and then an inspection, which lasted not less than six hours, and during which an officer selected three more men, thirty-one women, and a boy of thirteen for deportation to the north. The cold was intense, and on the following day twenty-seven persons died.

As soon as the citizens of Chauny were interned at Le Brouage, the Germans gave themselves up to unbridled pillage in the town, carrying off furniture, ripping open strong boxes, and sacking churches; and for a fortnight they proceeded to destroy the houses methodically by mines and incendiarism. For the past two months they had made notes of the dimensions of all the cellars, and so knew exactly what quantities of explosives were necessary for the execution of their infamous task.

Nothing is left of the Church of St. Martin but some portions of the wall. In Notre Dame, only a part of which was injured by explosion, the three alms-boxes are broken, and the marks of the instruments used to force them are very noticeable. The locks of the cupboards set in the paneling of the transept are forced. In the sacristy the chaos is indescribable; the presses are smashed, the drawers pulled out, and polluted sacerdotal ornaments are strewn on the ground.

On the 20th the enemy, having effected his retreat, began to bombard Le Brouage with batteries placed on the heights of Rouy. The bombardment continued for two and a half days, and was directed more especially against the Institute of St. Charles, which the Germans themselves had allotted as an asylum for the sick and aged, and on the roof of which they had painted enormous red crosses. Several persons were killed and others were wounded more or less seriously.

Even in the towns and villages they have not completely razed to the ground, the Germans made frantic efforts to destroy the factories and ruin agriculture. At Roye, for instance, where the fighting had caused no irreparable damage, they burned the sugar-refineries and took systematic steps to ruin all the industries, first by seizing all bronze, zinc, lead, copper and tin, and then by carrying off all the pieces of mechanism of any value, and smashing all

the castings.   At Ham, again, where they blew up the bell
tower and the château, they also blew up the two sugar-
refineries of Messrs. Bocquet and Bernot, the Sebastopol
distillery, M. Dive's oil refinery and M. Serré's brewery.
They acted in the same manner in many other places, notably
at Flavy-le-Martel and at Ourscamp, which are models of
devastation.   Nearly everywhere the fruit trees in the open
country and in gardens have been cut down, savagely hacked
about, or barked in such a way as to kill them.   Long rows
of great poplar-trees, sawn through at the base, strew the
fields adjoining the roads.   The approaches to the villages
are blocked by agricultural implements irretrievably damaged.   Near what was once the railway station of Flavy-le-
Martel we saw a vast orchard entirely devastated, and made
a dumping ground for a large number of plows, harrows,
mowing and reaping machines, mechanical rakes and sowers
which have been wrecked, the damage being of such a kind
that they are beyond repair.   Here and there a certain number of these machines had been piled on bonfires.   The iron
wheels were sprung, the mechanism smashed, and the wooden
parts charred by the flames.

One has only to look at all these ruins to recognize that
they were not heaped one upon another merely for military
reasons, and that the desire to injure was the essential motive.   A German army doctor, Professor Benneke, said
one day to Sister St. Romauld, the Sister Superior of the
hospital at Noyon: "You would not accept peace, so now
we have orders to make war on civilians"; and at Guiscard
a non-commissioned officer, who seemed intelligent and well
educated, expressed himself as follows: "As Germany's
peace offers have been rejected, the war is about to enter
on a new phase.   Henceforth we shall respect nothing."

Such words reveal a very poor psychology.   Nowhere,
indeed, among those who have undergone such cruel trials,
have we noted any indication of lassitude or discouragement; we have met with no sentiment but that of patriotic
enthusiasm and a fierce determination to obtain by victory
the reparation for this multitude of crimes.

BY FREDERIC C. PENFIELD

Former U. S. Ambassador to Austria-Hungary

By invitation of Premier Ribot I went to the French front to witness the great drive slowly but surely forcing the German invaders from French soil, and to view the area recently evacuated by the Germans. Secretary Frazier of the American Embassy and I were sent in a military automobile in charge of a high official from the Foreign Office. We had been told much of the ruthless devastation, prompted by military necessity or custom, but no oral account could give more than a suggestion of what we saw that day.

We traveled practically all over the Department of the Aisne, and approached to within eight miles of the lines of the German Crown Prince near St. Quentin. A terrific artillery battle was in progress. Many observation balloons were above us and military flyers seemed battling as fiercely in the sky as were the artillerists from their hidden positions. It was a sight never to be forgotten.

We visited Noyon, Péronne, Ham, Coucy, Chauny—in fact practically every town between the British front on the west and Verdun on the east. Scores of towns and villages, isolated châteaux and factories were razed to the ground. The entire Aisne Department seemed destroyed beyond repair.

The Germans appeared to have an antipathy to Catholic churches, for battering had reduced all to shapeless piles of débris. The destruction everywhere was complete, outrageous, fiendish. During the day we saw no living thing native to the land—no cow, sheep or horse; no dog, cat or fowl.

We visited many stately châteaux that had been destroyed beyond man's ability to repair. At one place we found the private chapel of a historic family of France whose coffins had been opened by vandals searching for plunder. Everywhere French soldiers told us that it had been only five weeks earlier when the rout of the Germans had become so urgent that they hastened through villages plundering and burning as they went—but not until all art objects and furniture of value had been dispatched beyond the Rhine.

Critics of Germany claim that one has but to visit the northern departments of France to learn that the refinement of barbarism is not confined to Germany's program on the seas, for it is expressed in the invaded zone of France in a manner causing revulsion to witness. From every town and village men and women had been driven into Germany like animals by the infuriated and beaten Teutons.

As I saw the destruction and thought of the generosity of my country people, I wondered if liberal Americans would not be glad to rebuild or assist in restoring some of the ruined towns and villages of the Aisne and Champagne. There can be no form of charity half as useful at this time.

The most ruthless and revolting thing that a visitor to the evacuated area perceives is the total destruction of all trees, fruit-bearing and ornamental. Nearly every tree in the Aisne Department has been felled, and for what purpose? There can be but one—to cripple the restoration of Northern France to usefulness. Men and money can rebuild the homes and factories in a year or two, but to restore the orchards and other useful trees will call for a half century. What the Germans did to tree life in Northern France was the systematic murdering of Nature, nothing less.

Our automobile broke a tire near a village that had been the appanage of a once splendid château, and when the chauffeur was making the repairs six or eight children gathered about the machine to witness the work. Two lads were better dressed than the others and wore neat suits of cotton corduroy. I engaged the elder of these brothers in conversation by asking where the garments came from and he promptly replied: "From the American Relief Clearing House Committee, which has fed and clothed us since the Boches were driven away."

"Have you any relatives?" I inquired. To this the boy answered: "Yes, my poor mother lies sick in that cottage there," pointing to a poor peasant house. "Have you sisters?" I asked, and this was the reply: "Two, aged 19 and 21. Both were outraged by the Germans and carried off by the retreating army. Our poor father, who tried to protect our sisters, was shot dead by the Boches, who said he was disobedient, and his body lies buried there by the roadside."

To me this incident in an Aisne village was more convincing of the barbarity and fiendishness of the men of military Germany than all the books and newspaper exposures I had ever read. I returned that night to Paris and decided in my belief that God would never permit the ferocious Kaiser William to succeed in his mad assault upon civilization. As an illustration of German *Kultur,* Belgium may present brutal instances in excess of those of the evacuated regions in France, but not many, I am sure. The deportations have been fewer from France, but fully as cruel in character.

BY WILLIAM SHARP

U. S. Ambassador to France in 1917

PARIS, April 1, 1917.
Secretary of State,
        Washington.

Accepting an invitation, kindly extended to me several days ago, I yesterday visited many of the French towns recently retaken in the invaded territory, making the trip in a military automobile. I was accompanied by military attaché Boyd. I regret to say that I found the various reports in circulation here, and doubtless forwarded to American newspapers, of the deplorable conditions in those towns are in no way exaggerated. With very few exceptions the places visited by me, though few in comparison, numbering upwards of thirty, had been quite destroyed by the Germans before evacuating them. The destruction wrought in the larger towns of Roye, Ham, and particularly the once thriving and attractive city Chauny, was complete. In many of the other smaller villages scarcely a house remains with its roof intact. A scene of desolation reigns everywhere over the reconquered territory. This is true not alone where the possibly excusable military operations carried out by the Germans protected their retreat, by the blowing up of

Shattered Relic

German shell strikes the Chateau du Ham, injuring the carefully preserved window from which Napoleon III escaped from imprisonment.

all the bridges and the destruction of the means of telegraphic and telephonic connections, including portions of railway lines, and the blocking of highways by the felling of many trees, but also where, as far as the eye could see, nearly all the fruit trees had either been cut down or exploded so as to completely ruin them. Not only were the towns destroyed for no seeming military reason, but every private house along the country highways, including some of the most beautiful châteaux of great value, had been completely gutted by explosives or by fires systematically planned. I am told that before the retreat commenced the agricultural implements found on the farms were also destroyed. Blackened walls of what must have been extensive manufacturing establishments were to be seen in many places, the salvage of which, including likewise that of most of all the other structures destroyed, would scarcely pay for the removal of the débris. The churches and cathedrals in some of the towns had been reduced to a mass of ruins by the Germans either by heavy charges of explosives or by fires.

At Ham I was told by the mother of six children that her husband and two daughters, one of the age of fifteen and the other eighteen, had been carried away by the Germans at the time of their evacuating the town, and upon her remonstrating she had been told that as an alternative she might find their bodies in the canal in the rear of her home. The same woman informed me that out of that town's total population several hundred people had been compelled to accompany the Germans, nearly half of whom were women and girls above fifteen years of age. There is the belief that a large number of French people in the evacuated towns and surrounding country were forced by the Germans to go with them in their retreat, from the fact that so comparatively few are now to be found.

After traversing a distance of more than one hundred miles in this invaded territory, I left with the conviction that history records no parallel in the thoroughness of destruction wrought either by a victorious or a vanquished army.

THE ZIMMERMANN WAR SCHEME EXPOSED

GERMANY URGES MEXICO AND JAPAN TO ATTACK THE UNITED STATES

FEBRUARY 28TH

DR. ALFRED ZIMMERMANN   THEODOR WOLFF
COUNT TERAUCHI

Time clears our perspective upon many matters. The Zimmermann note was an official letter sent secretly by Zimmermann, Germany's Secretary of Foreign Affairs, to her Minister in Mexico, directing him to attempt to unite Mexico and Japan with Germany in war against the United States. This document was captured by the United States secret service upon the Texas border, and was disclosed to the American public on February 28th, at the height of the brief interval of indignation and uncertainty between America's breaking of diplomatic relations and her declaring war.

Thus revealed, the note had a profound psychological effect. More than anything else, it hardened the peace-loving American people to the conviction that war with Germany was an absolutely necessary step. Many Americans regarded the note as another piece of German treachery, like the blowing up of their factories and placing bombs upon their ships; and they voiced their renewed anger against the false foe who encouraged secret murder while wearing the mask of peace. To-day, however, most statesmen would agree that the note lay well within Germany's rights. It expressly stated that the alliance against the United States was only to be attempted if and after the fact was certain that there was to be "an outbreak of war."

The deeper influence of the note upon Americans, therefore, depended not so much upon its evidence of Germany's evil methods of attack, but upon its revelation that she had no intention whatever of limiting her U-boat warfare so as to placate them. She had "counted the cost." If she could coax or frighten them into submitting to this U-boat destruction, good; if not, she meant to fight. Of America's backing down from the diplomatic stand of 1916, with all its background of American patience and German violence and subterfuge, there was no possibility whatever. Americans knew that surely; though Germany apparently did not. Hence the Zimmermann note told them that the war, the Great War, had come to them at last.

What strikes one most about the Zimmermann note to-day is not its perfidy, but its folly, its utter folly and futility. Mexico knew well that no German ship, no aid in men or in munitions, could possibly reach her. She delighted much in annoying the United States; but what chance was there that she would deliberately invite destruction by declaring war to oblige Germany? Or, even if we conceive Mexico guilty of such murderous madness, what effect could it have upon the United States beyond the holding of a few thousand troops upon the southern border, while the rest of the nation turned with increased anger and determination to Germany's overthrow?

When to this we add the absurdity of supposing that Mexico could at all sway the policy of Japan, the Zimmermann note becomes so monumental a stupidity that many men did not believe it could possibly be genuine, until Herr Zimmermann himself acknowledged it. It would seem more logical to assume that Germany meant the note for just what it achieved, meant it, that is, to be revealed and thus to confirm America's intent for war. We give therefore Dr. Zimmermann's defense of his note, and also the comment of Germany's most noted news-editor, Herr Wolff. We then give the Japanese Prime Minister's prompt rejection of the note and of all its suggestions. It is typical of the unfortunate Mexican attitude that no similar repudiation ever came from Mexico. C. F. H.

BY DR. ALFRED ZIMMERMANN

The Secret Note to Germany's Mexican Minister, Von Eckhardt

BERLIN, January 19, 1917.

ON the first of February we intend to begin submarine warfare unrestricted. In spite of this it is our intention to endeavor to keep neutral the United States of America.

If this attempt is not successful, we propose an alliance on the following basis with Mexico:

That we shall make war together and together make peace. We shall give general financial support and it is understood that Mexico is to reconquer the lost territory in New Mexico, Texas and Arizona. The details are left to you for settlement.

You are instructed to inform the President of Mexico of the above in the greatest confidence as soon as it is certain that there will be an outbreak of war with the United States, and suggest that the President of Mexico, on his own initiative, should communicate with Japan suggesting adherence at once to this plan; at the same time offer to mediate between Germany and Japan.

Please call to the attention of the President of Mexico that the employment of ruthless submarine warfare now promises to compel England to make peace in a few months.

(Signed) ZIMMERMANN.

Dr. Zimmermann's Speech of March 29th Defending His Mexican Note Against a Socialist Attack by Hugo Haase

I wrote no letter to General Carranza. I was not so naïve. I merely addressed, by a route that appeared to me to be a safe one, instructions to our representative in Mexico. It is being investigated how these instructions fell into the hands of the American authorities. I instructed the Minister to Mexico, in the event of war with the United States, to propose a German alliance to Mexico, and simultaneously to suggest that Japan join the alliance. I declared expressly that, despite the submarine war, we hoped that America would maintain neutrality.

My instructions were to be carried out only after the United States declared war and a state of war supervened. I believe the instructions were absolutely loyal as regards the United States.

General Carranza would have heard nothing of it up to the present if the United States had not published the instructions which came into its hands in a way which was not unobjectionable. Our behavior contrasts considerably with the behavior of the Washington Government.

President Wilson after our note of January 31, 1917, which avoided all aggressiveness in tone, deemed it proper immediately to break off relations with extraordinary roughness. Our Ambassador no longer had the opportunity to explain or elucidate our attitude orally. The United States Government thus declined to negotiate with us. On the other hand, it addressed itself immediately to all the neutral powers to induce them to join the United States and break with us.

Every unprejudiced person must see in this the hostile attitude of the American Government, which seemed to consider it right, before being at war with us, to set the entire world against us. It cannot deny us the right to seek allies when it has itself practically declared war on us.

Herr Haase says that it caused great indignation in America. Of course, in the first instance, the affair was employed as an incitement against us. But the storm abated slowly and the calm and sensible politicians, and also the great mass of the American people, saw that there was nothing to object to in these instructions in themselves. I refer especially to the statements of Senator Underwood. Even at times newspapers felt obliged to admit regretfully that not so very much had been made out of this affair.

The Government was reproached for thinking just of Mexico and Japan. First of all, Mexico was a neighboring State to America. If we wanted allies against America, Mexico would be the first to come into consideration. The relations between Mexico and ourselves since the time of Porfirio Diaz have been extremely friendly and trustful. The Mexicans, moreover, are known as good and efficient soldiers.

It can hardly be said that the relations between the United States and Mexico had been friendly and trustful.

But the world knows that antagonism exists between America and Japan. I maintain that these antagonisms are stronger than those which, despite the war, exist between Germany and Japan.

When I also wished to persuade Carranza that Japan should join the alliance there was nothing extraordinary in this. The relations between Japan and Mexico are long existent. The Mexicans and Japanese are of a like race and good relations exist between both countries.

When, further, the Entente press affirms that it is shameless to take away allies, such reproach must have a peculiar effect coming from powers who, like our enemies, made no scruple in taking away from us two powers and peoples with whom we were bound by treaties for more than thirty years. The powers who desire to make pliant an old European country of culture like Greece by unparalleled and violent means cannot raise such a reproach against us.

When I thought of this alliance with Mexico and Japan I allowed myself to be guided by the consideration that our brave troops already have to fight against a superior force of enemies, and my duty is, as far as possible, to keep further enemies away from them. That Mexico and Japan suited that purpose even Herr Haase will not deny.

Thus, I considered it a patriotic duty to release those instructions, and I hold to the standpoint that I acted rightly.

BY THEODOR WOLFF

The invitation to Mexico would have been a mistake even if it had not strayed from the right road. The fresh spirit of enterprise it shows, too impatiently eliminated sober judgment.

The Minister to Mexico was instructed to hold out the conquest of Texas, New Mexico, and Arizona to Carranza, and it would certainly be interesting to see the face of the wily Mexican when this offer was made. The idea, too, that through Carranza's mediation one could win over rather self-conscious Japan is somewhat strange. With Russia, England, and America, all leading powers in Eastern Asia, standing on the other side, Japan will certainly not be very amenable to Mexico's influence. It is not probable one can help along the world's history in this way.

Naturally no man says a word about morality in this connection; in the first place, morality has for a long time been that thing whose nonobservance is self-understood; secondly, it hasn't the least to do with the Mexican matter. It is not immoral to offer Mexico an alliance for the eventuality of war, and it would not be immoral even to ask Japan, "My yellow beauty, will you go with me?" One who does so is far from being a Machiavelli.

Likewise, nothing justifies the charge that the authors of the plan have touched the fuse to the American powder barrel. The development of things would have been approximately the same, even without the Mexican correspondence. Neither should one condemn an action because it fails. The greatest diplomatic geniuses have occasionally gone wrong.

After we have thus blown ourselves up with righteousness, we can quietly say that the jewel of statesmanship went lost between Berlin and Mexico.

BY COUNT TERAUCHI

The revelation of Germany's latest plot, looking to a combination between Japan and Mexico against the United States, is interesting in many ways. We are surprised not so much by the persistent efforts of the Germans to cause an estrangement between Japan and the United States as by their complete failure of appreciating the aims and ideals of other nations.

Nothing is more repugnant to our sense of honor and to the lasting welfare of this country than to betray our allies and friends in time of trial and to become a party to a combination directed against the United States, to whom we are bound not only by the sentiments of true friendship, but also by the material interests of vast and far-reaching importance.

The proposal which is now reported to have been planned by the German Foreign Office has not been communicated to the Japanese Government up to this moment, either directly or indirectly, officially or unofficially, but should it ever come to hand I can conceive no other form of reply than that of indignant and categorical refusal.

THE FALL OF BAGDAD

BRITAIN PIERCES TO THE HEART OF ASIATIC TURKEY

MARCH 11TH

GASTON BODART   SIR STANLEY MAUDE

EDMUND CANDLER

Our last volume told of the capture of the British army at Kut-el-Amara in 1916, and the disastrous effect of this upon the Allies' cause in Asia. Slowly and with splendid tenacity, Britain reorganized her eastern forces for another attack. Sir Stanley Maude was placed in command, and we give his own account of the decisive campaign which in three months carried him from the British base upon the Persian Gulf, northward up the Mesopotamian valley to the conquest of Bagdad. Moving up the great twin rivers of Bible fame, the Tigris and the Euphrates, the British approached Kut about mid-January, and after a month of stubborn fighting recaptured the town on February 24th. That was really their main battle.

Not until March 7th did the broken and fleeing Turks make another resolute stand. This was many miles farther up the valley, at Diala, just below Bagdad itself. Here came the "Battle for Bagdad." The Turks, defeated, fled again; and Bagdad was occupied on March 11th.

Content with this spectacular success, and made cautious by their previous disaster, the British did not attempt to follow the Turks into the mountainous regions further north. Instead they undertook the thorough reform and reconstruction of the vast captured region. Much of Persia also fell into their hands, and Sir Stanley Maude began a large administrative work. It was interrupted by his sudden death, probably by poison, before the end of the year. His successor completed the British conquest of Mesopotamia. The Teuton view of these events is given by Dr. Bodart, the official investigator for both Germany and Austria.

BY GASTON BODART

IT was to be expected that after the capture of Townshend's army England would strain every nerve to retrieve her prestige. Within the next seven months General Maude prepared with far greater care a much larger and better equipped expeditionary force. In the first place the rear lines of communication were improved, enlarged and made secure. For this purpose Basra was selected as an adequate base of operations. In conformity with the principle advocated by Lord Kitchener in his Khartoum enterprise, field railroads were constructed between Basra and the operating army, and the flotilla on the Tigris was correspondingly increased and equipped.

General Maude methodically grappled with the situation at Kut, attacking that position from two sides, east and south. Under continued pressure of the gunboats, he captured Kut on February 23rd, 1917. The badly shaken Turkish army did not offer any further resistance of consequence to the English advance; the right wing of the English army being protected as far as Kengawer by the Russian group of General Baratoff. The last Turkish position in the angle of the stream, formed by the junction of the Diala and the Tigris, was stormed, and it became necessary for the Turks to evacuate Bagdad. On March 11th the English entered the city of the Caliphs.

After a union with the Russians had been made by the occupation of Bakuba, and when Feludjah had been captured and the Euphrates made secure as far as Hit, the English continued their march toward Mosul. By a simultaneous advance of the principal columns along both banks of the Tigris and the victorious battle at Istabulat (April 21st, 1917) Samarra was reached, the two defeated Turkish corps being compelled to fall back to Mosul.

After a long pause, necessitated by the climatic conditions, Maude succeeded in nipping in the bud a design on the part of the Turks to deliver a blow against his left flank, in order to sever his rear communications. The powerful Turkish position on the Euphrates near Ramadieh was successful attacked on September 28th with sufficient forces (a former attempt had failed), was surrounded by the cavalry and forced to surrender, whereby the Turkish commander Achmed Bey and 3,500 men were taken prisoners. General Maude, the British commander-in-chief, died on November 19th in consequence of a camp malady, and was superseded by General Marshall. Under his command the English consolidated their control of Mesopotamia.

BY SIR STANLEY MAUDE

Briefly put, the enemy's plan appeared to be to contain our main forces on the Tigris, while a vigorous campaign, which would directly threaten India, was being developed in Persia. There were indications, too, of an impending move down the Euphrates toward Nasariyeh. It seemed clear from the outset that the true solution of the problem was a resolute offensive, with concentrated forces, on the Tigris, thus effectively threatening Bagdad, the center from which the enemy's columns were operating.

At the beginning of December the enemy still occupied the same positions on the Tigris front which he had held during the summer, and it was decided first to secure possession of the Hai River; secondly, to clear the Turkish trench systems still remaining on the right bank of the Tigris; thirdly, to sap the enemy's strength by constant attacks, and give him no rest; fourthly, to compel him to give up the Sannaiyat position, or in default of that to extend his attenuated forces more and more to counter our strokes against his communications; and, lastly, to cross the Tigris at the weakest part of his line as far west as possible, and so sever his communications.

The Hai position was seized with little difficulty in the middle of December, but the clearing of the Khadairi Bend, which was undertaken on January 6th, involved severe hand-to-hand fighting, and it was not until January 19th that the enemy, who had suffered heavy losses, was finally driven out.

On January 11th, while Lieut.-Gen. Cobbe was still engaged in clearing the Khadairi Bend, Lieut.-Gen. Marshall commenced preparations for the reduction of the Hai salient —the extensive trench system which the Turks held astride the Hai River near its junction with the Tigris, and for a fortnight we gained ground steadily in face of strong opposition, until, on the 24th, our trenches were within 400 yards of the enemy's front line.

On the 25th the enemy's front line astride the Hai was captured on a frontage of about 1,800 yards. On the eastern (or left) bank our troops extended their success to the Turkish second line, and consolidated and held all ground won in spite of counter-attacks during the day and following night. The enemy lost heavily, both from our bombardment and in violent hand-to-hand encounters. On the western (or right) bank the task was a severe one. The trench system was elaborate, and offered facilities for counter-attack. The enemy was in considerable strength on this bank, and guns and machine guns in skillfully concealed positions enfiladed our advance.

On February 3rd the Devons and a Ghurka battalion carried the enemy's first and second lines, and a series of counter-attacks by the Turks, which continued up till dark, withered away under our shrapnel and machine-gun fire. Our troops east of the Hai coöperated with machine-gun and rifle fire, and two-counter-attacks by the enemy on the left bank of the Hai during the day were satisfactorily disposed of. In the evening there were indications that he was contemplating withdrawal to the right bank, and by daybreak on the 4th the whole of the left bank had passed into our possession.

During this period the splendid fighting qualities of the infantry were well seconded by the bold support rendered by the artillery, and by the ceaseless work carried out by the Royal Flying Corps. These operations had again resulted in heavy losses to the enemy, as testified to by the dead found, and many prisoners—besides, arms, ammunition, equipment, and stores—had been taken, while the Turks now only retained a fast vanishing hold on the right bank of the Tigris.

February 6th to 8th were days of preparation, but continuous pressure on the enemy was maintained day and night. On the ninth the licorice factory was bombarded, and simultaneously the King's Own effected a lodgment in the center of the enemy's line, thereafter gaining ground rapidly forward and to both flanks. Repeated attacks by the enemy's bombers met with no success, and two attempted counter-attacks were quickly suppressed by our artillery. Further west the Worcesters, working toward Yusufiyah and west of that place, captured some advanced posts, trenches and prisoners, and established a line within 2,500 yards of the Tigris at the southern end of the Shumran Bend.

On February 3rd the Devons and a Ghurkha battalion west of the licorice factory, who had been subjected all night to repeated bombing attacks, began early to extend our hold on the enemy's front line. This movement was followed by a bombardment directed against machine guns located at Kut and along the left bank of the Tigris, which were bringing a galling fire to bear against our right. During this the Buffs and a Ghurkha battalion dashed forward, and, joining hands with the King's Own on their left, the whole line advanced northward. As communication trenches did not exist, any movement was necessarily across the open, and was subject to a hot fire from concealed machine guns on the left bank, but, in spite of this, progress was made all along the front to depths varying from 300 to 2,000 yards, our success compelling the enemy to evacuate the licorice factory. He withdrew to an inner line, approximately two and a half miles long, across the Dahra Bend, with advanced posts strongly held, and was finally inclosed in the Dahra Bend by February 13th.

An attack against the enemy's right center offered the best prospects of success, and this involved the construction of trenches and approaches for the accommodation of troops destined for the assault. Early on February 15th the Loyal North Lancashires captured a strong point opposite our left, which enfiladed the approaches to the enemy's right and center, the retiring Turks losing heavily from our machine-gun fire. An hour later the enemy's extreme left was subjected to a short bombardment and feint attack. This caused the enemy to disclose his barrage in front of our right, and indicated that our constant activity on this part of his front had been successful in making him believe that our main attack would be made against that part of his line. Shortly after the Royal Welsh Fusiliers and South Wales Borderers carried the enemy's right center in dashing style on a front of 700 yards, and extended their

success by bombing to a depth of 500 yards on a frontage
of 1,000 yards, taking many prisoners. Several half-hearted
counter-attacks ensued, which were crushed by our artillery
and machine guns, and it became evident that the enemy
had strengthened his left and could not transfer troops back
to his center on account of our barrage. A little later the
enemy's left center was captured by the Buffs and Dogras,
and, pushing on in a northeasterly direction to the bank of
the Tigris, they isolated the enemy's extreme left, where
about 1,000 Turks surrendered.

By nightfall the only resistance was from some trenches
in the right rear of the position, covering about a mile of
the Tigris bank, from which the enemy were trying to escape
across the river, and it had been intended to clear these remaining trenches by a combined operation during the night;
but two companies of a Ghurkha battalion, acting on their
own initiative, obtained a footing in them and took 98
prisoners. By the morning of the 16th they had completed
their task, having taken 264 more prisoners. The total
number of prisoners taken on the 15th and 16th was 2,005,
and the Dahra Bend was cleared of the enemy.

Thus terminated a phase of severe fighting, brilliantly
carried out. To eject the enemy from this horseshoe bend,
bristling with trenches and commanded from across the
river on three sides by hostile batteries and machine guns,
called for offensive qualities of a high standard on the part
of the troops. That such good results were achieved was
due to the heroism and determination of the infantry, and
to the close and ever-present support rendered by the artillery, whose accurate fire was assisted by efficient airplane
observation.

The enemy had now, after two months of strenuous
fighting, been driven entirely from the right bank of the
Tigris in the neighborhood of Kut. He still held, however,
a very strong position, defensively, in that it was protected
from Sannaiyat to Shumran by the Tigris, which also afforded security to his communications running along the
left bank of that river. The successive lines at Sannaiyat,
which had been consistently strengthened for nearly a year,

barred the way on a narrow front to an advance on our part along the left bank, while north of Sannaiyat the Suwaikieh Marsh and the Marsh of Jessan rendered the Turks immune from attack from the north.

On the other hand, we had, by the application of constant pressure to the vicinity of Shumran, where the enemy's battle line and communications met, compelled him so to weaken and expand his front that his attenuated forces were found to present vulnerable points, if these could be ascertained. The moment then seemed ripe to cross the river and commence conclusions with the enemy on the left bank. To effect this it was important that his attention should be engaged about Sannaiyat and along the river line between Sannaiyat and Kut, whilst the main stroke was being prepared and delivered as far west as possible.

While Lieut.-Gen. Marshall's force was engaged in the Dahra Bend, Lieut.-Gen. Cobbe maintained constant activity along the Sannaiyat front, and as soon as the right bank had been cleared orders were issued for Sannaiyat to be attacked on February 17th. The sodden condition of the ground, consequent on heavy rain during the preceding day and night, hampered final preparations, but the first and second lines, on a frontage of about 400 yards, were captured by a surprise assault with little loss. Before the captured trenches, however, could be consolidated they were subjected to heavy fire from artillery and trench mortars, and were strongly counter-attacked by the enemy. The first counter-attack was dispersed, but the second regained for the enemy his lost ground, except on the river bank, where a party of Ghurkhas maintained themselves until dusk, and were then withdrawn. The waterlogged state of the country and a high flood on the Tigris now necessitated a pause, but the time was usefully employed in methodical preparation for the passage of the Tigris about Shumran.

On February 22nd the Seaforths and a Punjabi battalion assaulted Sannaiyat, with the same objective as on the 17th. The enemy were again taken by surprise, and our losses were slight. A series of counter-attacks followed, and the first three were repulsed without difficulty. The fourth drove back our left, but the Punjabis, reënforced by an Indian Rifle battalion and assisted by the fire of the Seaforths, who were still holding the Turkish trenches on the right front, reëstablished their position. Two more counterattacks which followed were defeated. As soon as the captured position had been consolidated two frontier force regiments assaulted the trenches still held by the enemy in prolongation of, and to the north of, those already occupied by us. A counter-attack forced our right back temporarily, but the situation was restored by the arrival of reënforcements, and by nightfall we were in secure occupation of the first two lines of Sannaiyat. The brilliant tenacity of the Seaforths throughout this day deserves special mention.

Feints in connection with the passage of the Tigris were made on the night of the 22nd-23rd opposite Kut and at Magasis, respectively. Opposite Kut preparations for bridging the Tigris opposite the licorice factory, under cover of a bombardment of Kut, were made furtively in daylight, and every detail, down to the erection of observation ladders, was provided for. The result was, as afterward ascertained, that the enemy moved infantry and guns into the Kut peninsula, and these could not be retransferred to the actual point of crossing in time to be of any use. The feint at Magasis consisted of a raid across the river, made by a detachment of Punjabis, assisted by parties of sappers and miners and of the Sikh Pioneers. This bold raid was successfully carried out with trifling loss, and the detachment returned with a captured trench mortar.

The site selected for the passage of the Tigris was at the south end of the Shumran Bend, where the bridge was to be thrown, and three ferrying places were located immediately downstream of this point. Just before daybreak on February 23rd the three ferries began to work. The first trip at the ferry immediately below the bridge site, where the Norfolks crossed, was a complete surprise, and five machine guns and some 300 prisoners were captured. Two battalions of Ghurkhas, who were using the two lower ferries, were met by a staggering fire before they reached the left bank, but in spite of losses in men and pontoons they pressed on gallantly and effected a landing. The two down-stream ferries were soon under such heavy machine-gun fire that they had to be closed, and all ferrying was subsequently carried on by means of the upstream ferry.

By 7.30 a. m. about three companies of the Norfolks and some 150 of the Ghurkhas were on the left bank. The enemy's artillery became increasingly active, but was vigorously engaged by ours, and the construction of the bridge commenced. The Norfolks pushed rapidly upstream on the left bank, taking many prisoners, while our machine guns on the right bank, west of the Shumran Bend, inflicted casualties on those Turks who tried to escape. The Ghurka battalions on the right and center were meeting with more opposition, and their progress was slower. By 3 p. m. all three battalions were established on the east and west line one mile north of the bridge site, and a fourth battalion was being ferried over. The enemy attempted to counter-attack down the center of the peninsula and to reënforce along its western edge, but both attempts were foiled by the quickness and accuracy of our artillery. At 4.30 p. m. the bridge was ready for traffic.

By nightfall, as a result of the day's operations, our troops had, by their unconquerable valor and determination, forced a passage across a river in flood, 340 yards wide, in face of strong opposition, and had secured a position 2,000 yards in depth, covering the bridgehead, while ahead of this line our patrols were acting vigorously against the enemy's advanced detachments, who had suffered heavy losses, including about 700 prisoners taken in all. The infantry of one division were across and another division was ready to follow.

While the crossing at Shumran was proceeding, Lieut.-Gen. Cobbe had secured the third and fourth lines at Sannaiyat. Bombing parties occupied the fifth line later, and work was carried on all night making roads across the maze of trenches for the passage of artillery and transport. Early on February 24th our troops in the Shumran Bend resumed the advance, supported by machine guns and artillery from the right bank. The enemy held on tenaciously at the northeast corner of the peninsula, where there is a series of nalas in which a number of machine guns were concealed, but after a strenuous fight, lasting for four or five hours, he was forced back, and two field and two machine guns and many prisoners fell into our possession. Further west our troops were engaged with strong enemy forces in the intricate mass of ruins, mounds, and nalas which lie to the northwest of Shumran, and rapid progress was impossible, but toward evening the enemy had been pushed back to a depth of 1,000 yards, although he still resisted stubbornly.

While this fighting was in progress the cavalry, the artillery, and another division crossed the bridge. The cavalry attempted to break through at the northern end of the Shumran Bend to operate against the enemy's rear along the Bagdad road, by which airplanes reported hostile columns to be retreating, but strong Turkish rearguards entrenched in nalas prevented them from issuing from the peninsula. During this day's fighting at Shumran heavy losses had been inflicted on the enemy, and our captures have been increased in all to four field guns, eight machine guns, some 1,650 prisoners, and a large quantity of rifles, ammunition, equipment and war stores. The gunboats were now ordered upstream from Falahiyeh, and reached Kut the same evening.

While these events were happening at Shumran, Lieut.-Gen. Cobbe cleared the enemy's sixth line at Sannaiyat, the Nakhailat, and Suwada positions, and the left bank as far as Kut without much opposition.

The capture of the Sannaiyat position, which the Turks believed to be impregnable, had only been accomplished after a fierce struggle, in which our infantry, closely supported by our artillery, displayed great gallantry and endurance against a brave and determined enemy. The latter had again suffered severely. Many trenches were choked with corpses, and the open ground where counter-attacks had taken place was strewn with them.

Early in the morning of February 25th the cavalry and Lieut.-Gen. Marshall's force moved northwest in pursuit of the enemy, whose rearguards had retired in the night.

The gunboats also proceeded upstream. Our troops came in contact with the enemy about eight miles from Shumran and drove him back, in spite of stubborn resistance, to his main position two miles further west, where the Turks, strong in artillery, were disposed in trenches and nalas. Our guns, handled with dash, gave valuable support, but were handicapped in this flat country by being in the open, while the Turkish guns were concealed in gun pits. After a severe fight our infantry gained a footing in the enemy's position and took about 400 prisoners. The cavalry on the northern flank had been checked by entrenched infantry and were unable to envelop the Turkish rearguard. The Royal Navy, on our left flank, coöperated with excellent effect in the bombardment of the enemy's position during the day.

On the 26th one column, following the bend of the river, advanced to force any position which the enemy might be holding on the left bank of the Tigris, while another column of all arms marched direct to the Sumar Bend in order to intercept him. His retreat proved, however, to be too rapid. Stripping themselves of guns and other incumbrances, the Turks just evaded our troops, who had made a forced march across some eighteen miles of arid plain. Our cavalry came up with the enemy's rear parties and shelled his rearguard, entrenched near Nahr Kellak.

The gunboat flotilla, proceeding upstream full speed ahead, came under very heavy fire at the closest range from guns, machine guns and rifles, to which it replied vigorously. In spite of casualties and damage to the vessels, the flotilla held on its course past the rearguard position, and did considerable execution among the enemy's retreating columns. Further upstream many of the enemy's craft were struggling to get away, and the Royal Navy pressed forward in pursuit. The hostile vessels were soon within easy range, and several surrendered, including the armed tug *Sumana,* which had been captured at Kut when that place fell. The Turkish steamer *Basra,* full of troops and wounded, surrendered when brought to by a shell which killed and wounded some German machine gunners. His Majesty's ship *Firefly,* captured from us during the retreat from Ctesiphon in 1915, kept up a running fight, but, after being hit several times, she fell into our hands, the enemy making an unsuccessful attempt to set fire to her magazine. The *Pioneer,* badly hit by our fire, was also taken, as well as some barges laden with munitions. Our gunboats were in touch with and shelled the retreating enemy during most of the 27th, and his retirement was harassed by the cavalry until after dark, when his troops were streaming through Aziziyeh in great confusion.

The pursuit was broken off at Aziziyeh (fifty miles from Kut and halfway to Bagdad), where the gunboats, cavalry, and Lieut.-Gen. Marshall's infantry were concentrated during the pause necessary to reorganize our extended line of communication preparatory to a further advance. Lieut.-Gen. Cobbe's force closed to the front, clearing the battle-fields and protecting the line of march. Immense quantities of equipment, ammunition, rifles, vehicles, and stores of all kinds, lay scattered throughout the eighty miles over which the enemy had retreated under pressure, and marauders on looting intent did not hesitate to attack small parties who stood in their way.

Since crossing the Tigris we had captured some 4,000 prisoners, of whom 188 were officers; thirty-nine guns, twenty-two trench mortars, eleven machine guns, his Majesty's ships *Firefly, Sumana* (recaptured), *Pioneer, Basra* and several smaller vessels, besides ten barges, pontoons and other bridging material, quantities of rifles, bayonets, equipment, ammunition and explosives, vehicles, and miscellaneous stores of all kinds. In addition, the enemy threw into the river or otherwise destroyed several guns and much war material.

On March 5th, the supply situation having been rapidly readjusted, Lieut.-Gen. Marshall marched to Zeur (eighteen miles), preceded by the cavalry, which moved seven miles further to Lajj. Here the Turkish rearguard was found in an entrenched position, very difficult to locate by reason of a dense dust storm that was blowing and of a network of nalas, with which the country is intersected. The cavalry was hotly engaged with the enemy in this locality throughout the day, and took some prisoners. A noticeable feature of the day's work was a brilliant charge made, mounted, by the Hussars straight into the Turkish trenches. The enemy retreated during the night.

The dust storm continued on the 6th, when the cavalry, carrying out some useful reconnoissances, got within three miles of the Diala River, and picked up some prisoners. The Ctesiphon position, strongly entrenched, was found unoccupied. There was evidence that the enemy had intended to hold it, but the rapidity of our advance had evidently prevented him from doing so. Lieut.-Gen. Marshall followed the cavalry to Bustan (seventeen miles), and the head of Lieut.-Gen. Cobbe's column reached Zeur.

On March 7th our advanced guard came in contact with the enemy on the line of the Diala River, which joins the Tigris on its left bank, about eight miles below Bagdad. As the ground was absolutely flat and devoid of cover, it was decided to make no further advance till after sunset. Our gunboats and artillery, however, came into action against the hostile guns.

Measures for driving the enemy's infantry from the Diala were initiated on the night of March 7th-8th. It appeared as though the enemy had retired, but when the first pontoon was launched it was riddled by rifle and machine-gun fire. A second attempt was made with artillery and machine-gun coöperation. Five pontoons were launched, but they were all stopped by withering fire from concealed machine guns. They floated down stream, and were afterward recovered in the Tigris River with a few wounded survivors on board, and further ferrying enterprises were for the time being deemed impracticable. It now became evident that, although the line of the Diala was not held strongly, it was well defended by numerous guns and machine guns skillfully sited, and the bright moonlight favored the defense. To assist in forcing the passage a small column from the force under Lieut.-Gen. Marshall was ferried across the Tigris in order to enfilade the enemy's position with its guns from the right bank of that river.

During the night of the 8th-9th, after an intense bombardment of the opposite bank, an attempt was made to ferry troops across the Diala River from four separate points. The main enterprise achieved a qualified success, the most northern ferry being able to work for nearly an hour before it was stopped by very deadly rifle and machine-gun fire, and we established a small post on the right bank. When day broke this party of seventy of the Loyal North Lancashires had driven off two determined counter-attacks and were still maintaining themselves in a small loop of the river bend. For the next twenty-two hours, until the passage of the river had been completely forced, the detachment held on gallantly in its isolated position under constant close fire from the surrounding buildings, trenches, and gardens, being subjected to reverse as well as enfilade fire from distant points along the right bank.

On the 8th a bridge was constructed across the Tigris, half a mile below Bawi, and the cavalry, followed by a portion of Lieut.-Gen. Cobbe's force, crossed to the right bank in order to drive the enemy from positions which our airplanes reported that he had occupied about Shawa Khan, and northwest of that place, covering Bagdad from the south and southwest. The advance of our troops was much impeded by numerous nalas and water cuts, which had to be ramped to render them passable. During the forenoon of the 9th Shawa Khan was occupied without much opposition, and airplanes reported another position one and a half miles to the northwest, and some six miles south of Bagdad, as strongly held. Our attack against this developed later from the south and southwest in an endeavor to turn the enemy's right flank. The cavalry, which at first had been operating on our left flank, withdrew later, as the horses needed water; but our infantry were still engaged before this position when darkness fell, touch with the enemy being kept up by means of patrols, and the advance was resumed as soon as indications of his withdrawal were noticed.

On the morning of March 10th our troops were again engaged with the Turkish rearguard within three miles of Bagdad, and our cavalry patrols reached a point two miles west of Bagdad railway station, where they were checked by the enemy's fire. A gale and blinding dust storm limited vision to a few yards, and under these conditions reconnoissance and coördination of movements became difficult. The dry wind and dust and the absence of water away from the river added greatly to the discomfort of the troops and animals. About midnight patrols reported the enemy to be retiring. The dust storm was still raging, but, following the Decauville Railway as a guide, our troops occupied Bagdad railway station at 5.55 a. m., and it was ascertained that the enemy on the right bank had retired upstream of Bagdad. Troops detailed in advance occupied the city, and the cavalry moved on Kadhimain, some four miles northwest of Bagdad, where they secured some prisoners.

On the left bank of the Tigris Lieut.-Gen. Marshall had during the 9th elaborated preparations for forcing the passage of the Diala. At 4 a. m. on the 10th the crossing began at two points a mile apart, and met with considerable opposition, but by 7 a. m. the East Lancashires and Wiltshires were across and had linked up with the detachment of Loyal North Lancashires which had so heroically held its ground there. Motor lighters carrying infantry to attack the enemy's right flank above the mouth of the Diala grounded lower down the river, and took no part in the operation. The bridge across the Diala was completed by noon, and our troops, pushing steadily on, drove the enemy from the riverside villages of Saidah, Dibaiyi and Qararah—the latter strongly defended with machine guns—and finally faced the enemy's last position covering Bagdad along the Tel Muhammad Ridge. These operations had resulted in the capture of 300 prisoners and a large quantity of arms, ammunition, and equipment, while severe loss had been inflicted on the enemy in killed and wounded, more than 300 of his dead being found by our troops.

During the night of March 10th-11th close touch with the enemy was maintained by patrols, and at 1.30 a. m. on the 11th it was reported that the Turks were retiring. The Tel Muhammad position was at once occupied, and patrols pushed beyond it, but contact with the enemy was lost in the dust storm. Early on the 11th Lieut.-Gen. Marshall advanced rapidly on Bagdad, and entered the city amid manifestations of satisfaction on the part of the inhabitants. A state of anarchy had existed for some hours, Kurds and Arabs looting the bazaars and setting fire indiscriminately at various points. Infantry guards provided for in advance were, however, soon on the spot, order was restored without difficulty, and the British flag hoisted over the city. In the afternoon the gunboat flotilla, proceeding upstream in line ahead formation, anchored off the British Residency, and the two forces under Lieut.-Gens. Marshall and Cobbe provided for the security of the approaches to the city, being disposed one on either bank of the river.

For more than a fortnight before we entered Bagdad the enemy had been removing stores and articles of military value and destroying property which he could not remove, but an immense quantity of booty, part damaged, part undamaged, remained. This included guns, machine guns, rifles, ammunition, machinery, railway workshops, railway material, rolling stock, ice and soda water plant, pipes, pumps, cranes, winches, signal and telegraph equipment, and hospital accessories. In the arsenal were found, among some cannon of considerable antiquity, all the guns (rendered useless by General Townshend) which fell into the enemy's hands at the capitulation of Kut in April, 1916.

On the right bank of the Tigris the retreating enemy had entrenched a strong position south of Mushaidie railway station, some twenty miles north of Bagdad. A force under Lieut.-Gen. Cobbe carried this on March 14th, after a brilliant charge by the Black Watch and Ghurkhas. At Mushaidie station the enemy made his last stand, but the Black Watch and Ghurkhas rushed the station at midnight, and pursued the enemy for half a mile beyond. The enemy's flight was now so rapid that touch was not obtained again, and on March 16th our airplanes reported stragglers over a depth of twenty miles, the nearest being twenty-five miles north of Mushaidie.

On the same day a post was established on the right bank of the Diala, opposite Baqubah, thirty miles northeast of Bagdad, and four days later Baqubah was captured. On

March 19th our troops occupied Feluja, thirty-five miles west of Bagdad, on the Euphrates, driving out the Turkish garrison. The occupation of Feluja, with Nasariyeh already in our possession, gave us control over the middle Euphrates from both ends. During the remainder of the month minor operations were undertaken on the Diala, pending the arrival of the Russian forces advancing from Persia. The total number of prisoners taken during the period December 13th to March 31st was 7,921.

BY EDMUND CANDLER

The last fighting before Bagdad is likely to become historic on account of the splendid gallantry of our troops in the crossing of the Diala River. After the action at Lajj the Turkish rearguard fell back on Diala, destroying the bridge which crosses the stream at its junction with the Tigris. We pushed on in pursuit on the left bank, sending cavalry and two columns of infantry to work round on the right bank, and to enter Bagdad from the west. Speed in following up was essential, and the column attacking Diala was faced with another crossing in which the element of surprise was eliminated. The village lies on both banks of the stream, which is 120 yards wide. The houses, trees, nullah, and walled gardens made it impossible to build a road and ramps quickly and to bring up pontoons without betraying the point of embarkation. Hence the old bridge-head site was chosen. The attack on the night of the 7th was checked, but the quality of courage shown by our men has never been surpassed in war. Immediately the first pontoon was lowered over the ramp the whole launching party was shot down in a few seconds. It was a bright moonlight, and the Turks had concentrated their machine guns and rifles in the houses on the opposite bank.

The second pontoon had got into the middle of the stream, when a terrific fusillade was opened on it. The crew of five rowers and ten riflemen were killed and the boat floated down the stream. A third got nearly across, but was bombed and sank. All the crew were killed. But there was no holding back. The orders still held to secure the passage. Crew after crew pushed off to an obvious and certain death. The fourth crossing party was exterminated in the same way, and the pontoons drifted out to the Tigris to float past our camp in the daylight with their freight of dead. The drafts who went over were raised by volunteers from other battalions in the brigade. These and the sappers on the bank share the honor of the night with the attacking battalion. Nothing stopped them, save the loss of the pontoons. A Lancashire man remarked: "It is a bit hot here, but let's try higher up," but the gallant fellows were reduced to their last boat. Another regiment, which was to cross higher up, were delayed, as the boats had to be carried nearly a mile across country to the stream. After the failure of the bridge-head passage the second crossing was cancelled, but the men were still game.

On the second night the attempt was pursued with equal gallantry. This time the attack was preceded by a bombardment. Registering by artillery had been impossible on the first day in the speed of the pursuit. It was the barrage that secured us the footing—not the shells, but the dust raised by them. This was so thick that you could not see your hand in front of your face. It formed a curtain behind which ten boats were able to cross. Afterwards, in clear moonlight, when the curtain of dust had lifted, the conditions of the night before were reëstablished. Succeeding crossing parties were exterminated, and pontoons drifted away, but a footing was secured. The dust served us well. The crew of one boat which lost its way during the barrage were untouched, but they did not make the bank in time. Directly the air cleared a machine gun was opened on them, and the rowers were shot down, and the pontoon drifted back ashore. A sergeant called to volunteers to get the wounded out of the boat, and a party of twelve men went over the river bank. Every man of them, as well as the crew of the pontoons, were killed.

Some 60 men had got over, and these joined up and started bombing along the bank. They were soon heavily pressed by the Turks on both flanks, and found themselves between two woods. Here they discovered a providential

natural position. A break in the river bund had been repaired by a new bund built in a half-moon on the landward
side. This formed a perfect lunette. The Lancashire men,
surrounded on all sides but the river, held it through the
night, all the next day, and the next night against repeated
and determined attacks. Those attacks were delivered in
the dark or at dawn. The Turks only attacked once in the
daylight, as our machine guns on the other bank swept the
ground in front of the position. Twenty yards west of the
lunette there was a thin grove of mulberries and palms.
The pontoon was most vulnerable on this side, and it was
here that the Turkish counter-attacks were most frequent.
Our intense intermittent artillery fire day and night on the
wood afforded some protection. The whole affair was visible to our troops on the south side, who were able to make
themselves heard by shouting. Attempts to get a cable
across with a rocket for the passage of ammunition failed.

At midnight on the 9th and 10th the Turks were on top
of the parapet, but were driven back. One more determined
rush would have carried the lunette, but the little garrison,
now reduced to 40, kept their heads and maintained cool
control of their fire. A corporal was seen searching for
loose rounds and emptying the bandoliers of the dead. In
the end they were reduced almost to their last clip and one
bomb, but we found over 100 Turkish dead outside the
redoubts when they were relieved at daylight. The crossing on the night of the 9th and 10th was entirely successful. With our cavalry and two columns of infantry working round on the right bank the Turks were in danger of
being cut off, as at Sanna-i-Yat. Before midnight they had
withdrawn their machine guns, leaving only riflemen to dispute the passage. The crossing upstream was a surprise.
We slipped through the Turkish guard. He had pickets at
both ends of the river salient where we dropped our pontoons. But he overlooked essential points in it which offered us dead ground uncovered by posts up and down
stream. Consequently our passage here lost us no lives. The
other ferry near the bridge was also crossed with slight
loss, owing to a diversion upstream. The Turks, perceiving

that their flank was being turned, effected a general retirement of the greater part of their garrison between the two ferries. Some 250 in all, finding us bombing down on both flanks, surrendered. The upper crossing was so unexpected that one Turk was actually bayoneted as he lay covering the opposite bank with his rifle.

By 9.30 on the morning of the 10th the whole brigade had crossed. Soon after 11 the brigade was complete and the pursuit continued. The Turks continued their rearguard action, and in the afternoon there was fighting in the palm groves of Saidah, and the Turks were cleared with the bayonet, after artillery had combed the wood. The main body was holding the Tel Muhammad position, one and a half miles further north—a trench line running nearly four miles inland from the Tigris. We attacked this in front, while another column made a wide turning movement on the flank, and the enemy evacuated it at night. On the morning of the 11th we entered Bagdad. Our force on the right bank, after defeating the Turkish rearguard in two actions, reached the suburb on the opposite side of the Bridge of Boats. A brigade was ferried across in coracles, and at noon they hoisted the Union Jack on the citadel. Meanwhile the cavalry continued the pursuit and occupied Kadhimain after slight resistance. Four damaged aëroplanes and 100 prisoners were taken, in addition to the 300 captured on the left bank. The gunboats continued in pursuit of the enemy.

RUSSIA PROCLAIMS A REPUBLIC

AUTOCRACY DISAPPEARS FROM AMONG THE ALLIES

MARCH IITH-15TH

JOHN POLLOCK   CZAR NICHOLAS II.
              GRAND DUKE MICHAEL
STANISLAUS DE LAZOVERT   BORIS BAKHMETEFF

The exciting days of March 11th-15th in the Russian capital are
here described by John Pollock, a British newspaper correspondent
of high repute and authority, who witnessed much of what he here
depicts. The revolution had long been growing in every patriotic
Russian heart, because of the incompetence and suspected treachery
of the rulers and their palace favorites. Indeed, the active revolution
might well be reckoned as beginning with the killing of the "black
monk" Rasputin, the most evil of the foul knaves who enjoyed the
Czar's blinded protection. He was slain by desperate patriots on the
New Year's eve of 1917; and the story of that night is here given by
De Lazovert, a Russian colonel who took part in it. Of course the
colonel's story, while probable, lacks supporting evidence as to its details; but in some such fashion Rasputin died. His body was found
next day in the river.

Angered by Rasputin's death, the royal party increased its severity.
It is even probable that their police deliberately provoked a revolt,
for the sake of trampling on it. If so, they overshot their mark; for
discontent had pervaded the army as well as the civilian populace,
and when the latter were stirred to protest on March 11th, the army
sided with them. Against the army the police were powerless. Thus
the actual moment of the breaking forth of the revolution was acci-
dental, but the event itself was inevitable—unless the Czar could have
wholly changed his character and his entourage. In fact, the revolution was but a continuation of the unsuccessful outbreak of 1905. In
that year affairs had gone so far that the Czar had printed, but never
published, his abdication. Now abdication was promptly forced upon
him.

This revolution of March, 1917, was fortunate for the moment in
that Russia's most upright patriots were on hand to take immediate
control of its confused and ignorant forces. The national parliament,
or "Duma," was in session at the time, and was resolutely defying the
palace party, which had ordered its dispersal. The Duma had possessed neither legal nor military power to defend itself; but the soldiers
and populace, when they had defied the police, appealed to the Duma
to direct them, and the Duma took control.

Thus this first revolution, or this first stage in the increasing revo-

68

lution of the months that followed, brought to the front the strongest, wisest and most noble-minded men of Russia. Unfortunately neither their strength nor wisdom proved sufficient to protect and guide the densely ignorant masses. For the moment, however, everything looked bright. The country was declared a republic. Prince Lvoff, long the noblest champion of the people's rights, the leader of the Zemstvos, or local councils, was made Prime Minister. Professor Paul Milyukof, leader of the Democratic party in the Duma, became Foreign Minister. A. I. Guchkov, the parliamentary leader who had secured the Czar's peaceful abdication, made a most able and successful Minister of War; and the young Socialist lawyer, Kerensky, whose oratory had won him the confidence of the multitude, became Minister of Justice.

All that the new Democracy hoped to accomplish is here set forth by their official representative, Ambassador Bakhmeteff, who reached America in June. Uncle Sam had been prompt to recognize and welcome the new Democracy; and Bakhmeteff bore his country's message of thanks and plighted friendship.

BY JOHN POLLOCK

"DURING the last days disorders have taken place in Petrograd, followed by force and assaults on the lives of soldiers and members of the police.

"I forbid every kind of assembly in the streets.

"I warn the population of Petrograd that commands have been issued and repeated to the troops to use their arms and not to stop short of anything in order to assure tranquillity in the capital.—HABALOV, Lieutenant-General Commanding the Forces in the Petrograd Military Area, February 25, 1917."

The above proclamation was posted in the streets of Petrograd on the morning of February 26th-March 11th. Its effects were quickly seen. Before evening there were some three hundred dead, killed in the square opposite the Nicholas Station by machine-gun fire, and over a hundred more along the Nevsky Prospect. At night the streets, that had been unusually full of sightseers, were deserted, the Nevsky was guarded by troops from end to end, and a searchlight installed in the Admiralty illumined its waste and menacing length. The Government appeared to be securely in possession. On the following morning a proclamation was posted from General Habalov that if all the workmen did not resume work by the morning of March 13th they would be arrested and sent into the ranks. He received an answer no less prompt than startling. In less than twenty-four hours from the signing of his second threat, General Habalov was a prisoner and almost the whole of Petrograd in the hands of the populace and revolutionary soldiery.

In the midst of the most gigantic war one of the most momentous of known revolutions had been accomplished in the space of exactly seven days. Nevertheless, it began not as a revolution to change the form of government, but as a movement directed against the particular Government that was in power because the Government had become suspicious to all thinking and patriotic men. The first appeals made preserved the Emperor's authority, and the people showed no wish to change it; but events moved rapidly beyond this point. The immediate causes of the revolution are the reaction that has only gained in severity since the assassination of Rasputin, provocation by agents in the service of the Home Minister and probably bought by German money, and shortage of bread. It is the last that, acting on the exasperation produced by the two former, has brought about the explosion. An intimate connection links the three causes together, and all three are closely connected with the conduct of the War.

From an early stage in the War there has existed a strong pro-German element in the Russian Government, and much criminal negligence and actual treachery in high places. The mass of the nation, the huge unlettered peasant population, were inspired by vague feelings of patriotism, while among the small educated class all the progressive spirits looked to victory over the Germans as a priceless chance for the nation to raise itself toward self-consciousness and freedom. The first revelation of highly protected treachery was the plot of Colonel Myasoyedov, an intimate friend of the Minister of War, which gave the Germans the key to Lithuania. This was followed by the staggering news that the Minister himself, General Sukhumiloff, under the exalted ægis of the Imperial Inspector of Artillery, had failed to provide more than a fraction of the shells required by the Army. From that moment the nation wholly lost confidence in the Government, which proceeded to justify its distrust in the most thorough manner by a reversion to an almost daily increasing reaction. "From Goremykin onwards," said a conservatively minded Moscovite lawyer, "every change of Prime Minister has been for the worse."

The last straws on the back of Russian society were the events that attended the appointment as Home Minister of Protopopov, known to have held communication with enemy agents in Sweden, and the complete gag that he was allowed to put upon the Press. At the same time the other members of the gang, who, like Protopopov, owed their offices to the debauched charlatan and favorite of the Empress, Gregory Rasputin, were given a free hand to perpetrate numerous private and public crimes. In every rank of society it was freely said that the nation and the army were sold by the Empress's minions, and that she aimed at obtaining a regency to replace an Emperor whose weakness, garrulousness, and drunkenness had become a by-word. Should she succeed in this, it was thought certain that by fomenting disorder at home and obstructing the conduct of the war she would gain her desired object and force upon Russia a separate peace which, while ruining forever the hopes of progress, might save her native country, Germany, and would delight the ranks of reactionary bureaucrats. The policy pursued by the Empress was in the highest degree alarming to the circle of Grand Dukes, who almost unanimously protested against the banishment without trial of the Grand Duke Dmitri Pavlovich for his share in the murder of Rasputin in December, 1916. Many of their number, apart from this, not once, but often, represented to the Emperor that subservience to his wife must end in disaster. When these protests were disregarded it became generally believed that a Court revolution would take place and Nicholas the Second be dethroned in favor of his brother or his uncle. No one foresaw the immediate likelihood of a large popular movement, which, however, many thought to be inevitable after the war.

The first bread riot in Petrograd took place on the 8th of March. Its synchronization with the Emperor's departure for General Headquarters—for he was nominally Commander-in-Chief—was probably not due to chance, but was the sign of the deep causes at work; Protopopov's agents, on the one hand, provoking disorder, and on the other German money being spent with the same object among the Social Democrats, in whose ranks in Russia the claims of internationalism often call forth a readier response than those of patriotism. The rioting was so far confined to the Viborg side, the chief workmen's quarter of Petrograd, but in the center the tramway service had already become irregular. On the 9th the rioters stopped the trams across the river, terrorizing the drivers and throwing parts of the mechanism away, so that the service grew still more intermittent. Visits were paid to all the factories and the hands called out in a sympathetic strike against the sudden food shortage. On this day too a prefect of police (an official ranking above the district colonels of police and next to the prefect of the city) who threatened the crowd was killed. Strong Cossack squadrons patrolled Petrograd, and there was a collision on the Nevsky, in which the Cossacks used their whips, but they told the crowd they would not shoot so long as they only asked for bread. Alarmed at the attitude of the Cossacks, the authorities on the 10th brought troops of the line into the streets to support the police, posted machine guns on the Nevsky, and stopped traffic across it at many points.

Protopopov, approached by one who endeavored to convince him of the madness of his methods, only answered: "Do you know how splendidly machine guns work from the roof?" When the Duma met in February Protopopov had received the Emperor's special thanks for having kept order, which was effected by planting machine guns to command all approaches to the Duma. As it soon turned out, he had now had the roofs at every important street corner garrisoned by police with machine guns, and it is said that he promised a rise in pay of fifteen roubles a month and a present of fifty roubles to every man for his part in the bloody work that was expected. To Protopopov's disposition of the machine guns the success of the revolution is due. Had they been properly posted in the streets at strategic points and a sound scheme of coöperation arranged among the police and the gendarmes, some fifty thousand in strength, they could have swept every living thing from the streets: placed in dormer windows and behind parapets, the mitrailleuses were extremely difficult to train on their objective, and the police forces scattered throughout the city in innumerable small detachments were not in a position to support one another.

On the same day the first serious bloodshed took place, the police opening fire on a peaceful crowd opposite the Nicholas Station and inflicting some fifty casualties. Sunday, March 11th, began nervously. There were soldiers everywhere in the streets, and strong bodies held in reserve in courtyards. By now the trams had all stopped, and it was hardly possible to find a car. No newspapers appeared. About 3.30 p. m. the troops began to clear the streets round the Nevsky at the bayonet point, and soon afterwards the police turned their machine guns on to a crowd at the same place as the day before, but with more deadly effect, a Caucasian officer who was near by estimating the number of dead at 300. At the same time heavy firing took place further down the Nevsky, and opposite the Kazan Cathedral several score more people were killed. The crowd here retaliated with pistol shots, another prefect and a colonel of police, besides policemen and various innocent passers-by, being killed. It was significant that soldiers were seen among the crowd firing on the police, and a number of men and some fourteen officers of different detachments were arrested for refusing to support the police with arms. On the same afternoon a drunken officer of the Volynsky Regiment, named Lashkevich, ordered his men to fire on the crowd. They refused, but Lashkevich forced one of the soldiers to obey. His shot killed a woman. Thereupon the men returned to barracks and spent the night in great agitation. In the morning of Monday, March 12th, a detachment of gendarmes arrived to arrest the refractory soldiers. On this the battalion rose, overpowered the gendarmes, killed Lashkevich and some other officers, and at 8 a. m. left their barracks and rushed through the streets cheering. They were quickly joined by the Litovtsky and Preobrajensky Regiments, and in the course of the day by two or three others. First they marched to the artillery depot close by, then to the arsenal across the river, both of which they seized, burning the Courts of Justice on the way. The general in command of the artillery depot and several other persons were killed in the course of this. Beyond the district in which this occurred the event was not yet known.

At eleven o'clock the present writer, in company with a naval officer, drove in a motor car through the lines of the revolutionary troops and of the Government troops called out to meet them, unaware that anything more than rioting had taken place. The revolutionaries were in fair order, and the two sides watched one another curiously, without any hostile action.

When, soon after fighting began, it became apparent that no troops in Petrograd could be relied on by the Government, in the early afternoon the police began to fire on the soldiers, and among the troops adhesion to the revolutionary ranks became general. In order to avoid recognition many officers in the revolted regiments dressed like privates. There were by now no police on the streets, and crowds from across the river profited by the revolutionary troops having overpowered the bridge guards to come into the center and help to spread the spirit of revolution. Among their first objectives were the prisons where political prisoners were kept. These were released, but with them ordinary criminals also, to the number of some 15,000, and some of the prisons were burnt. Attention was next turned to the police stations, which were sacked, and the huge bonfires made by their contents, furniture and papers, lasted for more than a day and a night. The main police archives too were seized and burned and in the evening the contents of the prefecture itself, which had been the scene of much fighting, suffered the same fate. English readers must remember that the police of Petrograd were scarcely in any sense an instrument for preserving order, but were almost solely agents of political repression. By night the revolutionaries were in possession of the whole city, except the Winter Palace, the Admiralty, and the telegraph and telephone stations, the latter of which worked fairly well all through the day.   The guard regiments in Petrograd going over to the revolutionaries, these now numbered between thirty and forty thousand, and the only fear expressed was as to the attitude of the two divisions stationed at Tsarskoe Selo and of the troops at Moscow.   Those who wished ill to the movement confidently expected that the tables would soon be turned and with crushing effect.   Had these troops gone against the people, the revolutionaries, their discipline completely relaxed and many having given their rifles away to the crowd, must have succumbed.   When the immense excitement is considered, and the fact that, after years of reaction and months of the sternest repression of whatever kind of public expression, all authority was suddenly removed from the troops and populace alike, it must be thought wonderful that so little disorder occurred.   There was no general looting, well-dressed ladies who ventured out or dodged the fighting to get to their homes were not molested, and though officers were stopped and their arms taken from them, they were not for the most part ill-used.

As early as Saturday, March 10th, Rodzianko, the President of the Duma, had sent a telegram to the Emperor begging him to take measures to avert disaster and to allay feeling.   On the 11th he telegraphed again that the Government was paralyzed, that shooting was going on, that all public services were disorganized, and urged him to intrust the formation of a new government to some one enjoying the confidence of the country.   On the morning of the 12th he telegraphed: "Position growing worse.   Imperative take immediate measures, since to-morrow will be already too late.   The last hour has struck when the fate of the nation and of the dynasty will be decided."   To these telegrams only one answer was received.   On the morning of the 12th a decree was forwarded to Rodzianko from Prince Golitzin, the Premier, dated two days before from General Headquarters, and proroguing the Duma "to a date not later than April, 1917, dependent on extraordinary circumstances."   It was clear that Nicholas the Second and his advisers were bent on crushing the popular will, and believed that this could be done. Faced by a desperate position, Rodzianko rose to the greatness of his task with a promptitude for which the Allies should be forever grateful to him. He assumed a responsibility which had the revolution failed would undoubtedly have cost him his head, and disregarding the prorogation summoned a meeting of the Duma. The members of all parties but the Right met at 2.30 and proceeded to elect a Temporary or Executive Committee for the establishment of order in Petrograd, which assumed and during the next three days kept control of the government. Rodzianko had already telegraphed to the generals commanding the various fronts, and had received answers from General Brusiloff, on the southwestern, and from General Russky, on the northern front, that were at least not hostile. From General Evert, the lowest of the three in character and talent, he received no answer; and General Evert has since resigned his command. At 1 o'clock p. m. Prince Golitzin informed Rodzianko by telephone that he had resigned office, and was followed by almost all the other members of the Cabinet except Protopopov, who had vanished. The revolutionaries searched and pillaged the houses of ministers, the last-named only escaping a few minutes before their arrival. Before evening the president of the Council of the Empire, and former Minister of Justice, a man notorious for having debased justice and corrupted the courts, was arrested, and the beginnings of a national government already existed in Russia.

Throughout the day of March 13th fighting in Petrograd was general and heavy. The telephone was early captured and communication cut for the rest of the day. Every street corner became a trap for machine-gun and rifle fire from the police, ensconced in the upper part of the houses and shot at in their turn by parties of soldiers and civilians sheltering in doorways below. Soldiers in motor lorries or armored cars dashed to points where the fighting was fiercest, and in many places a furious battle raged all day. It was not until the afternoon of Wednesday, March 14th, the Winter Palace having been evacuated and the Admiralty captured on the evening of the 13th, that this gradually died

out as the effect of an order from the Duma Committee
that the owner and head-porter of any house from which
firing took place would be held responsible. These head-
porters, or dvorniki, were responsible to the police for the
identity of every inmate in their houses, and one of their
chief businesses was in fact spying for the police. It was
clear that the latter could not now have mounted guns upon
the roofs without their knowledge, and the prompt result of
the proclamation proved its wisdom. Even before this,
when in the course of the 13th and the morning of the 14th
it became known that the troops at Tsarskoe Selo, Pavlovsk,
Oranienbaum and Cronstadt had joined the people and later
that the garrison of Moscow too had thrown in its lot with
the revolution, feeling had become quieter. The autocracy
was left without serious defense, except in the unlikely event
of the soldiers at the Front declaring in its favor. Desultory but heavy outbursts of firing continued in Petrograd
till Thursday night, March 15th, when a detachment of five
hundred provincial police suddenly arrived, overpowered the
station guard, and marched through the city until dispersed
by armored motors. So recently as March 20th one or possibly more motor cars ornamented with black flags have been
dashing along the streets loosing off occasional belts of machine-gun cartridges at the passers, killing or wounding
many. But such piratical efforts are futile. Since March
14th the red flag flies everywhere in the capital.

It is at present impossible to arrive at an exact figure of
the numbers killed in and after the fighting, but it is certain
that the agreeable statements made as to the bloodlessness
are much exaggerated. The lowest estimate puts the number of dead at over two thousand; higher estimates at as
much as ten thousand, while the number of wounded must
also be considerable. The truth probably lies between four
and five thousand killed. In the two days before the revolution broke out, some five hundred were killed in the center
of the city; during the three days of fighting many more,
and this takes no account of the casualties beyond the river
on the Petrograd and Viborg sides. Many officers were
murdered by their men in the Baltic fleet as well as in the

army. Many policemen captured redhanded were made prisoners and taken to the Duma; but very many more were shot on the spot and their bodies flung into the canals. In the provinces the revolution was of a paper character, being mostly executed in the telegraph offices. Normal life was scarcely interrupted for more than one day in Moscow, and even less in other cities. It is none the less believed that not a few policemen and officers were disposed of in various parts, victims it may be in many cases of private revenge.

Warned by the fate of others, ministers and lesser servants of the old régime hastened to give themselves up to the Duma or were hunted out of hiding. Among the first was Stürmer, at whose residence a chest of coined money was discovered. Nor was he the only one to provide in hard coin against a rainy day, for at the house of Count Fredericks, the Minister of the Court and one of the chief props of the German system there, were discovered two boxes packed with gold. His house, full of objects of value, and probably also of highly interesting correspondence, was burnt to the ground. The wine cellar in the Grand Duchess Marie Pavlovna's palace, valued at half a million roubles, was destroyed for fear that the mob would sack the house. Kshesinska, the leading dancer of the Imperial Ballet and a former mistress of the Emperor, inspired by similar motives, took warning betimes and fled to Finland. The Hotel Militaire, ci-devant the Astoria, from which it was said that officers fired on the revolutionaries, had been attacked and captured on the 13th; its lower floors were gutted and several officers and civilians killed or wounded. The majority of the officers in Petrograd were quick to realize that the old order had passed away, and among the many processions of soldiers and employees who marched to the Duma to signify their adherence, none was more pleasing than that of a great number of officers, many colonels and even generals among them, who on the 14th, after a meeting at the Army and Navy Club, went to place themselves at the orders of the Duma Committee. On the same day the Grand Duke Cyril Vladimirovich, a man indeed of no political significance but much opposed to the Empress, signified to the Duma that he would whole-heartedly support the new régime with all the strength of the Navy Guards. Protopopov, who had spent the intervening two days since his disappearance in wandering about the streets, seeking refuge with his friends and being refused by all, had given himself up late the night before, and with his arrest the last shadow of the old government vanished. On the 14th the Duma Committee appointed Commissioners to take charge of the various ministries and other public offices and telegraphed the news to all the towns of Russia that it had temporarily undertaken the direction of affairs, and a municipal militia was established in the capital with its head office at the Town Hall.

Within a few hours of the appointment of the Executive Committee of the Duma, a Council of Workmen's Deputies was organized also at the Duma, composed of labor representatives, some soldiers, and a few stray sympathetic politicians. They divided the city into districts, to each of which a Commissioner was appointed, and representatives were invited to be sent from the factories and from every company. The object of the Commissioners was "the establishment of the popular power in the districts of Petrograd." "We call upon the population of the capital," their proclamation ran, "to gather round the Council, to organize local district committees, and to take into their hands the direction of all local affairs." By the 14th of March the Council was consolidated and enlarged into the Council of Workmen's and Soldiers' Deputies, and was making a bold bid to get the power over the army into its hands. Order No. 1 posted throughout Petrograd on the 15th of March ordained that in all their political concerns the military were subject to the Council, that committees were to be elected by every battalion or company to supervise the internal administration of the regiments, that all arms were to be under control of the committees and in no circumstances to be returned to officers as the Duma Committee had authorized, and that the orders of the Military Commission set up by the latter were only to be obeyed when they did not contradict the orders and resolutions of the Council of Workmen's and Soldiers' Deputies. On the 13th discipline was non-existent. Many of the soldiers had given up their arms to the crowd and were drifting listlessly about the streets watching the progress of the fight and in difficulties for food. On the 14th, though the food difficulty had increased, their behavior was better; they paraded in companies, though still many without arms, and preserved some outward orderliness. The adherence too of the officers on this day had its effect, and soldiers even began to salute again. But with the publication of the Council's Order an immediate deterioration became noticeable. The semblance of order preserved the day before vanished and was replaced by a sullen and occasionally a threatening attitude. There were no longer signs of respect for the officers, and the men went about asking for food and collecting money to support soldiers' tea-houses that had taken the place of many cafés. Small squads went round searching private apartments for arms, without, or refusing to show, the authority they should have had from the Duma: a fact greatly to the advantage of criminals, who dressed themselves up as soldiers and carried off valuables from citizens who dared not resist. It was known that a strong party for the immediate conclusion of peace existed among the workmen, and the gloomiest anticipations, freely entertained, were intensified by reports of the enemy having broken the Russian lines near Dvinsk. A counter-report, as it turned out equally untrue, that came late in the evening of a Russian advance in the same district, to some extent restored spirits, but the situation remained one of great tension.

From the very first day of the revolution, a news-sheet was issued with the imprint of the "Committee of Petrograd Journalists" and distributed gratis in the streets. This had to compete with the fuller sheet of the Workmen's Council, which though sold at five kopecks, enjoyed greater facilities for distribution, and it was not until Sunday the 18th that the publishers could arrange with the compositors to allow the regular papers to come out. The Council further forbade cabs, which began to be seen again on the streets on the 17th of March, to ply for hire after 7 p. m.; but they have had difficulty in enforcing this rule. Over the tramways, however, the Council had complete control; the wires, cut by bullets, were repaired by the 20th but no trams ran in the evening till some days later. The theaters too are sought to be brought under the workmen's heel: the Council flatly refused leave to any to open until the burial of certain victims of the fight in the cause of freedom, whom they proposed to inter in the great square opposite the Winter Palace.

By dint of much tact and forbearance on the part of the Duma Committee and of the new government announced by it on the 15th of March with Prince Lvoff, the President of the Union of Zemstvos, as prime minister, an open breach with the Council has hitherto been avoided. Frequent reports indeed are spread of the harmony reigning between the two bodies. But the mischief done in the first two days by the Council has spread very wide, and may prove irreparable. While many of the troops have returned to their duty, and fair discipline is kept, and work goes forward, the peace party among the socialists have not relaxed their efforts, and have succeeded in affecting some at least of the soldiers at the front. General Alexieff, nominally Chief of Staff and virtually Commander-in-Chief, has been called to task in the workmen's organ for issuing orders that unauthorized bands calling themselves deputies be prevented from disarming the railway gendarmes, which if allowed would give them control over the stations and the line. General Radko Dmitriev has found it necessary in two proclamations to remind his troops that in the face of the enemy, discipline must be preserved and that until new regulations are properly issued the old ones must remain in force. General Russky is said to have protested against the presence of socialist deputies who hold meetings among the soldiers. On the 23rd of March the papers contained separate appeals to the army and the nation from A. I. Guchkov, the new Minister of War, and from the whole Cabinet; and a third signed by Guchkov and General Alexieff. All three are couched in the most urgent terms and call upon citizens to do their duty at the front and at the rear, workmen and soldiers alike. They inform the nation that a tremendous effort of the enemy is to be expected, that Petrograd is threatened by pressing danger, and that should the Germans be victorious their victory will be gained not only over the Russian State but over the newly won freedom of the Russian nation. They passionately beg the soldiers to trust and follow their officers, who shared danger and hunger, and freely laid down their lives with their brothers. Guchkov's appeal ends: "The hour of trial approaches." In yet another appeal on the 24th the Minister of War wrote: "The enemy threatens the capital. . . . The danger is great."

Nevertheless obstinate rumors circulate that soldiers are leaving the Front, and that the officers are helpless to control them. The extreme socialists make no secret of their desire. Their program is "Down with the War at any cost, in any circumstances." In the third number of *Truth* (*Pravda*), the Moscow organ of this party, it is declared: "We hate every kind of despotism. We hate the despotism of William and of Briand, of Lloyd George and Ferdinand, just as we hate the despotism of the Romanoffs." In the fifth number (March 22nd) a leading article calls upon the soldiers in the trenches to raise the red flag, sing the International, refuse to attack, and fraternize "widely and systematically" with the soldiers on the other side. This party flatters or professes to flatter itself that if fighting is stopped on the Russian side there will be a revolution in Germany and the Emperor and the bourgeois régime will be overthrown. True, they are opposed by other sections of the socialists, but unfortunately under present conditions their quarrels are almost as pernicious as if all were united against the war. In spite of recent appeals by the Council of Workmen's Deputies, few of the factories in Petrograd had resumed work on the 21st of March, and the men may go out again at any moment.

March was the month when Paul the First was murdered. In March Alexander the Second was slain. And on the 1st of March Nicholas the Second set out for his last journey as Emperor from General Headquarters, with the object of reaching Tsarskoe Selo. It is said that Rod-

zianko's second and third telegrams were never delivered to
him, and that General Voyekov, one of his most intimate
advisers and a successful tool of the Empress, otherwise
chiefly known by having made a fortune out of an inferior
mineral water, only told him of the revolt in Petrograd
when forced to do so by General Pavel, who said that if
Voyekov refused he would burst into the Emperor's room
by force. Voyekov thereupon told the Emperor that students and revolutionaries had worked up the young con-
scripts to terrorize the Duma, but that the loyal regiments
from Tsarskoe would easily put the movement down. The
Emperor set out in one train with Generals Voyekov and
Pavel and Admiral Nivel, who appears to have been fuddled
with drink the whole time, the suite following in another.
Near the junction for Pskov, revolutionaries managed to
damage the engine of the second train, which could proceed
no further, and General Pavel insisted on telling the Emperor the whole truth, that Tsarskoe and Moscow equally
with Petrograd had abandoned his cause, that a telegram
had been received not to allow the train nearer to Petrograd,
and that the Emperor's position was hopeless. An attempt
was then made to return and to go to the front, but the line
had been blocked behind the last station and it had to be
abandoned. One thing only remained, to proceed to Pskov,
General Russky's headquarters, and there to await events.

Thither on the 15th of March A. I. Guchkov and V. V.
Shulgin proceeded from Petrograd with the Duma Committee's commission to negotiate with the Emperor. They
arrived at ten o'clock in the evening, and immediately had
an interview with the Emperor in his train, at which were also
present General Russky, Count Fredericks, and another General, who took notes, probably Voyekov. The once all-pow-
erful autocrat, who was in the uniform of a Caucasian regiment, listened to an exposition of the state of affairs by
Guchkov, who led up to the conclusion that he must abdicate in favor of his son, the Grand Duke Alexis, and nomi-
nate as regent his brother the Grand Duke Michael. When
Guchkov came to this point, General Russky bent towards
Shulgin and said, "That has already been decided." The

Emperor replied to Guchkov as follows: "I reflected all yesterday and to-day, and I have decided to abdicate from the throne. Until three o'clock to-day I was ready to abdicate in favor of my son. But then I understood that I was incapable of separating from my son." Then, after a little pause: "I hope you understand that." He continued: "Therefore I have decided to abdicate in favor of my brother." The deputies asked leave to consider this proposition, which was unexpected, in private, but after a short colloquy announced that they accepted it. They then presented a prepared form of abdication to the Emperor, who affixed his signature in pencil. The whole proceedings were simple, quiet, and evidently not unfriendly.

The next day, however, when the matter was laid before the Grand Duke Michael, the latter politely but firmly refused to accept the crown, except in the event of its being offered to him by a Constituent Assembly elected by the nation by universal, direct, and secret ballot. In this the Grand Duke (who passed some time in England and rented Lord Lytton's house at Knebworth) showed more political judgment than the new government had shown in attempting to keep his nephew Alexis on the throne. Events had already moved beyond the point where the workmen or the educated progressives or the soldiers in Petrograd would consent to see a Romanoff on the throne. Even the Grand Duke Nicholas, summoned from the Caucasus to take up again the chief command by the Duma Committee with the nominal authority of Nicholas the Second in one of his last acts, was compelled by the trend of events to lay it down. The nation has suffered too much from a dynasty which with but few exceptions has proved itself either cruel or effete, or both; which during the last forty years has expended every effort in repressing the smallest tendency towards westernization; and which has finally played foolishly or knavishly into the hands of the foe. It is unlikely in the extreme that a Romanoff will ever again wear the crown.

BY CZAR NICHOLAS II.

Abdication Proclamation of March 14, 1917

It has pleased God our Lord, in these days of great struggle with the external enemy, to visit Russia with new and severe trials. Popular disturbances which have begun among the masses of the people threaten to have a pernicious effect upon the further conduct of the war. The fate of Russia, the honor of our heroic army, the welfare of the people, and all the future of our dear country demand that the war should at all cost be brought to a victorious conclusion. The cruel enemy has bent his last energies, and the hour is near when our gallant army, in conjunction with our glorious Allies, would be able to crush him finally. In these decisive days in Russia's life we have deemed it to be a duty of our conscience to facilitate for our people a close union and consolidation of all forces for the speedy attainment of victory, and have, in agreement with the State Duma, thought it best to abdicate the throne of the Russian State and to renounce our supreme authority. Being reluctant to part from our beloved son, we have transferred the succession to our brother, the Grand Duke Michael Alexandrovitch, whom we bless on his accession to the throne of the Russian State. We bequeathe to our brother to rule the affairs of the State in complete and inviolable union with the representatives of the nation in the legislative bodies on principles to be determined by them, and to take an inviolable oath to that effect in the name of the ardently-beloved country. I call upon all the loyal sons of the fatherland to discharge their sacred duty towards him by obeying the Czar in this grave hour of national trial, and assist him and the representatives of the nation in the task of leading the Russian State on the path of victory, prosperity, and glory. May God our Lord help Russia!

NICHOLAS.

Pskov, March 14, 1917, 3 p. m.

Countersigned: FREDERICKS,

Minister of the Imperial Court.

PROCLAMATION OF MARCH 15TH BY DUKE MICHAEL

[When it became known in Petrograd that the Czar had been allowed to abdicate in favor of another Czar, his younger brother Michael, the Council of Workmen's and Soldiers' Deputies protested. The temporary government then consulted with Michael, and he refused the throne in the following words:]

A heavy burden has been imposed upon me by the will of my brother, who has transferred to me the Imperial throne of Russia at a time of unparalleled war and agitation of the people. Animated, together with the entire nation, by the view that the welfare of the country stands above everything else, I have taken the firm resolve to accept the supreme authority only in the case, if such be the will of our great people to which it pertains by right, through a Constituent Assembly elected by universal suffrage, to determine the form of government and the new fundamental laws of the Russian State. While invoking the blessing of God, I request all citizens to obey the Provisional Government which has been formed on the initiative of the State Duma, and which has been clothed with the plenitude of power until such time as a Constituent Assembly summoned at the earliest possible moment on the basis of universal, direct, equal, and secret suffrage has, by its decision on the form of government, made manifest the will of the nation.—MICHAEL. Petrograd, March 15, 1917.

BY DR. STANISLAUS DE LAZOVERT

The shot that ended the career of the blackest devil in Russian history was fired by my close and beloved friend, Vladimir Purishkevitch, Reactionary Deputy of the Duma.

Five of us had been arranging for this event for many months. On the night of the killing, after all details had been arranged, I drove to the Imperial Palace in an automobile and persuaded this black devil to accompany me to the home of Prince Yusupoff, in Petrograd. Later that night M. Purishkevitch followed him into the gardens adjoining Yusupoff's house and shot him to death with an automatic revolver. We then carried his riddled body in a sheet to the River Neva, broke the ice and cast him in.

The story of Rasputin and his clique is well known. They sent the army to the trenches without food or arms, they left them there to be slaughtered, they betrayed Rumania and deceived the Allies, they almost succeeded in delivering Russia bodily to the Germans. Rasputin, as a secret member of the Austrian Green Hand, had absolute power in Court. The Czar was a nonentity, a kind of Hamlet, his only desire being to abdicate and escape the whole vile business. Rasputin continued his life of vice, carousing and passion. The Grand Duchess reported these things to the Czarina and was banished from Court for her pains.

This was the condition of affairs when we decided to kill this monster. Only five men participated in it. They were the Grand Duke Dmitri Pavlovich, Prince Yusupoff, Vladimir Purishkevitch, Captain Suhotine and myself.

Prince Yusupoff's palace is a magnificent place on the Nevska. The great hall has six equal sides and in each hall is a heavy oaken door. One leads out into the gardens, the one opposite leads down a broad flight of marble stairs to the huge dining room, one to the library, etc. At midnight the associates of the Prince concealed themselves while I entered the car and drove to the home of the monk. He admitted me in person.

Rasputin was in a gay mood. We drove rapidly to the home of the Prince and descended to the library, lighted only by a blazing log in the huge chimney-place. A small table was spread with cakes and rare wines—three kinds of the wine were poisoned and so were the cakes. The monk threw himself into a chair, his humor expanding with the warmth of the room. He told of his successes, his plots, of the imminent success of the German arms and that the Kaiser would soon be seen in Petrograd.

At a proper moment he was offered the wine and the cakes. He drank the wine and devoured the cakes. Hours slipped by, but there was no sign that the poison had taken effect. The monk was even merrier than before. We were seized with an insane dread that this man was inviolable, that he was superhuman, that he couldn't be killed. It was a frightful sensation. He glared at us with his black, black eyes as though he read our minds and would fool us.

And then after a time he rose and walked to the door. We were afraid that our work had been in vain. Suddenly, as he turned at the door, some one shot at him quickly. With a frightful scream Rasputin whirled and fell, face down, on the floor. The others came bounding over to him and stood over his prostrate, writhing body. It was suggested that two more shots be fired to make certain of his death, but one of those present said, "No, no; it is his last agony now."

We left the room to let him die alone, and to plan for his removal and obliteration.

Suddenly we heard a strange and unearthly sound behind the huge door that led into the library. The door was slowly pushed open, and there was Rasputin on his hands and knees, the bloody froth gushing from his mouth, his terrible eyes bulging from their sockets. With an amazing strength he sprang toward the door that led into the gardens, wrenched it open and passed out.

As he seemed to be disappearing in the darkness, F. Purishkevitch, who had been standing by, reached over and picked up an American-made automatic revolver and fired two shots swiftly into his retreating figure. We heard him fall with a groan, and later when we approached the body he was very still and cold and—dead.

We bundled him up in a sheet and carried him to the river's edge. Ice had formed, but we broke it and threw him in. The next day search was made for Rasputin, but no trace was found. Urged on by the Czarina, the police made frantic efforts, and finally a rubber was found which was identified as his. The river was dragged and the body recovered.

I escaped from the country. Purishkevitch also escaped. But Prince Yusupoff was arrested and confined to the boundaries of his estate. He was later released because of the popular approval of our act. Russia had been freed from the vilest tyrant in her history; and that is all.

BY BORIS BAKHMETEFF
Words of Thanks from the Russian Democratic Government, Delivered
on June 20 and 23, 1917

In behalf of the Russian Provisional Government and
in behalf of all the people of new Russia, I have been first
of all sent here to express their gratitude to the Government of the United States for the prompt recognition of the
new political order in Russia.   This noble action of the
world's greatest democracy has afforded us strong moral
support and has created among our people a general feeling
of profound appreciation.   Close and active relationship between the two nations based upon complete and sincere understanding encountered inevitable obstacles during the old
régime because of its very nature.   The situation is now
radically changed with free Russia starting a new era in her
national life.

The Provisional Government is actively mobilizing all
its resources and is making great efforts to organize the
country and the army for the purpose of conducting the
war.   We hope to establish a very close and active coöperation with the United States, in order to secure the most
successful and intensive accomplishment of all work necessary for our common end.   For the purpose of discussing
all matters relating to military affairs, munitions and supplies, railways and transportation, finance and agriculture,
our mission includes eminent and distinguished specialists.

On the other hand, I hope that the result of our stay and
work in America will bring about a clear understanding on
the part of your public of what has happened in Russia and
also of the present situation and the end for which our
people are most earnestly striving.   The achievements of the
revolution are to be formally set forth in fundamental laws
enacted by a Constitutional Assembly, which is to be convoked as soon as possible.   In the meanwhile the Provisional
Government is confronted with the task of bringing into
life the democratic principles which were promulgated during the revolution.

New Russia received from the old Government a burden-
some heritage of economic and technical disorganization

which affected all branches of the life of the State, a disorganization which weighs yet heavily on the whole country. The Provisional Government is doing everything in its power to relieve the difficult situation. It has adopted many measures for supplying plants with raw material and fuel, for regulating the transportation of the food supply for the army and for the country, and for relieving the financial difficulties.

The participation in the new Government by new members who are active and prominent leaders in the Council of Workmen's and Soldiers' Delegates has secured full support from the democratic masses. The esteem in which such leaders as M. Kerensky and M. Tseretelli and others are held among the working classes and soldiers is contributing to the strength and stability of the new Government. The Constitutional-Democratic Party, the Labor Party, the Socialist-Populists, and, excepting a small group of extremists, the Social Democrats—all these parties, embracing the vast majority of the people, are represented by strong leaders in the new Government, thereby securing for it authority.

Plans of the Government

Firmly convinced that unity of power is essential, and casting aside class and special interests, all social and political elements have joined in the national program which the new Government proclaimed and which it is striving to fulfill. This program reads:

"The Provisional Government, rejecting, in accord with the whole people of Russia, all thought of separate peace, puts it openly as its deliberate purpose the promptest achievement of universal peace; such peace to presume no dominion over other nations, no seizure of their national property nor any forced usurpation of foreign territory; peace with no annexations or contributions, based upon the free determination by each nation of its destinies.

"Being fully convinced that the establishment of democratic principles in its internal and external policy has created a new factor in the striving of allied democracies for durable peace and fraternity of all nations, the Provisional Government will take preparatory steps for an agreement with the

Allies founded on its declaration of March 27th. The Provisional Government is conscious that the defeat of Russia and her allies would be the source of the greatest misery, and would not only postpone but even make impossible the establishment of universal peace on a firm basis.

"The Provisional Government is convinced that the revolutionary army of Russia will not allow the German troops to destroy our allies on the western front and then fall upon us with the whole might of their weapons. The chief aim of the Provisional Government will be to fortify the democratic foundations of the army and organize and consolidate the army's fighting power for its defensive as well as offensive purpose."

The last decision of the Russian Council of Workmen's and Soldiers' Delegates, the decision of the All-Russian Peasant Congress, the decision of the Duma, the voice of the country as expressed from day to day by almost the entire Russian press, in resolutions adopted at different conferences and congresses—all these confirm their full support to this national program and leave not the slightest doubt that Russia is decided as to the necessity to fight the German autocracy until the conditions for a general and stable peace in Europe are established. Such decision is becoming more and more evident each day by practical work and results and shows itself in the pressing and rapid reorganization of the army which is now being fulfilled under the firm and efficient measures adopted by Minister Kerensky.

New Russia, in full accord with the motives which impelled the United States to enter the war, is striving to destroy tyranny, to establish peace on a secure and permanent foundation and to make the world safe for democracy.

Does not one feel occasionally that the very greatness and significance of events are not fully appreciated, due to the facility and spontaneity with which the change has been completed? Does one realize what it really means to humanity that a nation of 180,000,000, a country boundless in expanse, has been suddenly set free from the worst of oppressions, has been given the joy of a free, self-conscious existence?

Instead of the old forms there are now being firmly established and deeply imbedded in the minds of the nation principles that power is reposed and springs from and only from the people. To effectuate these principles and to enact appropriate fundamental laws is going to be the main function of the Constitutional Assembly which is to be convoked as promptly as possible.

Guided by democratic precepts, the Provisional Government is meanwhile reorganizing the country on the basis of freedom, equality, and self-government, rebuilding its economic and financial structure.

The people are realizing more and more that for the very sake of further freedom law must be maintained and manifestation of anarchy suppressed. In this respect local life has exemplified a wonderful exertion of spontaneous public spirit. On many occasions, following the removal of the old authorities, a new elected administration has naturally arisen, conscious of national interest and often developing in its spontaneity amazing examples of practical statesmanship.

The latest resolutions, framed by the Council of Workingmen, the Congress of Peasants, and other democratic organizations, render the best proof of the general understanding of the necessity of creating strong power. The coalitionary character of the new Cabinet, which includes eminent Socialist leaders, and represents all the vital elements of the nation, therefore enjoying its full support, is most effectively securing the unity and power of the Central Government, the lack of which was so keenly felt during the first two months after the revolution.

As to foreign policy, Russia's national program has been clearly set forth in the statement of the Provisional Government of March 27th, and more explicitly in the declaration of the new Government of May 18th. With all emphasis may I state that Russia rejects any idea of separate peace. I am aware that rumors were circulated in this country that a separate peace seemed probable. I am happy to affirm that such rumors are wholly without foundation in fact.

THE UNITED STATES EXTENDS ITS TERRITORY

PURCHASE OF THE VIRGIN ISLES FROM DENMARK

MARCH 31ST

THEODOR DE BOOY   BISHOP CHARLES CURRIER

While the United States stood on the very edge of the War, there took place the final step in another event of importance, the addition of a new region to the territory of the United States. Denmark formally transferred to America the sovereignty over the Danish West Indies, over which there had been bargaining and hesitating for years. The treaty transferring them was finally signed in 1916; the people of the islands were called to vote their approval of the change, an approval their leaders had already expressed in words; and now, on March 31st, occurred the actual change of control. The account of it is given by a native of the isles, now a Danish missionary bishop. A review of the islands themselves is given by the well-known American geographical authority, Theodor De Booy.

The Danish West Indies had consisted of three main islands with their surrounding islets. Two of the islands had been visited by Columbus and named the Virgin Isles. So this name was now revived; and to the United States its new possessions are the Virgin Isles. They constitute the most southeastern of its extra-continental possessions, lying adjacent to and beyond Porto Rico to the south and east.

BY THEODOR DE BOOY [1]

THE most interesting historical relation of the Danish West Indies after 1815—their relation with the United States—is well known. In 1865 the United States offered the Danish Government the sum of $5,000,000 for the islands, which offer was increased to $7,500,000 two years later. The treaty providing for their purchase was ratified by the Danish parliament but for various political reasons was cancelled by the government at Washington. Again, in 1902 Denmark was offered $5,000,000 for the islands,

[1] Reprinted from the *Geographical Review* for November, 1917, published by the American Geographical Society, Broadway at 156th Street, New York.

and, had it not been for German influence in the upper house
of the Danish legislature, the sale would probably have been
consummated. It was not until January 17, 1917, that the
islands were finally sold to the United States. The sum
paid was $25,000,000; and the actual transfer to the United
States Government took place on March 31, 1917, when the
Stars and Stripes finally replaced the Dannebrog. It was
decided by the United States Government to name the acquired territory the Virgin Islands of the United States, and
they are now officially known by this name. It may be
pointed out, however, that the southernmost island, St. Croix,
in reality was not one of the Virgin Island group as named
by Columbus.

While negotiations between the United States and Denmark regarding the sale of the islands were in progress, considerable doubt was expressed by the general public as to
their value as an investment. The argument was advanced
that, with the exception of St. Croix, the islands were practically non-productive, and one periodical went so far as to
ask its readers if $25,000,000 was not too high a price to
pay for a bay rum factory. This latter remark, of course,
pertained to St. John, where bay rum is produced.

Whatever may be the intrinsic worth of the islands, there
can be no doubt that St. Thomas has an incalculable strategic
value, and that its possession is of the greatest protection
to the Panama Canal in the event of hostilities with any
European Power. It lies directly in the steamer routes between European ports and the Canal Zone, and a fleet stationed in the adjacent waters, with the wonderful harbor of
St. Thomas available for repairs and supplies, could dominate the approaches to the Caribbean. This fact appears to
have been overlooked by those who considered that too high
a price was paid for the islands.

It must of course be admitted that their mere commercial
importance did not warrant so large an amount. Nevertheless they have considerable commercial value. What their
resources are will be shown in the following pages, and, as
the three islands are totally different in their productions,
it will be necessary to discuss each island separately.

St. Thomas, the westernmost island of the group, is the second largest: it measures fourteen miles in length from east to west, and is from one to three miles broad. In reality it is nothing but a curved mountain ridge whose highest elevation is 1,550 feet. The island has a population of about 10,000, of which by far the greater part are negroes. Much could be written of its people: of their amiability, of their kindness and hospitality to strangers, and of their pride in their little island. It is undoubtedly a great satisfaction to the United States that the inhabitants of St. Thomas were practically unanimous in their desire to be transferred from the Danish Government to that of Washington, and the rejoicing when the actual transfer took place was great. For, while the St. Thomians had no reason to complain of the treatment accorded them by the Danes, it was always felt that Denmark was a long way off and that in consequence a long time had to elapse before the sanction of the home government could be obtained for any change that might be desirable. Furthermore, owing to the proximity to the United States and because of the numerous American vessels that have been coming to the port of St. Thomas for coaling or other purposes, the working classes of the island are familiar with Americans and American methods. As a consequence of all this, it is not probable that the change of government will cause much dissatisfaction among the islanders or that it will be long before the St. Thomians become accustomed to the new régime.

The mountain ridge which forms the island curves northward in the middle, leaving a corresponding basin on the south coast. It is this basin which forms the excellent harbor of Charlotte Amalia, as the town of St. Thomas is named. This harbor is unexcelled in the West Indies with the exception of Coral Bay on St. John. It offers complete protection to the largest ships, and the numerous inlets and smaller bays lend themselves admirably to the purposes of a naval base; large men-of-war may lie in the harbor itself, and smaller vessels, such as torpedo boats and supply ships, can take up positions in the inlets. With fortifications on the hills and mines in the approach to the harbor absolute safety may be insured.

The island of St. John, lying about three miles east of St. Thomas, is a little smaller in area than the latter. It is nine miles long and has an irregular breadth. The highest elevation is 1,300 feet, and, like St. Thomas, the whole island is hilly. The population consists of but 900 souls, and these lead a somewhat precarious and poverty-stricken existence.

St. John might well be termed the Cinderella of the Virgin Islands. If the average geographer be asked the name of the newly acquired Virgin Islands, he will reply: "St. Thomas, St. Croix," then pause and after deep thought add, "St. John." Published accounts of these additions to the territory of the United States make lengthy mention of the island of St. Thomas and its commercial and strategical importance, and of St. Croix with its agricultural possibilities, but dismiss St. John with a scant line or two telling of its bay trees and the poverty of its inhabitants.

The possibilities of exploiting St. John are great, however. In the first place, the bay tree flourishes on the little island. It has been found by actual experience that the bay tree is somewhat erratic and is most particular as to its habitat. Attempts have been made to grow this tree in various islands, and practically all attempts were failures. Even on St. John, small as it is, it seems that the trees do well in certain parts and are unable to gain a foothold in others. Why this is so has never been satisfactorily explained. But even with this drawback, there are to-day many regions on St. John where extensive cultivation of the bay tree would be highly profitable. The leaves of the bay tree are gathered and are distilled in the usual copper stills. This distillation results in the collecting of the natural oil, the bay oil, contained in the minute cells of the leaves. The bay oil is mixed with white rum in the ratio of about one quart of oil to five hundred quarts of rum, and the product is bay rum. Occasionally bay rum is made by distilling the bay leaves directly in the rum; but this method is slower and far more expensive and has practically been discontinued. The bay industry, therefore, presents one of the possibilities of St. John. While various proprietors are at present engaged in the cultivation of the trees and the distilling of the oil, there can be no doubt but that a greater exploitation of this industry would result in material benefit, especially if modern machinery for collecting the oil were employed.

Again, St. John offers great possibilities as a cattle-raising center. Perhaps no better-watered island exists in the Antilles. As a consequence, while the ground is generally steep and hilly, the slopes are covered with excellent grass of all varieties and offer feeding-grounds for thousands of heads of cattle. At the present time cattle raising seems to be neglected by practically the majority of the landowners. There can be no doubt that owing to the increased population of the neighboring island of St. Thomas through the prospective establishment of a naval station there, and also owing to the fact that no duty would have to be paid on cattle exported to Porto Rico now that the islands are under the same government, a ready market would be found for all cattle raised on St. John. St. Thomas can in no wise compare with St. John for pasturage or for water supply, and St. Croix is practically entirely given up to sugar cultivation.

St. Croix is the largest of the newly acquired islands and is 22 miles long and of irregular breadth. While the island has large flat plains, it also has one mountain ridge, the highest elevation of which is about 1,100 feet. The population consists of some 15,000 souls, the majority of whom are agricultural laborers.

St. Croix is the one agricultural possibility of the Virgin Islands. Its extensive and fertile plains make it especially well adapted for sugar cane cultivation, and those fields and hill slopes that are not given up to this purpose serve as pasturage for the numerous cattle that are used in the carts necessary for the transportation of the cane to the sugar mills. As a consequence St. Croix possesses very little waste land, and numerous large sugar factories dot the landscape with their huge chimneys.

The motoring possibilities of St. Croix are excellent, and the island boasts of many cars. A ride over one of the roads with its fringe of cocoanut trees is one of the delightful experiences lying in wait for the tourist. An automobile trip from Frederiksted, where all large steamers calling at the island anchor, to Christiansted, the seat of government, is a source of constant delight to the eye; and, while the wild magnificence of St. John is lacking, the more orderly landscapes of St. Croix are preferred by many.

St. Croix has two large towns, Frederiksted and Christiansted. Owing to the dangerous reef which shuts out the large ships, Christiansted is only visited by small sailing vessels and consequently does not exhibit the hustle and bustle so noticeable in Frederiksted on steamer days. On the other hand, Christiansted being the seat of government, its buildings are larger and more important-looking than those of Frederiksted and the inhabitants more sensible of their importance. Furthermore, Christiansted boasts of having been the home of Alexander Hamilton, and the inhabitants do not fail to point out his abode to the visiting tourist. Both Christiansted and Frederiksted have the usual forts of a style of architecture not unlike that of Fort Christian on St. Thomas; they serve to remind the tourist of the glories of bygone times, when buccaneers, privateers, and other enemies made life interesting to the more peaceful inhabitants of the Antilles.

In conclusion, a few words regarding the destructive hurricane which visited these islands on the night of October 9 to 10, 1916, may not be amiss. Any one familiar with West Indian literature becomes imbued with the idea that hurricanes of the most destructive variety are the common lot of settlers on those islands. As a matter of fact, but three major hurricanes have visited the Virgin Islands during historical times. The first one was in the latter part of the seventeenth century, the second was in 1867, and the last was that of 1916. Of course, minor hurricanes and heavy blows are not infrequent, but destructive hurricanes are rare indeed. When they do occur, a bountiful nature quickly succeeds in restoring vegetation to its normal aspect; as for the destroyed houses, their flimsy construction means that they can easily be replaced.

BY BISHOP CURRIER [2]

A letter came to me a short time ago written in the
hand of a correspondent in the Island of St. Thomas, bearing
a United States stamp. At first I thought it had been mailed
in the United States. Then the truth dawned upon me that
I must never expect to see again the old familiar Danish
stamp upon letters from the Virgin Islands, as they have
passed from the power of Denmark forever, and they are
now the property of the United States of America.

How strange it seems! The old Dannebrog flag, that
had been waving over St. Thomas for a period of 251 years,
has been lowered at last. The white cross has come down,
and the white stars have gone up.

Fifty years ago, when the writer was a child, a treaty
was concluded by which St. Thomas was to be purchased by
the United States. Many inhabitants of the island favored
it; we wore the United States colors to signify our satisfaction, the writer having as principal reason that he was
of American parentage. The treaty, however, was not ratified. The terrible hurricane and earthquake of 1867 came
to throw a damper on the proceedings, and we heard no
more of the purchase. The United States bought Alaska instead. The Danish fort, old Fort Christian, saluted the
national colors and the affair was at an end.

It is a long time since Christopher Columbus first caught
sight of these islands. It was in 1493, on his second voyage to America. He was sailing northward from Dominica,
where he first saw the Caribs, and as he went, hardly ever
out of sight of land, he gave the names of saints and sacred
places to the islands that he passed. Monserrat, Antiqua,
St. Christopher's, St. Eustachius, St. Martin followed, until
the island of the Holy Cross, Santa Cruz, was reached. Here
the Spaniards had an encounter with the fierce Caribs, and
hence they proceeded to Borinquen to which the name of St.
John was to be given, and which, in course of time, would
be better known as Porto Rico. On their way, the Spaniards

[2] Reprinted by permission from the *American Ecclesiastical Review*,
copyright, 1917.

passed a numerous group of islands, some of them mere rocks. The image of St. Ursula and her many virgins came to mind, and the group was collectively named the Virgin Islands, the two largest becoming known as St. Thomas and St. John.

For a long time, the Spaniards were so occupied with Santo Domingo, Jamaica, Cuba and Porto Rico, that they cared little for the smaller islands. Other nations, however, did not fail to grasp their opportunity, and at an early period we find the English, French, and Dutch busy in the work of colonization of the Windward and Leeward Islands.

The Dutch and the English appear to have settled in Santa Cruz or St. Croix, as this island is also called, about 1625. The early settlement of St. Thomas is wrapped in obscurity. The visitor to the island, as he enters the harbor of the town of Charlotte Amalia, the only one in St. Thomas, will observe three towers, two on the hills and one on the fort near the sea. These are respectively known as Blue Beard's, Black Beard's and Red Beard's tower. By whom were they erected? They have been attributed to the Buccaneers by some; by others to the Dutch; but their origin seems a mystery. Blue Beard's tower is surrounded by a kind of fort with mounted cannon.

Light begins to dawn with the advent of the Danes. On March 11, 1671, there was formed in Copenhagen the West India and Guinea Company, and in the same year the Danes took possession of St. Thomas as uninhabited. The English governor of the Leeward Islands protested, but King Charles II. of England directed his representatives in the West Indies not to interfere with the Danes. It appears from certain records that they had come to St. Thomas as early as 1666, before the establishment of the West India Company, and it is not unlikely that they, instead of the Dutch and Buccaneers, erected the towers to which allusion has been made. Thus did Denmark come into possession of St. Thomas, whence Danish colonization spread over the Virgin group and the Island of Santa Cruz.

From an agricultural standpoint, Santa Cruz grew to be the most important of the Danish islands. It is also the largest. There was comparatively little agriculture in St. Thomas, which is entirely mountainous, if you except the narrow strip of land through which Main Street runs, along the bay, with the level spaces beyond Cocoanut Square. But, if St. Thomas won little fame in agriculture, and if, for a long time, it was hardly known to the American public, except for the bay rum that bears its name, on the other hand it gained great renown as a commercial and maritime center, though this glory too has departed. Until about fifty years ago, St. Thomas was, perhaps, the busiest island in the West Indies, as far as trade is concerned; but it was a trade quite transitory in its nature. St. Thomas had little or nothing to export, but it served as a center, a depot for trade with other islands and with the Spanish Main, or Venezuela and Colombia. I can well remember how in the late 'sixties and early 'seventies, St. Thomas was overrun with buyers, mostly from Spanish America, with which she carried on a large wholesale business in goods imported from the various countries of Europe. There was no restriction on commerce, as free trade prevailed and import and export duties were hardly known. As far as I know, the revenues of the islands proceeded from taxes and licenses, while the Danish administration weighed lightly upon them. Few complaints were heard, and whatever disturbances arose were mostly among the turbulent negroes of Santa Cruz, and were of an economic nature.

Denmark was among the first of the nations of Europe to join in the anti-slavery movement, and she emancipated her slaves early in the nineteenth century. But slavery left behind an immense negro element in all the islands. To provide for labor, Santa Cruz adopted a contract system which was another form of slavery and which no doubt exerted an influence on the several negro rebellions that the island has known. After the emancipation of the negroes in the Dutch Islands in 1863, large numbers emigrated to Santa Cruz, allured by the change and the wages promised, but, no doubt, to find themselves disappointed.

In the meantime, little St. John, isolated from the world, continued its idyllic and monotonous existence, cultivating such fruits as home consumption needed or its neighbors might be willing to purchase.

With the emancipation, the plantations in St. Thomas declined, and the whole attention of the island was devoted to commerce. For the trades and the necessary manual labor generally, on land and water, the blacks of the island sufficed. Hence St. Thomas has never employed coolies, like the British and Dutch colonies, nor Chinese, except in very limited numbers.

The island, nevertheless, soon assumed a very cosmopolitan character, and people from every clime visited its shores, while foreign tongues were constantly heard. As headquarters for the Royal Mail Steam Packet Company, St. Thomas saw travelers to the West Indies and South America constantly coming and going. With the steamers of the English, French and Spanish lines repeatedly visiting her harbor, St. Thomas became a very important coaling station, as well for merchant steamers as for the many men-of-war of European and American nations that were frequently touching at the island. In those days sailing vessels were numerous, and the harbor was generally filled with them. I can well remember, moreover, the many side-wheel or paddle steamers that were then crossing the Atlantic. The first time I went to Europe, in 1871, it was in the old Royal Mail steam packet *Seine,* a ship of some 3,000 tons, propelled by side wheels. Soon after that screws became more numerous, and the old side-wheelers disappeared, though I recollect meeting the U. S. man-of-war *Powhattan,* a side-wheeler, as late as 1882 off the harbor of Santa Cruz.

I think that St. Thomas reached the climax of its prosperity in the late 'fifties, although it held its own quite well for ten years more. The greatest blow was received by the hurricane of 1867, followed about a month later by an awful earthquake and tidal wave. What the gale had spared, the earthquake destroyed. The former had played most havoc with the wooden houses, the latter sought out for its victims those built of stone. The loss of life in the hurricane was much greater than in the earthquake, especially among the shipping in the harbor. It was about this period, just after the Civil War, that the first negotiations had been set on foot between the United States and Denmark, looking toward a transfer of the islands.

The next blow that St. Thomas received was the removal of the Royal Mail Steam Packet Company to Barbados, whereby St. Thomas fell to be a very secondary port, especially since the Company began to run steamers to the Isthmus and to Colombia and Venezuela, thus destroying the trade of the Spanish Main that St. Thomas had enjoyed. Nor was this compensated for by the fact that the German Lloyd steamers began now to touch at the island.

At the period of its greatest prosperity St. Thomas was not particularly noted for health. Besides those diseases endemic in the tropics, it had occasional visits of smallpox and cholera, while yellow fever was hardly ever absent from its shores. With the advance of tropical hygiene, it stands to reason that St. Thomas has been benefited, like other countries in which yellow fever was once prevalent. It is now quite rare to hear of an epidemic of yellow fever anywhere.

Leaving aside such evils as these, the climate of St. Thomas is not disagreeable, while the winter months are cool. The elevation of the hills affords most desirable sites for beautiful residences, commanding some of the most superb views that mortal eye can desire. If the moral tone of the place can be raised, with the improvements, hygienic and other, that Americans would introduce, there is no reason why St. Thomas should not be an earthly paradise.

Speaking of the yellow fever reminds me that the United States once lost in St. Thomas a distinguished citizen by that terrible disease. I refer to Admiral Palmer, a fine gentleman of the old school who had fought in the Civil War. He was a man, as I heard, of deep religious sentiment. During the earthquake, in 1867, he lay with his flagship, the *Susquehanna,* in the harbor of St. Thomas, where she suffered some damage from the tidal wave, while the *Monongahela* at St. Croix was raised on the crest of the wave, and landed high and dry on the shore.

A new era has now dawned for the islands, that must henceforth be known as "The Virgin Islands of the United

States." They have been purchased from Denmark for the sum of twenty-five million dollars. On Saturday, March 31st, the old Dannebrog flag, the red with the white cross of Denmark, went up for the last time. Toward four in the afternoon a guard of honor from the Danish man-of-war, *Valkyrien,* under Lieutenant Jorgensen lined off on the pier. Another position was occupied by the Americans under Lieutenant Leach. Shortly after, in presence of many officials and of the officers of the *Valkyrien* and of the American ship *Hancock,* Commander Pollock met the Danish Governor, Konow, and the articles of transfer were read and signed. Then Governor Konow ordered the flag lowered. It came down at 4.45 p. m. mid the tears of the assembled multitude, the salute of twenty-one guns from the ships and the battery, and the playing of the Danish national anthem by the band from the *Valkyrien.* Again the ships and battery thundered out their salute of twenty-one guns, and, while the band of the *Olympia* rendered the "Star-spangled Banner," "Old Glory" floated up to the top of the pole, and the Virgin Islands had passed from Denmark to the United States. After the flag raising, Bishop E. C. Greider of the Moravian Church offered up a prayer and the benediction was pronounced by Bishop Charles B. Colmore, the Protestant Episcopal Bishop of Porto Rico. The churches represented by their clergy were the Lutheran, the Moravian, the Reformed Church, the Wesleyan Methodist, and the Catholic. The last named was represented by the Rev. Father Moris, C.SS.R., Superior of the Redemptorists. The Colonial Council had sent a farewell cable to Christian X., King of Denmark, to which the chairman received this reply: "Express my heartfelt thanks for kind telegram. God bless you all and best wishes for the prosperity of your islands."

John N. Lightbowm in his "Mail Notes," published in St. Thomas, writes: "It was a long time coming—this change—America's first effort at acquisition being made just fifty years ago, but it has come at last. For weal or for woe we are within the folds of 'Old Glory'—and we do trust that the islands may enjoy that 'happy and prosperous future' which both the King who has ceded them and the people of the United States who have acquired them hope for. We are taken under the Stars and Stripes, not as a conquered people, and neither do we expect to be treated as such. We have for these many years enjoyed the rights of a free and enlightened people, and of this freedom we expect no curtailment whatever. We shall give our loyalty unstintedly to the flag that now floats over us. From this moment on it is our flag and in every respect we demand every privilege, all the rights, and all the protection that it stands for."

St. Thomas has often been visited by distinguished personages, and not seldom has it given refuge to political exiles from various parts of Spanish America, such as Mexico, Venezuela and Santo Domingo. Prince Alfred of England, the "Sailor-prince"; Prince Waldemar of Denmark, a queen of the Hawaiians, then better known as the Sandwich Islands; De Lesseps of Panama Canal fame, and others have visited its shores. I have a recollection of reading somewhere that centuries ago it had also been visited by the great Dominican, St. Louis Bertrand.

In the nineteenth century, it was for some time the home of that turbulent Mexican spirit, the famous General Santa Ana who was a well-known character in the island, and who lived in a beautiful house on one of the hills. It has harbored ex-presidents and ex-governors from Venezuela and Santo Domingo, among them being the ex-priest and ex-president Morales of the latter country. Although Morales had left the ministry, he never in any way, so far as I know, showed himself hostile to the Church. Santo Domingo has also had other priests as president, such as the late Archbishop, and Monseigneur Nouel, the present Archbishop, who was recently Apostolic Delegate for Cuba and Porto Rico. As of especial interest to Americans we may also mention the fact that our Alexander Hamilton, a native of the island of Nevis, spent a portion of his boyhood in Santa Cruz.

With the change of government there will, no doubt, be a great influx of Americans to the islands and the Virgin group will become better known.

THE UNITED STATES ENTERS THE WAR

A UNITED DEMOCRACY ACCEPTS THE STERN NECESSITY OF BATTLE

APRIL 6TH

THE DECLARATION OF WAR

PRESIDENT WILSON	WILLIAM H. TAFT
VON BETHMANN-HOLLWEG	ROBERT MACHRAY
DAVID LLOYD GEORGE	ALEXANDER RIBOT

In this section of our work we give first the official Declaration of War, as passed by both Houses of Congress on April 6th. Then comes President Wilson's most celebrated speech, his official appeal to the Congress at its joint assembly, in which he outlined the events which he regarded as having made the war a necessity. For years past he had been doing his utmost to help Europe to make peace; but now even the peacemaker had become convinced that with Imperial Germany there could be no peace.

To show that the presidential address was no mere partisan speech but the genuine pronouncement of the entire nation, we follow it with the views of that other most honored statesman, the country's former President, Mr. Taft. Then comes the German official view as expressed by the Chancellor, Von Bethmann-Hollweg. His long rule over Germany was almost at an end. He had been Chancellor since the midsummer of 1909; but this last blunder turned even his own partisans against him, not because he had trampled on America's rights, but because he had undervalued America's power. When that became manifest, he resigned in July, 1917, and was followed by a succession of rapidly shifting chancellors. None of them, however, proved better able than he to rescue Imperial Germany from her impending fate. The system, not the individual, was driving her to ruin.

As the German Chancellor's statement is largely an attack on Britain, we give the British official commentary upon it, as also the popular British estimate of President Wilson's work at that time, before the Peace Negotiations had placed him before Europe in another light. The official voice of the French Government is expressed by the Prime Minister at the time, M. Ribot. He had succeeded to M. Briand in March; he resigned in September; and in November M. Clemenceau took the helm.

SIXTY-FIFTH CONGRESS OF THE UNITED STATES OF AMERICA;
At the First Session
Begun and held at the City of Washington on Monday, the
second day of April, one thousand nine hundred
and seventeen.

JOINT Resolution Declaring that a state of war exists between the Imperial German Government and the Government and the people of the United States and making provision to prosecute the same.

Whereas the Imperial German Government has committed
repeated acts of war against the Government and the
people of the United States of America; Therefore, be it
Resolved by the Senate and House of Representatives of
the United States of America in Congress assembled, That
the state of war between the United States and the Imperial
German Government which has thus been thrust upon the
United States is hereby formally declared; and that the
President be, and he is hereby, authorized and directed to
employ the entire naval and military forces of the United
States and the resources of the Government to carry on war
against the Imperial German Government; and to bring the
conflict to a successful termination all the resources of the
country are hereby pledged by the Congress of the United
States.
CHAMP CLARK,
Speaker of the House of Representatives.
THOS. R. MARSHALL,
*Vice President of the United States
and President of the Senate.*
Approved, April 6, 1917,
WOODROW WILSON.

BY PRESIDENT WILSON
Address Delivered at the Joint Session of the Two Houses of Congress, April 2, 1917

GENTLEMEN OF THE CONGRESS:
I have called the Congress into extraordinary session because there are serious, very serious, choices of policy to be

made, and made immediately, which it was neither right nor constitutionally permissible that I should assume the responsibility of making.

On the third of February last I officially laid before you the extraordinary announcement of the Imperial German Government that on and after the first day of February it was its purpose to put aside all restraints of law or of humanity and use its submarines to sink every vessel that sought to approach either the ports of Great Britain and Ireland or the western coasts of Europe or any of the ports controlled by the enemies of Germany within the Mediterranean. That had seemed to be the object of the German submarine warfare earlier in the war, but since April of last year the Imperial Government had somewhat restrained the commanders of its undersea craft in conformity with its promise then given to us that passenger boats should not be sunk and that due warning would be given to all other vessels which its submarines might seek to destroy, when no resistance was offered or escape attempted, and care taken that their crews were given at least a fair chance to save their lives in their open boats. The precautions taken were meager and haphazard enough, as was proved in distressing instance after instance in the progress of the cruel and unmanly business, but a certain degree of restraint was observed. The new policy has swept every restriction aside. Vessels of every kind, whatever their flag, their character, their cargo, their destination, their errand, have been ruthlessly sent to the bottom without warning and without thought of help or mercy for those on board, the vessels of friendly neutrals along with those of belligerents. Even hospital ships and ships carrying relief to the sorely bereaved and stricken people of Belgium, though the latter were provided with safe conduct through the proscribed areas by the German Government itself and were distinguished by unmistakable marks of identity, have been sunk with the same reckless lack of compassion or of principle.

I was for a little while unable to believe that such things would in fact be done by any Government that had hitherto subscribed to humane practices of civilized nations. International law had its origin in the attempt to set up some law which would be respected and observed upon the seas, where no nation had right of dominion and where lay the free highways of the world.   By painful stage after stage has that law been built up, with meager enough results, indeed, after all was accomplished that could be accomplished, but always with a clear view, at least, of what the heart and conscience of mankind demanded.   This minimum of right the German Government has swept aside, under the plea of retaliation and necessity and because it had no weapons which it could use at sea except these which it is impossible to employ as it is employing them without throwing to the wind all scruples of humanity or of respect for the understandings that were supposed to underlie the intercourse of the world.   I am not now thinking of the loss of property involved, immense and serious as that is, but only of the wanton and wholesale destruction of the lives of non-combatants, men, women and children, engaged in pursuits which have always, even in the darkest periods of modern history, been deemed innocent and legitimate.   Property can be paid for; the lives of peaceful and innocent people cannot be.   The present German submarine warfare against commerce is a warfare against mankind.

It is a war against all nations.   American ships have been sunk, American lives taken, in ways which it has stirred us very deeply to learn of, but the ships and people of other neutral and friendly nations have been sunk and overwhelmed in the waters in the same way.   There has been no discrimination.   The challenge is to all mankind.   Each nation must decide for itself how it will meet it.   The choice we make for ourselves must be made with a moderation of counsel and a temperateness of judgment befitting our character and our motives as a nation.   We must put excited feeling away.   Our motive will not be revenge or the victorious assertion of the physical might of the nation, but only the vindication of right, of human right, of which we are only a single champion.

When I addressed the Congress on the twenty-sixth of February last I thought that it would suffice to assert our neutral rights with arms, our right to use the seas against unlawful interference, our right to keep our people safe against unlawful violence. But armed neutrality, it now appears, is impracticable. Because submarines are in effect outlaws when used as the German submarines have been used against merchant shipping, it is impossible to defend ships against their attacks as the law of nations has assumed that merchantmen would defend themselves against privateers or cruisers, visible craft giving chase upon the open sea. It is common prudence in such circumstances, grim necessity indeed, to endeavor to destroy them before they have shown their own intention. They must be dealt with upon sight, if dealt with at all. The German Government denies the right of neutrals to use arms at all within the areas of the sea which it has proscribed, even in the defense of rights which no modern publicist has ever before questioned their right to defend. The intimation is conveyed that the armed guards which we have placed on our merchant ships will be treated as beyond the pale of law and subject to be dealt with as pirates would be. Armed neutrality is ineffectual enough at best; in such circumstances and in the face of such pretensions it is worse than ineffectual; it is likely only to produce what it was meant to prevent; it is practically certain to draw us into the war without either the rights or the effectiveness of belligerents. There is one choice we cannot make, we are incapable of making; we will not choose the path of submission and suffer the most sacred rights of our nation and our people to be ignored or violated. The wrongs against which we now array ourselves are no common wrongs; they cut to the very roots of human life.

With a profound sense of the solemn and even tragical character of the step I am taking and of the grave responsibilities which it involves, but in unhesitating obedience to what I deem my constitutional duty, I advise that the Congress declare the recent course of the Imperial German Government to be in fact nothing less than war against the Government and people of the United States; that it formally accept the status of belligerent which has thus been thrust upon it; and that it take immediate steps not only to put the country in a more thorough state of defense, but also to exert all its power and employ all its resources to bring the Government of the German Empire to terms and end the war.

What this will involve is clear. It will involve the utmost practicable coöperation in counsel and action with the governments now at war with Germany, and, as incident to that, the extension to those governments of the most liberal financial credits, in order that our resources may so far as possible be added to theirs. It will involve the organization and mobilization of all the material resources of the country to supply the materials of war and serve the incidental needs of the nation in the most abundant and yet the most economical and efficient way possible. It will involve the immediate full equipment of the navy in all respects but particularly in supplying it with the best means of dealing with the enemy's submarines. It will involve the immediate addition to the armed forces of the United States already provided for by law in case of war of at least five hundred thousand men, who should, in my opinion, be chosen upon the principle of universal liability to service, and also the authorization of subsequent additional increments of equal force so soon as they may be needed and can be handled in training. It will involve also, of course, the granting of adequate credits to the Government, sustained, I hope, so far as they can equitably be sustained by the present generation, by well-conceived taxation.

I say sustained so far as may be equitable by taxation because it seems to me that it would be most unwise to base the credits which will now be necessary entirely on money borrowed. It is our duty, I most respectfully urge, to protect our people so far as we may against the very serious hardships and evils which would be likely to arise out of the inflation which would be produced by vast loans.

In carrying out the measures by which these things are to be accomplished we should keep constantly in mind the wisdom of interfering as little as possible in our own preparation and in the equipment of our own military forces with the duty—for it will be a very practical duty—of supplying the nations already at war with Germany with the materials which they can obtain only from us or by our assistance. They are in the field and we should help them in every way to be effective there.

I shall take the liberty of suggesting, through the several executive departments of the Government, for the consideration of your committees, measures for the accomplishment of the several objects I have mentioned. I hope that it will be your pleasure to deal with them as having been framed after very careful thought by the branch of the Government upon whom the responsibility of conducting the war and safeguarding the nation will most directly fall.

While we do these things, these deeply momentous things, let us be very clear, and make very clear to all the world, what our motives and our objects are. My own thought has not been driven from its habitual and normal course by the unhappy events of the last two months, and I do not believe that the thought of the nation has been altered or clouded by them. I have exactly the same things in mind now that I had in mind when I addressed the Senate on the twenty-second of January last; the same that I had in mind when I addressed the Congress on the third of February and on the twenty-sixth of February. Our object now, as then, is to vindicate the principles of peace and justice in the life of the world as against selfish and autocratic power, and to set up among the really free and self-governed peoples of the world such a concert of purpose and of action as will henceforth insure the observance of those principles. Neutrality is no longer feasible or desirable where the peace of the world is involved and the freedom of its peoples, and the menace to that peace and freedom lies in the existence of autocratic governments, backed by organized force which is controlled wholly by their will, not by the will of their people. We have seen the last of neutrality in such circumstances. We are at the beginning of an age in which it will be insisted that the same standards of conduct and of responsibility for wrong done shall be observed among nations and their governments that are observed among the individual citizens of civilized States.

We have no quarrel with the German people. We have no feeling towards them but one of sympathy and friendship. It was not upon their impulse that their government acted in entering this war. It was not with their previous knowledge or approval. It was a war determined upon as wars used to be determined upon in the old, unhappy days when peoples were nowhere consulted by their rulers and wars were provoked and waged in the interest of dynasties or of little groups of ambitious men who were accustomed to use their fellowmen as pawns and tools. Self-governed nations do not fill their neighbor states with spies or set the course of intrigue to bring about some critical posture of affairs which will give them an opportunity to strike and make conquest. Such designs can be successfully worked out only under cover and where no one has the right to ask questions. Cunningly contrived plans of deception or aggression, carried, it may be, from generation to generation, can be worked out and kept from the light only within the privacy of courts or behind the carefully guarded confidences of a narrow and privileged class. They are happily impossible where public opinion commands and insists upon full information concerning all the nation's affairs.

A steadfast concert for peace can never be maintained except by a partnership of democratic nations. No autocratic government could be trusted to keep faith within it or observe its covenants. It must be a league of honor, a partnership of opinion. Intrigue would eat its vitals away; the plottings of inner circles who could plan what they would and render account to no one would be a corruption seated at its very heart. Only free peoples can hold their purpose and their honor steady to a common end and prefer the interests of mankind to any narrow interest of their own.

Does not every American feel that assurance has been added to our hope for the future peace of the world by the wonderful and heartening things that have been happening within the last few weeks in Russia? Russia was known by those who knew her best to have been always in fact democratic at heart, in all the vital habits of her thought, in all the intimate relationships of her people that spoke their natural instinct, their habitual attitude towards life. The autocracy that crowned the summit of her political structure, long as it had stood and terrible as was the reality of its power, was not in fact Russian in origin, character, or purpose; and now it has been shaken off and the great, generous Russian people have been added, in all their naïve majesty and might, to the forces that are fighting for freedom in the world, for justice, and for peace. Here is a fit partner for a League of Honor.

One of the things that has served to convince us that the Prussian autocracy was not and could never be our friend is that from the very outset of the present war it has filled our unsuspecting communities, and even our offices of government, with spies and set criminal intrigues everywhere afoot against our national unity of counsel, our peace within and without, our industries and our commerce. Indeed, it is now evident that its spies were here even before the war began; and it is unhappily not a matter of conjecture but a fact proved in our courts of justice that the intrigues which have more than once come perilously near to disturbing the peace and dislocating the industries of the country have been carried on at the instigation, with the support, and even under the personal direction of official agents of the Imperial Government accredited to the Government of the United States. Even in checking these things and trying to extirpate them we have sought to put the most generous interpretation possible upon them because we knew that their source lay, not in any hostile feeling or purpose of the German people toward us (who were, no doubt, as ignorant of them as we ourselves were), but only in the selfish designs of a Government that did what it pleased and told its people nothing. But they have played their part in serving to convince us at last that that Government entertains no real friendship for us, and means to act against our peace and security at its convenience. That it means to stir up enemies against us at our very doors the intercepted note to the German Minister at Mexico City is eloquent evidence.

We are accepting this challenge of hostile purpose because we know that in such a government, following such methods, we can never have a friend; and that in the presence of its organized power, always lying in wait to accomplish we know not what purpose, there can be no assured security for the democratic governments of the world. We are now about to accept the gauge of battle with this natural foe to liberty and shall, if necessary, spend the whole force of the nation to check and nullify its pretensions and its power. We are glad, now that we see the facts with no veil of false pretense about them, to fight thus for the ultimate peace of the world and for the liberation of its peoples, the German peoples included; for the rights of nations, great and small, and the privilege of men everywhere to choose their way of life and of obedience. The world must be made safe for democracy. Its peace must be planted upon the tested foundations of political liberty. We have no selfish ends to serve. We desire no conquest, no dominion. We seek no indemnities for ourselves, no material compensation for the sacrifices we shall freely make. We are but one of the champions of the rights of mankind. We shall be satisfied when those rights have been made as secure as the faith and the freedom of nations can make them.

Just because we fight without rancor and without selfish object, seeking nothing for ourselves but what we shall wish to share with all free peoples, we shall, I feel confident, conduct our operations as belligerents without passion and ourselves observe with proud punctilio the principles of right and of fair play we profess to be fighting for.

I have said nothing of the governments allied with the Imperial Government of Germany because they have not made war upon us or challenged us to defend our right and our honor. The Austro-Hungarian Government has, indeed, avowed its unqualified endorsement and acceptance of the reckless and lawless submarine warfare adopted now without disguise by the Imperial German Government, and it has therefore not been possible for this Government to receive Count Tarnowski, the Ambassador recently accredited to this Government by the Imperial and Royal Government of Austria-Hungary; but that Government has not actually engaged in warfare against citizens of the United States on the seas, and I take the liberty, for the present at least, of postponing a discussion of our relations with the authorities at Vienna. We enter this war only where we are clearly forced into it because there are no other means of defending our rights.

It will be all the easier for us to conduct ourselves as belligerents in a high spirit of right and fairness because we act without animus, not with enmity toward a people or with the desire to bring any injury or disadvantage upon them, but only in armed opposition to an irresponsible government which has thrown aside all considerations of humanity and of right and is running amuck. We are, let me say again, the sincere friends of the German people, and shall desire nothing so much as the early reëstablishment of intimate relations of mutual advantage between us,—however hard it may be for them, for the time being, to believe that this is spoken from our hearts. We have borne with their present government through all these bitter months because of that friendship, exercising a patience and forbearance which would otherwise have been impossible. We shall, happily, still have an opportunity to prove that friendship in our daily attitude and actions toward the millions of men and women of German birth and native sympathy who live among us and share our life, and we shall be proud to prove it towards all who are in fact loyal to their neighbors and to the Government in the hour of test. They are, most of them, as true and loyal Americans as if they had never known any other fealty or allegiance. They will be prompt to stand with us in rebuking and restraining the few who may be of a different mind and purpose. If there should be disloyalty, it will be dealt with with a firm hand of stern repression; but, if it lifts its head at all, it will lift it only here and there and without countenance except from a lawless and malignant few.

It is a distressing and oppressive duty, Gentlemen of the Congress, which I have performed in thus addressing you. There are, it may be, many months of fiery trial and sacrifice ahead of us. It is a fearful thing to lead this great peaceful people into war, into the most terrible and disastrous of all wars, civilization itself seeming to be in the balance. But the right is more precious than peace, and we shall fight for the things which we have always carried nearest our hearts. —for democracy, for the right of those who submit to authority to have a voice in their own governments, for the rights and liberties of small nations, for a universal dominion of right by such a concert of free peoples as shall bring peace and safety to all nations and make the world itself at last free. To such a task we can dedicate our lives and our fortunes, everything that we are and everything that we have, with the pride of those who know that the day has come when America is privileged to spend her blood and her might for the principles that gave her birth and happiness and the peace which she has treasured. God helping her, she can do no other.

BY WILLIAM HOWARD TAFT

Address at Union College, Schenectady, N. Y., June 13, 1917

Was there any other alternative for us than to declare war? I would like to begin with the fundamentals. That depends upon what in fact and in law the act of Germany was. What was the law? It is what is called international law; that is, a rule of conduct adopted by the acquiescence of all nations, of one nation toward another, both in peace and in war. The branch of international law in which we are concerned here is perhaps the most definitely fixed of any branch of that jurisprudence, which in some respects is indefinite. It is the branch that governs the capture of commercial vessels at sea. For a hundred years there has been very little doubt about the rules that control that field of jurisprudence. During the Napoleonic wars a great many commercial vessels were captured and in the procedure instituted they had to be brought into the domestic courts of prize where these rules were laid down. At the same time on our own side of the ocean our Supreme Court settled many of the cases. In our civil war, in the war between France and Germany, similar conditions were made. So that when we speak of that law we are speaking of a law that has some similitude to our domestic law.

In the first place, a belligerent—one of those engaged in war upon the high seas—may seize a commercial vessel of its enemy, may confiscate the vessel and its cargo, and, if necessity requires, may sink or burn it. The second is that a neutral vessel may be seized by a belligerent vessel upon the high seas and examined to see whether that neutral vessel is carrying contraband to the enemy of the captor, and if so, the contraband may be confiscated. Third, a belligerent vessel may blockade a port of its enemy. It must blockade it with visible vessels and a knowledge to the world that a blockade exists. Even if a neutral vessel enter this blockade it may be seized by the belligerent and the cargo confiscated.

These are the three rules that cover the whole field of capture of commercial vessels. But accompanying these rules is the limitation that in taking a commercial vessel which makes no response when hailed, which does not attempt to escape under the circumstances I have described, it is the bounden duty of the captor to see to it that the officers, the crew, and the passengers, all of the ship's company, shall be put in a safe place. The captor may, as I say, sink or burn the vessel at the time or it may take it into port and have it adjudged a prize, but in either case the captor is bound to secure the lives of those who are upon that commercial vessel.

Germany has violated that rule. It has deliberately caused the death of men, women and children on the high seas, under the American flag, and where they had a right to be. Killing against the law with deliberation is murder, and Germany has been guilty of murder of 200 of our fellow-citizens, innocent of any offense, national or international.

Now, what is our duty under these circumstances? The Constitution of the United States is interpreted by the Supreme Court to say the duty of the citizens of the United States is to render allegiance, to do service, to pay taxes, and support the Government, and the corresponding duty of the United States as a Government is to protect the rights of citizens of the United States at home and abroad. Because one citizen of the United States puts himself under the lawful jurisdiction of another country, the absolute right of protection is qualified by his voluntary submission to another jurisdiction. The necessity for protection is not entirely taken away, but it is qualified. When a man is on an American deck and under the American flag, a citizen of the United States, he is as much entitled to protection from the unlawful invasion of a foreign power as if he stood on the soil of the United States.

In view, therefore, of the murder of these 200 citizens and of the announcement of a policy to continue these murders, what alternative was there left open other than a declaration of war to the United States? Suppose this had been Guatemala which had sunk one of our vessels and had sent ten of our sailors to the bottom? How many hours do you think it would be before the President and the Secretary of the Navy would send a battleship down to Guatemala and be thundering at the ports of that republic and demanding restitution, demanding a promise of conduct hereafter, demanding damages for what had been done, and on failure to answer promptly, to begin a bombardment? Even pacifists would have justified that.

Now, what is the difference between that situation and this? None? Yes. A very great difference. The nation that has done this is the greatest military nation in the world. It is a nation with which, if we engage, we are likely to lose, it may be, a million men, and all that to resent the sacrifice of only 200 souls. That, it is said, is a trivial discrepancy. Is it? It is if you look at it from a grossly material and mathematical standpoint, but it is not if you understand what it means to consent to the murder of 200 of our citizens because there is a powerful nation you have to meet and overcome in order to vindicate the rights of our citizens. It means submission to the domination of another power; it means giving up the independence for which we fought in 1776 and which we made sacrifices to maintain in 1861.

There was great criticism of the Administration because we did not immediately act as we now have acted. I am not going into the pros and cons of that discussion. It suffices to say that the self-restraint, the deliberation, the tolerance, if you choose, which characterized that policy, has had this great and good effect. It has shown to the world, and it has shown to our people that in entering this war we have done it with the utmost reluctance, and in entering the war we are entirely void of offense. It has shown that we have been forced in and that the situation has been such that no self-respecting nation, no nation which appreciates what a government is formed for, could avoid doing what we are doing when the rights of our citizens, the preservation of which is the chief object of government, have been defiantly violated by a power that rests for its right upon might.

That is why we are in. There are many of us who think, "for my country, right or wrong; may she always be right, but always for my country." I do not care to discuss that philosophy, but I do think it important we should realize and take it home to our souls we do not need that kind of philosophy in fighting out the fight we are to fight now. In 1776 we were fighting for our own independence and the development of our future. In 1861 we tried to eliminate that living lie in the Declaration of Independence, which declared that "all men are born free and equal." It took us four years of a terrible struggle to demonstrate to the world what had been doubted. We demonstrated to the world that we could make sacrifices of lives and treasure for the maintenance of a moral principle and the integrity of the nation. We showed in the words of Lincoln, that "the rule of the people should not perish from the earth."

And then we went on and increased from 30,000,000 to 100,000,000 people, and we created a material expansion which has given us greater wealth than any other country. We have had comfort and luxury. Now the question was when this issue came on whether in that change from 30,-000,000 to 100,000,000, from comparative wealth to great wealth, we had lost the moral spirit we had before shown, we had become so enervated by our success that we felt it was not wise to risk the lives of those dear to us, to risk the destruction that war must bring in order to assert our rights. Now we have stepped to the forefront of nations, and they look to us.

Before we came into this fight Russia had become a

democracy, and we find ourselves fighting shoulder to shoulder with the democracies of the world. We find arrayed against us the military dynasties of the world, Germany, Austria, and Turkey. Of course, people say England has a King; so has Italy and other countries that are fighting on our side. A democracy is a country ruled by the people. The King of England and the King of Italy haven't any more influence over the policies of their country than an ex-President.

The issue at present is drawn between the democracies of the world and the military dynasties, and people like to characterize that as the issue. It is and it isn't. What I mean by that is: The United States is not a knight-errant country going about to independent people and saying, "We do not like your form of government, we have tried our own popular government and we think it is better for you to take it, and you have got to take it." That is a very unreasonable position, in so far as that form of government deals with only their domestic pursuits and their domestic happiness. If they like to have a Czar, if they prefer it, why, it isn't for us to take away their freedom of will. Otherwise we shall go back to the logic of the Inquisition, when they burned people in this world so that they might not burn in the next.

But when their form of government involves a policy which does not confine its opinions to the people who make the government or support it, but becomes a visible policy against the welfare and happiness of the rest of the world family, we have a right and a duty, standing with other nations as we do, to see to it that such a foreign policy is stopped and stamped out forever.

I will not minimize or confuse. Germany is not exhausted. That machine which it has been creating for fifty years is a wonderful machine. . . . It did not interfere with Austria until Austria showed some signs of coming into a conference, and then it said to Austria, "This is the time to strike." It had been creating this force for fifty years, and now seemed the time to make it most effective. . . .

This militarism is a cancer which must be cut out by a surgical operation. It shows its malignant character in the utter disregard of the rules of war. It shows itself in the violation of Belgium, in the policy of frightfulness in order to subjugate Belgium; in the violation of The Hague treaties, which forbid the dropping of explosives out of aërial craft, the planting of mines, the use of asphyxiating gases and flames, all spread out in The Hague treaties, and all violated promptly by this German military machine.

It is therefore a cancer which would absorb the wholesome life of the world unless it is cut out, and necessitates suffering and pain in ridding the world of it. There are other evidences of divine plan. Think of the battle of the Marne, where this matchless machine began to find France and England unprepared, and they turned at the Marne when the German hosts with their guns were heard in Paris, and by mere moral force they turned these German legions back. Think of the blindness of this absorption of gross materialism as brought into the intellect of the Germans.

They cannot understand other people. They cannot recognize a moral force that binds people together in a cause. They said England will not stand by Belgium; it has trouble with Ireland; they said France is torn with Socialism and it is a decadent nation. In both cases they made blunders. They said as regards Canada, Australia, New Zealand, and South Africa, England has no control over them by force; they are far removed from it and will follow the path of materialism and gain; they will follow where profit determines; they will not be held. And yet, nothing has been grander than this light bond which unites England with these independent dependencies, and they have rallied to the support of the mother country, responded out of gratitude for the liberty that it had conferred upon them, and they have made sacrifices which call for our profound admiration. Think of it. Canada has furnished upward of 400,000 men. Nearly every home in English Canada is mourning—their best and most beloved. If we furnish as many men as they have for this war our armies will reach 6,500,000 men.

If our contributions to the Red Cross, Y. M. C. A., and

other voluntary individual contributions, in addition to taxes, reach the figures which they have in Canada, we shall contribute $14 to $15 per capita.

My friends, those are the mistakes or blunders that Germany has made, self-imposed or imposed by a definite rule that when you subject yourself to grossly material considerations you lose the higher mental and spiritual forces which enable you to conquer in the end.

Now, the last blunder of all. In its determination to depend upon the devilish ingenuity of science in the development of war, the Germans said: "We can starve England out with this submarine." When it saw us it said, "There is a tango-loving nation, too fat to fight, too lazy to go into the trenches," and they have deliberately forced us into the ranks of their enemies. Think of it. They have been fighting for nearly three years. The exhaustion that has come to them has had no comparison in history. The war must be determined by the weight of wealth and resources and the courageous men which can be gathered together to fight it out and be sure of a victorious battle in the end. And yet, in the face of that fact, we should impress on them that they deliberately forced into the ranks of their enemies the nation which can furnish more wealth, more resources, more equipment, and more men than any other nation in the world.

My friends, we are going to make these sacrifices. We do not know what they are yet, and we shall not know until we see the bulletins. The English people watched the bulletins for May and saw a loss of 114,000 in the British Army; 26,000 privates killed and 16,000 officers killed in action; 76,000 privates wounded, and 3,600 officers wounded and 7,000 missing. When we watch a report like this, then it will come home to us in our souls and we shall understand the sacrifice we have to make.

BY CHANCELLOR VON BETHMANN-HOLLWEG

The directors of the American Nation have been convened by President Wilson for an extraordinary session of Congress in order to decide the question of war or peace between the American and German Nations.

Germany never had the slightest intention of attacking the United States of America, and does not have such intention now. It never desired war against the United States of America and does not desire it to-day.

How did these things develop? More than once we told the United States that we made unrestricted use of the submarine weapon, expecting that England could be made to observe, in her policy of blockade, the laws of humanity and of international agreements. This blockade policy, this I expressly recall, has been called illegal and indefensible by President Wilson and Secretary of State Lansing.[1]

Our expectations, which we maintained during eight months, have been disappointed completely. England not only did not give up her illegal and indefensible policy of blockade, but uninterruptedly intensified it. England, together with her allies, arrogantly rejected the peace offers made by us and our allies and proclaimed her war aims, which aim at our annihilation and that of our allies.

Then we took unrestricted submarine warfare into our hands; then we had to for our defense.

If the American Nation considers this a cause for which to declare war against the German Nation with which it has lived in peace for more than 100 years, if this action warrants an increase of bloodshed, we shall not have to bear the responsibility for it. The German Nation, which feels neither hatred nor hostility against the United States of America, shall also bear and overcome this.

BY LORD ROBERT CECIL
British Government Response to Bethmann-Hollweg

The German Chancellor claims that Germany in the past renounced the unrestricted use of her submarine weapon in the expectation that Great Britain could be made to observe in her blockade policy the laws of humanity and international agreements. It is difficult to say whether this statement is the more remarkable for its hypocrisy or for its falseness. It would hardly seem that Germany is in a po-

---

[1] Not the policy as a whole but some of its details were so characterized.

sition to speak of humanity or international agreements, since she began this war by deliberately violating the international agreement guaranteeing the neutrality of Belgium, and has continued it by violating all the dictates of humanity.

Has the Chancellor forgotten that the German forces have been guilty of excesses in Belgium, unparalleled in history, culminating in the attempted enslavement of a dauntless people, of poisoning wells, of bombarding open towns, torpedoing hospital ships and sinking other vessels with total disregard for the safety of noncombatants on board, with the result that many hundreds of innocent victims, including both women and children, have lost their lives?

The latest manifestation of this policy is to be seen in the devastation and deportations carried out by the Germans in their forced retreat on the Western front.

The Chancellor states that it is because the Allies have not abandoned their blockade and have refused the so-called peace offer of Germany that unrestricted submarine warfare is now decided on. As to this I will do no more than quote what the Chancellor himself said in the Reichstag, in announcing the adoption of unrestricted submarine war.

He said that as soon as he himself, in agreement with the supreme army command, reached the conviction that ruthless U-boat warfare would bring Germany nearer to a victorious peace, then the U-boat warfare would be started. He continued:

"This moment has now arrived. Last autumn the time was not ripe, but to-day the moment has come when, with the greatest prospect of success, we can undertake this enterprise. We must not wait any longer. Where has there been a change? In the first place, the most important fact of all is that the number of our submarines has been very considerably increased as compared with last spring, and thereby a firm basis has been created for success."

Does not this prove conclusively that it was not any scruple or any respect for international law or neutral rights that prevented unrestricted warfare from being adopted earlier, but merely a lack of means to carry it out?

I think it may be useful once again to point out that the illegal and inhuman attack on shipping by the Germans cannot be justified as a reprisal for the action of Great Britain in attempting to cut off from Germany all imports.

The submarine campaign was clearly contemplated as far back as December, 1914, when Admiral von Tirpitz gave an indication to an American correspondent in Berlin of the projected plan.

As for the plea that the Allies are aiming at the annihilation of Germany and her allies and that ruthless warfare is, therefore, justified, it is sufficient in order to refute this to quote the following passage from the Allies' reply of January 10, 1917, to President Wilson's note:

"There is no need to say that if the Allies desire to liberate Europe from the brutal covetousness of Prussian militarism, the extermination and political disappearance of the German people have never, as has been pretended, formed a part of their design."

BY ROBERT MACHRAY

If almost the latest in point of time, President Wilson is the most surprising as well as the most valuable discovery of the Allies. It is hardly an excess of language to say that he is one of the wonders of the War. He has accomplished that which in its way is among the most amazing feats of all history. To put it colloquially, he has swung into line with himself a free people of a hundred millions, the vast majority of whom not only were thoroughly pacific at heart but sincerely thought that their country had no special interest in, far less any vital concern with, the struggle, however much it was convulsing the rest of the world. It has taken him six months to bring about this prodigious result —not a long period when everything is considered. Events which occurred during these months have doubtless helped him materially, but previous events, not very dissimilar in their nature, had made no strong impression on the mass of American opinion. At the outset it might well have seemed an impossible undertaking. Germany was confident that it was impossible. More than that, she was certain, with that deadly infallibility of hers with respect to men and nations outside the Germanic pale which is one of the things working her ruin, that he would not fight at all.   What he had said and done, or left unsaid and undone, in the earlier stages of the War had given Count Bernstorff, her Ambassador at Washington, that conviction, and she herself, counting besides on the Germans and pro-Germans and other factors in her favor in the United States, was of the same mind. For about two years and a half nothing took place seriously to disturb her in that comfortable belief.   The feelings of pain and indignation evoked throughout America by the torpedoing of the *Lusitania,* in itself as sinister an incident as could be imagined, did not lead the President to take belligerent action.   Even when a year later, in his Note of April, 1916, after the sinking of the *Sussex,* he went so far as to threaten a rupture of relations, and Germany yielded to his demand for a restriction of submarine warfare, she was in reality as sure as ever that she had read him aright, and accordingly busied herself intensely in building fleets of U-boats—the lack of a sufficient number of which had been the true reason for her compliance.   Not that she neglected to take such steps as appeared to her likely to assist him in keeping the path of peace.   For example, immediately after the publication of the *Sussex* Note myriads of telegrams arrived at Washington, as many as a hundred thousand messages being received in a single day, all protesting against war, and all of them, it subsequently came out, inspired by Count Bernstorff and his friends.   This was only one of the numerous German plots and intrigues of which the United States had been and was then the field, and some at least of which must have been within Mr. Wilson's cognizance—as Germany knew perfectly, and was confirmed thereby in her conviction that he was not and never would be a fighter. She was to be undeceived, but for several months longer her belief in the unalterable character of the President's devotion to peace could not be said to be other than justified by the course which he adopted.

President Wilson took the stage as the protagonist of peace.   In May, 1916, he spoke in North Carolina in favor

of a negotiated settlement of the War. Later, in the same
month, at a meeting of the League to Enforce Peace, he
strongly urged a compromise on the belligerents. He said
that the United States was willing to become a partner in
any feasible association of the nations, and argued that had
such an association existed soon enough the War would never
have broken out. The idea of the League, which had been
developed by ex-President Taft, had found some support in
certain quarters in England, but obtained remarkably little
encouragement in the country of its origin. Neither in the
United States, which as a whole was still profoundly indifferent about the War, because still profoundly ignorant
of the menace to itself that was implicit in it, nor among the
Allied peoples, who realized the menace to themselves, and
wondered why Americans did not grasp the situation, was
there any marked response to Mr. Wilson's proposals.

In any case, all suggestions in response were quickly lost
sight of in the turmoil and excitement of the Presidential
election campaign, which started in July, 1916. The conflict between the Democrats and the Republicans was of infinitely more absorbing interest than the War, which, however, reacted on the political position. Led by Mr. Wilson,
who was standing for reëlection, the Democrats, with few
exceptions, were for peace almost at any price so far as
America was concerned, and passionately asserted that the
War was Europe's affair, not America's. Mr. Hughes, the
Republican candidate, preserved a discreet reticence, but Mr.
Roosevelt, one of his principal lieutenants, vigorously denounced the Germans, and pretty plainly indicated that if his
party came into power, and he had anything to do with the
influencing of its policy, there would be a marked alteration in the attitude of the United States towards the Central
Powers. The Republicans as a party were not exactly identified with an attitude of belligerency, for others of their leaders besides Mr. Hughes maintained a diplomatic reserve, but
popularly they were credited with views and aims that might
involve the country in the War. On the other hand, Mr.
Wilson and the Democrats were definitely regarded as the
peace party, as unchangeably determined to keep out of the

War. Very many Americans, especially in the West and in the South—the East was largely pro-Entente—supported Mr. Wilson's candidature on the specific ground that he had kept the United States at peace—and would continue to do so, as they were assured by fervent Democratic orators would be the case. Mr. Wilson's platform rather was that there was nothing in the War, once the submarining was restricted, that necessarily involved America.

At this time the comparative inactivity of the U-boats and the immunity of American vessels from their attacks could be and were adduced as proofs both of Mr. Wilson's wise statesmanship and of the friendship of Germany or, at any rate, of the absence of hostility on her part towards the United States. There would seem to have been no suspicion that the lull in the warfare of the submarines was a screen under cover of which these undersea vessels were being built in very large numbers—with intentions that were anything but amicable with regard to the Americans. In a speech delivered nearly a year afterwards Mr. Lansing, the Secretary of State, practically admitted that this was the fact. Yet in July and again in October of last year the Government and people of the United States saw two strange things happen on their Atlantic coast which might have given them an inkling of what was designed. The first was the arrival at Norfolk, Virginia, of the ocean-going submarine *Deutschland,* a U-boat of a new type; she was unarmed, and had a valuable if small cargo; perhaps innocent-looking enough, her real function was to act as a supply-ship, a depot, for the fighting submarines. The second of these strange things was the havoc wrought by the new ocean-going *U*-53 off the shores of New England on the 7th of October. Here were two indications—these large new submarines—of that intensification of the undersea war that was purposed by Germany. Moreover, the coming of the *Deutschland* informed the Americans that their littoral could easily be reached by the U-boats, and the depredations of *U*-53 emphatically pointed the moral that the United States would do well to keep out of the War. Republican "stalwarts" like Mr. Roosevelt found a fresh text for their denunciations of the German menace which, they declared, was now brought home to the national consciousness, but the Democratic leaders remained stubbornly pacific.

In that month of October Mr. Wilson, in the course of the electoral campaign, showed by his speeches that he had no belief in the reality of that menace, and that he still had not grasped the essential meaning of the War. Speaking at Omaha, he said, "The singularity of the present war is that its roots and origins and object never have been disclosed. . . . It will take the long inquiry of history to explain this war." In an address delivered at Cincinnati three weeks later, when the political contest was at its height, he asked his audience, "Have you ever heard what started the present war?" And he answered his query by stating, "If you have, I wish you would publish it, because nobody else has, so far as I can gather. Nothing in particular started it, but everything in general." Needless to say, President Wilson does not use such language now, but the point is that it was just such language as this that procured for him his second term. He was reëlected as a Peace President, with in effect a mandate to keep out of the War. It is only when this is understood that the magnitude of what the writer has characterized as President Wilson's Greatest Achievement can be realized. By his own words, his attitude, and his deeds or the want of them, he had made that achievement supremely difficult, yet he has succeeded in it—and succeeded magnificently. A splendid convert heads America.

Persons close to the President have intimated that he was always "pro-Ally," but the facts cannot be said to bear out this statement. To those already mentioned there has to be added another fact which is of the utmost significance in this connection—it was hinted at a few lines above in the phrase "deeds or the want of them." When by the joint resolution of Congress in April last the United States declared war on Germany it was not at all prepared for hostilities on a large scale, and was but ill-prepared for war even in a small way. That this was so must be put down very largely to President Wilson. In the *Sussex* Note he threatened Germany, but at the time and for months afterwards he took no military measures with a view to provide for the eventualities that might arise from carrying out that threat, as he believed he would never be called on to do anything of the kind. He was warned by the stalwarts that his belief might prove to be erroneous, and he was urged to be ready. He was reminded that weakness invited attack, and that even for self-defense the United States was in a lamentably poor position. Before this there had sprung up in America a strong movement for "national preparedness," the chief advocate and exponent of which was an organization called the National Security League, with not a few eminent men among its members. Taking as its rallying cry the statement that the country was in danger, the League strove with the utmost energy and earnestness to rouse the citizens of the United States to a sense of the dire possibilities of the situation. It pleaded with all its might for the immediate institution of universal military training as the only adequate remedy for the defenselessness of the Republic. It sent out eloquent speakers, it published convincing books and pamphlets, it inserted striking advertisements in the papers, it made excellent use of film-pictures. It did everything that could be done to influence the public, but the result in general was disproportionately small to the greatness of the effort essayed. Mr. Wilson did not give the movement his blessing, and the bulk of the population would have nothing to do with it. Yet it was not altogether a failure, for out of the "industrial preparedness" side of its campaign came the Advisory Commission of the Council of National Defense, which during the past seven or eight months has mobilized the industrial and commercial resources of the Union in the most marvelous manner.

After the *Sussex* Note, which in the retrospect stands out as crucial, President Wilson did little or nothing—practically nothing—to put the United States on a war footing. In Congress, during the summer of 1916, provision was made for a small increase of the regular army by five annual installments. But the army, after deducting from it the troops which garrisoned the Philippines, Panama, Hawaii, and Porto Rico and were on duty in China, was still around the

100,000-men mark, which for several years had been the standard of its strength in America. From the German point of view this army, so far as size went, was even more "contemptible" than that of Great Britain in 1914. The American second-line troops, consisting of the National Guard, which was the organized militia of the various States of the Union, comprised about 150,000 men, two-thirds of whom, it was estimated, could be placed in the field at a pinch. No steps were taken to increase the effectiveness of this force. With regard to the navy the story, if somewhat different, amounted in practice to the same thing. After suffering from some years of stagnation, the navy had been enlarged by the building of two capital ships a year. In 1916 Mr. Daniels, the Secretary of the Navy, obtained the authorization of Congress for a very large expansion of the Fleet, the money voted being nearly sixty-five millions sterling, or more than double the sum appropriated in the previous year. The program, which included the construction of ten first-class battleships of the largest size, sixteen cruisers, and many submarines and destroyers, was necessarily spread over a long period, and in 1917, when the United States went to war, there had not been time for any part of it to have materialized. Furthermore, the presence of so many very large ships in the program was in itself an indication, having regard to the stationary position of similar ships of the belligerents in European waters, that Germany could not be aimed at by the United States, for what was wanted in case of a war against her was a multitude of small but swift craft, such as destroyers and the "submarine-chasers," which afterwards were built by the Americans.

President Wilson was the ultimate source of the naval expansion program, and it was as easy for his countrymen to see from it, as from his speeches, that his thoughts were centered on peace. An organization called the Council of National Defense, and consisting of the Secretaries of War, of the Navy, of the Interior, of Agriculture, of Commerce, and of Labor, was given a legal status by Congress in August, 1916, and the same Act instituted an Advisory Commission to work with but under the Council. The formation of these bodies proved of incalculable importance in the mobilization of the United States, but six months passed before either body did anything. In their political origin they were nothing more than a diplomatic concession, at once sonorous and empty, to the stalwarts and the movement for national preparedness.

After Mr. Wilson was reëlected he continued to appear as a strenuous advocate of peace. In December, 1916, Germany began her first considerable "peace offensive," as it is very properly described, by the famous speech of Von Bethmann-Hollweg, then her Chancellor, suggesting a settlement. On the 20th of that month President Wilson invited the belligerents to say on what terms they would make peace. One of the paragraphs of the Note he addressed to the warring nations attracted particular notice and some unfavorable comment among the Allies; inferentially it demonstrated that he was still a disbeliever in the German menace to his own country. It stated:

"The President takes the liberty of calling attention to the fact that the objects which the statesmen of the belligerents on both sides have in mind in this War are virtually the same, as stated in general terms to their own people and to the world. Each side desires to make the rights and privileges of weak peoples and small States as secure against aggression or denial in the future as the rights and privileges of the great and powerful States now at war. Each wishes itself to be made secure in the future, along with all other nations and peoples, against the recurrence of wars like this, and against aggression or selfish interference of any kind."

This presentation of the case had some good effects. Germany, asked to come out into the open with her terms, declined to do so, whereas the Allies, after consulting together, boldly outlined theirs in a Note handed on the 10th of January, 1917, by the French Prime Minister to the American Ambassador at Paris. The Note was sent to the British Ambassador at Washington with a covering letter from Mr. Balfour, who shortly before had become Secretary for Foreign Affairs. A really great and illuminating State paper, Mr. Balfour's dispatch, after paying tribute to the

President's ideals, drove to the heart of the whole War by considering the main conditions which had made possible the calamities from which the world was suffering:

"These were the existence of a Great Power consumed with the lust of domination, in the midst of a community of nations ill-prepared for defense, plentifully supplied indeed with international laws, but with no machinery for enforcing them, and weakened by the fact that neither the boundaries of the various States nor their internal constitution harmonized with the aspirations of their constituent races, or secured to them just and equal treatment. . . . While other nations, notably the United States and Great Britain, were striving by treaties of arbitration to make sure that no chance quarrel should mar the peace they desired to make perpetual, Germany stood aloof. Her historians and philosophers preached the splendors of war; power was proclaimed as the true end of the State; the General Staff forged with untiring industry the weapons by which, at the appointed hour, power might be achieved. . . . Germany and Austria made the present War inevitable by attacking the rights of one small State, and they gained their initial triumphs by violating the treaty-guarded territories of another."

Mr. Balfour's letter, when given to the public, made an impression on many Americans, but apparently it made none on the President. On the 22nd of January, 1917, Mr. Wilson delivered a speech in the Senate in which he said, "There must be a peace without victory—a peace forced on the loser would leave a bitter memory, leave only a quicksand for the security of the world to rest on." Once more he brought forward the idea of the League to Enforce Peace, with limitations of armaments, and held out the prospect of the United States joining the nations in a world-wide guarantee of peace. By way of reply, Mr. Bonar Law said:

"What President Wilson is longing for we are fighting for, our sons and our brothers are dying for, and we mean to secure it. The hearts of the people of this country are longing for peace—a peace that will bring back in safety those who are dear to us, but a peace that will mean that those who will never come back shall not have laid down their lives in vain."

At the end of January the situation entered on a highly critical stage.   On the 31st Count Bernstorff presented a memorandum to Mr. Lansing in which, after referring in a complimentary manner to the speech of the President on the 22nd, and identifying German views with Mr. Wilson's aims and conceptions, it was announced that, owing to the failure of the Allies to respond satisfactorily to the overtures of peace, Germany was now compelled to continue the fight with the full employment of all the weapons at her disposal. Another memorandum elucidated this by declaring that no restriction would be placed on submarine warfare after the 1st of February.   By this time Germany had ready, or thought she had ready, these new submarines in numbers sufficient to force Great Britain to sue for peace in a few months, but the President knew nothing of that.   In consonance, however, with the *Sussex* Note he broke off relations with Germany, gave Count Bernstorff his passports, and withdrew from Berlin Mr. Gerard, the American Ambassador there.   This took place on the 3rd.   By his direction instructions were sent on the following day by Mr. Lansing to the American Ministers in neutral countries to notify the Governments to which they were accredited of what had occurred, and to tell them that he was "reluctant to believe" that Germany actually would carry out her threat against neutral commerce.   Though the document went on to say that if the threat should be carried out the President would "ask Congress to authorize the use of national power to protect American citizens engaged in their peaceful and lawful errands on the seas," it was evident from the foregoing that Mr. Wilson still had hopes of keeping the United States out of the War.   Relations were not broken off with Austria, as, so long as that did not happen, communications could be made through Vienna to Berlin.   On the 10th of February Mr. Lansing said in a speech, "There is always hope that our country may be spared the terrible calamity of being forced into a conflict."   That was the hope, indeed the expectation, of most Americans, although the President's dismissal of the German Ambassador had met with general approval. And as no preparations went forward at once for war, the expectation looked like a certainty. The majority of the people of the United States still were indifferent. Even the barbarous circumstances that attended the withdrawal of Mr. Gerard from Berlin did not rouse them to a desire for action. The trouble with the President himself was that he found it next to impossible to believe that Germanism—the German Government, as he would have put it —was the vile, brutal and inhuman thing it was, and that its aim was nothing less than the domination of the globe and the destruction of all human liberty. His Ambassadors in Europe must have told him what they knew, but they were unable to move him. It took the pressure of events coming nearer and nearer home to open his eyes. When his eyes were opened, he kept his face in the light.

"Only actual overt acts," said President Wilson, would overthrow his "inveterate confidence," and the acts came. Perhaps the first indication of his conversion was given on the 26th of February when, in an address to Congress, he asked for power to institute a policy of armed neutrality. After stating that two American vessels had been sunk in the barred zone, and that it was abundantly clear that Germany was determined to go on ruthlessly with her general submarine warfare, he requested authorization to use any instrumentalities or methods that might be necessary to protect ships and mariners of the United States "in their legitimate and peaceful pursuits on the seas." At the same time he struck a new note by remarking:

"I am thinking not only of the rights of Americans to come and go about their proper business by way of the sea, but also of something deeper, much more fundamental than that. I am thinking of those rights of humanity without which there is no civilization. My theme is of those great principles of compassion and protection which mankind has sought to throw about human lives, the lives of noncombatants, the lives of men who are peacefully at work keeping the industrial processes of the world quick and vital, the lives of women and children, and of those who supply the labor which ministers to their sustenance. We are speaking of no selfish material rights, but of rights which our hearts support and whose foundation is that righteous passion for justice upon which all law, all structures alike of family, of State, and of mankind must rest, as upon the ultimate base of our existence and our liberty. I cannot imagine any man with American principles at his heart hesitating to defend these things."

The bill which he submitted to Congress encountered considerable opposition. A week or so before, the Democratic leaders of both the Senate and the House of Representatives had told him that if he went to Congress for a declaration of war against Germany it was most probable that he would not get it. Both the "Pacifists" and the pro-Germans now spoke violently against his armed neutrality proposals. Then he played a strong card. Congress came automatically to an end at noon on the 4th of March, and the time was short. On the morning of the 1st all America was electrified by the publication of a dispatch, which had been intercepted by the U. S. Secret Service, from Zimmermann, then German Foreign Secretary, to Eckhardt, the German Minister in Mexico. This dispatch spoke of the unrestricted submarine warfare, and said that in spite of this an endeavor would be made to keep America neutral, but if the attempt failed an alliance between Germany and Mexico was to be proposed on the basis of financial help from the former to enable the latter to "reconquer her lost territory in New Mexico, Texas, and Arizona." Further, Mexico was to invite Japan to forsake the Allies, and arrange, after mediating between Germany and Japan, for her to join forces against the United States. The effect of this revelation of German intrigue—the first of a long series of official disclosures emanating from Washington—was that the people of the western and southern States now saw themselves directly affected, and were awakened to that consciousness of the peril of their country which had long been felt by most of the inhabitants of the eastern States. Congress was powerfully influenced. The Armed Neutrality Bill was passed in the House of Representatives by a large majority, but a dozen

"Pacifists," pro-Germans, and "cranks" contrived to talk it out in the Senate. "A group of willful men, representing no opinion but their own," commented President Wilson wrathfully, "have made the great Government of the United States helpless and contemptible." The majority in the Senate met the situation by new closure rules preventing the repetition of such an occurrence, and Mr. Wilson summoned Congress to an extraordinary session on the 16th of April, the date afterwards being advanced by a fortnight.

Meanwhile more American ships were sunk, more American lives lost by submarine action. The stalwarts clamored for war, and the "Pacifists" and pro-Germans organized counter-demonstrations throughout the land. Mr. Bryan came forward with a proposition that the question of peace or war should be settled by a referendum, but the chief organs of his party now joined with the Republican journals in urging the President to take a vigorous course. In the main the Americans still had not realized the necessity of going to war with Germany, and the result of a referendum might have been a pronouncement for peace. The President, to whom the full light had come, did not hesitate. He was under no illusions about Germany any longer, and great things were shaping themselves in his mind. Among the immediate steps he took was an order that the navy was to be recruited to its maximum, and another that the naval emergency fund of more than twenty millions sterling, which Congress had voted about two months previously, was to be expended on the construction, with all possible speed, of destroyers, submarine-chasers, and mosquito craft—just the ships required in the circumstances. He also began calling out the regiments of the National Guard, and under his hand the Council of National Defense, with its Advisory Commission, became endowed with life and energy. These were merely preliminary measures, but they showed that the United States was moving on to war. Some of its citizens expressed the hope that war would be on a "limited liability basis," with action confined to the protection of shipping and the assistance of the Allies with loans and supplies. On the 2nd of April when Congress—the Sixty-fifth—met, the President delivered an address, of which it has been well said that it will live forever, advising Congress to declare war on Germany.

BY DAVID LLOYD GEORGE
Address to the American Club in London, April 12, 1917

I am in the happy position of being, I think, the first British Minister of the Crown who, speaking on behalf of the people of this country, can salute the American Nation as comrades in arms. I am glad; I am proud. I am glad not merely because of the stupendous resources which this great nation will bring to the succor of the alliance, but I rejoice as a democrat that the advent of the United States into this war gives the final stamp and seal to the character of the conflict as a struggle against military autocracy throughout the world.

That was the note that ran through the great deliverance of President Wilson. It was echoed, Sir, in your resounding words to-day. The United States of America have the noble tradition, never broken, of having never engaged in war except for liberty. And this is the greatest struggle for liberty that they have ever embarked upon. I am not at all surprised, when one recalls the wars of the past, that America took its time to make up its mind about the character of this struggle. In Europe most of the great wars of the past were waged for dynastic aggrandizement and conquest. No wonder when this great war started that there were some elements of suspicion still lurking in the minds of the people of the United States of America. There were those who thought perhaps that Kings were at their old tricks—and although they saw the gallant Republic of France fighting, they some of them perhaps regarded it as the poor victim of a conspiracy of monarchical swashbucklers. The fact that the United States of America has made up its mind finally makes it abundantly clear to the world that this is no struggle of that character, but a great fight for human liberty.

They naturally did not know at first what we had endured in Europe for years from this military caste in Prussia. It never has reached the United States of America. Prussia was not a democracy. The Kaiser promises that it will be a democracy after the war. I think he is right. But Prussia not merely was not a democracy. Prussia was not a State; Prussia was an army. It had great industries that had been highly developed; a great educational system; it had its universities, it had developed its science.

All these were subordinate to the one great predominant purpose, the purpose of all—a conquering army which was to intimidate the world. The army was the spear-point of Prussia; the rest was merely the haft. That was what we had to deal with in these old countries. It got on the nerves of Europe. They knew what it all meant. It was an army that in recent times had waged three wars, all of conquest, and the unceasing tramp of its legions through the streets of Prussia, on the parade grounds of Prussia, had got into the Prussian head. The Kaiser, when he witnessed on a grand scale his reviews, got drunk with the sound of it. He delivered the law to the world as if Potsdam was another Sinai, and he was uttering the law from the thunder clouds.

But make no mistake. Europe was uneasy. Europe was half intimidated. Europe was anxious. Europe was apprehensive. We knew the whole time what it meant. What we did not know was the moment it would come.

This is the menace, this is the apprehension from which Europe has suffered for over fifty years. It paralyzed the beneficent activity of all States, which ought to be devoted to concentrating on the well-being of their peoples. They had to think about this menace, which was there constantly as a cloud ready to burst over the land. No one can tell except Frenchmen what they endured from this tyranny, patiently, gallantly, with dignity, till the hour of deliverance came. The best energies of domestic science had been devoted to defending itself against the impending blow. France was like a nation which put up its right arm to ward off a blow, and could not give the whole of her strength to the great things which she was capable of. That great, bold, imaginative, fertile mind, which would otherwise have been clearing new paths for progress, was paralyzed.

That is the state of things we had to encounter. The

most characteristic of Prussian institutions is the Hindenburg line. What is the Hindenburg line? The Hindenburg line is a line drawn in the territories of other people, with a warning that the inhabitants of those territories shall not cross it at the peril of their lives. That line has been drawn in Europe for fifty years.

You recollect what happened some years ago in France, when the French Foreign Minister was practically driven out of office by Prussian interference. Why? What had he done? He had done nothing which a Minister of an independent State had not the most absolute right to do. He had crossed the imaginary line drawn in French territory by Prussian despotism, and he had to leave. Europe, after enduring this for generations, made up its mind at last that the Hindenburg line must be drawn along the legitimate frontiers of Germany herself. There could be no other attitude than that for the emancipation of Europe and the world.

It was hard at first for the people of America quite to appreciate that Germany had not interfered to the same extent with their freedom, if at all. But at last they endured the same experience as Europe had been subjected to. Americans were told that they were not to be allowed to cross and recross the Atlantic except at their peril. American ships were sunk without warning. American citizens were drowned, hardly with an apology—in fact, as a matter of German right. At first America could hardly believe it. They could not think it possible that any sane people should behave in that manner. And they tolerated it once, and they tolerated it twice, until it became clear that the Germans really meant it. Then America acted, and acted promptly.

The Hindenburg line was drawn along the shores of America, and the Americans were told they must not cross it. America said, "What is this?" Germany said, "This is our line, beyond which you must not go," and America said, "The place for that line is not the Atlantic, but on the Rhine —and we mean to help you to roll it up."

There are two great facts which clinch the argument that this is a great struggle for freedom. The first is the fact

that America has come in.   She would not have come in
otherwise.   The second is the Russian revolution.   When
France in the eighteenth century sent her soldiers to America to fight for the freedom and independence of that land,
France also was an autocracy in those days.   But Frenchmen
in America, once they were there—their aim was freedom,
their atmosphere was freedom, their inspiration was freedom.   They acquired a taste for freedom, and they took it
home, and France became free.   That is the story of Russia.
Russia engaged in this great war for the freedom of Serbia,
of Montenegro, of Bulgaria, and has fought for the freedom
of Europe.   They wanted to make their own country free,
and they have done it.   The Russian revolution is not merely
the outcome of the struggle for freedom.   It is a proof of
the character of the struggle for liberty, and if the Russian
people realize, as there is every evidence they are doing,
that national discipline is not incompatible with national freedom—nay, that national discipline is essential to the security of national freedom—they will, indeed, become a free
people.

I have been asking myself the question, Why did Germany, deliberately, in the third year of the war, provoke
America to this declaration and to this action—deliberately,
resolutely?   It has been suggested that the reason was that
there were certain elements in American life, and they were
under the impression that they would make it impossible for
the United States to declare war.   That I can hardly believe.   But the answer has been afforded by Marshal von
Hindenburg himself, in the very remarkable interview which
appeared in the press.

He depended clearly on one of two things.   First, that
the submarine campaign would have destroyed international
shipping to such an extent that England would have been
put out of business before America was ready.   According
to his computation, America cannot be ready for twelve
months.   He does not know America.   In the alternative,
that when America is ready, at the end of twelve months,
with her army, she will have no ships to transport that army
to the field of battle.   In Von Hindenburg's words, "America

carries no weight." I suppose he means she has no ships to
carry weight. On that, undoubtedly they are reckoning.

Well, it is not wise always to assume that even when the
German General Staff, which has miscalculated so often,
makes a calculation it has no ground for it. It therefore
behooves the whole of the Allies, Great Britain and America in particular, to see that that reckoning of Von Hindenburg is as false as the one he made about his famous
line, which we have broken already.

The road to victory, the guarantee of victory, the absolute assurance of victory is to be found in one word—ships;
and a second word—ships; and a third word—ships. And
with that quickness of apprehension which characterizes your
nation, Mr. Chairman, I see that they fully realize that, and
to-day I observe that they have already made arrangements
to build one thousand 3,000-tonners for the Atlantic. I
think that the German military advisers must already begin
to realize that this is another of the tragic miscalculations
which are going to lead them to disaster and to ruin. But
you will pardon me for emphasizing that. We are a slow
people in these islands—slow and blundering—but we get
there. You get there sooner, and that is why I am glad to
see you in.

But may I say that we have been in this business for
three years? We have, as we generally do, tried every blunder. In golfing phraseology, we have got into every bunker.
But we have got a good niblick. We are right out on the
course. But may I respectfully suggest that it is worth
America's while to study our blunders, so as to begin just
where we are now and not where we were three years ago?
That is an advantage. In war, time has as tragic a significance as it has in sickness. A step which, taken to-day, may
lead to assured victory, taken to-morrow may barely avert
disaster. All the Allies have discovered that. It was a new
country for us all. It was trackless, mapless. We had to
go by instinct. But we found the way, and I am so glad
that you are sending your great naval and military experts
here, just to exchange experiences with men who have been
through all the dreary, anxious crises of the last three years.

America has helped us even to win the battle of Arras. Do you know that these guns which destroyed the German trenches, shattered the barbed wire—I remember, with some friends of mine whom I see here, arranging to order the machines to make those guns from America. Not all of them—you got your share, but only a share, a glorious share. So that America has also had her training. She has been making guns, making ammunition, giving us machinery to prepare both; she has supplied us with steel, and she has got all that organization and she has got that wonderful facility, adaptability, and resourcefulness of the great people which inhabits that great continent. Ah! It was a bad day for military autocracy in Prussia when it challenged the great Republic of the West. We know what America can do, and we also know that now she is in it she will do it. She will wage an effective and successful war.

There is something more important. She will insure a beneficent peace. I attach great importance—and I am the last man in the world, knowing for three years what our difficulties have been, what our anxieties have been, and what our fears have been—I am the last man to say that the succor which is given to us from America is not something in itself to rejoice in, and to rejoice in greatly. But I don't mind saying that I rejoice even more in the knowledge that America is going to win the right to be at the conference table when the terms of peace are being discussed. That conference will settle the destiny of nations—the course of human life—for God knows how many ages. It would have been tragic for mankind if America had not been there, and there with all the influence, all the power, and the right which she has now won by flinging herself into this great struggle.

I can see peace coming now—not a peace which will be the beginning of war; not a peace which will be an endless preparation for strife and bloodshed; but a real peace. The world is an old world. It has never had peace. It has been rocking and swaying like an ocean, and Europe—poor Europe!—has always lived under the menace of the sword. When this war began two-thirds of Europe were under autocratic rule. It is the other way about now, and democracy means peace. The democracy of France did not want war; the democracy of Italy hesitated long before they entered the war; the democracy of this country shrank from it—shrank and shuddered—and never would have entered the caldron had it not been for the invasion of Belgium. The democracies sought peace; strove for peace. If Prussia had been a democracy there would have been no war. Strange things have happened in this war. There are stranger things to come, and they are coming rapidly.

There are times in history when this world spins so leisurely along its destined course that it seems for centuries to be at a standstill; but there are also times when it rushes along at a giddy pace, covering the track of centuries in a year. Those are the times we are living in now. To-day we wage the most devastating war earth has ever seen; to-morrow—perhaps not a distant to-morrow—war may be abolished forever from the category of human crimes. This may be something like the fierce outburst of winter which we are now witnessing before the complete triumph of the sun. It is written of those gallant men who won that victory on Monday—men from Canada, from Australia, and from this old country, which has proved that in spite of its age it is not decrepit—it is written of those gallant men that they attacked with the dawn—fit work for the dawn!—to drive out of forty miles of French soil those miscreants who had defiled it for three years. "They attacked with the dawn." Significant phrase!

The breaking up of the dark rule of the Turk, which for centuries has clouded the sunniest land in the world, the freeing of Russia from an oppression which has covered it like a shroud for so long, the great declaration of President Wilson coming with the might of the great nation which he represents into the struggle for liberty are heralds of the dawn. "They attacked with the dawn," and these men are marching forward in the full radiance of that dawn, and soon Frenchmen and Americans, British, Italians, Russians, yea, and Serbians, Belgians, Montenegrins, will march into the full light of a perfect day.

BY ALEXANDER RIBOT

Address of the French Prime Minister Before the French Senate

What particularly touches us is that the United States has always kept alive that friendship toward us which was sealed with our blood. We recognize with joy that the bond of sympathy between the peoples is inspired by ideals which can be cultivated in the heart of democracy. The starry flag is going to float beside the tricolor. Our hands shall join and our hearts shall beat in unison.

President Wilson makes it plain to all that the conflict is truly one between the liberty of modern society and the spirit of the domination of military despotism. It is this which causes the President's message to stir our hearts to their depths as a message of deliverance to the whole world. The people who in the eighteenth century made a declaration of rights under the inspiration of the writings of our philosophers, the people who placed Washington and Lincoln among the foremost of its heroes, the people who in the last century liberated the slaves, is well worthy to give the world such an exalted example.

For us, after such death and ruin, such heroic suffering, the words of the President mean renewal of the sentiments which have animated and sustained us throughout this long trial. The powerful and decisive assistance which the United States brings us will be not material aid alone; it will be moral aid, above all, a veritable consolation. As we see the conscience of the whole world stirred in mighty protest against the atrocities of which we are victims, we feel that we are fighting not alone for ourselves and our allies, but for something immortal; that we are striving to establish a new order of things. And so our sacrifices have not been in vain. The blood poured out so generously by the sons of France has been shed in order to spread the ideals of liberty and justice, which will establish concord among nations.

In the name of all the country, the Government of the French Republic addresses to the Government and people of the United States an expression of its gratitude, and its most ardent greetings.

THE WORLD UNION AGAINST GERMANY

OTHER NEUTRALS ACCEPT THE LEAD OF THE UNITED STATES

APRIL 7TH

GENERAL MARIO MENOCAL   RAMON VALDEZ
DOMICIO DA GAMA   NILO PECANHA

The official list of nations which severed diplomatic relations with Germany in 1917, after the United States had done so, is as follows: Brazil, April 10th; Bolivia, April 13th; Guatemala, April 29th; Liberia, May 8th; Honduras, May 17th; Nicaragua, May 18th; Santo Domingo, July; Costa Rica, September 21st; Argentine, September 25th; Peru, October 6th; Uruguay, October 7th; and Ecuador in 1918 on December 8th.

The list of those which declared war is: Cuba, April 7, 1917; Panama, April 7, 1917; Greece, July 2, 1917; Siam, July 22, 1917; Liberia, August 4, 1917; China, August 14, 1917; Brazil, October 26, 1917; Guatemala, April 23, 1918; Haiti, July 15, 1918.

Other States, such as Chile and Colombia, which did not go so far as the above, still registered some form of disapproval of German aggression. The little border States surrounding Germany took no decisive action against her, partly perhaps through racial sympathy, but chiefly because they were too immediately within her grip to be able to defy her. Perhaps the only really neutral government remaining in the world was that of Spain, where a pro-German court was balanced against a pro-Ally people.

This attitude of Spain in opposition to that of South America had a far-reaching effect. Spanish-Americans became far more divided from the ancient motherland of Spain and far more inclined to follow the leadership of the United States. America as a whole became more united.

Of course the direct warlike aid of South America against Germany was negligible, as was that of China and Siam. But the moral effect of the course taken by all these countries was strong; and perhaps those which merely severed diplomatic relations made quite as much impression as those which declared war. Germany was now branded as a thing apart from humanity; and the German people felt the meaning of that brand. When the United States declared war, the Germans could still feel that this was only one more wicked nation attacking them unjustly. They raged against her in her turn, and their Government heaped up against her opprobrious charges which they eagerly believed. But against all these many nations which had so manifestly no wish for war and no profit to be reaped, how could they lash themselves into insensate rage? They read the somber writing on the wall.   C. F. H.

BY MARIO GARCIA MENOCAL
President of Cuba

CUBA cannot remain neutral in this supreme conflict, because the declaration of neutrality would oblige her to treat all the belligerents equally, refusing them with equal rigor any access to her ports and imposing on them the same restrictions and prohibitions, which would be in the present case contrary to public sentiment, to the essence of the pacts and moral obligations, moral rather than legal, which bind us to the United States; and would result, lastly, because of our geographical location, in being the cause of innumerable conflicts, the consequences of which it is easy to predict for a friendly and allied nation, and which would prove an inexcusable weakness and condescension for the attitude of implacable aggression unconditionally proclaimed by the Imperial German Government against the rights of all neutral peoples and against the principles of humanity and justice, which constitute the highest note of modern civilization.

Cuba's Declaration of War

Article I. Resolved, That from to-day a state of war is formally declared between the Republic of Cuba and the Imperial Government of Germany, and the President of the Republic is authorized and directed by this resolution to employ all the forces of the nation and the resources of our Government to make war against the Imperial German Government with the object of maintaining our rights, guarding our territory and providing for our security, prevent any acts which may be attempted against us, and defend the navigation of the seas, the liberty of commerce, and the rights of neutrals and international justice.

Article II. The President of the Republic is hereby authorized to use all the land and naval forces in the form he may deem necessary, using existing forces, reorganizing them or creating new ones, and to dispose of the economic forces of the nation in any way he may deem necessary. Article III. The President will give account to Congress of the measures adopted in fulfillment of this law, which will be in operation from the moment of its publication in the Official Gazette.

BY RAMON VALDEZ
President of Panama

Our indisputable duty in this tremendous hour of history is of a common ally, whose interests and existence as well are linked indissolubly with the United States. As the situation creates dangers for our country, it is the duty of the Panaman people to coöperate with all the energies and resources they can command for the protection of the canal and to safeguard national territory.

The attitude of the people was foreseen and interpreted faithfully in a resolution unanimously approved by the National Assembly on February 24th, and confirmed by later laws, and the moment has arrived for the Executive to act in accordance with the declarations of the supreme body. I therefore declare that the Panaman Nation will lend emphatic coöperation to the United States against enemies who execute or attempt to execute hostile acts against the territory of the canal, or in any manner affect or tend to affect the common interests.

The Government will adopt adequate measures in accordance with the circumstances. I consider it the patriotic duty of all Panaman citizens to facilitate the military operations which the forces of the United States undertake within the limits of our country. Foreigners, resident or transient, will be obliged to submit to the conditions of this declaration.

BY DOMICIO DA GAMA
Brazilian Ambassador to the United States

June 4, 1917.

Mr. Secretary of State: The President of the republic has just instructed me to inform your Excellency's Government that he has approved the law which revokes Brazil's neutrality in the war between the United States of America and the German Empire. The republic thus recognized the fact that one of the belligerents is a constituent portion of the American Continent and that we are bound to that belligerent by traditional friendship and the same sentiment in the defense of the vital interests of America and the accepted principles of law.

Brazil ever was and is now free from warlike ambitions, and, while it always refrained from showing any partiality in the European conflict, it could no longer stand unconcerned when the struggle involved the United States, actuated by no interest whatever but solely for the sake of international judicial order, and when Germany included us and the other neutral powers in the most violent acts of war.

While the comparative lack of reciprocity on the part of the American republics divested until now the Monroe Doctrine of its true character, by permitting of an interpretation based on the prerogatives of their sovereignty, the present events which brought Brazil even now to the side of the United States at a critical moment in the history of the world are still imparting to our foreign policy a practical shape of continental solidarity, a policy, however, that was also that of the former régime whenever any of the other sister friendly nations of the American Continent was concerned. The republic strictly observed our political and diplomatic traditions and remained true to the liberal principles in which the nation was nurtured.

Thus understanding our duty and Brazil taking the position to which its antecedents and the conscience of a free people pointed, whatever fate the morrow may have in store for us, we shall conserve the Constitution which governs us and which has not yet been surpassed in the guarantees due to the rights, lives, and property of foreigners.

In bringing the above-stated resolution to your Excellency's knowledge, I beg you to be pleased to convey to your Government the sentiments of unalterable friendship of the Brazilian people and Government.

BY NILO PEÇANHA

Public Note Addressed by Dr. Peçanha, Brazil's Minister of Foreign
Affairs, to Brazil's Ambassador to Pope Benedict in Rome, ex-
plaining to the Pope Brazil's Entry into the War

The Brazilian Nation, which has never engaged in a
war of conquest, but has consistently advocated arbitration
as the solution for external conflicts in the constitution of
the republic, and has no grievances and sufferings past or
present to revenge; which has solved with serenity all questions regarding territorial limits, and with a precise knowledge of what belongs to her and an accurate acquaintance
with the extent of her vast territory; which, thanks to
the labor not only of her own sons, anxious to prove themselves worthy of so rich a patrimony, but of that of all
foreigners whom our hospitality has assimilated; this nation, your Excellency can assure his Holiness, would have
remained apart from the conflict in Europe in spite of the
sympathy of public opinion for the Allies' liberal cause had
Germany not extended the war to America and thereby
prevented intertrading between all neutral countries.

Without renouncing her obligations as an American nation, this country could not fail to assume the position of
a belligerent as a last resource, without hatred or any interest
other than the defense of our flag and our fundamental
rights.

Happily to-day the republics of the New World are more
or less allied in their rights, but all, equally menaced in their
liberties and their sovereignty, draw closer the bonds of the
solidarity which formerly was merely geographic, economic,
and historic, and which the necessities of self-defense and
national independence now make political as well.

For such reasons Brazil can no longer maintain her
isolated attitude, and now, in close solidarity as she must
be and really is with the nations on whose side she has
ranged herself, she can even speak as an individual entity.

No Brazilian heart can receive without emotion the eloquent appeal of his Holiness in the name of the Almighty
to the belligerents in the cause of peace. Though no State
religion has been adopted by Brazil, and all creeds are

equally free, none the less Brazil is the third Catholic country of the world, and has maintained unbroken for centuries relations with the Government of the Holy See: Brazil, therefore, recognizes the generous motives that inspired the appeal of his Holiness asking that by disarmament and arbitration and the establishing of a régime in which the brute force of armies shall give way to the force of moral law, the restoration of France and Italy should be granted, and the Balkan problem and the restitution of liberty to Poland be considered.

Only the countries most deeply interested in these questions can judge if the honor of their arms has been saved in this war, or if these modifications of the political map of Europe are likely to restore tranquillity.

So long as the political and military organization that suspended living law the world over and suppressed spiritual conquests supposed to be established beyond question —so long as this power continues to abuse the alleviating functions of war and to destroy the Christian spirit that inspired the society of nations, only these nations can say whether confidence in treaties has disappeared and whether any other force excepting some new spirit of order can be accepted as a guarantee of peace.

Through the sufferings and the disillusions to which the war has given rise a new and better world will be born, as it were, of liberty, and in this way a lasting peace may be established without political or economic restrictions, and all countries be allowed a place in the sun with equal rights and an interchange of ideas and values in merchandise on an ample basis of justice and equity.

CANADA STORMS VIMY RIDGE

GREAT BRITISH-FRENCH SIMULTANEOUS ATTACK AT ARRAS AND CHAMPAGNE

APRIL 9TH

PHILIP GIBBS   CANADIAN WAR RECORDS REPORT
GENERAL VON LUDENDORFF   EMPEROR WILLIAM II.
GENERAL VON JANSON   PAUL PAINLEVÉ

The battles of Arras and Champagne were the Allies' military response to the Hindenburg Retreat. The first step in this widespread combined attack was the brilliant attack upon Vimy Ridge on April 9th. This is usually reckoned as Canada's greatest victory of the War. So it is here described from both the Canadian and the British viewpoint. To the German leaders, of course, Vimy was not to be depicted as a separate battle lest its result be too disheartening to the German soldiers. Hence General Ludendorff groups this with the larger Arras battle which extended over weeks, and which in the end showed no substantial profit for either side.

The attack of the French was launched from the south bank of the Aisne River on April 16th. But here, as General Ludendorff points out, the Allies were even less successful than at Arras, and Emperor William found opportunity for another of his characteristic proclamations glorifying his own family and his private god, and reasserting to his people that the War was fought only to preserve them from annihilation. The French view of this second great battle on the Aisne is here frankly stated by the Minister of War at the time, M. Painlevé.

The French attack spread from Soissons in the west to Rheims in the east. It carried, at enormous cost, the first German lines, sweeping them back from the bank of the Aisne, which they had held ever since the great Aisne Battle of 1914. Forced from the valley, the Germans defended themselves upon the heights to the northward, where ran the famous Ladies' Road, or *Chemin des Dames*. This had been built along the picturesque heights by King Louis XV, as a pleasant drive for the ladies of his court. Back and forth across these heights the battle swayed all through the year. The first tremendous assault, however, ended in May. After that there were no more reckless French attacks. On October 23rd, the French under General Pétain gained so much of the *Chemin des Dames* that the Germans abandoned the entire road. They withdrew across the next northward river, the Ailette, and there established their winter quarters on another and equally solid line of defense.

To Americans there is one point of particular interest about that first Canadian assault on Vimy Ridge. When it began on April 9th, the United States had been but three days in the War—officially,

153

and could not possibly have troops abroad. But as our previous volumes have shown, many a United States volunteer had privately joined
the War. One such gallant lad was with the Canadians, and as he
charged up Vimy he unrolled a tiny flag of stars and stripes and carried it on his bayonet. Hundreds of his comrades saw it there and
cheered it. That was the first American flag upon the battle line.

BY PHILIP GIBBS

TO-DAY, at dawn, our armies began a great battle, which,
if Fate has any kindness for the world, may be the beginning of the last great battles of the war. Our troops
attacked on a wide front between Lens and St. Quentin,
including the Vimy Ridge, that great, grim hill which dominates the plain of Douai and the coalfields of Lens and the
German positions around Arras. In spite of bad fortune
in weather at the beginning of the day, so bad that there
was no visibility for the airmen, and our men had to struggle forward in a heavy rainstorm, the first attacks have been
successful, and the enemy has lost much ground, falling back
in retreat to strong rearguard lines, where he is now fighting desperately. The line of our attack covers a front of
some 12 miles southwards from Givenchy-en-Gohelle, and is
a sledge-hammer blow, threatening to break the northern end
of the Hindenburg line, already menaced round St. Quentin.
As soon as the enemy was forced to retreat from the country east of Bapaume and Péronne, in order to escape a decisive blow on that line, he hurried up divisions and guns
northwards to counter our attack there, while he prepared a
new line of defense, known as the Wotan line, as the southern part of the Hindenburg line, which joins it, is known as
the Siegfried position, after two great heroes of old German
mythology. He hoped to escape there before our new attack
was ready, but we have been too quick for him, and his own
plans were frustrated.

So to-day began another titanic conflict which the world
will hold its breath to watch because of all that hangs upon
it. I have seen the fury of this beginning, and all the sky
on fire with it, the most tragic and frightful sight that men
have ever seen, with an infernal splendor beyond words to
tell. The bombardment which went before the infantry as-

sault lasted for several days, and reached a great height yesterday, when, coming from the south, I saw it for the first time. Those of us who knew what would happen to-day, the beginning of another series of battles greater, per-haps, than the struggle of the Somme, found ourselves yes-terday filled with a tense, restless emotion, and some of us smiled with a kind of tragic irony because it was Easter Sunday. In the little villages behind the battle lines the bells of the French churches were ringing gladly because the Lord had risen, and on the altar steps the priests were reciting the splendid old words of faith. *"Resurrexi et adhuc tecum sum. Alleluia"* ("I have arisen and I am with thee al-ways. Alleluia"). The earth was glad yesterday. For the first time this year the sun had a touch of warmth in it, though patches of snow still stayed white under the shelter of the banks, and the sky was blue and the light glinted on wet tree-trunks and in the furrows of the new-plowed earth. As I went up the road to the battle lines I passed a battalion of our men, the men who are fighting to-day, standing in hollow square with bowed heads while the chaplain con-ducted the Easter service. Easter Sunday, but no truce of God. I went to a field outside Arras and looked into the ruins of the cathedral city. The cathedral itself stood clear in the sunlight, with a deep black shadow where its roof and aisles had been. Beyond was a ragged pinnacle of stone, once the glorious Town Hall, and the French barracks and all the broken streets going out to the Cambrai road. It was hell in Arras, though Easter Sunday.

The bombardment was now in full blast. It was a beauti-ful and devilish thing, and the beauty of it, and not the evil of it, put a spell upon one's senses. All our batteries, too many to count, were firing, and thousands of gun flashes were winking and blinking from hollows and hiding-places, and all their shells were rushing through the sky as though flocks of great birds were in flight, and all were bursting over the German positions with long flames which rent the darkness and waved sword-blades of quivering light along the ridges. The earth opened, and great pools of red fire gushed out. Star shells burst magnificently, pouring down golden rain. Mines exploded east and west of Arras and in the wide sweep from Vimy Ridge to Blangy southwards, and voluminous clouds, all bright with a glory of infernal fire, rolled up to the sky. The wind blew strongly across, beating back the noise of the guns, but the air was all filled with the deep roar and slamming knocks of the single heavies and the drum fire of the field guns.

The hour for attack was 5.30. Officers were looking at their wrist watches as on a day in July last year. The earth lightened. A few minutes before 5.30 the guns almost ceased fire, so that there was a strange and solemn hush. We waited, and pulses beat faster than the second-hands. "They're away," said a voice by my side. The bombardment broke out again with new and enormous effects of fire and sound. The enemy was shelling Arras heavily, and black shrapnel and high explosive came over from his lines, but our gunfire was twenty times as great. Around the whole sweep of his lines green lights rose. They were signals of distress, and his men were calling for help.

It was dawn now, but clouded and storm-swept. A few airmen came out with the wind tearing at their wings, but could see nothing in the mist and driving rain. I went down to the outer ramparts of Arras. The suburb of Blangy seemed already in our hands. On the higher ground beyond our men were fighting forward. I saw two waves of infantry advancing against the enemy's trenches, preceded by our barrage of field guns. They went in a slow, leisurely way, not hurried, though the enemy's shrapnel was searching for them. "Grand fellows," said an officer lying next to me on the wet slope. "Oh, topping!" Fifteen minutes afterwards groups of men came back. They were British wounded and German prisoners. I met the first of these walking wounded afterwards. They were met on the roadside by medical officers, who patched them up there and then before they were taken to the field hospitals in ambulances. From these men, hit by shrapnel and machine-gun bullets, I heard the first news of progress. They were bloody and exhausted, but claimed success. "We did fine," said one of them. "We were through the fourth lines before I was knocked out."

"Not many Germans in the first trenches," said another, "and no real trenches either after shelling. We had knocked their dug-outs out, and their dead were lying thick, and the living ones put their hands up." All the men agreed that their own casualties were not high, and mostly wounded.

The Next Day.

By three in the afternoon yesterday the Canadians had gained the whole of the ridge except a high strong post on the left, Hill 145, which was captured during the night. Our gunfire had helped them by breaking down all the wire, even round Heroes' Wood and Count's Wood, where it was very thick and strong. Thélus was wiped utterly off the map. This morning Canadian patrols pushed in a snow-storm through the Farbus Wood, and established outposts on the railway embankment. Some of the bravest work was done by the forward observing officers, who climbed to the top of Vimy Ridge as soon as it was captured, and through a sea of heavy barrage reported back to the artillery all the movements seen by them on the country below.

In spite of the wild day, our flying men were riding the storm and signaling to the gunners who were rushing up their field guns. "Our 60-pounders," said a Canadian officer, "had the day of their lives." They found many targets. There were trains moving in Vimy village, and they hit them. There were troops massing on the sloping ground, and they were shattered. There were guns and limbers on the move, and men and horses were killed. Beyond all the prisoners taken yesterday by the English, Scottish and Canadian troops, the enemy losses were frightful, and the scenes behind his lines must have been and still be hideous in slaughter and terror.

The Battle of Arras is the greatest victory we have yet gained in this war and a staggering blow to the enemy. He has lost already nearly 10,000 prisoners and more than half a hundred guns,[1] and in dead and wounded his losses are great. He is in retreat south of the Vimy Ridge to defensive lines further back, and as he goes our guns are smashing

[1] Increased to 19,343 prisoners and 257 guns on May 2nd.

him along the roads. It is a black day for the German armies and for the German women who do not know yet what it means to them. During last night the Canadians gained the last point, called Hill 145, on the Vimy Ridge, where the Germans held out in a pocket with machine guns, and this morning the whole of that high ridge, which dominates the plains to Douai, is in our hands, so that there is removed from our path the great barrier for which the French and ourselves have fought through bloody years. Yesterday, before daylight and afterwards, I saw this ridge of Vimy all on fire with the light of great gunfire. The enemy was there in strength, and his guns were answering ours with a heavy barrage of high explosives.

This morning the scene was changed as by a miracle. Snow was falling, blown gustily across the battlefields and powdering the capes and helmets of our men as they rode or marched forward to the front. But presently sunlight broke through the storm-clouds and flooded all the countryside by Neuville-St. Vaast and Thélus and La Folie Farm up to the crest of the ridge where the Canadians had just fought their way with such high valor. Our batteries were firing from many hiding-places, revealed by the short, sharp flashes of light, but few answering shells came back, and the ridge itself, patched with snowdrifts, was as quiet as any hill of peace. It was astounding to think that not a single German stayed up there out of all the thousands who had held it yesterday, unless some poor wounded devils still cower in the great tunnels which pierce the hillside.

OFFICIAL ANNOUNCEMENT BY THE CANADIAN WAR RECORDS
OFFICE

Again the Canadians have "acquired merit." In the capture of Vimy Ridge on April 9th, as in the lesser action of Courcelette in September of last year, they have shown the same high qualities in victorious advance as they displayed in early days in desperate resistance on many stricken fields. At half-past five on Easter Monday morning the great attack was launched with terrible fire from our massed artillery and from many field guns in hidden advanced positions.

Our "heavies" bombarded the enemy positions on and beyond the ridge, and trenches, dugouts, emplacements, and roads, which for long had been kept in a continual state of disrepair by our fire, were now smashed to uselessness. An intense barrage of shrapnel from our field guns, strengthened by the indirect fire of hundreds of machine guns, was laid along the front.

At the same moment the Canadian troops advanced in line, in three waves of attack. Flurries of snow drifted over the battlefield as the Canadians left their jumping-off trenches behind the rolling barrage. The light was sufficient for maneuvering purposes and yet obscure enough to obstruct the range of vision and lessen the accuracy of fire of the German riflemen and machine gunners.

The troops on the extreme left made a start under conditions as favorable as those in the center and right, but they were soon confronted by a strong and constantly strengthening opposition. The advance of these troops was soon checked between its first and second lines of objectives by heavy fighting, which was more formidable against the center of the line than against the flanks.

A dip in the ground caused a change of direction, which swung these troops off their central objectives. They reached their goals on the flanks, only to find themselves subjected to heavy, close-range fire of machine guns and rifles. To be enfiladed from the center and the north was bad enough, but to add to the situation, caves, or a tunnel, in the hostile line over which we had already advanced now disgorged Germans, who promptly reoccupied their old front and opened fire on our rear. The enemy at these points fought with unusual vigor and resolution.

These troops on the extreme left fought all day against the Huns, and by 10 o'clock at night succeeded in disposing of the enemy in their rear and capturing the major portion of the enemy trenches in their center. "The Pimple," in the north, still remained to the enemy, but by then snow was falling heavily and it was wisely decided to consolidate the hard-won gains and prepare for a counter-attack rather than to undertake a further assault that night. "The Pimple" would keep for the morrow.

In the meantime the other troops fought forward to one line after another without serious check, but with many brisk encounters and not without casualties. Most of these were the result of shrapnel fire, only a small percentage were fatal, and the majority of the wounds were of a minor character.

On the German second line the troops drew breath and consolidated their gains. Our barrage was laid before them steady as a wall. Fresh troops came up and deployed into position. They waited for the barrage to lift at the ordained minute and lead them on. The enemy's artillery fire—their counter-barrage and bombardment of our gun positions— was not strong as strength in such things is considered to-day. Prisoners were already hurrying to our rear in hundreds, pathetically and often ludicrously grateful to the fortunes of war that had saved them alive for capture. They surrendered promptly and willingly.

The barrage lifted, and the two divisions on the right followed it forward to the German third line. Here again they paused for a time, then advanced again, behind the ever-ready and unslackening barrage, for a distance of about 1,200 yards. This advance included the capture of several villages, Hill 140, a number of fortified woods, and several trenches and belts of wire. And still the enemy surrendered by hundreds and scuttled rearward to safety. Their resistance grew feebler, their hands more eager to relinquish their weapons and ascend high above their heads, at each stage of our advance.

At 10 o'clock snow fell heavily from black clouds sweeping low across the ridge. Half an hour later the snow ceased, the clouds thinned, and the sun shone fitfully over the shattered and clamorous battlefield. Word was received at the advanced headquarters that the British division on our immediate right was enjoying a degree of success in its operations equal to the Canadian success.

Events continued to develop with rapidity and precision. By 1 o'clock every point in the enemy's third line of our

objectives had been reached and secured. By this time the
troops on the right had consolidated their gains and advanced strong patrols. From their new positions they commanded a wide view of enemy territory to the eastward.
They reported a massing of Germans on a road in the new
field of vision, and our heavy guns immediately dealt with
the matter. By noon one of the battalions of a division had
received and dealt drastically with three counter-attacks. Its
front remained unshaken. Shortly after this the Canadian
Corps was able to state that the prisoners already to hand
numbered three battalion commanders, 15 other officers, and
more than 2,000 noncommissioned officers and men—with
plenty more in sight—making for our "cages" as fast as
their legs could carry them.

The final stage of the attack of the troops on the right
was now made. They passed through the wide belts of enemy wire which fringed the plateau by way of wide gaps
torn by our heavy artillery at fixed intervals. So they issued
on the eastern slopes of Vimy Ridge—the first allied troops
to look down upon the level plain of Douai since the German
occupation in 1914. They saw the villages of Farbus, Vimy,
and Petit Vimy at their feet, and beyond these the hamlets
of Willerval, Bailleul, Oppy, and Mericourt. They pressed
on to Farbus Wood and Goulot Wood, and possessed themselves of several hostile batteries and much ammunition.

By an early hour of the afternoon all our objectives,
save those of the left of the attack, were in our possession,
and the task of consolidating and strengthening our gains
was well in hand. Throughout the day the most courageous
and devoted coöperation was rendered to the Canadian Corps
by a brigade and a squadron of the Royal Flying Corps.

The night saw all of Vimy Ridge, with the exception of
a few trenches on Hill 145, secure in Canadian hands.

BY GENERAL VON LUDENDORFF
Official Announcement of April 28, 1917

A very heavy drum fire, which was begun before daybreak over the whole front from Lens as far as Queant,
was the prelude to a battle by which the British for the

third time hoped to pierce the German lines near Arras. By midday the great battle was decided by a heavy defeat of the British.

At dawn, on a front of about thirty kilometers, British storming columns followed curtains of steel, dust, gas, and smoke, which had been advanced by degrees. The weight of the enemy thrust north of the Scarpe was directed against our positions from Achéville as far as Roeux, where the battle raged with extraordinary violence. The British forced their way into Arleux-en-Gohelle and Oppy and near Gavrelle and Roeux, occupied by us as advanced positions. They were met by a counter-attack by our infantry. In a severe hand-to-hand struggle the enemy was defeated. At some points he was driven beyond our former lines, the whole of which, with the exception of Arleux-en-Gohelle, is again in our hands.

South of the Scarpe, in the lowlands, a desperate battle also raged. In their wrecked positions our brave troops withstood the British charges, repeated several times. Here also the British attacks failed. On the wings of the battlefield enemy attacking waves broke down under destructive fire. The British losses were extraordinarily heavy. April 28th was a new day of honor. Our infantry powerfully led and excellently supported by its sister and auxiliary arm, showed itself fully equal to its tasks.

Unfortunately, the violence of the enemy fire prevents us from repairing our trenches. Any attempt to do so merely exhausts the fighting force of our men prematurely. From the outset of a battle another method of construction must be applied. A defensive zone extended in depth must be substituted for the old system of positions which can be destroyed by the enemy. This system, with its organizations concealed as far as possible from the enemy's observation, and with the troops holding it echeloned in depth so that their numbers, scanty in the front, increase progressively towards the rear, should enable us to pass from the defensive to the offensive with the troops from the rear. During the battle all idea of having a continuous front-trench line must be abandoned. This must be replaced by shell-crater nests, held by groups of men and isolated machine guns, disposed like the squares on a chess-board. The shelter provided by the shell-craters will be extended by tunneling into the sides, or by linking them to adjacent craters by means of tunnels, supported by timber props. The earth dislodged should be thrown into unoccupied craters near by, or, if the nature of the position permits it, should be spread over the ground between them. If timbered galleries cannot be built owing to the wetness of the ground, one must be content with very simple organizations to afford protection against shrapnel.

For this purpose old shelters, dug before the new order of things, may be used, but if none are available the men must obtain shelter as best they can on the open ground. There should be a line of barbed wire in front of the first line of shell-craters, and the empty craters in front of it should be girdled with wire to prevent the assaulting infantry from occupying them.

BY EMPEROR WILLIAM II.

Congratulatory Telegram of April 22, 1917, to the Crown Prince, Commanding in Champagne

The troops of all the German tribes under your command, with steel-hard determination and strongly led, have brought to failure the great French attempt to break through on the Aisne and in Champagne. Also there the infantry again had to bear the brunt, and, thanks to the indefatigable assistance of the artillery and other arms, has accomplished great things in death-defying perseverance and irresistible attack. Convey my thanks and those of the Fatherland to the leaders and men. The battle on the Aisne and in Champagne is not yet over, but all who fight and bleed there shall know that the whole of Germany will remember their deeds, and is at one with them to carry through the fight for existence to a victorious end. God grant it.

BY GENERAL VON JANSON

Field-Marshal von Hindenburg has announced that the great Franco-British offensive has apparently come to an

end. The Kaiser, in an address on June 2nd to the two
commanders on the battle front, the German Crown Prince
and the Crown Prince of Bavaria, has expressed his own
and the country's thanks to the troops who parried the blow.
High honors have been paid to First Quartermaster General
Ludendorff in recognition of the farsighted measures of the
General Staff, which made the success possible. It seems
the proper time, therefore, to sum up an account of the
spring offensive in the west.

Three hundred thousand English with numerous tank
squadrons attempted to force a break through on the line
Achéville-Queant, on both sides of the Scarpe. The attack
was preceded by the usual artillery preparation, which aimed
to destroy our defenses by the use of an enormous number
of shells and mines; and strong reserves were held in readiness to exploit the hoped-for victory. Their efforts were
confined to vigorous local thrusts, ending in hot contests
around certain towns, notably around Bullecourt, which had
been reduced long since to a heap of ruins.

The offensives of the enemy are usually marked by lack
of coördination due to the divided leadership, but on this
occasion the fourth battle of Arras had hardly begun when
the increased activity of the French artillery signaled a
nearly simultaneous attempt at a break through on the Aisne
front. The main attack was launched on the fifth of May
along a line thirty-five kilometers long between the Ailette
and Craonne. As with the British at Arras, the result was
a failure. During the first few days of the offensive the
French managed to conquer the northern side of the long
contested height near Craonne. The Germans, however, in
an irresistible assault, soon retook it and retained the whole
position in their hands. After a brief pause French reenforcements made new local attacks farther east, between
Corbeny and Berry-au-Bac, and on the Aisne-Marne canal,
and later renewed the attack against the *Chemin des Dames*
and in Champagne.

In all three sectors—the Arras region, the Aisne front,
and Champagne—events took a similar course up to June
1st. The battle raged back and forth around the old places

which had been so often fought over. At times the enemy succeeded in winning advantageous positions, but he could not keep them long; except for some unimportant points his gains were soon wrested from him. His losses piled up quite out of proportion to ours. Our troops, in spite of their undeniable sacrifices, preserved their fighting spirit magnificently; they had no need of the artificial stimulation which was sometimes supplied to the enemy's supporting forces, many of whom scarcely knew what they were fighting for.

After the great attempt at a break through had been halted and the fighting became purely local, the aggressiveness of our troops expressed itself in attempts to improve their positions. Every blow and counter-blow was part of a deliberate plan, not to advance the line wherever possible, but to conquer those places which would facilitate the defense of our positions or an attack upon the enemy's. One operation of this kind was successfully carried out on the southern slope of the *Chemin des Dames,* and another was for the heights near Nauroy, in Champagne, which eventually remained in our hands.

Such was the situation when Hindenburg announced that the English-French offensive was stopped. Let us try to realize what that meant. Three months before, the German High Command had drawn back and reformed the line on a great section of the front, at the same time instituting new defense tactics made up largely of offensive elements. This policy gave to the tactical conduct of the war a new turn, to which the enemy must accommodate himself whether he liked or not. It enabled the Germans, though on the defensive, to impose their will on the attacking enemy and to keep their own freedom of decision of action, which practically amounted to a reversal of the usual relationship between the attack and defense.

For the enemy, the result of the new tactics was the failure of an offensive pushed for two months by forces greatly superior to ours in numbers and supplied with seemingly inexhaustible war material. For our part, we were enabled to maintain our whole position in the enemy's territory and to keep our freedom of action for the future.

The extent of the success is only fully apparent when one considers how much better able the enemy was to replace his exhausted troops with fresh forces, and with what desperate recklessness he sacrificed his men. Of course the lack of technical skill of the English is well known, but so are their courage and tenacity; the French are traditionally as brave as they are well-schooled and versatile. Our own strength, that which made our victory possible, lay in the unity of command which has been established within our quadruple alliance—a unity never created by the Entente. Even in the west, where only Germans are engaged, the effect of this unity has been felt in the assurance that no disturbing measures could be instituted by our allies in other theaters of war.

BY PAUL PAINLEVÉ
Address by the French Minister of War, Delivered July 7, 1917

Grave mistakes were made in the course of our last offensive. We care neither to deny nor to minimize them. France is sufficiently sure of herself to be able to look the truth in the face. Yes, the price paid for the results that were obtained were paid for too dearly. It is true we suffered heavy losses, which, though they fell short of the fantastic figures that have been set about no one knows by whom, were unnecessarily heavy losses which could have been avoided and must be avoided in the future. The heads of the army on whom falls the responsibility for these mistakes have, in spite of the glorious services to which they might have appealed, been relieved of their command.[2]

We must have done with rash plans whose grandiose conception hardly hides their emptiness and lack of preparation. We must have a rational and positive war policy, endowed with a prudence that is quite consistent with energy, but does not force impossibilities from human flesh and blood. Such a policy more than ever necessary now is to be that

[2] On May 17th General Nivelle was withdrawn from command and General Pétain appointed in his stead. General Foch was made Pétain's Chief of Staff.

of the Government. This policy will enable us to keep strong until the final battles, and it will enable us to give our army a powerful armament of munitions and of heavy artillery. This policy, fruitful in results but economical in human life, we now know for certain will be followed in the future, since the General who is now at the head of the army has made himself the protagonist of it. After the attack on Carency, one of the most glorious episodes in this war, General Pétain did not shrink from declaring that infantry was powerless against entrenchments that had not been overthrown by artillery, and in consequence he has never failed to employ these tactics of artillery preparation for attack.

Our Allies, he said, know that nothing can bend the will of France. Whatever happens she will not fail in her task. But they know also that our army is like an army which protects civilization, and that its blood is flowing in streams. This thought, more than any other, determined the United States to enter the struggle. They did not wish France to resemble the funeral pile which illumines the world while consuming itself. The Government can give you the assurance that France will be able to reconcile her military effort and her economic effort. Victory is certain on the one condition that the morale in the country remains intact. Our soldiers must fight, resist, and die at their posts. History will say that they reached the limits of human courage. Our Republican army must know why it is fighting. Victory or submission, as President Wilson said, that is the alternative. There is no other. If our will should seem to bend, if a crack should seem to appear in the military *bloc* of the Allies, you would see the engaging smiles of Herr Scheidemann succeeded by the atrocious grimace of pan-Germanism.

We shall not allow Prussian militarism to lay its heel on our neck. Until now France has victoriously borne the trial and has resisted the most monstrous attempt. No nation has shown more perfect discipline. It is necessary that that should continue until the hour of final victory. No impatience and no maneuver must intervene to defeat our union.

We have to fight, and whoever advises us now to lay down our arms makes himself the accomplice of our foe.

THE UNITED STATES NAVY IN THE WAR

"DESTROYERS" DEAL THE FIRST ACTIVE STROKES FOR AMERICA

MAY 4TH-JUNE 22ND

JOSEPHUS DANIELS   COMMANDER C. C. GILL
GEORGE CREEL

Profoundly significant of the changing organization of the world was the sudden appearance in British waters of the United States "destroyer" fleet on May 4th. For America to be aiding in the protection of Europe was an evidence that the former frontier land had become a chief center of Civilization.

These destroyers did the first directly warlike work of America, and they did it well. So ready to the moment were they, that when the British authorities asked them where they would dock and refit before joining the British destroyers at work, their commanders were all able to reply that they needed not to dock at all, but preferred to go U-boat hunting at once.

Then when the first U. S. troops were ready to sail for France in June, the destroyers, with other members of the fleet this time, were again called on to guard the transports from the dreaded U-boat attack. The story of how they met that attack is here told as it was first announced by the U. S. official publicity bureau under George Creel. Later announcements from this bureau were toned down into a harmony with the severely accurate French and British official statements. This first one caused considerable comment by its flamboyant style, and there have been naval critics who doubted whether any submarines were sunk in this attack, and even if any submarines were sighted. The whole affair may possibly have sprung from a false alarm—but at least it demonstrated the "preparedness" of the destroyers.

The general work of the navy is here summed up by its responsible chief, Mr. Daniels, in a more sober style. The work of the transport service is given with semi-official authority by Commander Gill, his account having been authorized by Rear-Admiral Gleaves, who had charge of that department.

BY JOSEPHUS DANIELS
Official Report Made After the Armistice

THE operations of our navy during the world war have covered the widest scope in its history. Our naval forces have operated in European waters from the Mediterranean to the White Sea. At Corfu, Gibraltar, along the French Bay of Biscay ports, at the English Channel ports, on the Irish Coast, in the North Sea, at Murmansk and Archangel our naval forces have been stationed and have done creditable work. Their performance will probably form the most interesting and exciting portion of the naval history of this war, and it is the duty which has been most eagerly sought by all of the personnel, but owing to the character of the operations which our Navy has been called upon to take part in, it has not been possible for all of our naval forces, much as they desired it, to engage in operations at the front, and a large part of our work has been conducted quietly, but none the less effectively, in other areas. This service, while not so brilliant, has still been necessary, and without it our forces at the front could not have carried on the successful campaign that they did.

Naval men have served on nearly 2,000 craft that plied the waters, on submarines, and in aviation, where men of vision and courage prevent surprise attacks and fight with new-found weapons. On the land, marines and sailors have helped to hold strategic points, regiments of marines have shared with the army their part of the hard-won victory, and a wonderfully trained gun crew of sailors has manned the monster 14-inch guns which marked a new departure in land warfare.

In diplomacy, in investigation at home and in all parts of the world by naval officers and civilian agents, in protecting plants and labor from spies and enemies, in promoting new industrial organizations and enlarging older ones to meet war needs, in stimulating production of needed naval craft—these are some of the outstanding operations which mark the heroic year of accomplishment.

The employment of the fighting craft of the navy may be summed up as follows:

1. Escorting troop and cargo convoys and other special vessels.

2. Carrying out offensive and defensive measures against enemy submarines in the Western Atlantic.

3. Assignment to duty and the dispatch abroad of naval

vessels for operations in the war zone in conjunction with the naval forces of our allies.

4. Assignment to duty and operation of naval vessels to increase the force in home waters. Dispatch abroad of miscellaneous craft for the army.

5. Protection of these craft en route.

6. Protection of vessels engaged in coastwise trade.

7. Salvaging and assisting vessels in distress, whether from maritime causes or from the operations of the enemy.

8. Protection of oil supplies from the Gulf.

In order to carry out successfully and speedily all these duties large increases in personnel, in ships of all classes and in the instrumentalities needed for their production and service were demanded. Briefly, then, it may be stated that on the day war was declared the enlistment and enrollment of the navy numbered 65,777 men. On the day Germany signed the armistice it had increased to 497,030 men and women, for it became necessary to enroll capable and patriotic women as yeomen to meet the sudden expansion and enlarged duties imposed by war conditions. This expansion has been progressive. In 1912 there were 3,094 officers and 47,515 enlisted men; by July 1, 1916, the number had grown to 4,293 officers and 54,234 enlisted men, and again in that year to 68,700 in all. In granting the increase Congress authorized the President in his discretion to augment that force to 87,800. Immediately on the outbreak of the war the navy was recruited to that strength, but it was found that under the provisions of our laws there were not sufficient officers in the upper grades of the navy to do the war work. At the same time the lessons of the war showed it was impossible to have the combatant ships of the navy ready for instant war service unless the ships had their full personnel on board and that personnel was highly trained.

In addition to this permanent strength recourse was had to the development of the existing reserves and to the creation of a new force.

Up to 1913 the only organization that made any pretense of training men for the navy was the Naval Militia, and that was under State control, with practically no Federal supervision. As the militia seemed to offer the only means of producing a trained reserve, steps were at once taken to put it on a sound basis, and on February 16, 1914, a real Naval Militia under Federal control was created, provision being made for its organization and training in peace, as well as its utilization in war. As with all organized militia, the Naval Militia, even with the law of 1914, could not, under the Constitution, be called into service as such except for limited duties, such as to repel invasion. It could not be used outside the territorial limits of the United States. It is evident then that with such restrictions militia could hardly meet the requirements of the navy in a foreign war, and to overcome this difficulty the "National Naval Volunteers" were created in August, 1916.

Under this act members of Naval Militia organizations were authorized to volunteer for "any emergency," of which emergency the President was to be the judge. Other laws included the same measure, provided for a reserve force, for the automatic increase of officer personnel in each corps to correspond with increases in enlisted men, and for the Naval Flying Corps, special engineering officers, and the Naval Dental and Dental Reserve Corps. It also provided for taking over the lighthouse and other departmental divisions by the navy in time of war. Briefly, then, on July 1, 1917, three months after the declaration of war, the number of officers had increased to 8,038—4,694 regulars, 3,344 reserves—and the number of enlisted men to 171,133—128,-666 regulars, 32,379 reserves, 10,088 National Naval Volunteers.

The expansion of aviation in the navy has been of gratifying proportions and effectiveness. On July 1, 1917, naval aviation was still in its infancy. At that time there were only 45 naval aviators. There were officers of the navy, Marine Corps, and Coast Guard who had been given special training in and were attached to aviation. There were approximately 200 student officers under training, and about 1,250 enlisted men attached to the Aviation Service. These enlisted men were assigned to the three naval air stations in this country then in commission. Pensacola, Fla., had about

1,000 men, Bay Shore, Long Island, N. Y., had about 100, and Squantum, Mass., which was abandoned in the fall of 1917, had about 150 men. On July 1, 1918, there were 823 naval aviators, approximately 2,052 student officers, and 400 ground officers attached to naval aviation. In addition, there were more than 7,300 trained mechanics, and more than 5,400 mechanics in training. The total enlisted and commissioned personnel at this time was about 30,000.

On the day war was declared 197 ships were in commission. To-day there are 2,003. In addition to furnishing all these ships with trained officers and men, the duty of supplying crews and officers of the growing merchant marine was undertaken by the navy. There has not been a day when the demand for men for these ships has not been supplied—how fit they were all the world attests—and after manning the merchant ships there has not been a time when provision was not made for the constantly increasing number of ships taken over by the navy.

During the year the energy available for new construction was concentrated mainly upon vessels to deal with the submarine menace. Three hundred and fifty-five of the 110-foot wooden submarine chasers were completed during the year. Fifty of these were taken over by France and fifty more for France were ordered during the year and have been completed since July 1, 1918. Forty-two more were ordered about the end of the fiscal year, delivery to begin in November and be completed in January.

Extraordinary measures were taken with reference to destroyers. By the summer of 1917 destroyer orders had been placed which not only absorbed all available capacity for more than a year, but required a material expansion of existing facilities. There were under construction, or on order, in round figures, 100 of the thirty-five-knot type.

During the year, including orders placed at navy yards, the following have been contracted for: Four battleships, 1 battle cruiser, 2 fuel ships, 1 transport, 1 gunboat, 1 ammunition ship, 223 destroyers, 58 submarines, 112 fabricated patrol vessels (including 12 for the Italian Government), 92 submarine chasers (including 50 for the French Gov-

ernment), 51 mine sweepers, 25 seagoing tugs and 46 harbor
tugs, besides a large number of lighters, barges, and other
auxiliary harbor craft.   In addition to this, contracts have
been placed for twelve large fuel ships in conjunction with
the Emergency Fleet Corporation.

Ships launched during the year and up to October 1, 1918,
include 1 gunboat, 93 destroyers, 29 submarines, 26 mine
sweepers, 4 fabricated patrol vessels, and 2 seagoing tugs.
It is noteworthy that in the first nine months of 1918 there
were launched no less than 83 destroyers of 98,281 tons aggregate normal displacement, as compared with 62 destroyers of 58,285 tons during the entire nine years next preceding
January 1, 1918.

There have been added to the navy during the fiscal
year and including the three months up to October 1, 1918,
2 battleships, 36 destroyers, 28 submarines, 355 submarine
chasers, 13 mine sweepers and two seagoing tugs.   There
have also been added to the operating naval forces by purchase, charter, etc., many hundred vessels of commercial
type, including all classes from former German transat-
lantic liners to harbor tugboats and motor boats for auxiliary
purposes.

Last year the construction of capital ships and large
vessels generally had been to some extent suspended. Work
continued upon vessels which had already made material
progress toward completion, but was practically suspended
upon those which had just been begun, or whose keels had
not yet been laid.   The act of July 1, 1918, required work
to be actually begun upon the remaining vessels of the three-
year program within a year.   This has all been planned
and no difficulty in complying with the requirements of the
act and pushing rapidly the construction of the vessels in
question is anticipated.   Advantage has been taken of the
delay to introduce into the designs of the vessels which had
not been laid down numerous improvements based upon war
experience.

War was declared on April 6, 1917.   On the 4th of May a
division of destroyers was in European waters.   By January
1, 1918, there were 113 United States naval ships across,

and in October, 1918, the total had reached 338 ships of all classes. At the present time there are 5,000 officers and 70,000 enlisted men of the navy serving in Europe, this total being greater than the full strength of the navy when the United States entered the war. The destroyers upon their first arrival were based on Queenstown, which has been the base of the operations of these best fighters of the submarines during the war. Every facility possible was provided for the comfort and recreation of the officers and men engaged in this most rigorous service.

During July and August, 1918, 3,444,012 tons of shipping were escorted to and from France by American escort vessels; of the above amount 1,577,735 tons were escorted in and 1,864,677 tons were escorted out of French ports. Of the tonnage escorted into French ports during this time, only 16,988 tons, or .009 per cent., were lost through enemy action, and of the tonnage escorted out from French ports only 27,858, or .013 per cent., were lost through the same cause. During the same period, July and August of this year, 259,604 American troops were escorted to France by United States escort vessels without the loss of a single man through enemy action. The particulars in the above paragraph refer to United States naval forces operating in the war zone from French ports.

During the same time—July and August—destroyers based on British ports supplied 75 per cent. of the escorts for 318 ships, totaling 2,752,908 tons, and including the escort of vessels carrying 137,283 United States troops. The destroyers on this duty were at sea an average of 67 per cent. of the time, and were under way for a period of about 16,000 hours, steaming approximately an aggregate of 260,-000 miles. There were no losses due to enemy action.

The history of the convoy operations in which our naval forces have taken part, due to which we have been able so successfully to transport such a large number of our military forces abroad, and so many supplies for the army, is a chapter in itself. It is probably our major operation in this war, and will in the future stand as a monument to both the army and the navy as the greatest and most difficult troop transporting effort which has ever been conducted across seas.

This entire force, under command of Rear Admiral Albert Gleaves, whose ability and resource have been tested and established in this great service in coöperation with the destroyer flotilla operating abroad, has developed an anti-submarine convoy and escort system the results of which have surpassed even the most sanguine expectations.

American and British ships have carried over two million American troops overseas. The United States did not possess enough ships to carry over our troops as rapidly as they were ready to sail or as quickly as they were needed in France. Great Britain furnished, under contract with the War Department, many ships and safely transported many American troops, the numbers having increased greatly in the spring and summer. A few troops were carried over by other allied ships. The actual number transported in British ships was more than a million.

Up to November 1, 1918, of the total number of United States troops in Europe, 924,578 made passage in United States naval convoys under escort of United States cruisers and destroyers. Since November 1, 1917, there have been 289 sailings of naval transports from American ports. In these operations of the cruiser and transport force of the Atlantic fleet not one eastbound American transport has been torpedoed or damaged by the enemy and only three were sunk on the return voyage.

Our destroyers and patrol vessels, in addition to convoy duty, have waged an unceasing offensive warfare against the submarines. In spite of all this, our naval losses have been gratifyingly small. Only three American troopships—the *Antilles,* the *President Lincoln,* and the *Covington*—were sunk on the return voyage. Only three fighting ships have been lost as a result of enemy action—the patrol ship *Alcedo,* a converted yacht, sunk off the coast of France November 5, 1917; the torpedo boat destroyer *Jacob Jones,* sunk off the British coast December 6, 1917, and the cruiser *San Diego,* sunk near Fire Island, off the New York coast, on July 19, 1918, by striking a mine supposedly set adrift by a German submarine. The transport *Finland* and the destroyer *Cassin,* which were torpedoed, reached port and were soon repaired and placed back in service. The transport *Mount Vernon,* struck by a torpedo on September 5th, proceeded to port under its own steam and was repaired.

The most serious loss of life due to enemy activity was the loss of the Coast Guard cutter *Tampa,* with all on board, in Bristol Channel, England, on the night of September 26, 1918. The *Tampa,* which was doing escort duty, had gone ahead of the convoy. Vessels following heard an explosion, but when they reached the vicinity there were only bits of floating wreckage to show where the ship had gone down. Not one of the 111 officers and men of her crew was rescued, and, though it is believed she was sunk by a torpedo from an enemy submarine, the exact manner in which the vessel met its fate may never be known.

Secretary Daniels' Report as to the First Destroyers

The first actual war service undertaken by the navy was the sending of our destroyers over to the other side for actual participation in the hostilities at sea. This was done in spite of the theory that the place of the destroyers was with the battleship, that every dreadnought should have at least four destroyers to act as her eyes and scouts, and screen her with their smoke. But a great many former theories have had to be revised in this war; so we sent the type of craft that, under normal conditions, would have been the last to go, and our allies were greatly elated by our decision.

Both the English and French Commissions told us that the smaller vessels of our navy would be the most useful to them, and they expressed the hope that we might be able to send destroyers, although they did not expect it. But after consultation with Admiral Benson, Chief of Naval Operations, and later with Admiral Mayo, Commander in Chief of the Atlantic Fleet, I ordered the destroyers to go, even though it seemed a somewhat risky thing to do.

They were all manned by picked officers and men. Nobody was allowed to go on this expedition who had not had experience on destroyers, which is in these days the hardest

and most exacting service in the navy. But it develops a
wonderful breed of men. They are young, alert, ambitious.
The Captain of a destroyer is generally a Lieutenant Commander, and it is a great thing for a youngster of that rank
to be in command of his own ship. The best of them strive
for it, and the other officers of the destroyer are of the same
stamp, and the personnel of the crew is a good match for them.
It was because of the quality of these officers and men and because of the splendid construction and equipment of the
ships themselves that they were able to surprise the English
with the statement that they were ready to go to work immediately upon their arrival on the other side. The spirit
of the men in this part of the navy had been greatly improved by the organizing of the destroyers into a flotilla of
their own, and they had had the great inspiration of serving
under Admiral Sims when he was in command of that
flotilla, and later under Admiral Gleaves.

It was Sims who declared at a dinner in London about
fifteen years ago that blood was thicker than water and that
if war ever came England could count upon America as an
ally. Germany resented that officially through diplomatic
channels, and Sims was reprimanded. Of course, he should
have been reprimanded. I told him so myself not so very
long ago, and then selected him to go to England and
France before America entered the war. Even then I thought
I could see the clouds and felt the need of getting in touch
with the British and French Admiralties.

BY COMMANDER CHARLES C. GILL

Previous to 1916 the idea of a United States overseas
expeditionary force numbered by millions would have been
generally regarded as a remote if not impossible contingency. Consequently no extensive peace-time preparations
had been made for such an undertaking. The task of providing a transport fleet was, therefore, a pioneer work. Ships
had to be obtained, officers and crews enrolled and trained.
It was necessary to provide docks, storehouses, lighters and
tugs, coaling equipment, repair facilities, and all the varied
machinery for operating and maintaining a large transporta-

tion service. An efficient administrative organization had to be developed.

Such, in brief, was the problem confronting Rear Admiral Albert Gleaves, then Commander of the Destroyer Force of the Atlantic Fleet, when, on May 29, 1917, he received orders designating him Commander of United States Convoy Operations in the Atlantic in addition to his other duties.

The work of the navy in connection with the transportation of troops to France constitutes a distinct phase of the present war. The attending political and military circumstances incident to the collapse of Russia, the critical situation on the Western front, and the threat of the German submarine combined to make this phase of special significance. Throughout the year following the entry of the United States into the war the military and naval developments were such that the safe transportation across the Atlantic of troops and supplies became a problem of more and more pressing importance.

The United States Army in France was a decisive factor in obtaining speedy victory. The transportation of this army overseas under naval protection was, therefore, a major operation of first importance. A large share of this urgent mission devolved on the United States Navy, and its successful accomplishment in the face of great difficulties is another page to the record of the service in keeping with its past history and traditions.

Much confusion of thought has existed as to just how the vast work of transporting a United States Army numbering 2,079,880 souls to Europe has been accomplished. It is unfortunate that misinformation should be disseminated respecting an operation in which the different organizations concerned performed their respective functions in utmost harmony and coöperation. All have done their allotted parts splendidly and efficiently. All share in the satisfaction resulting from the successful accomplishment of a difficult and urgent undertaking.

At the time the United States entered the war the enormous toll of shipping gathered by the U-boat in the East

Atlantic and the boast of Von Hindenburg that the submarine blockade of England would starve her out and win the war, indicate the seriousness of the naval situation in those waters at that time. Inasmuch as the principal field of British naval activities was the North Sea and English Channel, the task of breaking the U-boat blockade in the Atlantic naturally became the immediate mission of the United States Navy. The prompt dispatching of destroyers, yachts, and all other available craft of a type useful against the submarine to the East Atlantic, and the splendid work these vessels and others later sent to augment their strength have done in cleaning up these waters of U-boat devastation is a matter of record, the importance of which in winning the war is conceded from all quarters. This was the first step in preparation for sending the United States Army overseas.

The next step was the development of the transport service and the convoy and escort system. In this work the Cruiser and Transport Force coöperated with the destroyers and other anti-submarine craft abroad. In addition, Great Britain, France, and Italy supplied troopships. As would be expected from Great Britain's enormous merchant marine, she was able to supply the greatest carrying capacity. She had the ships ready for this use, and 48¼ per cent. of the American Army was transported in British steamers; 2½ per cent. were carried in French ships, and 3 per cent. in Italian. The remaining 46¼ per cent. were carried in United States ships, and all but 2½ per cent. of these sailed in United States naval transports.

All the troops carried in United States ships were escorted by United States men-of-war; that is, cruisers, destroyers, converted yachts, and other anti-submarine craft. Also for the most part the troops carried in British, French, and Italian ships were given safe conduct through the danger zones by United States destroyers. Roughly, 82¾ per cent. of the maximum strength of the naval escorts provided incident to the transportation of United States troops across the Atlantic was supplied by the United States Navy, 14⅛ per cent. by the British Navy, and 3⅛ per cent. by the French Navy.

The declaration of war with Germany found the United States without a transport fleet and without a merchant marine capable of supplying ships for transporting a large military expedition. It is a remarkable and noteworthy example of American ingenuity and zeal that, starting with almost nothing at the beginning of the war, a United States naval transport service has been built up which has carried almost a million soldiers to Europe. In spite of the determined efforts of submarines to prevent it this has been accomplished without the loss of a single soldier by the hand of the enemy.

The splendid coöperation of the army has made this possible. The army organized and developed an efficient system for loading and unloading the ships at the terminal ports. The navy transported the troops and safeguarded them en route.

On homeward-bound voyages, however, we have not been so fortunate. In a measure this has been due to need of concentrating maximum naval escort protection on troop-laden convoys. Frequently this necessitated lighter escort for the ships returning, and it was on these homeward-bound vessels that the submarines scored their successes. The United States Naval Transports *Antilles, President Lincoln,* and *Covington* were torpedoed and sunk. The *Finland* and *Mount Vernon* were torpedoed, but were able to reach port for repairs. The United States armored cruiser *San Diego* struck a mine laid by a German submarine and was sunk.

The service was not without hazard, as is shown by the fact that more than half of the war casualties in the United States Navy were suffered in the Cruiser and Transport Force. Nor were enemy guns and torpedoes the only menace —danger from fire and internal damage was enhanced by the machinations of enemy secret agents, and the likelihood of collision was increased by the necessity of maneuvering without lights in convoy formation vessels manned for the most part by inexperienced crews.

In connection with the operation of the ships special mention should be made of the volunteer and reserve personnel, particularly the officers and men from the United States merchant marine service who enrolled in the navy for the period of the war. These have rendered splendid service, and the interests of the United States for the future require that the cordial relations of coöperation established between the merchant marine and the navy be maintained. In the larger transports it was the policy of the department to have the Captains, executive officers, chief engineers, gunnery officers, senior medical officers, and senior supply officers detailed from the regular navy and the remainder of the officer complement filled from the various classes of reserve and volunteer officers. This worked very well, and too much credit cannot be given the latter for the loyal service rendered and the aptitude shown in adapting themselves to naval war conditions.

In special cases it was possible, after a certain amount of experience had been gained, to relieve heads of departments, originally assignments of regular naval officers, by reserve officers. For example, in the case of the *Harrisburg, Louisville, Plattsburg, Manchuria, Mongolia,* and *Finland,* after a few trips the reserve Captains took over command of the ships. Credit is also due the navy yards, provisions and clothing depots, medical supply depots, and the ship repair plants which supplemented the navy yards in performing the work incident to making ready and keeping in service this large United States Naval Cruiser and Transport Force, commanded by Rear Admiral Gleaves, and numbering, at the time of the armistice, twenty-four cruisers and forty-two transports, manned, exclusive of troops carried, by about 3,000 officers and 42,000 men.

BY GEORGE CREEL

Official Announcement by the U. S. Government Press Bureau Under Mr. George Creel, Describing the Defense by "Destroyers" Accompanying the First U. S. Transport Fleet to France

German submarines attacked the transports in force. They were outfought by the American escorting destroyers, and at least one submarine was destroyed.

No American ship was hit, and not a life lost. The

German submarines attacked twice. On both occasions the U-boats were beaten off with every appearance of loss. One boat was certainly sunk, and there is reason to believe that the accurate fire of our gunners sent others to the bottom.

For the purposes of convenience the expedition was divided into contingents. Each contingent was composed of troopships and a naval escort designed to keep off such German raiders as might be met with. An ocean rendezvous was arranged with the American destroyers now operating in European waters in order that the passage through the danger zone might be attended by every possible protection.

The first attack occurred at 10.30 p. m. on June 22nd. What gives it a peculiar and disturbing significance is that our ships were set upon at a point well on this side of the rendezvous, in a part of the Atlantic which might have been presumed free from submarines.

The attack was made in force, and although the night made it impossible to arrive at an exact count, it was clear that the U-boats had gathered for what they deemed would be a slaughter. The heavy gunfire of the American destroyers scattered the submarines. It is not known how many torpedoes were launched, but at least five were counted.

The second attack was launched a few days later against another contingent, the point of attack being beyond the rendezvous. Not only did the destroyers hold the U-boats at a safe distance, but their speed resulted in the sinking of at least one submarine. Grenades were used, firing a charge of explosives timed to go off at a certain distance under water. In one instance the wreckage covered the surface of the sea after a shot at a periscope, and reports claim that the boat was sunk.

Protected by our high-seas convoy, destroyers, and by French war vessels, the contingent proceeded and joined the others at the French port. The whole nation will rejoice that so great a peril was passed by the vanguard of the men who will fight our battles in France.

CONSCRIPTION IN THE UNITED STATES

DEMOCRACY ACCEPTS COMPULSORY MILITARY SERVICE

MAY 18TH

OFFICIAL GOVERNMENT ANNOUNCEMENT
SAMUEL GOMPERS

On May 18th, Congress passed the law adopting military conscription, and the President immediately issued the proclamation given herewith, directing how it should be enforced. Never before had the United States employed other than a volunteer army, except for that brief period in the Civil War when such states or districts as could not secure their allotted quota of soldiers by volunteering, resorted to the "draft." Then there had been "draft riots" in New York City and other places. So that now there was considerable anxiety lest a similar opposition should find riotous voice.

Nothing of the sort occurred. The nation had gone too wholeheartedly into the War. Moreover, the question of the righteousness of calling upon every citizen to serve the country instead of allowing some to shift the burden upon others had been fully discussed. Practically every American had seen the double justice, first, of making every man assume an equal share of risk and service, and second, of building the entire nation into an army. So the draft was welcomed and made rather a national festival than an occasion for angry protest.

Men already in the National Guard, or militia of the States, were taken at once into the National Army. Others who wished were allowed to join this army at once as volunteers. But no distinction was made between enlisted and drafted men. The registration for the draft took place on June 5th. About 9,500,000 men registered, representing practically the entire young manhood of the nation, the age limits of this first draft being twenty-one and thirty. As only a small proportion of these could be used at once, the Government on July 20th had a formal drawing of lots to decide which ones should be first called. The first number, drawn from a great glass jar by Secretary Baker in person, was 258. So all over the country the young men who had been numbered 258 in their local drafting board records were summoned; and other numbers were drawn until the army was as large as was required. Not all whose numbers were drawn were sent to the army, for this was a "selective draft," and all who really ought to have been excused for physical or financial reasons were left until a later extremity might demand their service also. The local draft boards all over the country passed upon each case; and while errors were doubtless made, yet upon the whole, these boards achieved a most wonderful work. Its justice, mercy, watchful shrewdness and high honesty crowned the members of these boards with a well-deserved glory.

Later drafts reached out for older and younger men, the age limits gradually spreading between eighteen and forty-five. These later classes were not really called for service. But they would have been had the War continued long enough to require them; and at no time was there any slightest unreadiness shown by the men of the nation to abide by this method of gradually putting into the battlefield the entire manhood of America.

C. F. H.

THE PRESIDENTIAL PROCLAMATION ESTABLISHING CONSCRIPTION

WHEREAS, Congress has enacted and the President has on the 18th day of May, one thousand nine hundred and seventeen, approved a law, which contains the following provisions:

SECTION 5.—*That all male persons between the ages of 21 and 30, both inclusive, shall be subject to registration in accordance with regulations to be prescribed by the President: And upon proclamation by the President or other public notice given by him or by his direction stating the time and place of such registration it shall be the duty of all persons of the designated ages, except officers and enlisted men of the regular army, the navy, and the National Guard and Naval Militia while in the service of the United States, to present themselves for and submit to registration under the provisions of this act: And every such person shall be deemed to have notice of the requirements of this act upon the publication of said proclamation or other notice as aforesaid, given by the President or by his direction: And any person who shall willfully fail or refuse to present himself for registration or to submit thereto as herein provided shall be guilty of a misdemeanor and shall, upon conviction in the District Court of the United States having jurisdiction thereof, be punished by imprisonment for not more than one year, and shall thereupon be duly registered; provided that in the call of the docket precedence shall be given, in courts trying the same, to the trial of criminal proceedings under this act; provided, further, that persons shall be subject to registration as herein provided who shall have attained their twenty-first birthday and who shall not have attained their thirty-first birthday on or before the day set for the registration; and all persons so registered shall be and remain subject to draft into the forces hereby authorized unless excepted or excused therefrom as in this act provided; provided, further, that in the case of temporary absence from actual place of legal residence of any person liable to registration as provided herein, such registration may be made by mail under regulations to be prescribed by the President.*

SECTION 6.—That the President is hereby authorized to utilize the service of any or all departments and any or all officers or agents of the United States and of the several States, Territories, and the District of Columbia and subdivisions thereof in the execution of this act, and all officers and agents of the United States and of the several States, Territories, and subdivisions thereof, and of the District of Columbia; and all persons designated or appointed under regulations prescribed by the President, whether such appointments are made by the President himself or by the Governor or other officer of any State or Territory to perform any duty in the execution of this act, are hereby required to perform such duty as the President shall order or direct, and all such officers and agents and persons so designated or appointed shall hereby have full authority for all acts done by them in the execution of this act by the direction of the President. Correspondence in the execution of this act may be carried in penalty envelopes, bearing the frank of the War Department. Any person charged, as herein provided, with the duty of carrying into effect any of the provisions of this act or the regulations made or directions given thereunder who shall fail or neglect to perform such duty, and any person charged with such duty or having and exercising any authority under said act, regulations, or directions, who shall knowingly make or be a party to the making of any false or incorrect registration, physical examination, exemption, enlistment, enrollment, or muster, and any person who shall make or be a party to the making of any false statement or certificate as to the fitness or liability of himself or any other person for service under the provisions of this act, or regu-

lations made by the President thereunder, or otherwise evades or aids another to evade the requirements of this act or of said regulations, or who, in any manner, shall fail or neglect fully to perform any duty required of him in the execution of this act, shall, if not subject to military law, be guilty of a misdemeanor, and upon conviction in the District Court of the United States having jurisdiction thereof be punished by imprisonment for not more than one year, or, if subject to military law, shall be tried by court-martial and suffer such punishment as a court-martial may direct.

Now, Therefore, I, Woodrow Wilson, President of the United States, do call upon the Governor of each of the several States and Territories, the Board of Commissioners of the District of Columbia, and all officers and agents of the several States and Territories, of the District of Columbia, and of the counties and municipalities therein, to perform certain duties in the execution of the foregoing law, which duties will be communicated to them directly in regulations of even date herewith.

And I do further proclaim and give notice to all persons subject to registration in the several States and in the District of Columbia, in accordance with the above law, that the time and place of such registration shall be between 7 a. m. and 7 p. m. on the fifth day of June, 1917, at the registration place in the precinct wherein they have their permanent homes. Those who shall have attained their twenty-first birthday and who shall not have attained their thirty-first birthday on or before the day here named are required to register, excepting only officers and enlisted men of the regular army, the navy, the Marine Corps, and the National Guard and Navy Militia, while in the service of the United States, and officers in the Officers' Reserve Corps and enlisted men in the Enlisted Reserve Corps while in active service. In the Territories of Alaska, Hawaii, and Porto Rico a day for registration will be named in a later proclamation.

And I do charge those who through sickness shall be unable to present themselves for registration that they apply on or before the day of registration to the County Clerk of the county where they may be for instructions as to how they may be registered by agent. Those who expect to be absent on the day named from the counties in which they have their permanent homes may register by mail, but their mailed registration cards must reach the places in which they have their permanent homes by the day named herein. They should apply as soon as practicable to the County Clerk of the county wherein they may be for instructions as to how they may accomplish their registration by mail. In case such persons as, through sickness or absence, may be unable to present themselves personally for registration shall be sojourning in cities of over 30,000 population, they shall apply to the City Clerk of the city wherein they may be sojourning rather than to the Clerk of the county. The Clerks of counties and of cities of over 30,000 population in which numerous applications from the sick and from nonresidents are expected are authorized to establish such agencies and to employ and deputize such clerical force as may be necessary to accommodate these applications.

The power against which we are arrayed has sought to impose its will upon the world by force. To this end it has increased armament until it has changed the face of war. In the sense in which we have been wont to think of armies, there are no armies in this struggle, there are entire nations armed. Thus, the men who remain to till the soil and man the factories are no less a part of the army that is France than the men beneath the battle flags. It must be so with us. It is not an army that we must shape and train for war; it is a nation.

To this end our people must draw close in one compact front against a common foe. But this cannot be if each man pursues a private purpose. All must pursue one purpose. The nation needs all men; but it needs each man not in the field that will most pleasure him, but in the endeavor that will best serve the common good. Thus, though a sharpshooter pleases to operate a trip-hammer for the forging of great guns and an expert machinist desires to march with the flag, the nation is being served only when the sharpshooter marches and the machinist remains at his levers.

The whole nation must be a team, in which each man shall play the part for which he is best fitted. To this end, Congress has provided that the nation shall be organized for war by selection; that each man shall be classified for service in the place to which it shall best serve the general good to call him.

The significance of this cannot be overstated. It is a new thing in our history and a landmark in our progress. It is a new manner of accepting and vitalizing our duty to give ourselves with thoughtful devotion to the common purpose of us all. It is in no sense a conscription of the unwilling; it is, rather, selection from a nation which has volunteered in mass. It is no more a choosing of those who shall march with the colors than it is a selection of those who shall serve an equally necessary and devoted purpose in the industries that lie behind the battle line.

The day here named is the time upon which all shall present themselves for assignment to their tasks. It is for that reason destined to be remembered as one of the most conspicuous moments in our history. It is nothing less than the day upon which the manhood of the country shall step forward in one solid rank in defense of the ideals to which this nation is consecrated. It is important to those ideals no less than to the pride of this generation in manifesting its devotion to them, that there be no gaps in the ranks.

It is essential that the day be approached in thoughtful apprehension of its significance, and that we accord to it the honor and the meaning that it deserves. Our industrial need prescribes that it be not made a technical holiday, but the stern sacrifice that is before us urges that it be carried in all our hearts as a great day of patriotic devotion and obligation, when the duty shall lie upon every man, whether he is himself to be registered or not, to see to it that the name of every male person of the designated ages is written on these lists of honor.

In witness whereof, I have hereunto set my hand and caused the seal of the United States to be affixed. Done at the City of Washington this 18th day of May in the year of our Lord one thousand nine hundred and seventeen, and of the Independence of the United States of America the one hundred and forty-first.

By the President.

BY SAMUEL GOMPERS

I have counted myself happy in the companionship of the men and women who called themselves pacifists. There was not a State or national or international peace society of which I was not a member, and in many instances an officer. As a trade unionist, with its practices and its philosophies, I have been in happy accord with our movement for international peace.

At a great gathering in Faneuil Hall, Boston, some years ago, I gave utterance to my soul's conviction that the time had come when great international wars had been put to an end, and I expressed the opinion that in the last analysis, if those who are the profit-mongers by "war" undertook to create a war, the working people of the countries of the world would stop work simultaneously, if necessary, in order to prevent international war. . . .

I was sent as a delegate from the American Federation of Labor to the International Congress of Labor in 1909, held at Paris, France, and there at that conference, incidental to it, there was arranged one of the greatest mass-meetings I have ever attended, at which the representatives of the labor movement of each country declared that there would not be another international war.

And I went home, happy in the further proof that the time of universal peace had come. And I attended more peace conferences. I was still firmly persuaded that the time had come, and until 1914 I was in that Fool's Paradise. I doubt if there were many who were so thoroughly shocked to the innermost depths of their being as I was with the breaking out of the European War. But it had come! And as it went on, ruthlessly, we saw a terrific conflict in which the dominating spirit was that the people attacked must be subjugated to the will of the great autocrat of his time regardless of how our sympathies ran, and that men who had given the best years of their lives in the effort to find some means, some secret of science or of nature, so that the slightest ill or pain of the most insignificant of the race might be assuaged, turned to purposes of destruction. At the call of this autocrat, His Imperial Majesty the Emperor of Germany, men were set at attack, and we found that these very men were clutching at each other's throats and seeking each other's destruction. . . .

The United States has declared that she can no longer live in safety when there is stalking throughout the earth this thunderous machine of murder. The United States authoritatively has declared that peace is desirable and should be brought about, but that peace is impossible so long as life and liberty are challenged and menaced. The Republic of the United States has cast her lot with the Allied countries fighting against the greatest military machine ever erected in the history of the world.

I am made ill when I see or hear any one suffering the slightest pain or anguish, and yet I hold that it is essential that the sacrifice must be made that humanity shall never again be cursed by a war such as the one which has been thrust upon us.

TRIUMPHS OF THE AIR AGE

THE GREATEST FEAT OF THE GREATEST FRENCH ACE, GUYNEMER

MAY 25TH

PAUL DESCHANEL   HENRI BORDEAUX
CLAUDE GRAHAME-WHITE

The remarkable development of the air machines during the Great War has made this indeed the opening of the Air Age. The main steps in its progress are here outlined by the celebrated British leader in aviation development, Mr. Claude Grahame-White.

The most impressive single feat in aviation during the War was perhaps that of the chief French aviator, Georges Guynemer, who on May 25, 1917, brought down four enemy battle-planes in quick succession on a single day. Other aviators are said to have since equaled this brilliant record, but in no such completely proven fashion. Guynemer remains the chief aviator hero of the War as to the number of his victories, their dramatic completeness, and the impression that his daring successes had upon the minds of men. This inspirational effect of his victories and of his death is here described by M. Paul Deschanel, poet, orator, and Member of the French Academy, who in 1920 became President of France. The special deeds of Guynemer's one greatest day are presented from the detailed account of M. Henri Bordeaux, the noted French patriotic writer.

BY PAUL DESCHANEL

DEAR and sublime lad, thy frail body, worn by a hundred combats, wounded by bullets, battered unceasingly by the fury of the elements and the greater fury of men, has been stricken down at length by the assault of the enemy; but thy superb and intrepid spirit still leads to victory thy comrades of the fight; and thy immortal *escadrille,* the *escadrille* of the "Storks," still announces from on high in the blue of the heavens the deliverance of Alsace.

Yes, from the mud and misery of our hallowed trenches, our heroes still follow thy flights with eager pride and enthusiasm. Flying above them still in spirit, you lead them to combat across the German lines; and they find victory through you. They love you, as does all France.

Dear lad, thy brilliant path across the sky, so swift and so full of glory that it epitomizes, as naught else before, the history of our race, thy flaming epic, will be to the eyes of future generations a double sign. The art of aviation, despite its miracles, is still in its infancy. Already it has changed the existence of humanity and doubtless that which we see is but little compared to that which shall be seen by our children. But the name of Guynemer, summing up in a word the splendid exploits of the youth of our day, will remain as long as the earth carries thinking beings, the symbol of the heroism of France in the greatest of all wars. It will be also a symbol of the magnificent discoveries which, in giving to man wings, have opened to him life.

From the first day of Guynemer's arrival on the battle front his bravery was clearly revealed; but as he advanced in the skill of his chosen work, he added to his courage and audacity a wealth of experience and an ever increasing mastery over his opponents. In eight months, from June, 1915, to March, 1916, he fought twenty-one aërial combats and brought down eight enemy aëroplanes. Thereafter the rhythm of his victories grew swifter; triumphs rushed upon him; adventures crowded fast as in an epic tale of glory.

In May, 1916, Guynemer was attached to the army of Verdun; then in June he appeared on the Somme battle front, always with the escadrille of the Storks. In September, 1916, he reached the summit of his powers. On September 22nd, at a height of over three thousand meters he attacked three enemy planes at once. At twenty-two minutes past eleven he destroyed the first foe; at twenty-two and a half minutes past eleven he destroyed the second foe; and at twenty-seven minutes past eleven he put to flight the third. The enemy artillery opened fire upon him, and a shell struck his machine. A splinter wounded him in the knee, and his machine fell to the earth. Yet even then by his skill he managed to guide it to a safe landing.

His wounds did not long hold him from the field. On the last day of 1916 he was promoted to be lieutenant of his squadron; and in 1917, on the Somme and in Lorraine, the series of his triumphs recommenced. In three days, from the 23rd to the 26th of January, he was five times victorious and destroyed five enemy planes. On the 8th of February, he undertook to fight single handed against a triplane armed with three machine guns, and he forced it to descend as a captive within our lines.

His reward was his commission as Captain, which he obtained on the 18th of February, at twenty-two years of age. After this he was withdrawn from the front line for a short time to superintend the installation of a new aëroplane device which he had invented; but he returned hastily to the front for the great spring battle in Champagne.

Here on the 25th of May he surpassed himself and achieved the most memorable of his many victories. He destroyed four of the enemy battle-planes in a single day. This exploit, unique in the annals of military aviation, won for him the officer's cross of the Legion of Honor.

By the end of the summer of 1917, his service record included the destruction of fifty-three enemy aëroplanes; he had been twenty-five times cited with honor in the proclamations of the army, and he had been twice wounded. The number of his victories was always far larger than the total of those officially registered, and probably exceeded a hundred. His final official record was to contain but one more victory and one more citation.

His leadership in his squadron was irresistible. He was by his example, by his mere appearance, a marvelous encourager of men. At sight of him the soldiers of the army always became enthusiastic; they were thrilled to a splendid height of enthusiasm. During a big attack he would fly ahead of the soldiers, close to earth, straight toward the enemy positions, pointing the way to the eager masses of infantry who rushed forward in his path.

Seeing him return unharmed from so many perils, we came to believe him invincible. In August of 1917, he was with the Franco-British offensive in Flanders. On the 6th of September he brought down his fifty-fourth victim, his last.

On the 11th of September in the morning, he set out in his machine on a reconnoissance. About half-past nine while accompanied by the machine of his comrade, Lieutenant Bozon-Verduraz, he perceived an enemy aëroplane, and with his usual intrepidity drove straight at the foe. Suddenly from the morning fog appeared several of the German planes speeding to the help of their comrade. Lieutenant Bozon-Verduraz, seeing the danger of Guynemer, boldly attacked these new adversaries and succeeded in scattering their forces. Then he returned to seek his comrade. He searched the sea of clouds, he explored the far horizon; but Guynemer and his plane had disappeared.

As one of his comrades in arms has said, "Even in the tragic mystery which surrounds his last moments, Fame, whose favorite child he was, proved generous toward him, and carried him away on her own wings. The deeps of the sky, those strangely fascinating oceans which he had so often explored, had wrapped him in their impenetrable mists, as if to steal from earth the child who belonged to them."

Thus ended, in the apotheosis of a great aërial combat, the career of Guynemer, brilliant with youth and heroism.

Citation of Honor Issued to Guynemer by the French Government

GEORGES GUYNEMER

FALLEN ON THE FIELD OF HONOR ON SEPTEMBER 11, 1917. A LEGENDARY HERO, FALLEN FROM THE VERY ZENITH OF VICTORY AFTER THREE YEARS' HARD AND CONTINUOUS FIGHTING. HE WILL BE CONSIDERED THE MOST PERFECT EMBODIMENT OF THE NATIONAL QUALITIES FOR HIS IN-DOMITABLE ENERGY AND PERSEVERANCE AND HIS EXALTED GALLANTRY. FULL OF INVINCIBLE BELIEF IN VICTORY, HE HAS BEQUEATHED TO THE FRENCH SOLDIER AN IMPERISH-ABLE MEMORY WHICH MUST ADD TO HIS SELF-SACRIFICING SPIRIT AND WILL SURELY GIVE RISE TO THE NOBLEST EMU-LATION.

"To deserve such a citation and die!" exclaimed a young officer after reading it.

BY HENRI BORDEAUX [1]

On May 25th Guynemer, on his morning patrol, met three German airplanes flying towards the French lines. They were two-seaters, less nimble, no doubt, than one-seaters, but provided with so much more dangerous arms. Yet he pounced upon his three opponents, who promptly turned back. However, he overtook one, began making evolutions around him, succeeded in getting slightly below him, fired, and with his first volley succeeded in bringing him down in flames north of Corbeny (northeast of Craonne).

The danger for a one-seater is to be surprised from behind. Just as Guynemer veered round, he saw another machine flying after him. He again fired upwards, and the airplane fell in flames, like the first, only a few seconds having elapsed between the two fights. Guynemer then returned to camp.

But he was excited by these two fights; his nerves were strained and his will was tense. He soon started again. Towards noon a German machine appeared above the camp itself. How had it been able to get there? This is what the airmen down below were asking themselves. It was useless to chase it, for it would take any of them longer to rise than the German to escape. So they had to content themselves with looking up, some of them searching the sky with binoculars. Everybody was back except Guynemer, when somebody suddenly cried: "Here comes Guynemer!"

"Then the Boche is done for."

Guynemer, in fact, was coming down upon his prey like lightning, and the instant he was behind and slightly beneath him, he fired. Only one shot from the machine gun was heard, but the enemy airplane was already spinning down, its engine going full speed, and was dashed into the earth at Courlandon near Fismes. The pilot had been shot through the head.

In the afternoon Guynemer started for the third time,

and towards seven o'clock, above the Guignicourt market gardens (that is to say, in the enemy lines), he brought down another machine in flames.

Guynemer, when returning to camp after a victory, generally announced his success by making his engine work to some tune. This time the cadence was the tune of the *Lampions*. All the neighboring airplane sheds understood, also the cantonments, parks, depots, dugouts, field hospitals and railway stations; in a word, all the communities scattered behind the lines of an army. This time the motor was singing so insistently that everybody, with faces upturned, concluded that their Guynemer had been "getting them."

In fact, the news was already spreading like wildfire, as news has the mysterious capacity for doing. No, it was not simply one airplane he had set ablaze; it was two, one above Corbeny, the other above Juvincourt. And people had hardly realized the wonderful fact before the third machine was seen falling in flames near Fismes. It was seen by hundreds of men who thought it was about to fall upon them, and ran for shelter. Meanwhile, Guynemer's engine was singing.

And for the fourth time it was heard again at twilight. Could it be possible? Had Guynemer really succeeded four times? Four machines brought down in one day by one pilot was what no infantry-man, gunner, pioneer, territorial, Anamite or Senegalese had ever seen. And from the stations, field hospitals, dugouts, depots, parks and cantonments, while the setting sun lingered in the sky on this May evening, whoever handled a shovel, a pickax or a rifle, whoever laid down rails, unloaded trucks, piled up cases, or broke stones on the road, whoever dressed wounds, gave medicine or carried dead men, whoever worked, rested, ate or drank —whoever was alive, in a word—stepped out, ran, jostled along, arrived at the camp, got helterskelter over the fences, broke into the sheds, searched the airplanes, and called to the mechanicians in their wild desire to see Guynemer. There they were, a whole town of them, knocking at every door and peeping into every tent.

Somebody said: "Guynemer is asleep."

Whereupon, without a word of protest, without a sound, the crowd streamed out and scattered in the darkening fields, threading its way back to the quiet dells behind the lines. So ended the day of the greatest aërial victory.

BY CLAUDE GRAHAME-WHITE
The Dawn of the Air Age in 1918

The world hardly sees yet a shadow of the revolution in its habits and customs which is impending, and will follow the use of the air as a highway. The aircraft industry, weak and struggling no longer, thanks to the stimulus of war, is planning already the building of machines which will be sufficiently powerful and airworthy to maintain regular services by air for passengers, mails, and light express goods. More experience in construction has been gained during two and a-half years of war than would have been possible under peace conditions in many years. The industry is now organized, and stronger financially; and only a year or so should elapse after the war before the first air services are run on a commercial basis between London and the Continent, and also between London and the cities of the Midlands and the North. This is no longer the dream of an enthusiast. The recent constructional progress has been such that passenger services by air could be organized even at the present time, were the industry not preoccupied with its work in connection with the war.

By means of technical improvements which have become feasible, and which need only peace conditions to enable them to be carried into effect, it should be possible, almost immediately after the war, to build passenger aircraft which will carry twenty-five or fifty people at an average speed of nearly 100 miles an hour. And this will form a stepping-stone to larger craft, fitted with motors developing thousands of horse-power, which should attain speeds of 200, 250, and perhaps even 300 miles an hour. Time and money —not forgetting the skill of designers and constructors, and an infinite patience and perseverance—are all that are required to bring about this era. We have sufficient knowledge at the present time to indicate that there are no technical difficulties which should prove insuperable.

The demand of the commercial world, for years prior to the war, was for greater speed in transit. Time, representing money, had been growing daily more valuable. After the war, huge schemes of reconstruction will become necessary, and there should be an immense quickening of trade activity in all quarters of the globe. With the employment of commercial aircraft, able to pass without deviation above land, sea, forests, or mountains, the question of distance, or of the difficulty of communication through natural obstacles, will cease to be a barrier between nations.

The first use of commercial aircraft should be as mail-carriers; and it is possible that the first experimental services will be attempted over localities remote from large centers of population, where the nature of the country makes it difficult to maintain regular communication by land; also to link up by air-mail the widely scattered communities such as exist in our dominions oversea.

America, France, and Italy are concerning themselves already with the question of establishing air-mail services; and the British Government, with foreign possessions in which air-mail services might be established with great convenience to the inhabitants, has every reason to do the same. The recent appointment of the Civil Aërial Transport Committee is an indication that the authorities are now becoming alive to the importance of commercial aëronautics. The main task of this Committee is to recommend to the Government what steps shall be taken, when the war is over, to develop civil flying in all its aspects.

The American Government, it is understood, intends to operate an air-mail, with a service twice weekly, between the Alaskan coast and certain of the inaccessible districts which lie inland. It is hoped, by means of the air service, to make journeys in five or six hours which, by land transport, have sometimes taken as long as three weeks.

The French Government has established a Committee which is investigating the whole question of transporting mails by air; and one of the aims of this Committee is to determine, if possible, at what cost per kilometer it would be possible to operate such services.

The Italian Government has, since the beginning of the war, connected several of her important commercial centers by means of a system of alighting-grounds; and along these "airways" already an experimental mail service is being operated—although, naturally, the needs of the moment are almost entirely military.

It will certainly be unwise, right at the beginning of commercial aviation, for Governments to expect an air service tc be completely self-supporting, or to operate at once with such profit as might be shown, say, by transport systems on land or sea—which, of course, have had years of organization and experience. What Governments must do, and particularly the British Government, is to insure to the operators of these first air-mail services a freedom from financial anxiety during the period when their main task will be to gain all the experience they can as to suitable types of machine, and to make any experiments, and incur any reasonable expense, which they may consider necessary for the improvement of their services.

And when the experience gained in these, and other ways, permits the running of passenger air services, the Government must be equally ready with assistance, and must make it one of its chief aims—undeterred by cries which may be raised for retrenchment in expenditure—to insure that commercial flying in all its aspects develops rapidly and successfully, and that no invention of importance is lost to us through a lack of financial aid. The rate-payer, when his money is spent to develop flying, need have no fear that it is being wasted, or that such expenditure is inadvisable. It will be a matter of vital necessity for us, on imperial as well as purely national grounds, to create and maintain a large fleet of commercial aircraft. We know how, in this present war, with the danger zones created by hostile submarines, we have had to rely on our great mercantile marine. And it may happen in some war of the future, with sea-blockades so efficient as to hold up traffic altogether, that we shall have to depend upon aircraft to bring us the supplies which cannot be obtained in any other way. Another important reason for a Government subsidy of the aircraft industry lies in the fact that the knowledge and experience which are gained in building and piloting commercial-type machines will be of extreme value in time of war; while it should be remembered that commercial craft could, in war-time, be converted quickly and without difficulty into cruiser-type machines, being fitted with bomb-sighting and releasing gear, and also with guns throwing explosive shells. And such converted machines would be extremely useful in attacking land positions, or in harassing an enemy's air and sea traffic.

It is difficult for us to realize the change in our habits, and in our routine of living, which will follow the coming of the air age. As soon as we have daily services by air operating on an adequate scale, it will be possible for city workers to live much farther afield than they can with any existing form of locomotion. And this will mean, in the course of time, that the outskirts of a city like London will cease to be dormitories for the workers, and will be given over almost exclusively to factories and workshops. The workers of the city, traveling at high speeds by air, will be able to live along the southern and southeastern seacoasts, or in the heart of the country. And this will be so beneficial to their health that their efficiency as workers will be materially increased; while the cost of aërial travel, in their daily journeys, will be outweighed by the fact that their rent and living expenses will be reduced, and that they will be able to cultivate produce in their own gardens. It will become feasible, in the air age, to populate evenly the whole of a country, instead of masses of people being congested— as they are now through the slowness of transit—within areas of only a few miles.

City men who are private owners of aircraft will be able to live a hundred miles or more away from town, and still attend their offices each day. Flying up in the morning to one of the aërodromes which will be situated on the outskirts of London, they will house their machines there, and then travel on into the heart of the city by one of the high-speed tubes (probably on the mono-rail system), which will act as "feeders" for the aërodromes, and will run to and fro constantly with passengers and goods. In the evening, the last of his letters signed, the business man will take tube to the aërodrome, ascending again in his aircraft, and reaching his home, somewhere in the heart of the country, in time for dinner.

The world has, at various times, been promised an ideal form of travel—such as the train, the motor-car, and the luxurious modern liner. But the train oscillates; its wheels grind and roar; it clangs through tunnels and over bridges; it lurches when rounding curves. With the motor-car, even on the best of roads, there is always the sensation of earth contact and of vibration—to say nothing of the dust and inconvenience of the traffic on main thoroughfares; while the ocean-going liner, pitching and rolling in a bad sea, causes acute discomfort to many of its passengers. The air will provide a luxurious form of travel such as the voyager of to-day has never known, and can scarcely imagine. There will be no vibration or noise from the machinery, and no sensation whatever of an earth contact. The only sound to reach a passenger's ears, as the machine sweeps through the air in a smooth, apparently effortless progress, will be the faint hum of the wind as it rushes past the hull. When they are on long journeys, aircraft will fly high, often above the clouds; and there will be no sign then of the earth below, and nothing to tell the eye that the machine is driving its way through the air at high speed.

Even in a 100-mile-an-hour aircraft, immediately one reaches the normal cross-country altitude of about 5,000 feet, the sensations of movement or of speed, in relation to the earth below, become almost imperceptible. The passengers, seated in luxuriously-appointed saloons, will be in just as much comfort, so far as any sense of movement is concerned, as though they were in their drawing-room at home. People complain often of train-tiredness after a long journey by rail. This is due to the oscillation, noise, and the constant flashing past of objects which are close to the carriage win-

dows. But there will be no such fatigue after an air journey, however long, for the reason that there will be none of
the discomforts which are encountered on land.

There are people still who think that, because a flying
machine passes through the air, unsupported by any earth
contact, there will always be an element of risk in aërial
travel. But in the future, when passenger-carrying machines
have been perfected, to travel by air will not only be as safe
as to travel by land or sea, but will be in certain respects
even safer. There will, for instance, be less danger from
collision. Craft traveling in different directions—north,
south, east, or west—will be required by the rules of the air
to fly at various altitudes. And these lanes of traffic, in which
all the machines will be traveling in the same direction, will
be so arranged that they are not immediately one above another, but are some little distance apart; and this will mean
that should a machine have to glide down from a high altitude, through some temporary breakdown of its machinery,
there would be little risk of its penetrating as it descended—
with a consequent risk of collision—any of the streams of
traffic which might be moving at lower altitudes and in different directions. Foggy weather, which presents such dangers for land or sea traffic, would only provide a risk in
aërial travel (one writes, of course, in a general sense) when
machines are ascending or alighting. At higher altitudes, as
a rule, it should be possible for them to escape the fog banks.
And at the landing grounds, when there are fogs, science
may find it possible to dissipate these, at any rate over limited areas; or by some system of powerful lights, or by signals from captive balloons which ascend above the fog banks,
it should be possible to regulate the flow of traffic in and out
of the aërodromes. An aircraft pilot under such conditions,
when approaching an aërodrome at a high altitude, well above
the fog, would watch for the signals sent up from the ground,
which would inform him whether all was clear for his descent, in the same way that a ship is signaled, telling it
whether it is safe to enter a harbor.

The attaining of high speeds by air implies a greater
safety rather than a greater risk—provided, of course, that

a machine is so built that it will withstand the air pressures it encounters. The higher the speed at which a machine is traveling, the more control its pilot has over it; while there is not the same risk in the air, as there is on land, of a vehicle oscillating when at a very high speed, and threatening to overturn or leave its track. The faster an aircraft flies the steadier is its motion. The momentum of its flight enables it to drive through adverse wind-gusts without these having any effect upon it; whereas a slow machine would pitch and roll. And there is not the risk with an aircraft, as with a land vehicle, of a wheel or axle breaking under the strains of a high speed, and thereby causing an accident.

In flying, of course, as in any other new form of transport, the purely experimental stage has been marred by accidents. Machines have collapsed in flight, or have been driven to earth and wrecked by wind-gusts; motors have failed, and caused disaster; pilots have been guilty of errors of judgment which have cost them their lives. But during all this time, experience and useful data have been accumulating. In learning to fly, men have been accumulating. In learning to fly, men have been breaking completely new ground— learning to navigate an entirely new element. But in the future we shall be bred and born to the air. We shall take to it just as naturally as, to-day, we travel by land or sea. With the aircraft of the future, which will be metal-built, the risk of structural breakage will be reduced practically to a vanishing point. And the inherent stability of these large machines, and the speeds at which they will fly, will enable them to weather safely even the heaviest of gales; while the multi-engine plants with which they will be fitted, enabling any one unit to be cut temporarily from the series, and repaired while the machine continues in flight under the power of its other motors, will eliminate for all practical purposes any need to descend owing to a mechanical breakdown. Assuming, however, that a machine should descend involuntarily, there will be chains of landing-grounds on all the main flying routes, and these will be so close together that a machine which is flying at a sufficient altitude will be able to reach one or other of them, in a glide, from any point at which its machinery may fail. Craft which are on ocean journeys, being built so that they can alight on the water, will follow certain given routes, and will be in constant touch with each other by wireless. Should a machine be obliged to descend on the water through a total breakdown of its machinery, it will be able to call to its assistance, if necessary, and in a very short time, any such craft as may be nearest to it on the flying route.

But such a total breakdown will be no more probable with a perfected aircraft than it would be with an ocean-going liner. On the liner, should one of her turbines run hot, this only reduces her speed temporarily, while the turbine is stopped and allowed to cool. The others continue to do their work and to propel the ship. With a liner, in fact, having many engines and boilers, and several propeller shafts, the risk of a total breakdown is practically eliminated. And in aircraft of the future, which will be fitted with multi-engines, driving a number of propellers, this risk will be equally remote.

In the a.r age we shall be able to take the map of Europe, and also of the world, and reduce journeys of weeks to days, and those of days to hours; and what this will mean to business men, who will be extending their interests farther and farther afield, one need scarcely emphasize. In the years following the war men who have great organizing ability—and they are certainly not legion—will find their services almost beyond price. Such men will need to have the whole world, and not any one country or continent, as the field for their operations; and, when they travel frequently to all parts of the globe, any saving of time in their journeys will be of extreme importance.

Here lies the future of aërial transit. It will supply a means of communication so rapid that the world will be able, after the war, to go ahead in the full stride of its reconstructive energy; though this period of reconstruction will, of course, occupy a number of years. Instead of being restricted to the old, slow methods of travel, the nations in their expansion will find this new and high-speed medium open to them—a medium in which rates of travel will be obtainable without risk which would be impossible by land or sea. Five days are required, at normal times, to traverse the sea route between England and America. A business man who has interests in the two countries, and needs to travel frequently between them, must set aside ten days at least of his valuable time in which to be transported across the ocean and back again. In the future, however, by way of the air, he will be able to travel from New York to London and back again, within a period of forty-eight hours.

The influence of high-speed air transit, facilitating business between various countries, will be beneficial to an extent which is almost incalculable. After the war we shall be establishing closer relations with Russia. But the traveler by land and sea, coming from Petrograd to London, has to face a long and wearisome journey, crossing a number of frontiers and being subjected to many delays. In the days of the Continental air service, however, a Russian business man, embarking at Petrograd in the morning on one of the aircraft which will run non-stop on such routes as these, will find himself in London the same evening, having made a smooth and easy journey, with no need to leave the saloon into which he stepped in his own city. In connection with such long, non-stop flights, in which passenger aircraft, while en route, will pass above frontiers without alighting, it may be necessary for the authorities of the various powers to have representatives at the points of departure, so that the flights of these express craft may be supervised, and the customs, passport, and other formalities complied with before the machines ascend.

The stream of traffic which passes at normal times between London and Paris, and will attain after the war an even greater volume, will be influenced to a remarkable extent by the establishment of a Continental air service. One need not dwell upon the discomforts and delay, during the winter months, which business men have had to suffer whose misfortune it has been to make this journey frequently by steamer and train. About seven hours are needed for the journey under favorable conditions. But, when there is a

Channel gale or fog, apart from the unpleasantness of the sea crossing, travelers have to reconcile themselves to many hours of delay. The Channel tunnel, if it is built, will obviate the discomforts of the sea passage, and also the delay of changing from train to steamer and from steamer to train. But no journey by land, even with the advantages of the tunnel, will offer such facilities in rapid transit as will be possible by air. A high-speed aircraft, flying in an absolutely straight line between the two cities, should be able to make the journey in slightly more than two hours! Aircraft will, of course, show to the greatest advantage in the matter of time-saving when on long rather than on short journeys, owing to the fact that a certain amount of time will have to be lost in gaining altitude before a maximum speed can be attained, and again in slowing down before alighting.

Instead of being a series of widely-scattered communities, knowing little of each other, and prone in consequence to suspicions and mistrust, humanity will find itself drawn closer and closer together through the speed of aërial transit. In the process of time the individual man will cease to regard himself as the citizen of any one nation, and will recognize that he is a unit in a world-wide organization, laboring not for the furtherance of purely selfish aims, or even of local or national ambitions, but for the betterment of conditions throughout the globe. That, at any rate, is the ideal. It will be some time, naturally, before it is realized, if it is ever realized. But this much is certain: it would never be possible to realize it at all were it not for the promise which is offered by the coming of the air age. After the war, therefore, every nation, as well as every individual, should work whole-heartedly for the development of flight. Though the aircraft now figures in our minds principally as an instrument of destruction, its rôle in the future will be that of a great instrument of construction—an instrument by means of which we may establish such a world-wide friendship, such a mutual understanding, that the ruthless ambitions of a few men will never again be able to throw millions of their fellow-citizens at each other's throats.

THE MAN-MADE EARTHQUAKE

THE BRITONS BLOW UP MESSINES RIDGE

JUNE 7TH

SIR DOUGLAS HAIG   FRANK FOX
FREIHERR VON DER OSTEN SACKEN

The Messines Ridge explosion of June 7th was the largest ever made by man. Back in October of 1885 American engineers had set an explosive record for the world when they blew up the "Hell Gate" reef which partly blocked one of New York City's waterways. At Hell Gate nine acres of rock were blown up by 140 tons of "rackrock." At Messines the combined mines contained over 450 tons of a similar explosive compound known as ammonal. When these were touched off all at once the noise was heard and the rocking of the earth was felt in England as well as all over northern France. Britain's Premier, Lloyd George, knowing of the time set for the explosion, waited through the night and listened, and heard the "boom" of this greatest gun ever fired by man.

The effect of this explosion and the swift assault that followed was to place the British in possession of all that was left of Messines Ridge. This was still the highest ground in the region around Ypres. That sector, which the British had so long held beneath the "strafing" of the German guns from Messines, was now secure. Indeed, the strategic position was sharply reversed. British guns now dominated the German lines, and gave the Allies such an advantage that less than two months later they began a new advance in this region, the great "Battle of Flanders."

BY SIR DOUGLAS HAIG

A SPECIAL feature of the attack on the Messines-Wytschaete Ridge, and one unique in warfare, was furnished by the explosion of nineteen deep mines at the moment of assault.

The inception of a deep mining offensive on the Second Army front dated from July, 1915; but the proposal to conduct offensive mining on a grand scale was not definitely adopted till January, 1916. From that date onwards, as the necessary labor became available, deep mining for offensive purposes gradually developed, in spite of great difficulties from water-bearing strata and active countermining by the enemy.

In all, twenty-four mines were constructed, four of which were outside the front ultimately selected for our offensive, while one other was lost as the result of a mine blown by the enemy. Many of these mines had been completed for twelve months prior to our offensive, and constant and anxious work was needed to insure their safety. The enemy also had a deep mining system, and was aware of his danger.

At Hill 60 continuous underground fighting took place for over ten months prior to our attack, and only by the greatest skill, persistence and disregard of danger on the part of our tunnelers were the two mines laid by us at this point saved from destruction. At the time of our offensive the enemy was known to be driving a gallery which ultimately would have cut into the gallery leading to the Hill 60 mines. By careful listening it was judged that if our offensive took place on the date arranged the enemy's gallery would just fail to reach us. So he was allowed to proceed.

At the Bluff also underground fighting went on incessantly. Between January 16, 1916, and June 7, 1917, twenty-seven camouflets were blown in this locality alone, of which seventeen were blown by us and ten by the enemy. After February 1, 1917, the enemy showed signs of great uneasiness, and blew several heavy mines and camouflets in the endeavor to interfere with our working. One of these blows destroyed our gallery to the Spanbroekmolen mine. For three months this mine was cut off, and was only recovered by strenuous efforts on the day preceding the Messines attack. The Spanbroekmolen mine formed the largest crater of any of those blown, the area of complete obliteration having a diameter of over 140 yards.

A total of 8,000 yards of gallery were driven in the construction of these mines, and over one million pounds of explosives were used in them. The simultaneous discharge of such an enormous aggregate of explosive is without parallel in land mining, and no actual experience existed of the effects which would be produced. In these circumstances, the fact that no hitch of any kind occurred in the operation, and that the effects of the discharges were precisely such as had been foretold, reflects the very highest credit upon those responsible for the planning and construction of the mines.

The group of hills known as the Messines-Wytschaete Ridge lies about midway between the towns of Armentieres and Ypres. Situated at the eastern end of the range of abrupt, isolated hills which divides the valleys of the River Lys and the River Yser, it links up that range with the line of rising ground which from Wytschaete stretches northeastwards to the Ypres-Menin road, and then northwards past Passchendaele to Staden.

The village of Messines, situated on the southern spur of the ridge, commands a wide view of the valley of the Lys, and enfiladed the British lines to the south. Northwest of Messines the village of Wytschaete, situated at the point of the salient and on the highest part of the ridge, from its height of about 260 feet commands even more completely the town of Ypres and the whole of the old British positions in the Ypres salient.

The German front line skirted the western foot of the ridge in a deep curve from the River Lys opposite Frelinghien to a point just short of the Menin road. The line of trenches then turned northwest past Hooge and Wieltje, following the slight rise known as the Pilckem Ridge to the Yser Canal at Boesinghe. The enemy's second-line system followed the crest of the Messines-Wytschaete Ridge, forming an inner curve.

In addition to these defenses of the ridge itself, two chord positions had been constructed across the base of the salient from south to north. The first lay slightly to the east of the hamlet of Oosttaverne, and was known as the Oosttaverne Line. The second chord position, known as the Warneton Line, crossed the Lys at Warneton, and ran roughly parallel to the Oosttaverne Line a little more than a mile to the east of it.

The natural advantages of the position were exceptional, and during more than two years of occupation the enemy had devoted the greatest skill and industry to developing them to the utmost. Besides the villages of Messines and Wytschaete, which were organized as main centers of resistance, numerous woods, farms and hamlets lent themselves to the construction of defensive points.

Captured documents and the statements of prisoners proved the importance attached by the enemy to the position. His troops in the line were told that the coming battle might well prove decisive, and that they were to resist to the last. They were assured that strong reserves were available to come to their assistance and to restore the battle should the British attack succeed in penetrating their lines.

At 3.10 a. m. on the 7th of June the nineteen mines were exploded simultaneously beneath the enemy's defenses. At the same moment our guns opened and our infantry assault was launched. Covered by a concentrated bombardment, which overwhelmed the enemy's trenches and to a great extent neutralized his batteries, our troops swept over the German foremost defenses all along the line.

The attack proceeded from the commencement in almost exact accordance with the time-table. The enemy's first trench system offered little resistance to our advance, and the attacking brigades—English, Irish, Australian, and New Zealand—pressed on up the slopes of the ridge to the assault of the crest line.

At 5.30 a. m. Ulster regiments had already reached their second objectives, including l'Enfer Hill and the southern defenses of Wytschaete, while on their left a South of Ireland Division fought their way through Wytschaete Wood. At 7 a. m. New Zealand troops had captured Messines. Men from the western counties of England had cleared the Grand Bois. Other English county regiments had reached the Dam Strasse, and all along the battle front our second objectives had been gained.

Only at a few isolated points did the resistance of the enemy's infantry cause any serious delay. Northeast of Messines our infantry were held up for a time by machine-gun fire from a strong point known as Fanny's Farm, but the arrival of a tank enabled our progress to be resumed. So rapid was the advance of our infantry, however, that only a few tanks could get forward in time to come into action. Heavy fighting took place in Wytschaete, and further north London troops encountered a serious obstacle in another strong point known as the White Chateau. This redoubt was captured while the morning was yet young, and before midday the two Irish Divisions had fought their way side by side through the defenses of Wytschaete.

Our troops then began to move down the eastern slopes of the ridge, and the divisions in the center of our attack who had farthest to go, gradually drew level with those on either flank. About 2,000 prisoners had already been brought in, and Australian and English troops had reached the first of the enemy's guns. Our own guns had begun to move forward.

Further fighting took place in Ravine Wood, where English county regiments and London troops killed many Germans, and short-lived resistance was encountered at other points among the many woods and farm houses. Bodies of the enemy continued to hold out in the eastern end of Battle Wood and in strong points constructed in the spoil banks of the Ypres-Comines Canal. Except at these points, our troops gained their final objectives on both flanks early in the afternoon. In the center we had reached a position running approximately parallel to the Oosttaverne Line and from 400 to 800 yards to the west of it. The guns required for the attack upon this line had been brought forward, and the troops and tanks detailed to take part were moving up steadily. Meanwhile the bridges and roads leading out of the triangle formed by the River Lys and the canal were kept under the fire of our artillery.

The final attack began soon afterwards, and by 3.45 p. m. the village of Oosttaverne had been captured. At 4 p. m. troops from the northern and western counties of England entered the Oosttaverne line east of the village and captured two batteries of German field guns. Half an hour later other English battalions broke through the enemy's position further north. Parties of the enemy were surrendering freely, and his casualties were reported to be very heavy. By the evening the Oosttaverne line had been taken, and our objectives had been gained.

The rapidity with which the attack had been carried through, and the destruction caused by our artillery, made it impossible at first to form more than a rough estimate of our captures. When the final reckoning had been completed, it was found that they included 7,200 prisoners, 67 guns, 94 trench mortars and 294 machine guns.

During the night our infantry consolidated the captured positions; while tanks patrolled the ground east of the Oosttaverne Line, and in the early morning of June 8th assisted in the repulse of an enemy counter-attack up the Wambeke valley. At 4 a. m. on the same morning our troops captured a small portion of German trench near Septieme Barn, where the enemy had resisted our first attack. That evening, at 7 p. m., after an intense bombardment, the enemy counter-attacked along practically the whole of our new line, but was repulsed at all points.

Consolidation and the establishment of advanced posts continued during the following four days, in the course of which Australian troops captured La Potterie Farm, southeast of Messines, and the hamlet of Gapaard was occupied.

Our progress on the right of the battle front made the enemy's positions between the Lys River and St. Yves very dangerous, and he now gradually began to evacuate them. Our patrols kept close touch with the enemy, and by the evening of June 14th the whole of the old German front and support lines north of the Lys had passed into our possession.

That evening we again attacked south and east of Messines and on both sides of the Ypres-Comines Canal, and met with complete success. The strong points in which the enemy had held out north of the canal were captured, and our line was advanced on practically the whole front from the River Warnave to Klein Zillebeke.

BY FRANK FOX

The Battle of Messines marked another step in the progressive deterioration of the German position on the Western front. The enemy had been hustled off the Somme ridges and had found himself compelled in consequence to evacuate the Somme district. He had been hustled off the Artois ridges and was able to keep the Lens coal basin and the Douai Plain below only by continuous sacrifice of men and material. He was now to be pushed off the ridges around Ypres, the last of his old bulwarks facing the British line. Of these ridges the Messines Ridge was the most formidable.

Messines Ridge may be described as the German point of concentration against Calais. It was wrested from us, after fierce fighting, during the first Battle of Ypres in 1914, and was supposed to give the enemy Ypres and the road to Calais. The French came to the rescue, retook Messines Ridge, and lost it again in December, 1914, since which date the Germans had held it without serious challenge. It did not give the Germans Ypres nor the road to Calais, because the stubborn British Army refused to recognize the "military impossibility" of holding Ypres with the enemy dominating the ruined town from Messines; but it did give the enemy the means to inflict constant and serious losses on our troops; and while they held it, the Germans could still pretend to hope for some future successful assault, which would win for them the French Channel ports and the means to compel Great Britain to peace. Now that hope was to be dissipated very plainly, so plainly as to make its message comprehensible to the dullest German. The Battle of Messines Ridge proclaimed that there was little hope of another German offensive on the Western front in this war, that the rôle of the German Army now is the dispiriting one of holding on to positions until it suits the attack to turn them out.

Advantage was taken of the delay to perfect preparations. The famous Mine of Messines, which was very literally to blast the German out of his front positions on June 7, 1917, was in 1916 already in being, though it was afterwards extended. The German still rages and grumbles about that Messines Mine. It infuriated him just as the tank infuriated him. The one supremacy that he felt sure was left to him in this war was in regard to science and material. He might not be able to put such good men into the line, might be beaten in the matter of quick adaptable courage in the field, but his Herr Professors, he reckoned, had an invulnerable supremacy. His machines would always be better.

Now, in this matter of the Mine of Messines, the Herr Geology Professors on the German side knew quite well that you could not mine to any extent around Messines. The water-logged strata would not allow of it, so Fritz could sleep easily in his trench, so far as mines were concerned; and Fritz, confident in his Herr Professors, altogether neglected any attempt to counter-mine. But on our side there was a Geology Professor who knew better, and the Messines Mine, the greatest ever used in warfare, was the result.

It was the only element of surprise in the battle. In the preparation of the Arras push the British forces had been able to introduce a good deal of the element of surprise. The Artois country made concealment of the preliminary operations (road-making, etc.) possible, and the last great deployment was protected from observation by a successful air offensive. In the preparation of the Messines Battle, effective concealment was out of the question. All the low marshy country on our side of the Messines Ridge was under constant enemy observation. We could not make a road nor push a light railway forward without the fact being known. And to give an offensive any chance at all in these marsh lands it was necessary to build many roads and many light railways to bring up supplies for guns and troops. In the Flanders plain country, barely above sea-level, always water-logged, traversed by innumerable ditches, wheeled traffic can never pass except by a built road, and only rarely can foot traffic leave the granite-paved roads with safety. To effect a big concentration of troops, roads and railways had to be multiplied, and this work done under German observation.

The Battle of Messines had, therefore, to be a "pitched

battle," with ample notice to the defense that an attack was preparing. Indeed, the date of the attack could be forecasted fairly accurately by the enemy (who was only one day out in his reckoning, as the event proved), and he was able to make the best preparation of which he was capable. He might be excused for viewing the position with some confidence. The ridge on which he sat was of great natural strength and formidably fortified. The marshy country through which we had to advance to any attack gave little cover; the routes which the advance must follow were accurately known and "registered" for artillery barrages.

Messines was distinguishable in the current account as an "Irish Day." The Wytschaete end of the ridge was taken by Irish battalions, in which were Ulster men and South of Ireland men, men who take different sides in the religious and political controversies which separate Ireland (not at all so sharply, in my humble opinion, as many think), but who took a common view as to the necessity of ending the German threat to human civilization. A very gallant gentleman, Major Willie Redmond, M.P., one of the leading figures in "Nationalist" Ireland, gave up his life in this battle, and around the place where he fell the Irishmen of the North and of the South were fighting in brotherly comradeship, showing an Irish unity which could not be questioned. An "Irish Day" certainly, Messines, and no one will grudge them the honor; least of all the Australians and New Zealanders who had, too, a big share in the victory, and who find themselves embarrassed sometimes by the amount of attention which is given to their exploits.

As for the English troops, who, of course, had the largest share in this and other battles on the Western front, they have never to expect a degree of popular notice commensurate with their work; and, to do them justice, I do not think they "grouse" to any extent at the working of the inexorable publicity law which deprives them of "paragraph value." Newspapers must give attention to the abnormal, the unusual, to the outstanding group rather than the mass.

Again, on the principle that it is the unusual that is "news," accounts of the Battle of Messines concentrate most attention on the great mine explosion which heralded the struggle. It was, of course, helpful—singularly so. But it was not the whole battle, nor even an essential to its success. Two pen-pictures of the great explosion follow:

From the *Morning Post:*—"The ground opened below the brim of Wytschaete as though the furnace door of Hades itself had been thrown back, and an enormous fountain of fire spurted into the sky. It was infinitely terrifying. Another fountain gushed on the right, and still another on the left. The black shadows of the slope turned to flame as the mines went up, and with them stout trenches. The scarred face of Hill 60, a score of redoubts, and long banks of wire vanished in the night, and when the dawn came there remained only dreadful gaps and fissures in the naked earth, where our men afterwards found embedded the bodies of many of their enemies. The earth rocked as though a giant hand had roughly shaken it. Then the guns began anew."

From Reuter's correspondent:—"At the prearranged moment the biggest thing ever attempted in mining operations rent the sky with a terrible glare and an ear-splitting crash as a long series of mines, some of which were dug over a year ago, were blown along the enemy positions. The aggregate total of the charges touched off in these earth-shattering eruptions was well over a million pounds of high explosives. The villages of Messines and Wytschaete have totally vanished. From the north of Hill 60 to the south of Ploegsteert the enemy's terrain looks like the face of the Long Valley at Aldershot after an August field-day. The spectacle is incredible. The whole geography of the district has been churned and blown and furrowed out of recognition, and how many stark Huns lie amid the hecatomb the Recording Angel alone can tell, for the enemy has been expecting this attack, and had brought up masses of troops to try to withstand the onslaught. The existence of these German soldiers for the past week baffles all efforts of imagination. Prisoners taken during raids state that no food worth speaking of has reached their front since the terrific bombardment began. They were reduced by hunger to the lowest ebb of morale."

Following the mine explosion, the artillery barrage began from the groups of artillery which kept to their positions, whilst other groups of artillery at once moved forward following on the heels of the infantry. A swarm of aëroplanes also rose and advanced on the enemy. It is not much to the discredit of the German soldier that in the first few minutes of the battle he did not "stick it." The gun-flogging he had had for a fortnight had got on his nerves. He had been kept short of food. He saw now thousands of his comrades blown up in the air by an explosion which made a record for this or any other war. We took the first system of the enemy's defenses with little trouble, collecting the remnants of the German front-line garrison as prisoners. The harvest of prisoners was unexpectedly rich. The enemy had reënforced his line considerably, and was further reënforcing it when we attacked. Some regiments had all their battalions in line (instead of one in line, one in support, and one in reserve). In one sector a Bavarian Division was relieving a Saxon Division at the hour of the attack, and we levied on both for the prisoners' cages.

Later in the day the German resistance stiffened. As captured documents showed, the German Command had given instructions that the positions on Messines Ridge were to be held at all hazards; and to keep up the courage of the front-line troops it was announced to them that great reserves were collected to come to their aid whenever an attack was developed. The opinion has been ventured in a previous section that probably the German plan was reconciled to the loss for a while of the front system of defenses and hoped that our attack would land us just that far, in an utterly ruined position from which we could be ejected with great loss by counter-attacks from the second system of defense. That opinion seemed to be borne out by the progress of the day's fighting. But even at the second line the resistance was not as stubborn as had been expected. In Wytschaete Wood, a wood in which every tree had been reduced to a splintered stump by our shell fire, a tough fight was put up by a Prussian battalion. The wood was studded with pill-boxes, and a wild tangle of wire and débris made the going underfoot exceedingly difficult. The pill-boxes were connected by galleries, and other galleries connected the far edge of the wood with the Hospice and with the cellars of Wytschaete. The artillery preparation had demolished some of the pill-boxes, but not all. At one moment it seemed as if the infantry would be held up here, but our men, rushing forward with bayonets, shouting the while, terrified the enemy, and the wood was cleared.

At Battle Wood, on the left wing of the attack, there was also some stubborn fighting. But on the whole Messines was a cheap victory. Careful organization had foreseen and provided for every contingency of the day, and we won a great result at a relatively small cost in casualties.

It was impossible for the Germans to allow the loss of this key-position to their Flanders coast-line to go unchallenged. But their effort to retake Messines was a dismal failure, and gave proof of a degree of demoralization that had never before been shown by the Germans in a big field of action. The counter-attack was made 36 hours after our initial success. That was too late to take advantage of the confusion which must follow in some degree a successful advance. It was too early to permit of a thorough preparation on the German part. Falling between the two stools of "early" and "thorough," it was a sheer waste of men, and must have added greatly to losses which were already huge. The full extent of those losses will probably never be known, so many bodies and guns rest under the débris of the giant mine.

BY FREIHERR VON DER OSTEN SACKEN

This article, by one of Germany's most noted critics, was published in the Fall of 1917

The plans of our enemies for a general offensive in the spring of 1917 were broken up by the Russian revolution, which took Russia for the time out of the war. England, however, actuated by the submarine danger, was unwilling to put off her own offensive, and France was completely dependent upon England.

So on the 9th of April, after very heavy artillery preparation, the English launched a mass attack on the Artois front. Resolved to force a break through between Douai and Cambrai, Sir Douglas Haig used twenty-eight divisions, consisting of 500,000 men, that is, half of the entire English infantry force in France, on a front of thirty-four kilometers, and later sent sixteen more divisions to their support. Overwhelming as was this force, it was destined to achieve only initial successes. By the second day its advance was stopped, and the battle broke up into limited local engagements. The most important of these took place on the 23rd, 27th, and 28th of April and the 5th of May. All of these were preliminary to a greater attack in June; but the preliminaries had proved so expensive that the main attack had to be delayed. After six weeks of fighting the British had lost 200,000 men, without having penetrated farther than our front trenches. Their effort had exhausted itself, though desultory fighting continued here and there.

Meanwhile the French offensive along a sixty-kilometer front on the Aisne and in Champagne was held up by insufficient artillery support, so that it did not begin until April 16th. The attackers sacrificed themselves without stint, but made progress only at the beginning, although General Nivelle drew from the other fronts all the troops that could possibly be spared. In the end he had engaged seventy-two divisions, amounting to 450,000 men, or two-thirds of his whole army. On April 17th he was obliged to cease his attacks, and was unable to renew them until the 5th and 6th of May. He then undertook a second assault, which was quite as costly and ineffectual as the first. In all, he lost 200,000 men. He was now succeeded by General Pétain, a man of ability but limited by the condition of the army, which he found greatly shaken by its terrible sacrifices and record of defeat. The slight gain of territory which the French could show for their efforts soon crumbled away.

Matters went no better for the French at Verdun, where we slowly made progress along the left bank of the Meuse. From Verdun eastward to the Swiss border the first half of 1917 was marked by minor engagements only.

In the meanwhile the English had prepared their great

new attack. Their objective this time was our position in the Wytschaete bend, which was naturally weak. On June 7th, after a severe bombardment lasting several weeks, accompanied toward the end by violent mine explosions, ten English divisions went over the top. Again their success in spite of great sacrifices was only temporary. The attack broke down against our positions between Hollebeke and Warneton and was not renewed.

Seldom has such vast effort met such little reward. Our nation has reason indeed to be satisfied with the High Commanding officers who have thus calmly turned back Britain's noisiest effort. We are convinced now that our line in the West is secure against all that our enemies can do. We have still before us the opportunity and the power to "win the War in the East."

GREECE ENTERS THE WAR

VENIZELOS SUPERSEDES KING CONSTANTINE

JUNE 12TH-JULY 2ND

AUGUSTE GAUVAIN   COMMISSIONER JONNART
KING CONSTANTINE   KING ALEXANDER

In 1914 Greece had been vigorously pro-Ally in sentiment. She was only held back from the War by her German-descended king, Constantine. To accomplish this, he overthrew the constitution and dismissed the people's chosen leader, Venizelos. This, as our 1916 volume showed, brought on a revolution in Greece, and Venizelos had made eastern Greece a republic. In Athens itself, however, the disastrous fate of Serbia and Rumania had led the people to give approval to their king's high-handed course, since it had kept them from any such disaster. Hence Constantine's popularity increased.

The Ally view, on the other hand, was that Constantine's falsity to his constitutional oath and to the original will of his people, had caused all the Balkan disasters. Greek aid at the beginning, instead of Greek opposition, would have enabled them to checkmate Turkey, prevent Bulgaria entering the War, and so saved all the Balkans from ravage and starvation. Hence, as Constantine grew more defiant, the Allied Powers grew more severe in blockading Greece and in supporting Venizelos.

Autocratic Russia had upheld autocratic Greece. With the downfall of Russian Autocracy and the entry of American Democracy into the War, the Allies resolved suddenly to endure no more of Constantine's clearly proven duplicity. The account of their changing attitude and of the strife in Athens is here given by the French Minister who saw it all, M. Gauvain.

The Allies named a French Senator and former Governor of Algeria, M. Jonnart, as their High Commissioner to act for them in deposing Constantine and restoring the disrupted constitutional régime under Venizelos. The Commissioner's official statements are given here, as also the parting words of King Constantine and the pledges with which his second son, Alexander, assumed the throne.

There had been much discussion as to whether Greece should continue as a monarchy or as a republic, Venizelos having already set up republican forms in eastern Greece. Ultimately the Allies and Venizelos agreed that the Greek people would be best satisfied if no present revolution were enacted, but only the old régime restored as it had been before Constantine defied the constitution. Hence the parliament which Constantine had arbitrarily dismissed nearly two years before, was recalled to office; Venizelos became again Prime Minister, and

221

the crown was transferred to young Alexander, who had not been prominently connected with his father's arbitrary proceedings. Monarchy was frankly declared to be having its last trial. Could a Greek king really reign after the British instead of the German model?

Alexander's opening proclamation seemed to promise that he would imitate his father. Later, however, it was learned that this proclamation had been written for him by one of his father's pro-German friends. Alexander repudiated it, and delivered a throne speech pledging himself to reign in subordination to the parliament, instead of in defiance of its laws.

The new-old parliament promptly, on July 2nd, voted to join the Allies in the War.

BY AUGUSTE GAUVAIN

DURING the last days of November, 1916, there was extreme confusion in Athens. The Military League was reconstituted. The officers stirred up the soldiers in their barracks, the reservists were armed, the disorderly elements were enrolled by the agents of General Dousmanis. Fights broke out in the streets; many Venizelists were roughly handled. On the 26th a detachment of 200 French marines came to reënforce the little contingent encamped at the Zappeion. In the capital an artificial excitement increased hour by hour. In the provinces, where none existed, the government counterfeited it. It pictured an uprising of the peasants in Thessaly, a massacre of the soldiers at Ecaterini. Now, nowhere had the Thessalian peasants stirred, and the very prefect of Larissa himself acknowledged that not a word had been heard about rebellion in his province. As for the evzones (light-armed troops in native costume), not one had been harmed. That did not, however, hinder the Gounarists from ordering a solemn requiem—forbidden at the last minute—to "celebrate the entrance into immortality of the heroes who had fallen gloriously in a battle against the traitors." By dint of these tragi-comedies an agitation was produced which threatened at any instant to be transformed into riots and massacres. During the night of the 27th very many houses in which Venizelists lived were marked with red circles. The leaders of the reservists proclaimed that they would hinder by force the surrender of weapons even if the government permitted it. Trenches were dug in the immediate neighborhood of Athens, and emplacements for machine guns and artillery were prepared.

In spite of all these unfavorable signs, the confidence of Admiral Dartige and of General Bousquier, the French military attaché, in an amicable solution appeared unshaken. On the 29th the admiral had a somewhat long interview with the king. On the 30th the general too was given an audience by Constantine I. In the course of these conversations both were convinced that the king desired only that they should force his hand and that a simple outward manifestation of force would make it possible to gain all that they had demanded. The king, it was said, had formally declared that the Greek troops would offer no resistance; he had even had this assurance given in writing by the marshal of the court. During the 30th vessels carrying French troops cast anchor in the harbor of Pireus. They had orders to disembark the next morning and, without cannon or convoy of munitions and supplies, to go and occupy certain positions and take charge of a prescribed amount of war material that was to be handed over to them. The expedition was organized like an ordinary field maneuver in time of peace, with the conviction that it would encounter no resistance. Admiral Dartige, in fact, expressed to some newspaper correspondents "his full conviction" that the cannons would be delivered without any disturbance of the peace. He added that he "had not the slightest intention of resorting to force."

This optimism was not shared by the Athenians. Since the night of the 29th the troops of the garrison of Athens had left their barracks to take up positions in the environs of the city, especially at Goudi and Chalandri. By authority of a decree published on the 29th, authorizing voluntary engagements, an indirect mobilization was effected. More than 10,000 men "volunteered" the first day and were at once incorporated in the force. The instructions given to the military authorities prescribed that they should not hinder the disembarking of the Allied troops, but should follow them in equal numbers and oppose the execution of the orders of Admiral Dartige. The principal buildings of Athens

were occupied by Greek marines. The inhabitants of the
city who were witnesses of these preparations and of a multitude of little characteristic incidents, got the impression
that a conflict was inevitable. The newspapers informed
their readers to this effect.

On Thursday, the 30th of November, at half-past six
in the afternoon, Admiral Dartige received the official reply
of the Greek Government, elaborated in several successive
meetings of the Cabinet. It was a refusal. The admiral was
not surprised, for he believed that Constantine I. wanted to
have his hand forced by a demonstration of military force.
Consequently, on the morning of Friday, December 1st, several French detachments, equipped as though for a dress
parade, disembarked and advanced in different directions.
They soon clashed with troops entrenched along the two principal roads that lead from the sea to Athens. The Greek
soldiers blocked their way and opened fire. Immediately the
royalists posted on the emplacements began to fire volleys
with their machine guns not only upon the Allied detachments but also on the French quartered at the Zappeion and
on the annex of the English Legation, which served as the
headquarters of the Anglo-French police. The Anglo-French
defended themselves valiantly. But, caught by treachery,
they endured cruel losses, for which, however, they made
the enemy pay dearly. I shall not go into numbers here, nor
shall I describe the vicissitudes of this deplorable day. I
shall limit myself to a few statements of fact. The Greeks,
whether reservists or soldiers of the standing army, took the
initiative in firing without the slightest provocation, and
even before the Allies had tried to take away a single cannon. They fired on troops quartered in a public building and
engaged in peaceful occupations. They fired through the
windows at those of the Allies who had taken refuge in
buildings where, on the word of Greek officers, they had believed themselves safe, they acted exactly as though they
had received definite orders. They were posted in such positions that it was almost impossible to reply to their fire
without hitting some of the most celebrated monuments of
Athens. They had taken the ground immediately surround-

ing the Acropolis as their base of operations. If the fleet, moored before Salamis with its vessels broadside toward the Acropolis, had wished to destroy with its shells the batteries or the massed troops, it would have run great risk of blowing up a part of the celebrated temple. Even if the sacred marbles had received only some slight scratches from shrapnel, the Allies would none the less have been denounced to the whole world, especially to hesitating neutrals, as barbarians that had fallen lower than Vandals or Huns.

In lack of preliminary arrangements or of orders issued in the course of the drama, the grand Allied fleet remained almost inert. Only a few shells were fired on the garden of the Royal Palace. Blockaded in the Zappeion, to which he had gone at the beginning of the day, Admiral Dartige was neither able to go out from the Zappeion so as to go directly to the palace, which was near at hand, nor to have orders sent down to the fleet. The ministers of the Entente were no whit wiser or bolder than he. We should like to be able to blot out this page of our history. While our soldiers were falling under the blows of assassins, negotiations began once more.

This was a surrender. Count Bosdari, Minister of Italy, agreed to it only upon the insistence of his colleagues. "It made me blush for France," he said a few hours later to one of our countrymen. Not only were our decimated detachments forced to beat a sad retreat, leaving to others the duty of burying their dead and of caring for their wounded, but our companies, encamped at the Zappeion, and all our other posts were reëmbarked. Admiral Dartige left the Zappeion about seven o'clock in the morning to return on board his vessel. The survivors of the companies who had stayed with him the entire day (December 1st) endured the depth of humiliation. As they possessed no means of transport for their material, military trucks were furnished them by the Minister of War of Constantine I. on the request of the admiral and the French minister. Along with the soldiers of the different branches of the Allied control, these brave men, among whom were to be seen many who had fought at Verdun or at Dixmude, regained the quay of embarkation under the escort of Greek soldiers.

The 2nd of December beheld even worse horrors. According to the testimony of a witness, "the hunting out of the Venizelists was a truly horrible business to which nothing can be compared unless it be the Massacre of Saint Bartholomew's Eve." The prominent Venizelists of Athens and Pireus were massacred, tortured and imprisoned. Their houses were pillaged from garret to cellar. The offices and presses of the liberal newspapers were destroyed. No help was given to the pursued. They were forced to endure outrages and sufferings of all kinds without having the consolation of hearing or seeing any help coming from the powers who ought to have protected their country. The mayor of Pireus, escaping from torture, said to a Frenchman: "In the whole history of France there is not a single example of a similar abandonment."

It was true. There certainly is not in the history of France an example of a like humiliation accepted so resignedly. After the retreat of all our contingents, the evacuation of all our posts and the abandonment of the control of all public utilities, there was an exodus of our nationals. The French of Attica, the personnel of the French School of Archæology, our merchants and our journalists fled, with the surviving Venizelists, from that land where Constantine I. ruled in blood. On the 4th of December a cortège of Venizelists in chains marched past the French School. French citizenship, which had been respected for a hundred years in all Greek lands, had become an object of derision.

While these new negotiations were hanging fire, Constantine I. and his accomplices gloried loudly in their triumph. The pursuit of the Venizelists, though less savage, continued and the pillage of their houses went on. Taking the diplomatic offensive, the Lambros Cabinet sent to its representatives abroad a dispatch in which it claimed that it had been compelled to repress an insurrection. "The investigation which is being actively pushed," said this communication, "will show the existence of an antidynastic plot, fomented by the Venizelist party, which took advantage of the riots resulting from the skirmishes in the streets. It was only owing to the measures taken by the government that the conspirators could be arrested and the perfect order that now reigns could be restored." A repression so moderate of a rebellion so criminal certainly deserved congratulation, and the Minister of War actually did congratulate the troops of the Athens garrison and "the other combatants" in an order of the day, of which these passages are worth remembering: "It is with a heart overflowing with gratitude that, by order of his majesty the king, your commander-in-chief, I address to you my felicitations and congratulations on your exemplary conduct during those never-to-be-forgotten days, the 1st and 2nd of December. Your loyalty, your spirit of self-sacrifice and your courage have saved our fatherland jeopardized by enemies who hoped to disturb public order and overthrow the dynasty. Our enemies must now realize that such valiant troops are invincible, and I can from now on view the future with confidence."

On their part the royalist newspapers celebrated in big headlines, "the retreat of the Allied forces before the irresistible attack of the Greek troops," and enumerated the prisoners taken on the 1st of December. Others were glad "that the heroes of Kilkish had had the honor of fighting the heroes of the Somme and Verdun." The newspaper *Nea Hemera* wrote: "The 1st and 2nd of December have been, we are proud to say, two of the greatest, the holiest, the most splendidly glorious days in all Greek history. They may be regarded as the dawn of the real independence of Greece, delivering her from the most hateful yoke which has ever menaced the existence of our race."

The Allies, who had been represented to the Greek people as having confiscated the instruments of national defense, —in particular, the French and English allies (for care was taken not to raise disturbances in the neighborhood of the Italian and Russian embassies),—were denounced, through the machinations of the king, as enemies of the Greek people. Constantine I. had cunningly persuaded us to formulate claims that were sure to wound Greek national pride and had urged us to proceed to the execution of our demands by force. He had then thrown against our unsuspecting soldiers bands of highly excited Greeks, and in short, thus killing two birds with one stone, he had suppressed those Venizelists whom he had resolved to hinder, even by fire and sword, from regaining power by legal means.

On the 16th of January, after a Crown Council, which had been specially called, the government of Athens decided to yield. It declared "that it had no idea of procuring any limitations to the acceptance of the demands formulated by the powers and that it gave its adherence to the precise terms as announced." On the 24th of January the *Official Journal* of Athens published a decree deposing from office General Callaris, commanding the 1st corps of the army. On the 25th Mr. Zalocostas addressed the following letter to the representatives of the Quadruple Entente: "Conformably to the promise given in its reply to the ultimatum of the Allied governments dated January 8th, the royal government presents formal apologies to their excellencies, the Ministers of France, Great Britain, Italy and Russia because of the regrettable incidents of the 1st of December, 1916." On the 29th, in the presence of the ministers and before detachments of the land and sea forces of the four powers, in Zappeion Square, the Greek troops commanded by a Greek general and Prince Andrew, the king's brother, marched solemnly by and saluted the Allied colors. On the same day, Mr. Zalocostas informed M. Guillemin that the dissolution of the societies of reservists had been declared and that the judiciary had been charged with the extension of this measure.

Such was the outcome of this long diplomatic duel. We obtained a nominal satisfaction, but in reality Constantine I. came out of the conflict not only exonerated but with reputation enhanced. Under the inspiration of his hidden councilors who were always with him, he continued to elude the effective execution of the guarantees accepted by his government.

This diplomatic bickering was succeeded by skirmishing between the Allies and the administration. The time-limit of fifteen days, set by the declaration of the 8th of January, elapsed, but the prescribed transfers of troops and war material had not been effected, the controls which had been provided for had not been established, and the reparation to the victims of the 1st and 2nd of December had not been made. Mr. Lambros and his civil and military coadjutors employed every artifice to avoid the execution of the conditions laid down by the Entente. The soldiers transported to the Peloponnesus made their way back again in citizen's dress or on military leave of absence; or better yet, such men as were needed north of the Isthmus of Corinth were dressed up as police, if indeed they were not turned into comitadjis outright. Lies were told about the contents of cases of weapons, and arms were cached in the earth. Informed of this by the Allied controllers, General Caubone, the new military attaché of France, presented claim on claim. Messrs. Lambros and Zalocostas dissimulated, denied, protested their good-will, evaded the issue and were profuse in promises. Meanwhile, the royalist newspapers invented calumny on calumny against the Allies. Their principal argument was furnished them in the continuation of the blockade; they proclaimed that the Entente was starving the people; they organized indignation meetings, and saw that repeated entreaties and petitions were sent to the king. In order not to permit public opinion to be led astray, the ministers of the Entente, on the 19th of February, caused to be published in the newspapers a declaration to the Greek people summing up the situation as follows:

"The representatives of the Allies have already called the attention of the royal government to the hostile attitude of the Greek press and to the danger that Greece will incur if she persists in fostering public excitement and in making attacks that are as often as not founded on calumny and lies. For example, in the matter of the blockade, certain newspapers are trying to spread the impression that this is unjustly maintained since Greece has, as they say, fulfilled all her engagements. This is manifestly inexact. The military control of the Allies cannot take the responsibility of declaring that the promised guarantees have been given, while there remains in continental Greece a great quantity of arms, the existence of which is recognized by the Greek Government itself since it has prescribed to the authorities the date on which they must be surrendered. The Allied control is all the less justified in consenting to leave these arms on this side of the Peloponnesus, since they might be employed by the hostile organizations which continue to exist in all parts of Greece and especially in Thessaly, where they constitute a perpetual menace to the oriental army. Other important facts have been brought directly to the knowledge of the Greek Government by the chief of the Allied control,—for example, the laying of mines on the banks of the Corinth canal. In these circumstances the Greek people ought not to be surprised that the Allies, in default of that correct attitude which they have a right to expect on the part of Greece, cannot regard the guarantees stipulated in the note of January 8th as having yet been yielded. Nevertheless, far from being indifferent to the sufferings of an innocent people, the Allied powers have already looked into the question of what measures they will take to furnish Greece with food supplies just as soon as circumstances will permit. In consequence, the Allied ministers call the attention of the Greek Government once more to the grave responsibility that it would incur if it tolerated any longer the excesses of the anti-Venizelist press, which seems to have no other design than to delude public opinion and thus hinder the reëstablishment of friendly relations between Greece and the Allied powers."

This appeal to common sense provoked in Greece a redoubling of recriminations and calumnies. New journals were even created specially charged with vilifying the Allies. Ever since the 2nd of December the Venizelist newspapers had ceased to appear. The public could only look for information to the organs of King Constantine. It was thus kept in an utterly abnormal state of ferment. The Lambros Cabinet took advantage of this to oppose to the demands of the Allies exceptions or contestations that were increasingly irritating.

On the 19th of April, in a meeting at Saint-Jean-de-Maurienne, Messrs. Ribot, Lloyd George, Boselli and Sonnino discussed, among other subjects, the Greek question. Their decision was not divulged, but a few days later the

court at Athens showed symptoms of uneasiness. The
rumor of Mr. Lambros' resignation was current. Mr.
Lambros, a mere tool of the king, had no special reason for
withdrawing nor even any desire to do so. If the power left
his hands, it was because the monarch judged it advantageous
to sacrifice this minister to the supposed rancor of the Entente. There was some talk of Mr. Zaïmis, who had become
once more the governor of the National Bank, as future
Prime Minister. These tentative moves had a somewhat
cool reception in the French press. The change of person,
as proposed, would have brought us no satisfaction. For
some time, there was no further mention of it. But another
rumor spread. An intention to abdicate in favor of the
Crown Prince was attributed to Constantine I. The French
press observed that neither Greece nor the Entente would
gain anything by the change. Since, after the appointment
of the Ribot ministry, the censor had allowed greater freedom to the press, it demanded the definitive and radical
settlement of the Greek question. It demanded of the powers
that had signed the declaration of the 8th of January to
reclaim their liberty of action in accordance with the formal
clause that had provided for this eventuality, and to act
vigorously in Attica, or at least to permit the provisional
government to act by its own agencies in Thessaly and the
rest of the kingdom. These articles in the French journals
were much commented on in Athens. People believed that
they saw in them the precursors of grave measures.

On the first of May the Congress of Hellenic Colonies, assembled at Paris, declared Constantine I. and all
his dynasty deposed from the throne and from all royal
prerogatives. At the same time it "appealed to the benevolence of the Allied powers no longer to hinder any province
from giving its adherence freely to the national government
at Salonika" and begged them "to recognize the Greek Republic just as soon as the assembly called to constitute it
should have proclaimed it." Then the Zaïmis clique appeared
once more, and was accepted on the 3rd of May. After
long parleys Mr. Zaïmis consented to leave his position at
the National Bank to take upon himself once more the prime

ministry with the portfolio of foreign affairs. Almost all
his colleagues were professed anti-Venizelists.

Mr. Zaïmis had very little support in the press. Treated
as a suspect by the royalist editors who had been besought
to conceal their sentiments so as not to bring discredit on
the new royal cabinet, he was described by most of the Venizelists as a man of straw. The *Makedonia* characterized
him as "the Pilate of crucified Greece." In France a marked
distrust of him was evinced. Although he declared that
his entire program consisted in the reëstablishment of
friendly relations with the Entente, he was suspected of holding to these friendly relations only in order to permit the
king to gain more time and to corner the grain-harvest of
Thessaly for the exclusive advantage of the royalists. Besides, General Dousmanis, Colonel Metaxas, Messrs. Streit,
Mercouris and Co. kept hold of the power both public and
secret, and with it remained in the confidence of Constantine I. Mr. Zaïmis did, to be sure, immediately put at the
disposal of the commission on indemnities a meeting place
for which they had up to that time looked in vain. He did,
to be sure, announce that measures had been taken against
the armed bands that were overrunning Thessaly, and he
also let it be known that he was going to send away from
Athens seven colonels who were known to be hostile to the
Entente. Very small guarantees these to the Entente!

As a matter of fact, during the entire month of May, the
agents of control under General Cauboue kept discovering
arms and ammunition concealed in the capital itself, or in
the suburbs or the provinces. The police continued to dress
themselves up as comitadjis, and the comitadjis to disguise
themselves as police. The officers of Constantine's staff
elaborated as assiduously as ever the plans for coöperating
with the Germano-Bulgarians against the day so eagerly
longed for, the day when the soldiers of William II. would
descend on Salonika. Though to all appearance dissolved,
the League of Reservists was reconstituted under the direction of a nephew of Mr. Gounaris by the name of Sayas.
In reply to objections on the part of the Minister of the Interior, Mr. Sayas threatened the government "with an ex-

plosion of popular anger." As a substitute for the League
of Reservists or as a superstructure on it, there was formed,
under the auspices of Mr. Livieratos, a retired magistrate,
a so-called "Federation" of the syndicates of the different
trades and professions and of popular societies. The royalists gave out that this was a union of labor organizations,
but the real labor organizations entered a protest. Messrs.
Sayas and Livieratos, however, negotiated with Mr. Zaïmis
none the less freely, because of this fact, on an absolutely
equal footing. They issued a manifesto against the dismissal
of the seven colonels.

These were not the only indications of a dangerous situation. The authorities themselves assumed a provocative attitude. On the 21st of May a decree of arrest issued by the
grand jury brought before the assizes the director and man-
ager of the newspaper *Patris* on the score of having published in 1916 some letters that established the part taken by
Deputy Callimassiotis, a friend of Mr. Gounaris, in supplying the German submarines. On the 29th of May the navy
war-council sent forth an order for the arrest of Admiral
Coundouriotis for the crime of high treason. At the end
of the same month some Venizelists were beaten and imprisoned on the island of Ægina by the police. During the
night of the 30th-31st an attempt was made to assassinate
two English officers. A few days later some French officers
of the military control, on a tour of search, were obliged to
turn back before a party of reservists. The newspaper *Scrip*
accused the Senegalese of the expeditionary force of kid-
naping little children, killing and eating them.

At the same time the Constantine cult became a sort of
idolatry. On the 27th of May the second anniversary of
the miraculous cure of the king by the wonder-working
picture of the Panagia of Tenos, a thanksgiving service was
held at the Metropolitan Church, which the *Embros* reported
in the following words: "When the reverend orator, in-
comparable in the force of his logic and the brilliance of his
rhetoric, had affirmed in thundering words that King Constantine was not destined to be dethroned but to be crowned
with the imperial diadem in Constantinople, when he had fin-

ished chanting the hymn: 'Be victor, thou emperor and king,' the throng rushed forward to kiss the hands of the prelate, while on all sides reëchoed these cries: 'Down with the tyrants! Long live our adored king!'" On the 3rd of June, the king's fête, the followers of Constantine were carried away by another outburst of devotion to their sovereign. The Federation of Workingmen presented the monarch with an iron cross, begging him to wear it whenever he appeared before the troops with the bâton of a German field marshal in his hand. After the *Te Deum* at the cathedral Constantine I. betook himself to the University to take part in the dedication of his own bust. Two other busts of him were to be dedicated in the course of the month, one at the barracks of the 7th regiment of infantry and the other at the Chamber of Deputies. Fate, however, was reserving for Constantine a ceremony of quite a different nature.

During the month of May the Cabinets of Paris and London had come to an agreement. Their chiefs had held additional conferences in Paris and in London. Assured of the agreement of Russia and the consent of Italy, they had resolved on radical measures. Their decisions, the outcome of secret deliberations, became known only after they had been put in execution, and even then not fully. We may quite certainly say that they had a double object: the sequestration of the harvests in Thessaly so that they would profit all Greece, and the reëstablishment of the constitutional régime. Suspecting what was to happen as to the first part of the program, Mr. Zaïmis proposed to yield to the Allies a portion of the Thessalian harvest. As to the second part, the government in Athens did not know exactly in what this reëstablishment of the constitutional régime consisted. But it flattered itself that it could bring it to naught. The time has not come to tell what supreme efforts were put forth in order to make the Allies' enterprise miscarry as it had done in the month of June, 1916. This time these efforts failed.

On Wednesday, June 6th, the Athenians suddenly learned of the arrival in Greek waters of M. Jonnart, a French senator, invested with the rank of High Commissioner of the protecting powers. Then they noticed a great movement of

warships in the bay of Salamis, the Saronic Gulf and the
Gulf of Corinth. The royalists insinuated that it was going
to be just the same with the Jonnart mission as with the
earlier demonstrations of the Allies. Then they saw the
vessel that carried the High Commissioner, after a short stop
at Salamis, sail off to Salonika. What passed between M.
Jonnart, Mr. Venizelos and General Sarrail is not known.
On the 10th M. Jonnart returned to Salamis. On the 11th,
in the morning, the lightning struck. In an interview with
Mr. Zaïmis, the High Commissioner of the three protecting
powers demanded in their name the abdication of King Constantine and the designation of his successor, to the ex-
clusion of the Crown Prince. What then became of the tens
of thousands of heroes who had sworn to defend the king,
their idol, to the very last drop of their blood. They raised
a hue and cry, turbulent throngs filled the streets, but there
was no breach of the peace. What were the thoughts that
passed through the mind of Constantine I.? After bitter
reflections on the vicissitudes of mundane affairs, he decided
to submit. On Tuesday, between 9 and 10 in the morning,
Mr. Zaïmis informed M. Jonnart that "His Majesty the
King, solicitous as ever of the interests of Greece alone, has
decided to leave the country along with the Crown Prince
and has designated as his successor Prince Alexander," his
second son.

Constantine I. did not officially abdicate nor did his eldest
son resign his claim to the throne. They hoped without
doubt to be restored to Greece by William II., the Conqueror.
They left the throne in the meantime to a complacent prince
who would keep the crown for them, and they left the political power to a minister who would care for their interests.
But they went away without daring to defend themselves
or to have any defense made for them. They fled before
the storm, carrying with them the curse of Hellas. Embarked for Italy, they had not yet reached the residence of
their choice when their hopes were dashed. While they
slipped out of Lugano amid manifestations of public scorn,
Mr. Venizelos was starting for Athens. After a brief consultation, the High Commissioner decided, with Mr. Veni-

zelos and Mr. Zaïmis agreeing, that halfway measures would do no good and that the best thing was to restore the power to Mr. Venizelos, who would reassemble the Chamber elected June 13, 1915. No sooner said than done. In consequence of the publication of a proclamation in which he boasted of his desire to follow in the footsteps of his illustrious father, Alexander I. was required to apologize and to declare his willingness to respect the Constitution. He is now only the shadow of a king, obliged to content himself with signing the papers that his Prime Minister puts before him. The latter, acclaimed by the crowd, which, according to the statement of the paid agents of the German propaganda, hated him and was sure to tear him in pieces, has taken up with a firmer hand than ever, and with an increased prestige, the direction of national affairs.

BY COMMISSIONER JONNART
Ultimatum presented on June 11, 1917

The protecting powers of Greece have decided to reconstitute the unity of the kingdom without impairing the monarchical constitutional institutions that they have guaranteed to Greece. His Majesty King Constantine, having manifestly on his own initiative violated the Constitution of which France, England, and Russia are the trustees, I have the honor to declare to your Excellency that his Majesty the King has lost the confidence of the protecting powers, and that the latter consider themselves free toward him from the obligations resulting from their right of protection.

I have in consequence the mission, with a view of re-establishing the real Constitution, to ask for the abdication of his Majesty King Constantine, who will himself designate, together with the protecting powers, a successor among his heirs. I am under the obligation to ask from you an answer within twenty-four hours.

ATHENIAN PRESS REPORT

June 11th.

At 11.30 o'clock the Crown Council began, there being present, besides M. Zaïmis, M. Skouloudis, M. Lambros,

M. Dimitrakopoulos, M. Gounaris, M. Stratos, M. Kalogheropoulos, M. Rallis, and M. Dragoumis—all ex-Prime Ministers.

When they were seated, the king read to them the demands of the Allies. It is difficult to be quite sure of what happened, but it seems certain that when the king pronounced the fateful words demanding his abdication he turned toward them as for their opinion, and M. Gounaris [the pro-German leader] half rose and said: "Impossible! It is impossible that——" when the king stopped him, raised his hand, and said: "I have decided to accept."

The Council lasted till 2.30 o'clock, the Ministers insisting on seeing if a way of satisfying the Allies' demands could not be found without the abdication of the king, but it all ended in their recognizing the hopelessness of the situation, and the Council was dismissed by the king.

The demeanor of the Ministers as they came out showed the throng of waiting journalists that they had heard grave news, but they would not speak. M. Gounaris seemed incapable of speaking. M. Skouloudis, under whose Premiership Fort Rupel was handed over to the Bulgarians and the disasters of to-day largely prepared, was pale and shaking, and had to be assisted into his motor car. When he reached home he remained prostrate for a considerable time.

June 14th.

The departure of ex-king Constantine, with Queen Sophie, the Crown Prince, the princesses, and Prince Paul, which I witnessed this morning at Oropos, a small port in the Gulf of Eubœa, took place very quietly.

Oropos is a tiny fishing village with a small jetty. All the night and all the morning motor cars had been bringing the king's luggage. A number of the king's personal friends came to see him off. The late King George's yacht *Sphakteria* was refitted rapidly to receive the royal family, and lay off Oropos this morning escorted by two French destroyers whose Tricolors flapped broadly against the Eubœan hills.

The ex-king and queen and the Crown Prince arrived in motor cars shortly after 11 o'clock. The king wore a general's uniform and got slowly out of the car, which drew up close to the jetty, where two French officers stood rigidly. A small group of country people and schoolgirls mingled with M. Zaïmis, the Prime Minister, courtiers, and official personages.

The king was pale, but erect and composed. He took a bouquet of flowers which a small child on the top of a wall thrust out to him. People gave subdued cheers, and peasants on the jetty knelt as the king and queen passed them. The king made way for the queen, bidding the people let them pass. The royal family then quickly entered a waiting motor launch and were borne to their vessel.

The king was dignified and bowed and saluted, but he scarcely uttered a word from the moment of his arrival till the launch cast off. Several of his friends were weeping. One man threw himself in the water in an endeavor, apparently, to follow the royal boat, but he was rescued.

BY KING CONSTANTINE
Farewell proclamation of June 14, 1917

Yielding to necessity, accomplishing my duty towards Greece, and having in view only the interests of the country, I am leaving my dear country with the Crown Prince, leaving my son Alexander on the throne.

Still, when far from Greece, the queen and I will always preserve the same love for the Hellenic people. I beg all to accept my decision calmly and quietly, trusting in God, whose protection I invoke for the nation.

In order that my bitter sacrifice for my country may not be in vain, I exhort you, for the love of God, for the love of our country, if you love me, to maintain perfect order and quiet discipline, the slightest lapse from which, even though well-intentioned, might be enough to cause a great catastrophe.

The love and devotion which you have always manifested for the queen and myself, in days of happiness and sorrow alike, are a great consolation to us at the present time. May God protect Greece.

PROCLAMATION BY KING ALEXANDER

At the moment when my venerated father, making to the Fatherland the supreme sacrifice, intrusts me with the heavy duties of the Hellenic throne, I pray that God, granting his wishes, may protect Greece and permit us to see it once more united and strong.

In the grief of being separated in such painful circumstances from my well-beloved father I have the single consolation of obeying his sacred command. With all my energy I shall try to carry it out by following along the lines which so magnificently marked his reign, with the help of the people on whose love the Greek dynasty rests.

I have the conviction that, in obeying the will of my father, the people by their submission will contribute to our being able together to draw our well-beloved country out of the situation in which it now is.

PROCLAMATION BY COMMISSIONER JONNART

France, Great Britain, and Russia desire to see Greece independent, great, and prosperous, and they mean to defend the noble country, which they have liberated, against the united efforts of the Turks, Bulgarians, and Germans. They (the Entente Allies) are here to circumvent the maneuvers of the kingdom's hereditary enemies; they want to end the repeated violations of the Constitution and of the treaties and the deplorable intrigues which have resulted in the massacre of soldiers of the united countries.

Berlin until now has commanded Athens and has been gradually bringing the people under the yoke of the Bulgarians and Germans. We have resolved to reëstablish the constitutional rights and unity of Greece. The protecting powers have in consequence demanded the abdication of King Constantine. But they do not intend to touch the constitutional monarchy. They have no other ambitions than to assure the regular operation of the Constitution to which King George of glorious memory had always been scrupulously faithful and which King Constantine has ceased to respect.

Greeks! the hour of reconciliation has come. Your destinies are closely associated with those of the protecting powers. Your ideal is the same. Your hopes are the same. We appeal to your wisdom and patriotism. The blockade is now raised. Every reprisal against the Greeks, no matter by whom, will be pitilessly suppressed. No attempt against the public order will be tolerated. The property and liberty of all will be safeguarded. A new era of peace and work is opening before you.

Know that the protecting powers, respectful of the national sovereignty, have no intention of imposing upon the Greek people a general mobilization.

Long live Greece, united, great, and free!

BY KING ALEXANDER

Address to the Greek Parliament, delivered after taking the coronation oath on August 4, 1917

It is with sincere joy that I address this first greeting to the representatives of the nation. You know the events which brought about some months ago the division of the Hellenic State, but the benevolent solitude of the protecting powers of Greece succeeded, without sacrifices or an internal struggle, in reconstituting the national unity by the reëstablishment of liberal institutions. The conditions upon which the transmission of the royal power was effected have clearly shown the path to be followed in the future. They render necessary the appeal to the national sovereignty, so as to revise and consolidate at the same time as the throne a form of government established on the basis demanded by the popular will, to decide in the most precise fashion the extent of the sovereign rights of the people as well as the extent of the royal authority as defined by the Constitution, by giving it the democratic character which is the desire of the dynasty. "The royal power resides in the love of the people," but foreign events did not permit the immediate convocation of the National Assembly, and that is why, in order to inaugurate the new constitutional era which we are entering, we have repealed the decree which by a violation of the Constitution dissolved the Chamber, and have convoked this Chamber for its regular second session.

Gentlemen, I am glad to inform you that my Government, faithful to national tradition, has already given its foreign policy the orientation approved by the people at the elections of May 31 and ratified by the Chamber. After two glorious wars Greece desired peace, of which she had great need, in order to retrieve her sacrifices and to regain her strength with a view to reorganizing the State recently enlarged, and to render it capable of accomplishing its great civilizing mission in the East. Greece was therefore grieved to see a new war break out which would result in a general conflagration, setting against one another two worlds, two civilizations, and two opposed conceptions of nationalities and of humanity. Indeed, it would have been sufficient for little Greece to remember her traditions, her history, and her duty in order not to hesitate spontaneously to offer her feeble forces to that group in the conflict whose war aim was to defend the rights of nationalities and the liberty of peoples.

But more imperious obligations called Greece into the same camp, and she has therefore now adopted an attitude which duty and honor imposed upon her toward the brave and chivalrous ally—the defense of the rights of Hellenism and the debt of gratitude contracted for her original liberation and for the protection which she has always enjoyed. If it had been given to the entire nation to follow as soon as possible such a policy, it would more rapidly and more effectively have assured the defense of the country against the hereditary enemy. Part of the Greek Army has fortunately had occasion to prove at the front its value and morale by heroic acts, thanks to which Greece has been able to regain the esteem of the allied armies and foreign public opinion, and her prestige, until then so deeply sullied, and to avoid the national catastrophes which were threatening her. The heroism and self-sacrifice of the troops at the front are a most happy augury for the ultimate fate of the struggle undertaken by united Greece, for they are evidence of the fine pride and gallantry of the Hellenic Army.

Faithful to this policy, my Government has already recalled the representatives of Greece from the capitals of the enemy countries. The first result of this policy has been the decision taken at the last conference in Paris to re-establish in its integrity the sovereignty of the State by the abolition of all the controls recently imposed, and by the evacuation of the Epirus and the other regions occupied by the Allies. Greece is justly proud to have found in this conference the same consideration as her powerful protectors and allies. My Government will submit to you the legislative measures necessitated by the needs of the war, convinced that it will have your whole support, but the country has other needs than these as the result of the existence of a state of war.

I appeal to your unanimous aid in studying the measures indicated in the present circumstances as regards the economical situation of the State and the country. Gentlemen, never has the country passed through a more serious period. Greece has to defend her territory against barbarous aggressors. But if in the trials of the past Greece has been able, thanks to the civilizing strength of the morale of the race, to have overcome the conquerors and to rise free amidst the ruins, to-day it is quite a different matter. The present cataclysm will decide the definite fate of Hellenism, which, if lost, will never be restored. I am convinced that to accomplish the great and difficult task which the country has undertaken it will have assistance equal to the danger of which you are aware. I am also certain that the self-sacrifice of the Hellenic people will rise to the heights demanded by the struggle to which we have been called by the supreme care of our national defense, and for which I wish success by invoking the Divine assistance.

RUSSIA'S MILITARY BREAKDOWN

IGNORANCE AND PACIFISM DESTROY RUSSIA'S DEMOCRACY

JULY 1ST-20TH

ALEXANDER GUCHKOV   ALEXANDER KERENSKY
RUSSIAN COUNCIL OF WORKMEN AND SOLDIERS
GENERAL BRUSILOFF   GENERAL DENIKINE
FREIHERR VON DER OSTEN SACKEN

No tragedy of the War exceeded that of the breakdown of the Russian army. Pathos mingled here with horror. Splendor and glory shone side by side with gross bestiality and the madness of ignorant despair.

From the time of the Revolution of March, a merely temporary Democratic cabinet had been ruling the country while awaiting the gathering of a General Assembly elected by the people. The real power lay with the "Council of Workmen's and Soldiers' Delegates," to which were later added "Farmers' Delegates" as well. This body issued its directions to the workmen and the soldiers, and was at first obeyed by them. Hence the temporary government ruled by its support. This Workmen's Council was, however, Socialistic in spirit; and its trust was given not to the Democrats in the government but to the Socialists, and primarily to the Socialistic orator Kerensky. So manifest was this, that gradually the non-Socialistic ministers were forced from office; and in July Kerensky supplanted Prince Lvoff as Prime Minister.

Not even Kerensky, however, could check the ever-increasing demands of the workmen and soldiers. They wanted peace and idleness and relief from all restraint; and beyond that they wanted drunkenness and plunder. In brief, though there were in Russia many noble and high-minded men, yet the masses were too ignorant and bestial for self-rule. They were unable to give persistent support to any organization, unable to subordinate momentary desires for the sake of larger but more distant advantages. They were capable only of the narrow beast life of aboriginal mankind. Their civilization was too big for them to understand; and they destroyed it.

Democratic leaders, like the able temporary War Minister Guchkov, cried a warning of the danger, as in his speech here presented. Even Kerensky cried out against the spreading anarchy, in the noted speech here given. Workmen were urged to toil and soldiers to fight. They were told that for freedom's sake they must beat back the Germans. The most celebrated of the older generals, Brusiloff, was made commander-in-chief; Kerensky journeyed to the front and roused the men with fiery orations; and a great "people's offensive" was begun, in the hope that Germany was to be beaten back forever. The attack opened brilliantly on July 1st. War Minister Guchkov had made excellent preparation. General Brusiloff had never planned better nor with greater forces under his command. The Austrian front crumbled before the Russians once again—but for the last time.

The advance began in Galicia on July 1st along the Dniester River. On July 6th the army of General Korniloff joined the assault, attacking south of the Dniester and sweeping forward almost unresisted. On July 10th Korniloff captured Halitch, and on July 11th Kaluse, which had been the Austrian headquarters. On July 16th the Germans to the northward began a counter-attack; and on that same day there arose in Petrograd the first revolt of the Maximalists, afterward better known as Bolsheviks. This first Maximalist street tumult was easily suppressed.

Suddenly, as Generals Brusiloff and Denikine here tell us, the Russian soldiers stopped the great military advance. German emissaries and the advocates of the new anarchy of Bolshevism whispered everywhere among the soldiers that this fighting, this risking of their lives, was unnecessary. They were told that the men who led them on toward death were their real enemies, and the Germans were their friends. So thousands of them abandoned the advance, leaving their more loyal comrades to perish in unsupported attacks.

Many a gallant deed was done by some single gallant soul. Many a veteran, private as well as officer, gave his life for the army he could no longer save or serve. On the other hand, there was endless rioting. Many a retreating regiment slew its officers; many companies plundered and recklessly squandered their own supplies. All organization was lost, and the advancing Teutons were able to seize befuddled and bewildered prisoners by thousands. The Germans' publicity writer, Von der Osten, declares this to have been one of their most glorious triumphs.

C. F. H.

BY A. I. GUCHKOV

Address of May 10, 1917

UNFORTUNATELY the first feeling of radiant joy evoked by the revolution has given place to one of pain and anxiety. The Provisional Government explained the cause of this in its recent declaration, in which it was pointed out that the destruction of the old forms of public life, to which an end had been put by the revolution, had been effected more rapidly than had the creation of new forms to replace them.

It is especially regrettable that the destruction has touched the political and social organization of the country before any life center has had time to establish itself and to carry out the great creative work of regeneration.

How will the State emerge from this crisis? That is the question for solution and on which will depend not only the consolidation of the liberties won, but the issue of the war and the destinies of the country. In any case, the duality of power—and even polyarchy—and the consequent anarchy now prevailing in the country make its normal existence difficult.

Our poor country is fighting at an extraordinary hard conjuncture of an unparalleled war and internal troubles such as we never have seen before, and only a strong Governmental power able to rely on the confidence of the nation can save it.

We received a terrible legacy from the old régime, which was incapable of governing in time of peace and still less was able to do so while waging war.

We all know the conditions in which our valiant army defended every foot of Russian territory and how it still is carrying on a truly heroic but not hopeless struggle. One more effort and an effort by the whole country and the enemy will be beaten, but we have got to know first of all whether we can make this effort.

The *coup d'état* found echoes in the army and navy which, believing in their creative strength, unanimously adhered to the new régime and set to work on a radical reform of the armed forces of the country.

For the moment we hoped our military powers would emerge from the salutary process regenerated and renewed in strength and that a new reasonable discipline would weld the army together, but that has not been the case, and we must frankly face the fact that our military might is weakened and disintegrated, being affected by the same disease as the country, namely, duality of power, polyarchy, and anarchy, only the malady is more acute.

It is not too late to cure it, but not a moment must be lost. Those who, either deliberately or not realizing what they were doing, have cast into our midst the subversive *mot d'ordre* "peace at the front and war in the country," those people, I say, are carrying on a propaganda of peace at any price and civil war, cost what it may.

That *mot d'ordre* must be smothered by another, that being "war at the front and peace within the country."

Gentlemen, some time ago the country realized that our motherland was in danger. Since then we have gone a step further, for our motherland is on the edge of an abyss.

BY ALEXANDER KERENSKY
Address of May 14th

I came to you because my strength is at an end. I no longer feel my former courage, nor have my former conviction that we are conscientious citizens, not slaves in revolt. I am sorry I did not die two months ago, when the dream of a new life was growing in the hearts of the Russian people, when I was sure the country could govern itself without the whip.

As affairs are going now, it will be impossible to save the country. Perhaps the time is near when we will have to tell you that we can no longer give you the amount of bread you expect or other supplies on which you have a right to count. The process of the change from slavery to freedom is not going on properly. We have tasted freedom and are slightly intoxicated. What we need is sobriety and discipline.

You could suffer and be silent for ten years, and obey the orders of a hated Government. You could even fire upon your own people when commanded to do so. Can you now suffer no longer?

We hear it said that we no longer need the front because they are fraternizing there. But are they fraternizing on all the fronts? Are they fraternizing on the French front? No, comrades, if you are going to fraternize, then fraternize everywhere. Are not enemy forces being thrown over on to the Anglo-French front, and is not the Anglo-French advance already stopped? There is no such thing as a "Russian front," there is only one general allied front.

We are marching toward peace and I should not be in the ranks of the Provisional Government if the ending of the war were not the aim of the whole Provisional Government; but if we are going to propose new war aims we must see we are respected by friend as well as by foe. If the tragedy and desperateness of the situation are not realized by all in our State, if our organization does not work like a machine, then all our dreams of liberty, all our ideals, will be thrown back for decades and maybe will be drowned in blood.

Beware! The time has now come when every one in the depth of his conscience must reflect where he is going and where he is leading others who were held in ignorance by the old régime and still regard every printed word as law. The fate of the country is in your hands, and it is in most extreme danger. History must be able to say of us, "They died, but they were never slaves."

MANIFESTO OF MAY 15TH, BY THE COUNCIL OF WORKMEN
AND SOLDIERS

Soldiers and comrades at the front, we speak to you in the name of the Russian revolutionary democracy. The people did not wish the war, which was begun by the Emperors and capitalists of all countries, and, therefore, after the abdication of the Czar, the people considered it urgent to end the war as rapidly as possible. Do not forget, soldiers and comrades, that the regiments of William are destroying revolutionary Russia. Do not forget that the loss of free Russia would be a catastrophe, not only to us but to the working classes of the entire world. Defend, therefore, revolutionary Russia with all your power.

The Council of Workmen's and Soldiers' Delegates leads you toward peace in another way. By calling for a revolution of the workmen and peasants of Germany and Austria-Hungary we will lead you to peace after having obtained from our Government a renunciation of the policy of conquest and after demanding a similar renunciation from the allied powers. But do not forget, soldiers and comrades, that peace cannot be achieved if you do not check the enemy's pressure at the front, if your ranks are pierced and the Russian revolution lies like an inanimate body at William's feet. Do not forget, you in the trenches, that you are defending the liberty of the Russian revolution and your brother workmen and peasants.

Now, how are you to accomplish this defense if you remain inactive in your trenches? Frequently only an offensive can repel or check a hostile offensive, frequently those who await an attack perish. Soldiers and comrades, having sworn to defend Russian liberty, do not renounce the offensive. Fight and struggle for this liberty, and while fighting and struggling fear the enemy's traps. The fraternizing which is taking place at present at the front can easily become a trap. Do not forget that revolutionary troops have only the right to fraternize with troops who are also revolutionary and who are also ready to die for peace and liberty.

The German Army is not a revolutionary army if it is still blindly following William and Charles, Emperors and capitalists. You are fraternizing openly, not with enemy soldiers but with officers of the enemy's General Staff, disguised as common soldiers. Peace will not be obtained by separate treaties or by the fraternizing of isolated regiments and battalions. This will only lead to the loss of the Russian revolution, the safety of which does not lie in a separate peace or armistice.

Reject, therefore, everything which weakens your military power, which distracts the army and lowers its morale. Soldiers, be worthy of the trust that revolutionary Russia puts in you.

MANIFESTO OF JULY 23RD

Fellow-soldiers: One of our armies has wavered, its regiments have fled before the enemy. Part of our front has been broken. Emperor William's hordes, which have moved forward, are bringing with them death and destruction.

Who is responsible for this humiliation? The responsibility rests with those who have spread discord in the army and shaken its discipline, with those who at a time of danger disobeyed the military commands and wasted time in fruitless discussions and disputes.

Many of those who left the line and sought safety in running away paid with their lives for having disobeyed orders. The enemy's fire mowed them down. If this costly lesson has taught you nothing, then there will be no salvation for Russia.

Enough of words. The time has come to act without hesitation. We have acknowledged the Provisional Government. With the Government lies the salvation of the revolution. We have acknowledged its unlimited authority and its unlimited power. Its commands must be law. All those who disobey the commands of the Provisional Government in battle will be regarded as traitors. Toward traitors and cowards no mercy will be shown.

Fellow-soldiers: You want a durable peace. You want your land, your freedom. Then you must know that only by a stubborn struggle will you win peace for Russia and all nations. Yielding before the troops of the German Emperor, you lost both your land and your freedom. The conquering, imperialistic Germans will force you again and again to fight for your interests.

Fellow-soldiers at the front: Let there be no traitors or cowards among you. Let not one of you retreat a single step before the foe. Only one way is open for you—the way forward.

Fellow-soldiers in the rear: Be ready to advance to the front for the support of your brothers, abandoned and betrayed, fleeing from their positions in the regiments. Gather all your strength for the struggle for a durable peace, for your land and your freedom. Without wavering, without fear, without disastrous discussions, carry out all military commands. At the time of battle disobedience and wavering are worse than treachery. Your ruin lies in them, the ruin of Russia.

Fellow-soldiers: You are being watched by those who work for Russia and by the whole world. The ruin of the Russian revolution spells ruin for all. Summon up all your manhood, your perseverance and sense of discipline and save the Fatherland.

MANIFESTO OF JULY 25TH

Lack of discipline and open treachery at the front are facilitating Field-Marshal von Hindenburg's new offensive. The serious defeats inflicted on our army are opening the way to the enemy for increasing the general panic and preparing the soil in which the poisonous seeds of counter-revolution may come into full bloom. Already an attack is being organized by the strong bourgeoisie; already the jackals and hyenas of the old régime are howling.

We turn to you, our representatives, with a passionate appeal for aid. Support the revolutionary authority; try to secure the full submission of workingmen, soldiers, and peasants to all the decisions of democracy's majority. Inspire them; awaken enthusiasm in them. Exert your entire will, your entire energy. Rally round our All-Russian centers and we will show the country and the world that the nation which created the greatest revolution in the world can not and shall not perish.

BY GENERAL BRUSILOFF

Address to the "Revolutionary Army" summoning them to the attack of July 1st

Since you could fight bravely and beat the enemy for the old régime, under the threat of being shot, surely you will not now hesitate and doubt as to defending our freedom and exalting our great Revolution. Surely you do not want to justify the shameful assertion of the enemy, that freedom has undone us, that we are not worthy of it, that the Russian Revolutionary army is not a threatening force, but a weak, distracted crowd of people unworthy of freedom.

No, I know the Russian nation and the Russian soldier. I myself am a Russian soldier, and I can answer to the Russian nation for their Fatherland. I answer that we will fulfill our duty to the victorious end, and will attain for our Fatherland an honorable peace, crowned with the aureole of resplendent freedom, which we will guarantee to ourselves forever. We will be ready, then, to sacrifice ourselves to defend at whatever cost that which we have won, and, where it may be necessary, to hurl ourselves upon the enemy and crush him.

Then all hail to our Mother Russia, and long may she live. And hail to our Provisional Government, and our War Minister, Kerensky, whose hope is in us. And I, comrade soldiers and officers, vouch for it to them that we will honorably, faithfully, and gallantly fulfill our duty.

He who advances vanquishes, but he who awaits the attack of the enemy perishes ingloriously. To vanquish is our desire.

General Brusiloff's Announcements of the July Attack

July 7th.—In the direction of Zloczow [on the Lemberg-Tarnopol railway], in the region of Batkow-Manajow, after artillery preparation, our infantry attacked the strongly fortified positions of the enemy and occupied three lines of trenches, but towards evening the enemy succeeded, by a series of counter-attacks, in pressing back our detachments.

On the sector of the heights north of Presowce, Lawrykowce, Trawotloki, Hodow [all near Zborow and north of Brzezany], and the wood to the west of Koniuchy, our detachments conducted an offensive and engaged in a stubborn battle throughout the day of July 6th. Fortified positions constantly changed hands. The enemy bringing up fresh reserves, executed a series of counter-attacks. The more formidable of these counter-attacks came from the direction of the village Urlow and the woods to the west of Koniuchy, where in certain places the enemy succeeded in pressing back our attacking detachments.

Towards the evening there remained in our hands the heights to the northwest of Presowce, the villages of Lawrykowce and Trawotloki, and the heights to the east of Hodow.

In the battle of July 6th we captured 17 officers and 672 men.

In the direction of Zloczow during the night of July 6th-7th the enemy launched energetic counter-attacks on the front of Hodow and in the wood to the west of Koniuchy, attempting to dislodge our troops from the positions which they captured in the battle on July 6th. All these attacks

were repelled.   Attacks by dense enemy columns supported
by armored motor-cars west of Byszki, were also repelled.

July 10th.—Direction of Dolina.—On July 8th, about
midday, after artillery preparation, the troops of Gen. Korniloff's army attacked the fortified positions of the enemy to
the west of Stanislau, on the Jamnica front, and, having
pierced the foremost and most important position of the
enemy, our troops advanced and captured in battle the small
town of Jezupol [on the Bystrzyca] and the villages of Cie-
sow, Pawelcze, Rybno, and Stary Lysiec [all west of or on
the same river].

Our cavalry, giving immediate pursuit to the retreating
enemy, reached the River Lukwa [about eight miles behind
the enemy first line].

During the course of the day 131 officers and 7,000 rank
and file were taken prisoners; 48 guns (including 12 heavy
guns) and numerous machine guns were also captured.

July 10th.—Yesterday the troops of Gen. Korniloff continued the offensive in the region west of Stanislau.   The
Austro-Germans offered an energetic resistance, launching
desperate counter-attacks.

Fighting of a most stubborn and sanguinary character
took place on the roads leading to Halicz in the vicinity of
the villages of Huciska, Pacykow and Pawelcze.   In the
streets of the last-named village hand-to-hand fighting occurred, which ended in the complete defeat of the enemy.

In yesterday's fighting we captured more than 1,000 Austro-German prisoners, three field guns, and a large quantity of trench engines, machine guns and engineering and
war material.

The gallant conduct of our troops was beyond praise and
the officers were everywhere in the forefront.

July 19th.—West of Halicz the detachments occupying
the village of Bludniki retired, whereupon the enemy, profit-
ing by this movement, occupied the place.   The effort to win
back this village was unsuccessful.

According to supplementary reports received, on July
17th about 7 o'clock in the evening, when the enemy took
the offensive and seized the height to the south of the vil-

lage of Nowica (south of Kalusz), one of our regiments began to leave.

Maj.-Gen. Prince Gagarin, commanding the Caucasian Native Horse Division, seeing the critical situation, at once moved forward a battalion of the Ukhnoff Regiment, placing himself at its head and disposing three of his regiments— the Daghestanians on the right, the Circassians and the Kabardians on the left. With a furious onslaught the Ukhnoff Regiment and the horsemen rushed forward, bearing also with them the Russian regiment which had retired.

The general onslaught soon changed the situation in our favor. The advancing enemy fled in disorderly fashion, and our former position was restored. The brilliant work of the artillery of this command contributed decisively to the success.

July 21st—NORTHEAST GALICIA.—After strong artillery preparation, the enemy persistently attacked our detachments on the Pieniaki-Harbuzow front [on both sides of the head-waters of the Sereth and 20 miles south of Brody]. At first all these attacks were repelled.

At 10 o'clock, July 19th, the 607th Mlynoff Regiment, situated between Batkow and Manajow (in the same region), left their trenches voluntarily and retired, with the result that the neighboring units had to retire also. This gave the enemy the opportunity for developing his success.

Our failure is explained to a considerable degree by the fact that under the influence of the extremists (Bolsheviks) several detachments, having received the command to support the attacked detachments, held meetings and discussed the advisability of obeying the order, whereupon some of the regiments refused to obey the military command. The efforts of the commanders and committees to arouse the men to the fulfillment of the commands were fruitless.

July 22nd.—Our troops, having manifested absolute disobedience to the commanders, continued to retreat to the River Sereth, part giving themselves up as prisoners. Only the 155th infantry division in the district of Dolzanka-Domamoricz, and the armored cars which fired on the German cavalry on the Tarnopol road, put up any opposition to the enemy. With immense superiority in forces and technic on our side in the sections attacked, the retreat continued almost without a break. This was due to the absolute instability of our troops and discussions as to whether to obey or not to obey orders of commanders, and to the criminal propaganda of the Bolsheviks.

BY EYE-WITNESSES
Account of the capture of Kalisz, the Austrian Headquarters

On all sides there was evidence of the precipitate flight of the Headquarters of the Third Austrian Army, situated in the suburbs on the banks of the Lomnica. Gen. von Tersztyansky evidently considered himself safe from attack.

During the day we strengthened and extended our position on the west bank of the Lomnica in preparation for the arrival of the enemy's reserves. That evening heavy rain began, necessitating the suspension of the advance. The Lomnica was transformed into a boiling torrent and all the bridges were swept away. The Germans brought up six batteries and shelled our communications, but the following day our guns silenced them and covered our positions across the river. Rain continuing, it became necessary to withdraw the bulk of our forces, a move which was safely carried out on the night of July 15th.

Meanwhile we have extended our lines in the valley of the Lomnica, which will be useful for the eventual resumption of the offensive. Our present line includes the whole of the Lomnica from the Dniester to its sources, so that the enemy is confined to the hills.

According to the statements of prisoners the enemy has transferred hither the Jäger Reserve Division from Vilna, the remnants of the German 75th Reserve Division from Brzezany, and the Austrian 5th Division from the Carpathians. During our attacks on July 8th, 9th and 10th the Austrian 15th Division lost 80 per cent., the German 33rd Division 40 per cent., and the Austrian 16th Division 50 per cent., and the Austrian 36th Division lost 30 per cent., while the Austrian 2nd Cavalry Division lost little. The enemy had altogether 44 battalions with 32,000 bayonets, of which they lost over 16,000 including 12,000 prisoners. Our losses are about one-third. We have taken over 100 guns.

Our further successes will depend on the measures that may be taken to restore a proper spirit of subordination among the men at the front and the reserves. This question is bound up with the whole political situation of Russia. The Army has done better than was expected, but the present committee system has failed.

Account by a British Observer of the Russian Retreat

From the words of an officer captured near Brzezany a fortnight ago we understood that the Germans were preparing an artful stroke in conjunction with their agents in Petrograd and in our armies. "You will see that your troops will run away when the time comes, and we shall have a walk over," he declared.

Events have fully borne out this prophecy. Lenine and his crew have well earned their pay. The disturbances in Petrograd, organized on the 16th inst., were obviously directed from Berlin so as to coincide with the German plan. The thunderbolt fell almost on the day when the high command on this front changed hands, and the harvest in Eastern Galicia and Bukovina had almost been gathered.

A whole day before the news of the crisis in Petrograd reached us, Lenine's agents were acquainted with it through traitors in the wireless service. They spread a report among the troops that the Bolsheviks were in control of the Government, and that the war was at an end. The execution of the German plan became ridiculously easy.

The enemy entered at our most sensitive point near Zborow, in the direction of Trembowla. The wedge thus driven in would sever the Tarnopol-Buczacz railway and the highways, disuniting the Eleventh and Seventh Armies and exposing the right flank of the latter to serious peril.

Our line was opened on the morning of the 19th inst. at Zwyzen, north of Zborow. The 6th Grenadier Division deserted wholesale, and fled. On the 18th General Brusiloff, who had come to Tarnopol, summoned General Korniloff and ordered him to take over the command from General

Gutor. The rupture was represented to be a slight affair, as we had eight divisions in reserve. The Staffs of the neighboring armies were left in the dark. General Korniloff, however, realized that the danger was great. But he had to go to Stanislau in order to transfer his command of the Eighth Army to General Tcheremisoff. Much precious time had to be wasted in journeys.

Having rejoined the British Armored Car Headquarters on the 17th inst., I left again for Stanislau on the afternoon of the 20th inst. Nothing was then known of the rupture of the front at a point only 25 miles distant on the previous morning, and the first report of it reached Commander Locker-Lampson late on the 20th. At Stanislau rumors began to circulate during the afternoon of the 22nd that Tarnopol was in danger, but nothing positive was known at the Staff.

General Tcheremisoff assumed command of the Eighth Army that morning. I saw him at noon. He was disquieted by the defections among his own men, but said not a word of the rupture in the front of the Eleventh Army. On the morning of the 23rd the Staff had information that left no doubt as to the magnitude of the catastrophe.

My first thought was to rejoin the British section, whose position was extremely perilous. Abandoning all impedimenta, I jumped into the first car going to Buczacz in the hope of meeting the British contingent as it fell back through Podhajce.

At Buczacz I came across our transport and Colonel Valentine of the British Air Service. From them I heard the full story of the disaster. The officers had safely removed the aëroplanes and the aëronautical stores from the zone of the Eleventh Army under the full blast of the Russian panic.

We were destined to witness some strange scenes on the road from Buczacz eastward, although the enemy was still 30 miles distant. A man on a white horse dashed through the town yelling: "German cavalry are behind, save yourselves." He was afterwards arrested, and proved to be a German spy. Indescribable confusion ensued. A multitude of deserters and transport cars, lorries, and ambulances headed eastward at top speed. The roadway was littered with impedimenta. Through this inferno, through burning dust, and under a scorching sun, we literally fought our way, using our sticks and fists, and brandishing revolvers at the deserters who repeatedly tried to storm our cars, until we had got ahead of the rout. Then placing our lorries across the road, we dammed the tide of panic.

Leaving Buczacz at 5 p. m., we reached Proskurow in Russia only at 8 o'clock the following morning.

Narrative of M. Lembitch, Chief Russian Observer at the Front

July 21st.—Every hour there comes more and more alarming news from the field of battle.

The retirement of our troops yesterday in the direction of Tarnopol was like a panic-stricken flight.

The catastrophe took place so unexpectedly that a man had to be made of iron not to lose his head through all the hellish madness and confusion which had been created in the army by a treacherous and venal mob of rascals and traitors, turning units that were once the best into crowds of revolted slaves, flying like sparrows at the first round of the enemy's guns. Let the Russian public know to what an appalling pass the Leninites have brought the Russian Army by their heinous agitation, and it will quickly say the word of power.

I have only just heard from the most certain source particulars of the catastrophe. Only a short time ago I witnessed the elemental enthusiasm with which the revolutionary troops hurled themselves against the defenses of the enemy, throwing every obstacle from their path. And there are no words to express the feeling of immense gladness that filled us then. We all, journalists and generals, officers and soldiers, doctors and dressers, in a word, all the representatives of the Staff and organizing forces of the army, as we looked at the hurricane attack on the Brzezany heights, congratulated one another with tears in our eyes on the marvelous resurrection of the restored Russian Army.

Alas! the sweet dream was short-lived. The first impulse over, the best and most honorable fighters for freedom laid low by the bullets and shells of the enemy, and the hydra of confusion, work of German hirelings—Bolsheviks and mere good-for-nothings keeping company with them—raised its head anew. Enthusiasm for victory turned out to be too little by itself. Absence of discipline and, consequently, of steadiness made us give back to the enemy almost without a fight all that had been won by whole thousands of fallen heroes. . . . The piercing of our front was caused by sheer treachery of whole units of troops on the one hand, and, on the other hand, the absence of discipline and steadiness in the present army. It is now established that the piercing of the lines at Zwyzen, between the Graberk and Sereth, developed in the course of a day into a great catastrophe, was carried out by the Germans with most inadequate and purely local forces, without the help of the great reserves stationed near Brzezany. The Germans, it is evident, only intended to make a big demonstration with the intention of diverting our forces from the Stanislau front. But when units of the 6th Grenadier Division, which was not long before in a state of revolt after it had been brought up to strength with men from Petrograd, treacherously left their positions and went away, the Germans rushed in without opposition through the breach that had been made and began to advance deep into our positions.

The line had been pierced on a comparatively small section and the harm done might have been retrieved by steadiness and discipline on the part of the troops. The high command at once gave orders to move perfectly adequate forces to the place where the breach had been made, with the design of getting the Germans, who, it appears, were rushing forward, in a vise and to cut them off from retreat on two sides. But then it was that took place that horrible thing that has now been given in the army the name of "Meeting strategy." The majority of the troops ordered to the breach either did not leave their quarters or began to assemble meetings to decide the question whether they should go to the positions indicated or not by means of voting. Two regiments, who had been given a more responsible task than others, considered the question until late at night, and the men, not being able to come to a decision, separated. During this time the Germans, not encountering any serious resistance, penetrated 12 versts [8 miles] to the rear of our lines, began to capture batteries and a number of prisoners, and to outflank Jezierna, the headquarters of the Staff.

In the evening of this unhappy day panic began to spread in the army, deliberately encouraged by certain suspicious characters, Bolsheviks in uniform, who flooded the army in the days of the Revolution. The rumor was circulated that the Germans had pierced our front at two points and that the way of retreat to Tarnopol was cut off. One after the other the divisions sent to encounter the Germans refused to attack, or, on the first encounter with the enemy, began to desert without any sense of responsibility, breaking up in disorder, creating great uproar and confusion. The cavalry and artillery alone rose to the height of their duty and with the greatest steadfastness supported the few heroic units of infantry who covered the retreat. Yesterday one valiant Cossack regiment saved the position in an exceptional way, and, in horse and foot formation, repelled all the violent attacks of the Germans.

Yesterday at 10 in the evening the breach in the lines was already 30 versts [20 miles] in length, from the banks of the Graberk to the region south of Zborow. Our units by this time had retreated to the positions of last year, Gliadki-Worobiewka. In the course of a day the enemy had penetrated 25 versts [17 miles] into the rear, inflicting on us immense loss. Commanders of units, officers and army committees made desperate efforts to bring the units who had forgotten their duty to their senses, and to stop those who were fleeing. Military commissioners of the army and the front came posthaste to the scene of the catastrophe with the same purpose.

The only hope is in the firmness of General Korniloff.

July 22nd.—The German light and heavy artillery is bombarding Tarnopol. There is unimaginable panic in the town. The whole night the organizations stationed there have been evacuating the place. Trains are leaving overflowing with passengers—persons serving in the Red Cross, members of the Zemstvo Union, and of various public and military organizations. Most people are fleeing on foot or in carts.

The retreat of our army continues with the same rapidity. Immense bands of deserters are breaking into shops and private houses in the towns and villages. The misery caused by the retreat is colossal.

Units, faithful to their duty to the Fatherland, are performing miracles of valor, trying to withstand the pressure of the enemy and to give our infantry the chance of successfully getting away from it. A few traitorous units have given themselves up as prisoners to the enemy. There only remain 200 men of the traitorous 6th Grenadier Division. The rest have either given themselves up as prisoners or deserted, spreading panic where they go.

BY GENERAL DENIKINE
Report of July 28th to the Russian Government

Well aware of my great responsibility, and with a heart full of the deepest feelings, I have written this report. Be patient. In the presence of the autocratic Czar, I could ever speak honestly and without fear; in the presence of the revolutionary autocracy, my words shall be of the same kind.

The troops were in a state of complete disorganization, I discovered when called to the command. This amazed me because neither the reports that had reached the headquarters of the General Staff, nor in fact my own observations, had caused me to suspect so tragic a situation. However, it is easily accounted for: the soldiers committed no serious excesses when they had only to give a passive acquiescence. But, when they were ordered to prepare for attack, and the time for active duty came, the animal instinct cried aloud and the truth was revealed!

Ten divisions at least did not take their positions for departure as ordered. Thereupon a tremendous furor arose among officers of every rank, and the committees, and the agitators. There were endless commands and arguments.

Before any action could be taken, the number of troops in revolt must be lessened. The greater part of a month was consumed in this way, and but a part of the divisions obeyed the order to go into battle. The 2nd Corps from the Caucasus, and the 160th Infantry Division revolted. Thus many companies degenerated from their former appearance, and some even lost human semblance! Never shall I forget the scenes I watched in the 703rd Regiment!

Eight to ten distilleries of alcohol existed in some regiments. Consequently drunkenness, gambling, pillage and assault of all descriptions, even murder, occurred. I decided to send the 2nd Caucasian Corps to the rear, excepting the 51st Infantry Division, and to reorganize it as well as the 160th, thus, from the outset, losing a force of about 130,000 bayonets. In the same sector with the Caucasian Infantry Corps were the 28th and 29th Infantry Divisions, which were considered the best on the front. The 29th went into position as ordered, but the day following almost two and a half regiments returned to the rear. The 28th Division agreed to send one of its regiments to hold the vacant position, but that regiment voted on its own account not to occupy the position; it withdrew instead.

Everything was done to persuade the men. The Commander-in-Chief came in person, and after interviews with the committees and delegates of the two corps retired with the impression that the soldiers were sound, but that the officers were frightened, and had lost their heads. This was false; the officers had done all in their power in this unprecedented and painful predicament.

A meeting was held by the 1st Siberian Corps, at which the address made by the Commander-in-Chief was received enthusiastically; but he was unaware that the meeting was continued after his departure, and that the soldiers listened to other speakers who commanded them not to listen to—I ask your pardon, but this is the word used—"the old bourgeois." His name was loaded with insults; and such speeches met with tremendous applause.

M. Kerensky, Minister of War, while on a tour of inspection, delivered an inspiring appeal to glory, and received a staunch welcome from the 28th Infantry Division. One-half hour after this orator's departure, a deputation from one of the regiments in this division was sent after him with a resolution they had taken, declaring they would not attack. Even more misleading in its temporary enthusiasm was the sight of the 28th Infantry Division breaking into wildest enthusiasm when the red flag was returned to the commander of the regiment from Poti. The soldiers kneeled to receive it, and vowed that they would die for their country. This they affirmed by repeated oaths and by the fiery speeches of three orators. On the first day of the attack, without even going into the front trenches, this regiment made a half-face and marched off some six or seven miles to the rear of the battle.

The morale of the men should have been upheld by the soldiers' committees and the political commissaries; but in reality these deputies led them into complete demoralization. Perhaps there were among the commissaries a few "black Swans" who really were of assistance by not meddling in what was no concern of theirs. But this very institution, involving as it did two powers, creating friction, interfering banefully and unsolicited, could not help but be a cause of disintegration in the army.

Another cause of demoralization lies in the committees. That some of these do remarkable work with intense regard for their duty, I do not deny. Many of their members set superb examples of heroic death. But such usefulness, I reaffirm, does not compensate, except in a minor way, for the enormity of the evil to army discipline caused by the committees by reason of their oligarchy, of their division of power, their hostile interference in war affairs, and their overthrow of all authority. Although I could give hundreds of examples of their weakening and disorganizing work, I will limit myself to the most characteristic:

On June 8th a committee at the front decided not to attack. Then, shifting, it decided for an attack. On June 1st the committee of the Second Army decided not to attack, and on June 20th changed this decision. The Soviet of Workmen's and Soldiers' Delegates at Minsk refused to authorize the attack, by a vote of 123 to 79. All the committees of the 169th Infantry Division voted a lack of confidence in the Provisional Government, and declared that they considered an attack on the enemy to be "treason to the revolution." Many dismissals of commanding officers resulted from this breach of authority, dismissals in which in most cases the committee took part. Thus a corps commander, a chief of the General Staff, and the head of a division intrusted with an important attack, had to renounce their commands at the very outset of military operations. About sixty officers were deposed as commanders of army corps or heads of regiments.

The total of evil done by the committees is difficult to estimate. No firm discipline any longer exists. If a patriotic and soldierly decision is made by a majority vote, this amounts to nothing. Another vote will soon change it. Hiding behind their privilege as members of the committee, the Bolsheviki sow revolt and trouble everywhere. In a word, idleness and ever-shifting talk! The military leader with all his authority discredited is elevated and then cast down. Yet he is expected to be powerful enough to conduct the troops to vigorous battle.

This was the real preparation which preceded the operations. Enemy pressure on the southwest front made immediate assistance necessary, although the deployment was not finished. My front lost three or four divisions which disappeared before the enemy's attacks; so I decided to attack with the remaining troops who seemed faithful to their duty.

During three days our artillery thundered against the enemy trenches, tearing them up frightfully and inflicting heavy losses against the Germans, and pounding out a road for our infantry. The entire front zone was nearly carried. Our chain of troops reached the enemy batteries. The breach seemed about to be widened; it was the long promised victory. Suddenly, however, the advance stopped. New regiments failed to appear. Men fled on every side. A gap yawned in our lines; and without any advance by the enemy, we were compelled to withdraw.

During this reverse, the lessening of our man-power increased. By nightfall it took on huge proportions. The soldiers, weary, unnerved, unaccustomed to the roar of cannon after months of inaction, of fraternization, and of meetings, deserted the trenches *en masse,* throwing away their rifles and machine guns, and stampeding like a wild herd to the rear. The cowardice and panic reached such depths that several generals requested the artillery fire be stopped, fearing the noise of our own cannon would cause further panic among our soldiers.

The offensive thus resulted disastrously, yet never before had I had the good fortune to fight with greater numerical superiority in bayonets and materials. Never had success seemed more assured. On thirteen miles of front I had 184 batteries, against 29 enemy batteries; 900 guns against 300; the batteries that were to go into the attack were 138 against 17. All this was reduced to annihilation.

The generals' reports showed that the mental condition of the troops immediately following the operation defied analysis. I called the army commanders together three days later, and asked these questions: "Will our armies be able to resist a serious German attack by increased numbers?" Answer: "No." "Can our armies sustain an organized attack of the Germans if the enemy forces remain the same as now?" Two commanders gave vague answers in conditional terms. The consensus of opinion was: "We no longer have any infantry." I will make that statement stronger and say, "We no longer have any army, and one must be created at any price."

Paragraph 6, of the "Declaration of the Soldiers' Rights," says all printed matter without exception shall be forwarded to the person addressed. Thus the spirit of the whole army is fed with incendiary literature, with which the Bolshevists deluge it. It is plain that official funds, funds of the people and of the Military Bureau at Moscow, have been invested in this vicious propaganda and sent to the front. There arrived 7,000 copies of the *Pravda,* 2,000 copies of the *Soldatskaia Pravda,* and over 30,000 of the *Social Democrat,* between March 24th and May 1st. Between May 1st and June 11th there were again 7,000 copies of the *Pravda,* 32,000 of the *Social Democrat,* and over 61,000 of the *Soldatskaia Pravda.* These sheets were handed out to every one by the soldiers themselves.

Paragraph 14 of the new military code declares that no one is to be punished without trial. In practice, however, this right belongs only to the private soldiers. Officers have been repeatedly condemned without trial. The result is that all military tribunals are at a standstill; they dare not act in the most ordinary cases. The officers have lost all authority, and the courts which were to have been composed solely of private soldiers, have not even been selected. The men have either neglected them or in other places openly voted to have no courts at all. In brief, the idea of Justice has been quite thrust out of the army. These new laws and methods have utterly destroyed all authority and all discipline, have placed the officers in a shameful position, and deprived them of all consideration and all honor.

Of the sufferings of the officers, it is very painful for me to speak; and I will be brief. Sokoloff, writing of them, said: "I could not have imagined martyrs such as your officers; I bow before them." It is true. Not even in the darkest days of the Czar did the secret police employ upon those whom they regarded as most criminal, such tortures, such jeers, as are now inflicted upon faithful officers by the fury of drunken soldiers and revolutionary mobs. Insulted at every turn, they are often struck and even lashed. No murmur of complaint escapes them, though they are moved by shame, mortal shame. Many a one, alone, weeps over his misfortune and to escape such humiliations seeks death upon the battlefield. Here is a passage from a report of the 38th Army Corps. Does it not breathe of the heroic epic! "The officers who were marching in advance, tried vainly to rally their men. At that instant, a white flag was hoisted by our soldiers in Redoubt 3. Thereupon fifteen officers, with a little group of soldiers, marched forward alone. Their fate is unknown. They were not seen again."

May the blood of these heroes be upon the heads of those who caused their untimely death, willingly or unwillingly! Peace to their noble souls! Powerful measures must be taken, if the army is to be rescued from its ruins.

BY FREIHERR VON DER OSTEN SACKEN

Signs of awakening activity were perceptible along the Russian front in June. Britain and America, by threatening to withdraw their support from the government then in control of Russia, had determined it to join in the war again. Secondary attacks were to be launched in the North and in Rumania, while the main blow was struck at Lemberg and the oil fields around Drohobycz, a region which it was highly important for us to retain in our possession. In pursuance of this plan, Kerensky, the Minister of War, and Brusiloff, the Commander-in-Chief, put the army again upon a fighting basis, repairing as well as they could the disintegration caused by the Revolution and succeeding events. Fighting on the front increased in violence, though it was at first confined within narrow limits. Artillery duels on the Galician front increased in intensity from the middle of June.

On June 29th, the Russian bombardment swelled to drum fire, and the Eleventh and Seventh Russian Armies, composed supposedly of thirty-eight divisions, which if filled out would number 600,000 infantry, attacked the positions of the Central Powers stretching from the Lemberg-Tarnopol railway through Koniuchy and Brzczany to Halicz. At Brzczany the Russians were defeated by Bothmer's army, and at Koniuchy they won only initial successes. Between Koniuchy and Zborow, however, they penetrated the lines of the Second Austro-Hungarian Army and were only stopped by the reserves.

On July 3rd they attacked again near Brzczany without success; then, having suffered enormous losses, they paused. When on the 6th the northern wing renewed the attack, it met with a severe defeat. With losses estimated at 250,000 men, Brusiloff had now had enough. Until the 19th, therefore, there was quiet, broken only by artillery duels.

South of the Dniester the fighting was all the livelier for this period of calm on the other fronts. The Eighth Russian Army pressed the Third Austro-Hungarian Army from west of Stanislav back behind the Lomnica; then, on July 16th, was itself obliged by the approach of German reenforcements to withdraw to the east bank at Kalusz. There ensued heavy fighting, in the course of which, on the 17th, the heights of Novica were wrested from the enemy.

The Russians in Galicia now met their fate. Our High Command resolved to lay for all time the danger threatening from that direction. Without the knowledge of the Russians, the commander of our Eastern army, Prince Leopold of Bavaria, collected several German army corps north of the Lemberg-Tarnopol railroad near the source of the Strypa and the Sereth. On the 19th of July he led them in a southeasterly direction against the bent-back right wing of the Eleventh Russian army, and inflicted on it a decisive defeat.

His left wing next pressed the Russians, retreating in disorder, back upon Tarnopol and captured incalculable booty. His right wheeled to the south against the flank of the Russian main front. Staggered by the combined force of this pressure on their flank and the frontal attacks of our other armies, which had advanced 250 kilometers to the Tartar Pass, the Russians quickly started a retreat. On the 23rd and 24th, after some hot fighting which cost them dear, they were forced back across the Sereth between Trembowla and Tarnopol. Continuing to withdraw before us, they next crossed the Zbrucz, which forms the frontier. On the 29th, we also forced the passage of the Zbrucz, and established ourselves firmly on the right bank. Galicia was liberated; Podolia was invaded.

The concentric advance of the Third Austro-Hungarian Army and the left wing of Archduke Joseph's army now forced the Russians, still fighting spiritedly, to draw back in Bukowina also. Czernowitz was taken by our allies on the morning of August 3rd. The frontiers of Bessarabia and Moldavia were overrun. In Bukowina as in Galicia the Russians had terribly laid waste the country.

"IN FLANDERS FIELDS"

THE GREAT CANADIAN ASSAULT ON PASSCHENDAELE

JULY 31ST-NOVEMBER

GENERAL DAVIDSON   GENERAL LUDENDORFF
MAX OSBORN   SIR DOUGLAS HAIG

GENERAL SIR DAVID WATSON

The "Battle of Flanders", the third great struggle around Ypres, ranks with the Somme as Britain's main effort of the War. It lasted through almost all of the second half of 1917. So heavy were the British losses here, so slight was the British advance, that no battle has been more criticised than this in England. Its true value lay of course in its being an "offensive of defense". That is to say, it engulfed all the German strength and prevented Ludendorff from striking elsewhere. This he himself admits in the portion of his "Memoirs" here presented.

Britain here for half a year bore the brunt of the War. Russia was collapsing. France was exhausted by her terrible losses in the first half year at the Aisne. The United States was still unready. Except for Britain's mighty attack in Flanders, Germany might have won complete victory in the East, crushed France, or overrun, as she so nearly did overrun, Italy.

The climax of this great Flanders battle was the storming of Passchendaele by the Canadians on November 6th, their costliest triumph of the War. Their story is here told by their own beloved general, since deceased, Sir David Watson. The critical British view of the whole battle is expressed by General Sir John Davidson, and General Haig's celebrated official report gives the details. The German view is given not only by General Ludendorff, but by Max Osborn, the official German observer on the spot, and by an anonymous participant.

BY GENERAL SIR JOHN DAVIDSON

THE word "Passchendaele" was and has been used as a reproach to British generalship, and as a symbol of waste and useless suffering.

To the men who actually fought, such an attitude might be intelligible, for their horizon was limited by the expanse of mud and waste on every hand, by the incessant fire to which they were subjected, by the comparatively insignificant gains of ground at great sacrifice, and by the abnormal fatigue and hardship. Similarly to the wounded and to those who had lost their husbands, sons and brothers it appeared that heavy suffering had been inflicted and limbs and lives lost with little or no result so far as winning the war was concerned.

To the gunner during the latter period of the offensive, day in and day out handling his mud-spattered ammunition with unspeakable fatigue, constantly endeavoring to save his guns from disappearing into the morass, serving his pieces clustered round the only solid means of approach, the duckboard pathway, under a concentrated and almost continuous hail of enemy projectiles; to the infantryman heavily equipped staggering through an interminable sea of mud towards what appeared to him as certain death, the physical and mental strain was well-nigh unbearable. A blank wall on every side and no apparent end to the misery.

Ludendorff states in reference to the last phase of the operations, "What the German soldier experienced, achieved and suffered in the Flanders battle will be his everlasting monument of bronze erected by himself in the enemy's land."

What the British soldier achieved was something far greater. This was the bitterest campaign of the whole war, the one in which the British single-handed shouldered the whole burden, and of which the British nation may most justly feel proud; the one in which the British held the German Army in its grip, closed with it, and fixed it to its ground, thus preventing the enemy from taking the initiative in such a manner as to gain the decision elsewhere.

Let us examine the facts.

The objects before the British in delivering the offensive in Flanders were briefly, from a strategical point of view, to pin the German Army to the British front in the North and draw in their Reserves; and from a tactical point of view:

(a) To free Ypres by gaining the Passchendaele ridge which lies in a semi-circle round the eastern side and dominates the town and surrounding country;

(*b*) To gain the Passchendaele ridge, thereby commanding with long-range gunfire the enemy's communications through Roulers and his submarine bases at Ostend and Zeebrugge.

(*c*) To exploit to the full any tactical success gained (for this special preparations were made).

In order to gain strength for offensive purposes and to increase the number of our available reserves we had entered into negotiations with the French to take over part of our defensive front. This, however, they were unwilling to do, but requested to be allowed to take a small part in the Flanders offensive. It was considered advisable to acquiesce in their demands, but this was done with great reluctance and disappointment, for the mixture of French, Belgian and British troops in a confined area was not conducive to success, and their infantry, guns and ammunition arrived late, thereby delaying the commencement of operations until the 31st of July and involving the loss of many days of valuable summer weather which would have been of incalculable advantage in view of the exceptionally bad weather experienced in August.

It is difficult to see how in the circumstances described any other course could justifiably be advocated, though the air was full of the cries of "No more Somme battles," "We must wait for the Americans," and so on. Had the British Commander accepted this advice, presented from influential quarters, and had he not forced on a *British battle* on the *British front,* it is more than likely we should have been involved before many weeks had elapsed in a defensive *battle of German making,* at a point chosen by the enemy, where it would be most difficult for the British forces to operate in parrying the blow.

It will be convenient to divide the operations into five periods as has been done roughly in the official despatch and by Ludendorff in his *War Memories:*

First period: July 31st to August 16th.

Second period: August 17th to September 19th.

Third period: September 20th to October 4th.

Fourth period: October 5 to October 24th.

Fifth period: October 25th to November 10th.

As ill-luck would have it, after we had waited patiently for many days to open the attack for reasons given above, the weather broke on the afternoon of the 31st of July and rain continued incessantly for four days. However, very considerable results were achieved on the opening day and the enemy continued to counter-attack violently for some days with great loss. The British delivered their second attack, also successfully, on the 16th of August, but thereafter the abnormally wet weather necessitated a cessation of the operations for a whole month; this constitutes the first two periods. Fortunately the weather improved in September and the 20th ushered in the third period with a British attack on a wide front. The culmination of our efforts came in the fourth period, between the 22nd and 25th of October. Then the capture of Passchendaele was the final stroke.

In reference to these periods some extracts from Ludendorff's *Memories* are instructive. Ludendorff and his subordinate commanders were greatly puzzled at our tactics, and the deliberate manner in which the German counter-attacks were repeatedly smashed with heavy loss, and were constantly discussing and altering the tactics of the defence so as to minimize the loss. Not only does he admit this in his memoirs, but documents captured at the time showed that the German High Command recognized the failure of their methods.

BY GENERAL VON LUDENDORFF

The fighting on the western front became more severe than any the Germany army had yet experienced. In the east we had to keep on hammering at Russia in order to bring about the fall of the Colossus. From the 31st of July till well into September was a period of tremendous anxiety. On the 31st of July the English, assisted by a few French Divisions on their left, had attacked on a front of about 31 kilometres, but besides the loss of from two to four kilometres along the whole front, it caused us very heavy losses in prisoners and stores, and a heavy expenditure of reserves.

On the 16th we sustained another great blow. The English pressed on beyond Poelcapelle, and even with an extreme exertion of strength on our part, could only be pushed back a short distance. It had cost us heavily.

The costly August battles imposed a heavy strain on the Western troops. In spite of all the concrete protection they seemed more or less powerless under the enormous weight of the enemy's artillery. At some points they no longer displayed that firmness which I in common with the local commanders had hoped for. The enemy managed to adapt himself to our method of employing counter-attack Divisions. There were no more attacks with unlimited objectives, such as General Nivelle had made in the Aisne-Champagne battle. He was ready for our counter-attacks and prepared for them by exercising restraint in the exploitation of success.

I was myself being put to a terrible strain. The state of affairs in the West appeared to *prevent the execution of our plans elsewhere.* Our wastage had been so high as to cause grave misgivings and exceeded all expectation. *The attack on the Dvina had to be postponed repeatedly.* Indeed, it became a question whether we could continue to bear the responsibility of retaining those Divisions in the East.

After a period of profound quiet in the West, which led some to hope that the battle of Flanders was over, another terrific assault was made on our lines on the 20th of September. The third bloody act of the battle had begun. The main force of the attack was directed against the Passchendaele-Gheluvelt line. Obviously the English were trying to gain the high ground between Ypres and the Roulers-Menin line, which affords an extensive view in both directions. These heights were also exceptionally important for us, as they afforded us ground observation posts and a certain amount of cover from hostile view.

The enemy's onslaught on the 20th was successful, which proved the superiority of the attack over the defence. The power of the attack lay in the Artillery, and in the fact that ours did not do enough damage to the hostile Infantry as they were assembling, and, above all, at the actual time of the assault.

Another English attack on the 21st was repulsed; but the 26th proved a day of heavy fighting, accompanied by every circumstance that could cause us loss. We might be able to stand the loss of ground, but the reduction of our fighting strength was again all the heavier. Once more we were involved in a terrific struggle in the West. October came and with it one of the hardest months of the war. I had not known what joy meant for many a long day. The actions of the Third battle of Flanders had presented the same set-piece characteristics. The depth of penetration was limited so as to secure immunity from our counter-attacks, and the latter were then broken up by the massed fire of the Artillery. As regards the battle on the 4th of October, again we only came through it with enormous loss.

The wastage in the big actions of the fourth Battle of Flanders was extraordinary high. In the West we began to be short of troops. Two Divisions that had been held in readiness in the East and were already *on their way to Italy were diverted to Flanders. The Italian operation could not be started before the 22nd,* and the weather held it up until the 24th. These days were the culminating point of the crisis.

BY MAX OSBORN

July 31st.

Never-ending howls and piercing screams are rending the air from the sea to the River Lys, while accessory noises like growls and blows seem to spring from everywhere on the Yser, in front of Dixmude and Langemarck, around Hollebeke and Warneton. The whole of West Flanders is one large, steaming pot, in which death and devastation are brewing. With the sun smiling its brightest at us, terrific, never-ending thunderstorms are raging over the land. Amid noises such as the old earth never heard before, a crop of new battles and new wars between nations is growing to maturity.

What were the battles of the Somme, Arras, the Aisne,

and Champagne against this earthquake of Flanders? Millions of capital are blown up in the air and explode in the ground. It is like a Cyclopean concert of unheard-of brutality, to celebrate with becoming fitness the end of the third years of universal madness. The louder the desire of the nations for peace begins to express itself, the wilder the thunder of the guns at England's command to drown any cry of hope. Sometimes one thinks the end of the bloody intoxication is coming, but there are still graduations of description for which there are no words. We thought we had got accustomed to the atrociousness of all this, and at home you may forget the monstrous events. At the front for days our senses and nerves must certainly have suffered from these awful three years. Spirit and feelings seek to escape the intolerable horror, but it is no use. Here, up against the worst form of slaughter, again these nameless noises bring it home to you with overpowering force.

This battle has lasted for days; now it is again that continuous roar that effaces, or rather, consumes, all individual noises, that makes even fierce explosions close by you indistinguishable. Everything disappears in one loud, rolling, threatening volume of sound. The air carries it a hundred miles distant, and tremblingly they listen, south and north, west and east, where they cannot see the horror of all this.

But if you come nearer, it is like the bowels of the earth exploding. Our soldiers sit in their dugouts, and cannot do anything but trust to luck. Just now the infantry must keep quiet; only the big guns are talking. The waiting infantry is, as it were, locked in prison. The men cannot get out, nor can anybody approach them. The way to them is fraught with fearful danger. All around spatter steel splinters, shrapnel bullets, stones and earth. If you are hit you are dead or crippled. What shall one do? One smokes incessantly, until the air in the narrow shaft is heavy enough to cut. That is bad, but somehow it helps one to endure the horrors of the situation.

You live for days in the closest contact with your comrades in a contracted space. You cannot move, and are unable to think clearly. Never did I realize how difficult it can be to lead a human life. There is nameless agony in it.

Suddenly there is a terrible explosion quite near you. The earth is moving. Splinters drop from nowhere. Our works have been hit at an adjacent point, but thank Heaven! there are no wounded. Nobody was stationed there when the projectile struck.

There is still another explosion, this time the other side of us. Nine dugouts have been hit and have collapsed.

Then there is one of those rare lulls in the cannonade, and quite distinctly we make out some of our comrades struggling in the ruins of a wrecked dugout. We rush to their aid, heedless of the shells bursting around us. Another of those deadly beasts strikes almost at our feet, but it does not explode. We don't stop; we rush on; we shout to our friends, who are buried under the earth, stones, and timber, and we set to work digging them out.

"Nobody is seriously hurt," they cry joyously, when we drag them, covered with scratches and contusions, to daylight again. We do not always fare so well as this. Sometimes we dig them from cellars and earthworks as corpses, sometimes fearfully mutilated, or just in time to draw their last breath.

But after all, our losses are not so large—certainly not compared with the mass of munitions exploded. Our men have become masters in the art of dodging and using cover. They certainly have had experience enough. But still too many sons of German mothers must yield up their young lives mutely without a chance of defending themselves. But they all realize that only the Fatherland counts; that the individual cannot claim special attention here. The heavy twenty-four-centimeter projectiles of the enemy care not where they strike, be it human life, wire entanglements, or trench, and sometimes they hit our nerves though they strike many meters distant.

There is one consolation: Our artillery pays them back with interest, and the hellish noises at our rear are almost music to the ears of our men in our dugouts. Once upon a time infantrymen used to swear at artillery in battles; nowadays you hear nothing of the kind. Our infantry

knows that those men behind their guns are having a hell
of a time, while the infantryman is comparatively safe in
his dugout.

But even the artillery needs our infantryman. He must
carry munitions to positions that are inaccessible to horses
and carts. The infantryman must watch the approaches
to the artillery positions from all sides, and must be at his
post when the sign is given for a general advance. Is this
the end of terror, or merely the lull before the attack?
Fiercely your fist grips gun and hand grenade. The eyes of
the men on guard pierce the dense darkness ahead. There
rises a green fireball. Is it ours? Is it theirs? Nobody
seems to know its meaning, but all of a sudden the English
begin to rain steel again. We give them tit for tat. The artillery on each side seems to try to surpass that on the
other. What has happened? Nothing particular, but since
they were at it, they thought they might as well keep hammering, and that one long roar continues until the sun rises
again on a new day as cruel as yesterday. Nobody will
ever forget the horror of it.

August 1st.

The great brutal force of the initial blow has been parried. We survived the grewsome tension occasioned by the
uncanny artillery fire, and we are able again to hold our
heads high as the battle of living men is resumed. The
struggle has now reached the phase of human effort, after
unseen mechanical death has been knocking at the door day
and night for weeks. The German fighting spirit was fully
awakened, and heroes flung themselves from the islands of
defense in the conquered district against the advancing
masses and seriously weakened the flanks of the oncoming
troops. Millions of shells have been spent, and now comes
the test of strength and nerves.

The mainspring which impelled the German fighting man
was the strong realization that he was here called upon to
defend the German U-boat—to serve the mightiest, most
promising weapon of his country and bar the path to it

with his life. The German troops counter-attacked in frightful bayonet and hand grenade combats. It was the mightiest counter-thrust, following the mightiest impact, which the world has ever seen.

Nightfall witnessed the happy German achievement. The foe had won German trenches, had gained control of Bixschoote, and had carried off prisoners, but he lay bleeding at the foot of the wall he desired to scale.

BY SIR DOUGLAS HAIG

At 3.50 a. m. on the morning of the 31st of July the combined attack was launched. English, Irish, Scottish and Welsh troops delivered the main assault on the British front.

Preceded at zero hour by discharges of thermit and oil drums, and covered by an accurate artillery barrage from a great number of guns, the Allied infantry entered the German lines at all points. The enemy's barrage was late and weak, and our casualties were light.

On the greater part of the front of the main attack the resistance of the German infantry was quickly overcome and rapid progress was made. The difficult country east of Ypres, where the Menin Road crosses the crest of the Wytschaete-Passchendaele Ridge, formed, however, the key to the enemy's position, and here the most determined opposition was encountered. None the less, the attacking brigades, including a number of Lancashire battalions, regiments from all parts of England, and a few Scottish and Irish battalions, fought their way steadily forward through Shrewsbury Forest and Sanctuary Wood and captured Stirling Castle, Hooge and the Bellewarde Ridge.

Farther north British and French troops carried the whole of the first German trench system with scarcely a check, and proceeded in accordance with the time-table to the assault of the enemy's second line of defense. Scottish troops took Verlorenhoek, and, continuing their advance, by 6 a. m. had reached Frezenberg, where for a short time stiff fighting took place before the village and the strong defenses round it were captured. South of Pilckem a Prussian Guard battalion was broken up by Welsh troops after a brief resistance and Pilckem was taken. Sharp fighting occurred also at a number of other points, but in every instance the enemy's opposition was overcome.

At 9 a. m. the whole of our second objectives north of the Ypres-Roulers Railway were in our possession, with the exception of a strong point north of Frezenberg, known as Pommern Redoubt, where fighting was still going on. Within an hour this redoubt also had been captured by West Lancashire Territorials. On our left French troops made equal progress, capturing their objective in precise accordance with program and with little loss.

By this time our field artillery had begun to move up, and by 9.30 a. m. a number of batteries were already in action in their forward positions. The Allied advance on this portion of our front was resumed at the hour planned. English county troops captured St. Julien, and from that point northwards our final objectives were reached and passed. Highland Territorials, Welsh and Guards battalions secured the crossings of the Steenbeek, and French troops, having also taken their final objectives, advanced beyond them and seized Bixschoote. A hostile counter-attack launched against the point of junction of the French and British Armies was completely repulsed.

Meanwhile, south of the Ypres-Roulers Railway, very heavy and continuous fighting was taking place on both sides of the Menin Road.

After the capture of the German first line system our troops on this part of our front had advanced in time with the divisions on their left against their second objectives. Great opposition was at once encountered in front of two small woods known as Inverness Copse and Glencorse Wood, while further south a strong point in Shrewsbury Forest held out against our attacks till the morning of the 1st of August. North of Glencorse Wood English troops continued their advance in spite of the enemy's resistance and reached the village of Westhoek.

Later in the day heavy counter-attacks began to develop from south of the Menin Road northwards to St. Julien.

Our artillery caused great loss to the enemy in these attacks, although the weather was unfavorable for aëroplane work, and observation for our batteries was difficult. At Inverness Copse and Glencorse Wood a few tanks succeeded in reaching the fighting line, in spite of exceedingly bad ground, and came into action with our infantry. Fierce fighting took place all day, but the enemy was unable to shake our hold upon the ridge.

At the end of the day, therefore, our troops on the Fifth Army front had carried the German first system of defense south of Westhoek. Except at Westhoek itself, where they were established on the outskirts of the village, they had already gained the whole of the crest of the ridge and had denied the enemy observation over the Ypres plain. Farther north they had captured the enemy's second line also as far as St. Julien. North of that village they had passed beyond the German second line, and held the line of the Steenbeek to our junction with the French.

On our left flank our Allies had admirably completed the important task allotted to them. Close touch had been kept with the British troops on their right throughout the day. All and more than all their objectives had been gained rapidly and at exceptionally light cost, and the flank of the Allied advance had been effectively secured.

Meanwhile, the attack on the Second Army front had also met with complete success. On the extreme right New Zealand troops had carried La Basse Ville after a sharp fight lasting some fifty minutes. On the left English troops had captured Hollebeke and the difficult ground north of the bend of the Ypres-Comines Canal and east of Battle Wood. Between these two points our line had been advanced on the whole front for distances varying from 200 to 800 yards.

Over 6,100 prisoners, including 133 officers, were captured by us in this battle. In addition to our gains in prisoners and ground we also captured some 25 guns, while a further number of prisoners and guns were taken by our Allies.

The weather had been threatening throughout the day,

and had rendered the work of the aëroplanes very difficult from the commencement of the battle. During the afternoon, while fighting was still in progress, rain began, and fell steadily all night. Thereafter, for four days, the rain continued without cessation, and for several days afterwards the weather remained stormy and unsettled. The low-lying, clayey soil, torn by shells and sodden with rain, turned to a succession of vast muddy pools. The valleys of the choked and overflowing streams were speedily transformed into long stretches of bog, impassable except by a few well-defined tracks, which became marks for the enemy's artillery. To leave these tracks was to risk death by drowning, and in the course of the subsequent fighting on several occasions both men and pack animals were lost in this way. In these conditions operations of any magnitude became impossible, and the resumption of our offensive was necessarily postponed until a period of fine weather should allow the ground to recover.

As had been the case in the Arras battle, this unavoidable delay in the development of our offensive was of the greatest service to the enemy. Valuable time was lost, the troops opposed to us were able to recover from the disorganization produced by our first attack, and the enemy was given the opportunity to bring up reënforcements.

During the night of the 31st of July and on the two following days, the enemy delivered further counter-attacks against our new line, and in particular made determined efforts to dislodge us from the high ground between the Menin Road and the Ypres-Roulers Railway, and to recover his second line system between Frezenberg and St. Julien. In this he completely failed. The violence of his artillery fire compelled us, however, to withdraw temporarily from St. Julien, though we retained a bridgehead across the Steenbeek, just north of the village.

In spite of these counter-attacks and the great but unavoidable hardships from which our troops were suffering, steady progress was made with the consolidation of the captured ground, and every opportunity was taken to improve the line already gained.

On the 3rd of August St. Julien was reoccupied without serious opposition, and our line linked up with the position we had retained on the right bank of the Steenbeek further north. A week later a successful minor operation carried out by English troops gave us complete possession of Westhoek. Seven hostile counter-attacks within the following four days broke down before our defense.

During this period certain centers of resistance in the neighborhood of Kortekeer Cabaret were cleared up by our Allies, and a number of fortified farmhouses, lying across the front of the French position, were reduced in turn.

Towards the middle of August a slight improvement took place in the weather, and advantage was taken of this to launch our second attack east of Ypres. Thereafter unsettled weather again set in, and the month closed as the wettest August that has been known for many years.

On the day preceding this attack at Ypres a highly successful operation was carried out in the neighborhood of Lens, whereby the situation of our forces in that sector was greatly improved. At the same time the threat to Lens itself was rendered more immediate and more insistent, and the enemy was prevented from concentrating the whole of his attention and resources upon the front of our main offensive.

At 4.25 a. m. on the 15th of August the Canadian Corps attacked on a front of 4,000 yards southeast and east of Loos. The objectives consisted of the strongly fortified hill known as Hill 70, which had been reached, but not held, in the battle of Loos on September 25, 1915, and also the mining suburbs of Cité Ste. Elizabeth, Cité St. Emile, and Cité St. Laurent, together with the whole of Bois Rase and the western half of Bois Hugo. The observation from Hill 70 had been very useful to the enemy, and in our possession materially increased our command over the defenses of Lens.

Practically the whole of these objectives were gained rapidly at light cost, and in exact accordance with plan. Only at the farthest apex of our advance a short length of German trench west of Cité St. Auguste resisted our first assault.

This position was again attacked on the afternoon of the following day and captured after a fierce struggle lasting far into the night.

A number of local counter-attacks on the morning of the 15th of August were repulsed, and in the evening a powerful attack delivered across the open by a German reserve division was broken up with heavy loss. In addition to the enemy's other casualties, 1,120 prisoners from three German divisions were captured by us.

Close upon the heels of this success, at 4.45 a. m. on the 16th of August our second attack was launched east and north of Ypres; on a front extending from the northwest corner of Inverness Copse to our junction with the French south of St. Janshoek. On our left the French undertook the task of clearing up the remainder of the Bixshoote peninsula.

On the left of the British attack the English brigades detailed for the assault captured the hamlet of Wijdendrift and reached the southern outskirts of Langemarck. Here some resistance was encountered, but by 8.00 a. m. the village had been taken, after sharp fighting. Our troops then proceeded to attack the portion of the Langemarck-Gheluvelt Line which formed their final objective, and an hour later had gained this also, with the exception of a short length of trench northeast of Langemarck. Two small counter-attacks were repulsed without difficulty.

The attack of the First French Army delivered at the same hour was equally successful. On the right a few fortified farms in the neighborhood of the Steenbeek again gave trouble, and held out for a time. Elsewhere our Allies gained their objectives rapidly, and once more at exceptionally light cost. The bridge-head of Drie Grachten was secured, and the whole of the peninsula cleared of the enemy.

In the center of the British attack the enemy's resistance was more obstinate. The difficulty of making deep-mined dugouts in soil where water lay within a few feet of the surface had compelled the enemy to construct "pill-boxes" built of reënforced concrete often many feet thick.

In the interval, on the 19th, 22nd and 27th of August, positions of considerable local importance in the neighborhood of St. Julien were captured with some hundreds of prisoners, as the result of minor attacks conducted under the most unfavorable conditions of ground and weather. The ground gained represented an advance of about 800 yards on a front of over two miles. In combination with the attack of the 22nd of August, English troops also attacked astride the Menin road, and after six days of continuous local fighting established themselves in the western edge of Inverness Copse.

Meanwhile, in pursuance of my policy of compelling the enemy to guard himself on other fronts, successful minor operations had been undertaken elsewhere. On the Lens front, Canadian troops attacked on the 21st of August, and carried the line of German trenches skirting the town to the southwest and west, taking 200 prisoners. Further south, north-country troops attacked on the 26th of August east of Hargicourt, and captured the enemy's advanced positions on a front of a mile. In this operation 136 prisoners were taken, and on the 9th and 11th of September our gains were extended and further prisoners secured.

At the beginning of September the weather gradually improved, and artillery and other preparations for my next attack proceeded steadily. Both the extent of the preparations required, however, and the need to give the ground time to recover from the heavy rains of August rendered a considerable interval unavoidable before a new advance could be undertaken. The 20th of September was therefore chosen for the date of our attack, and before that day our preparations had been completed.

The front selected extended from the Ypres-Comines Canal north of Hollebeke to the Ypres-Staden Railway north of Langemarck, a distance of just over eight miles along the line then held by us. The average depth of our objectives was 1,000 yards, which increased to a depth of a mile in the neighborhood of the Menin road. Australian, English, Scottish and South African troops were employed in the attack, and gained a success conspicuous for precision and thoroughness of execution.

During the night of the 19th-20th of September rain again fell steadily, and when dawn broke thick mist made observation impossible. Despite this disadvantage, the assembling of our troops was carried out in good order, and at 5.40 a. m. on the 20th of September the assault was launched.

Good progress was made from the start, and as the morning wore on the mist cleared. Our aëroplanes were able to establish contact with our infantry, to assist them by engaging parties of the enemy with machine-gun fire, and to report hostile concentrations and counter-attacks to our artillery.

On our right Welsh and west country troops advanced down the spur east of Klein Zillebeke, and after sharp fighting in the small woods north of the Ypres-Comines Canal gained the whole of their objectives. English battalions pushed through the eastern portions of Shrewsbury Forest and reached their objectives in the valley of the Bassevillebeek. Regiments from the southeast counties of England had some trouble from snipers and machine guns early in their advance, but ultimately fought their way forward across the upper valley of the Bassevillebeek and up the slopes of Tower Hamlets. Here strong opposition was encountered, with heavy machine-gun fire from Tower Hamlets and the Veldhoek Ridge.

In the meantime, however, north country troops had already carried Inverness Copse, and after beating off a counter-attack in the neighborhood of Dumbarton Lakes captured Veldhoek and the line of their final objectives some 500 yards farther east. Their progress assisted the southeast county battalions on their right to establish themselves across the Tower Hamlets spur.

On the left of the north country division Australian troops carried the remainder of Glencorse Wood and Nonne Boschen. Before 10 a. m. they had taken the hamlet of Polygonveld and the old German third line to the north of it. This advance constituted a fine performance, in which the capture of a difficult piece of ground that had much delayed us was successfully completed. Sharp fighting took place at a strong point known as Black Watch Corner at the southwestern end of Polygon Wood. By midday this had been captured, the western portion of Polygon Wood had been cleared of the enemy, and the whole of our objectives on this part of our front had been gained.

On the Fifth Army front our attack met with equal success. Scottish and South African troops, advancing on both sides of the Ypres-Roulers Railway, stormed the line of fortified farms immediately in front of their position, and, pressing on, captured Zonnebeke and Bremen Redoubts and the hamlet of Zevenkote. By 8.45 a. m. our final objectives on this front had been gained.

West Lancashire Territorial battalions found the ground southeast of St. Julien very wet and heavy after the night's rain. None the less, they made steady progress, reaching the line of their final objectives early in the afternoon. North of the Zonnebeke-Langemarck Road London and Highland Territorials gained the whole of their objectives by midday, though stiff fighting took place for a number of farms and strong places.

As the result of this most successful operation the whole of the high ground crossed by the Menin Road, for which such desperate fighting had taken place during our previous attacks, passed into our possession. Important positions were won also on the remainder of our front, by which the right of our attack was rendered more secure, and the way opened for the advance of our left. In the attack, as well as in the repeated counter-attacks which followed, exceedingly heavy casualties were inflicted on the enemy, and 3,243 prisoners, together with a number of guns, were captured by us.

The enemy did not abandon these important positions without further severe struggles. During the afternoon and evening of the 20th of September no less than eleven counter-attacks were made without success against different parts of our new front, in addition to several concentrations of hostile infantry, which were broken up by our artillery before any attack could be launched.

East of St. Julien the enemy at his third attempt succeeded in forcing back our troops to the west of Schuler Farm, but on the following day the farm was retaken by us and our line reëstablished. Northeast of Langemarck stubborn fighting took place for the possession of the short length of trench which, as already recounted, had resisted our attacks on the 16th of August. It was not till the morning of the 23rd of September that the position was finally captured by us.

Fierce fighting took place also on the 21st of September in the neighborhood of Tower Hamlets. In the course of this and the following four days three powerful attacks were launched by the enemy on wide fronts between Tower Hamlets and Polygon Wood, and a fourth northeast of St. Julien. All these attacks were repulsed, except that on the 25th of September parties of German infantry succeeded in entering our lines north of the Menin Road. Heavy and confused fighting took place in this area throughout the day, in which English, Scottish, and Australian troops gradually drove the enemy from the limited foothold he had gained.

The enemy's casualties in these many counter-attacks, as well as in all those subsequently delivered by him on the Ypres front, were consistently very heavy. Our constant successful resistance reflects the greatest credit on the high fighting qualities of our infantry, on the courage and devotion of our airmen, and upon the excellence of our artillery arrangements.

All this heavy fighting was not allowed to interfere with the arrangements made for a renewal of the advance by the Second and Fifth Armies on the 26th of September.

The front of our attack on that date extended from south of Tower Hamlets to northeast of St. Julien, a total distance of rather less than six miles; but on the portion of this front south of the Menin Road only a short advance was intended. North of the Menin Road, our object was to reach a position from which a direct attack could be made upon the portion of the main ridge between Noordemdhoek and Broodseinde, traversed by the Becelaere-Passchendaele Road.

The assault was delivered at 5.50 a. m., and, after hard and prolonged fighting, in which over 1,600 prisoners were taken by us, achieved a success as striking as that of the 20th of September.

Australian troops carried the remainder of Polygon Wood, together with the German trench line to the east of it, and established themselves on their objectives beyond the Becelaere-Zonnebeke Road. On the left of the Australians, English troops took Zonnebeke Village and church, and North Midland and London Territorial battalions captured a long line of hostile strong points on both sides of the Wieltje-Gravenstafel Road.

South of Polygon Wood an obstinate struggle took place for a group of fortified farms and strong points. English, Scottish, and Welsh battalions of the same Divisions that had borne the brunt of the enemy's attacks in this area on the previous day gallantly fought their way forward. In their advance they effected the relief of two companies of Argyll and Sutherland Highlanders, who, with great courage and resolution, had held out in our forward line all night, although isolated from the rest of our troops. It was not until the evening of the 27th of September, however, that the line of our objectives in this locality was completely gained.

As had been the case on the 20th of September, our advance was at once followed by a series of powerful counter-attacks.

There is evidence that our operations had anticipated a counter-stroke which the enemy was preparing for the evening of the 26th of September, and the German troops brought up for this purpose were now hurled in to recover the positions he had lost. In the course of the day at least seven attacks were delivered at points covering practically the whole front from Tower Hamlets to St. Julien. The fiercest fighting prevailed in the sector between the Reutel-beek and Polygon Wood, but here, as elsewhere, all the enemy's assaults were beaten off.

On the 30th of September, when the enemy had recovered from the disorganization caused by his defeat, he recommenced his attacks. Two attempts to advance with *flam-menwerfer* north of the Menin Road were followed on the 1st of October by five other attacks in this area, and on the same day a sixth attack was made south of the Ypres-Roulers Railway. Except for the temporary loss of the two advanced posts southeast of Polygon Wood, all these attacks were repulsed with great loss. At dawn on the 3rd of October another attempt in the neighborhood of the Menin Road broke down before our positions.

The spell of fine weather was broken on the evening of the 3rd of October by a heavy gale and rain from the southwest. These conditions serve to emphasize the credit due to the troops for the completeness of the success gained by them on the following day.

At 6.00 a. m. on the 4th of October our advance was renewed, in accordance with plan, against the main line of the ridge east of Zonnebeke. The front of our principal attack extended from the Menin Road to the Ypres-Staden Railway, a distance of about 7 miles. South of the Menin Road a short advance was undertaken on a front of about a mile, with the object of capturing certain strong points required to strengthen our position in this sector.

The attack was carried out by Australian, New Zealand, and English Divisions, including among the latter a few Scottish, Irish and Welsh battalions, and was successful at all points.

On the right of the main attack troops from Kent, Devon and Cornwall, and a battalion of the King's Own Scottish Borderers carried their objectives after heavy fighting in the neighborhood of Polderhoek Château. Battalions from Yorkshire, Northumberland, Surrey and Lincolnshire cleared the small enclosures east of Polygon Wood and seized the village of Reutel, meeting with strong opposition. On their left Surrey, Staffordshire, Devon, Border and Highland troops, advancing across the crest of the ridge, captured the hamlet of Noordemdhoek.

Farther north, Australian troops advanced beyond the Becelaere-Passchendaele Road, storming Molenaarelsthoek and Broodseinde, and established themselves well to the east of the crest line. New Zealand troops carried Gravenstafel, and drove the enemy from a network of trenches and strong points on the Gravenstafel Spur.

On the whole of this front the enemy was met in great strength. In addition to the two German divisions already in line, the enemy had brought up three fresh divisions, with a view to launching an attack in force upon the positions captured by us on the 26th of September. Our advance anticipated this attack by ten minutes, and the German infantry were forming up for the assault when our artillery barrage opened. Very serious casualties were inflicted on the enemy by our artillery, and our infantry advancing with the bayonet quickly overcame the resistance of those of his troops who had escaped our shell fire. Great numbers of prisoners were taken.

On the left of our attack South Midland troops forced their way across the valley of the Stroombeek, in spite of difficulties due to the rain of the previous night, and gained their objectives according to program, with the exception of a single strong point at the limit of their advance. Other English Divisions, advancing on both sides of the Poelcappelle Road, stormed the western half of that village, including the church, and captured the whole of their objectives for the day. Tanks took part in the attack on Poelcappelle and contributed to the success of our troops.

On the extreme left considerable opposition was met with, and determined fighting took place for the possession of the rising ground known as 19 Meter Hill. Early in the afternoon a hostile counter-attack forced us back from a portion of this position, but later in the day our troops returned to the attack and recovered the lost ground.

Meanwhile, south of the Menin Road English troops had gained the whole of their limited objectives with the exception of two strong points. Soon after midday our final objectives had been gained, and large numbers of prisoners had already been brought in. The final total of German prisoners captured in these operations exceeded 5,000, including 138 officers. A few guns and many machine guns and trench mortars were also taken by us.

The destruction of the Divisions which the enemy had assembled for his intended attack made immediate serious counter-attacks impossible for him on a great part of our front. Between the Menin Road and the neighborhood of Reutel, however, no less than seven counter-attacks were beaten off in turn. Exceedingly heavy fighting took place in this area, and later in the day an eighth attack succeeded in dislodging us from Polderhoek Château and from the eastern portions of Reutel. Another determined counter-attack delivered in three waves early in the afternoon north of the Ypres-Roulers Railway was broken up by our artillery, rifle and machine-gun fire. Hostile concentrations east of Zonnebeke and west of Passchendaele were dispersed by our artillery.

The success of this operation marked a definite step in the development of our advance. Our line had now been established along the main ridge for 9,000 yards from our starting point near Mount Sorrel. From the farthest point reached the well-marked Gravenstafel Spur offered a defensible feature along which our line could be bent back from the ridge.

The year was far spent. The weather had been consistently unpropitious, and the state of the ground, in consequence of rain and shelling combined, made movement inconceivably difficult. The resultant delays had given the enemy time to bring up reënforcements and to organize his defense after each defeat. Even so, it was still the difficulty of movement far more than hostile resistance which continued to limit our progress, and now made it doubtful whether the capture of the remainder of the ridge before winter finally set in was possible.

On the other hand, there was no reason to anticipate an abnormally wet October. The enemy had suffered severely, as was evidenced by the number of prisoners in our hands, by the number of his dead on the battlefield, by the costly failure of his repeated counter-attacks, and by the symptoms of confusion and discouragement in his ranks.

In this connection, documents captured in the course of the battle of the 4th of October throw an interesting light upon the success of the measures taken by us to meet the enemy's new system of defense by counter-attack. These documents show that the German Higher Command had already recognized the failure of their methods, and were endeavoring to revert to something approximating to their old practice of holding their forward positions in strength.

After weighing these considerations, as well as the general situation and various other factors affecting the problem, among them the desirability of assisting our Allies in the operations to be carried out by them on the 23rd of October in the neighborhood of Malmaison, I decided to continue the offensive further and to renew the advance at the earliest possible moment consistent with adequate preparation.

Accordingly, I determined to deliver the next combined French and British attack on the 9th of October.

Unfortunately, bad weather still persisted in the early part of October, and on the 7th of October heavy rain fell all day. The unfavorable conditions interfered with our artillery preparations; but every effort was made to engage the enemy's batteries in their new positions, and on the date last mentioned our artillery coöperated effectively in the repulse of two hostile attacks.

On the 8th of October rain continued, and the slippery state of the ground, combined with an exceptionally dark night, made the assembling of our troops a matter of considerable difficulty. No interference, however, was encountered from the enemy's artillery, and at 5.20 a. m. on the 9th of October our attack was renewed on a front of over six miles, from a point east of Zonnebeke to our junction with the French northwest of Langemarck. On our left our Allies prolonged the front of attack to a point opposite Draaibank. At the same time, minor operations were undertaken on the right of our main attack, east and southeast of Polygon Wood.

The greatest depth of our advance was on the left, where the Allied troops penetrated the German positions to a distance of nearly one and a half miles. French troops and British Guards crossed the flooded valley of the Broenbeek, and, making steady progress towards their objectives captured the hamlet of Koekuit, Veldhoek, Mangelare, and St. Janshoek, besides woods and a great number of farmhouses and strong points. Early in the afternoon both French and British troops had established themselves on their final objectives on the outskirts of Houthulst Forest.

On the right of the Guards, other English Divisions made equal progress along the Ypres-Staden Railway and secured a line well to the east of the Poelcappelle-Houthulst Road. Stiff fighting took place around certain strong points, in the course of which a hostile counter-attack was repulsed.

Farther south, English battalions fought their way forward in the face of great opposition to the eastern outskirts of Poelcappelle village. Australian troops and East Lancashire, Yorkshire and South Midland Territorials carried our line forward in the direction of Passchendaele and up the western slopes of the main ridge, capturing Nieuwemolen and Keerselaarhoek and a number of strong points and fortified farms.

In the subsidiary attack east of Polygon Wood Warwickshire and H.A.C. battalions successfully regained the remainder of Reutel.

Over 2,100 prisoners were taken by the Allies in the course of these operations, together with a few guns.

Though the condition of the ground continued to deteriorate, the weather after this was unsettled rather than persistently wet, and progress had not yet become impossible. I accordingly decided to press on while circumstances still permitted, and arrangements were made for a renewal of the attack on the 12th of October. On the night of the 11th-12th of October, however, heavy rain commenced again, and after a brief interval during the morning continued steadily throughout the whole of the following day.

Our attack, launched at 5.25 a. m. on the 12th of October between the Ypres-Roulers Railway and Houthulst Forest, made progress along the spurs and higher ground; but the valleys of the streams which run westward from the main ridge were found to be impassable. I was therefore determined not to persist in the attack, and the advance towards our most distant objectives was cancelled.

Certain strong points and fortified farms on the western slopes of the ridge were captured on this day, and were incorporated in our line. Farther north, on both sides of the Ypres-Staden Railway, English County Divisions and the Guards gained their objectives in spite of all difficulties. Though for many hours the position of our advanced troops on this part of our front was uncertain, communication was at length established and the captured ground maintained.

Over 1,000 prisoners were taken by us in this attack, in which the troops employed displayed remarkable gallantry, steadfastness and endurance in circumstances of extreme hardship.

By this time the persistent continuation of wet weather had left no further room for hope that the condition of the ground would improve sufficiently to enable us to capture the remainder of the ridge this year. By limited attacks made during intervals of better weather, however, it would still be possible to progress as far as Passchendaele, and in view of other projects which I had in view it was desirable to maintain the pressure on the Flanders front for a few weeks longer.

To maintain his defense on this front the enemy had been obliged to reduce the garrison of certain other parts of his line to a degree which justified the expectation that a sudden attack at a point where he did not expect it might attain a considerable local success. The front for such an attempt had been selected and plans had already been quietly made. But certain preparations and movements of troops required time to complete, and the 20th of November had been fixed as the earliest date for the attack.

No large force could be made available for the enterprise. The prospects of success therefore depended on complete secrecy and on maintaining sufficient activity in Flanders to induce the enemy to continue his concentration of troops in that theater.

As has been indicated above, our Allies also had certain limited operations in view which would be likely to benefit by the maintenance of pressure on my front, and, reciprocally, would add to the prospects of success of my intended surprise attack. Accordingly, while preparing for the latter, operations of limited scope were continued in Flanders.

After the middle of October the weather improved and on the 22nd of October two successful operations, in which we captured over 200 prisoners and gained positions of considerable local importance east of Poelcappelle and within the southern edge of Houthulst Forest, were undertaken by us, in the one case by East County and Northumberland troops, and in the other by West County and Scots battalions in coöperation with the French.

The following two days were unsettled, but on the 25th of October a strong west wind somewhat dried the surface of the ground. It was therefore decided to proceed with the Allied operations which had been planned for the 26th of October.

At an early hour on that morning rain unfortunately began again and fell heavily all day. The assembling of our troops was completed successfully none the less, and at 5.45 a. m. English and Canadian troops attacked on a front extending from the Ypres-Roulers Railway to beyond Poelcappelle.

The Canadians attacked on the right on both sides of the small stream known as the Ravebeek, which flows southwestwards from Passchendaele. On the left bank of the stream they advanced astride the main ridge and established themselves securely on the small hill south of Passchendaele. North of the Ravebeek strong resistance was met on the Bellevue spur, a very strong point which had resisted our efforts in previous attacks. With splendid determination the Canadians renewed their attack on this point in the afternoon, and captured it. Two strong counter-attacks south and west of Passchendaele were beaten off, and by nightfall the Canadians had gained practically the whole of their objectives.

On the left of the Canadians the Royal Navy Division and battalions of London Territorials also advanced, and, in spite of immense difficulties from marsh and floods in the more low-lying ground, made progress.

In a subsidiary attack undertaken by us at the same hour English troops entered Gheluvelt and recaptured Polderhoek Château, with a number of prisoners. Our men's rifles, however, had become choked with mud in their advance, and when later in the morning strong German counter-attacks developed, they were obliged to withdraw.

The operations of our Allies on this day were limited to establishing bridgeheads across the floods of the St. Jansbeek. This was successfully accomplished, in spite of considerable opposition. Next day the French continued their advance in concert with Belgian troops, who crossed the Yser opposite Knockehoek, and captured Aschhoop, Kippe, and Merckem. The southern end of Blankaart Lake was reached on the same day, and early on the 28th of October French and Belgian troops completed the capture of the whole Merckem peninsula.

Over 400 prisoners were taken by our Allies in these operations, bringing the total Allied captures since the commencement of our attacks on the 26th of October to over 1,200.

At this date the need for the policy of activity outlined above had been still further emphasized by recent developments in Italy. Additional importance was given to it by the increasing probability that a time was approaching when the enemy's power of drawing reënforcements from Russia would increase considerably. In pursuance of this policy, therefore, two short advances were made on the 30th of October and the 6th of November, by which we gained possession of Passchendaele.

In the first operation Canadian and English troops attacked at 5.50 a. m. on a front extending from the Ypres-Roulers Railway to the Poelcappelle-Westroosebeke Road.

On the right the Canadians continued their advance along the high ground and reached the outskirts of Passchendaele, capturing an important position at Crest Farm on a small hill southwest of the village. Fighting was severe at all points, but particularly on the spur west of Passchendaele. Here no less than five strong counter-attacks were beaten off in the course of the day, our troops being greatly assisted by the fire of captured German machine guns in Crest Farm.

Farther north, battalions of the same London and Naval Divisions that had taken part in the attack on the 26th of October again made progress wherever it was possible to find a way across the swamps. The almost impassable nature of the ground in this area, however, made movement practically impossible, and it was only on the main ridge that much could be effected.

During the succeeding days small advances were made by night southwest of Passchendaele, and a hostile attack on both sides of the Ypres-Roulers Railway was successfully repulsed.

At 6 a. m. on the 6th of November Canadian troops renewed their attack and captured the village of Passchendaele, together with the high ground immediately to the north and northwest. Sharp fighting took place for the possession of "pill-boxes" in the northern end of the village, around Mosselmarkt, and on the Goudberg Spur. All objectives were gained at an early hour, and at 8.50 a. m. a hostile counter-attack north of Passchendaele was beaten off.

Over 400 prisoners were captured in this most successful attack, by which for the second time within the year Canadian troops achieved a record of uninterrupted success. Four days later, in extremely unfavorable weather, British and Canadian troops attacked northwards from Passchendaele and Goudberg, and captured further ground on the main ridge, after heavy fighting.

These operations concluded our Flanders offensive for the time being, although considerable activity was still continued for another fortnight for purposes already explained.

This offensive, maintained for three and a half months under the most adverse conditions of weather had entailed almost superhuman exertions on the part of the troops of all arms and services. The enemy had done his utmost to hold his ground, and in his endeavors to do so had used up no less than seventy-eight divisions, of which eighteen had been engaged a second or third time in the battle, after being withdrawn to rest and refit. Despite the magnitude of his efforts, it was the immense natural difficulties, accentuated manihold by the abnormally wet weather, rather than the enemy's resistance, which limited our progress and prevented the complete capture of the ridge.

What was actually accomplished under such adverse conditions is the most conclusive proof that, given a normally fine August, the capture of the whole ridge, within the space of a few weeks, was well within the power of the men who achieved so much. They advanced every time with absolute confidence in their power to overcome the enemy, even though they had sometimes to struggle through mud up to their waists to reach him. So long as they could reach him they did overcome him, but physical exhaustion placed narrow limits on the depth to which each advance could be pushed, and compelled long pauses between the advances. The full fruits of each success were consequently not always obtained. Time after time the practically beaten enemy was enabled to reorganize and relieve his men and to bring up reënforcements behind the sea of mud which constituted his main protection.

Notwithstanding the many difficulties, much has been achieved. Our captures in Flanders since the commencement of operations at the end of July amount to 24,065 prisoners, 74 guns, 941 machine guns and 138 trench mortars. It is certain that the enemy's losses considerably exceeded ours. Most important of all, our new and hastily trained armies have shown once again that they are capable of meeting and beating the enemy's best troops, even under conditions which favored his defense to a degree which it required the greatest endurance, determination and heroism to overcome.

BY GENERAL SIR DAVID WATSON

What a sacrifice this operation entailed, and yet so necessary in the great final victory. No one of us, who had previous experience of the Ypres Salient fighting, could anticipate without horror and dread, the orders received for the great effort and still greater sacrifices of Passchendaele. The approaches to the front, and on beyond, were simply beyond description. Wastes of mud, destroyed houses, roads torn up by constant shelling and above all, the vile weather conditions, that made life a burden.

Sir Douglas Haig, at a conference with the Canadian Generals some days prior to the attack, stated that the Canadian Corps would be the determining factor, for the date of the operation, as ours was the big effort, all the others being subsidiary to our main operation of the capture of Bellevue Spur, Crest Farm, and Passchendaele itself.

Our engineers at once started to lay our French Railways, guns were brought well forward, dumps of ammunition and supplies established, dressing stations located, and proper jumping off positions for the infantry were dug and prepared. Night and day the work progressed under most trying and difficult situations. It was decided to carry out the scheme in three staged operations, all of which as explained in the story following, were successfully accomplished and carried out precisely according to schedule.

It need hardly be a matter of surprise that the Canadians by this time had the reputation of being the best shock troops in the Allied Armies. They had been pitted against the select guards and shock troops of Germany and the Canadian superiority was proven beyond question. They had the physique, the stamina, the initiative, the confidence between officers and men (so frequently of equal standing in civilian life) and happened to have the opportunity. As Philip Gibbs said of the battle of Passchendaele, "The Canadians have had more luck than the English, New Zealand and Australian troops who fought the way up with most heroic endeavor, and not a man in the army will begrudge them the honor which they have gained, not easily, nor without the usual price of victory, which is some men's death and many men's pain. After an heroic attack by the Canadians, they fought their way over the ruins of Passchendaele and into the ground beyond it. Their gains held, the seal is set upon the most terrific achievement of war ever attempted and carried through by British arms."

At and around Passchendaele was the highest ground on the ridge, looking down across the sweep of plains into which the enemy had been thrust and where he had camps and dumps. Sir Douglas Haig's official report said: "Night operations were undertaken this morning (November 6th, 1917) by Canadian troops with complete success against the enemy's defences in and around Passchendaele and on the spur north and north-west of the village. The assembly of our troops for the attack was carried out successfully, and at 6 a. m., the assault was launched as arranged. The enemy had been ordered to hold this important position on the main ridge at all costs. Hard fighting took place at a number of points on the Goudberg Spur. None the less our troops made steady progress, and at an early hour the village of Passchendaele was captured with the hamlet of Mosselmarkt and Goudberg. Before mid-day all our objectives had been gained, and a number of prisoners had been taken."

The enemy might brush aside the advance for the moment as the taking of a mud patch, but to resist it had at one time or another put nearly a hundred divisions into the arena of blood; and the defence cost him legions in dead and wounded. To defend the ridge the Germans had massed great numbers of guns, machine guns which seemed absolutely without number, so incredible was their volume, and many of the finest divisions in the German army. Passchendaele was but a dot on the map, but that the British should not take it the enemy spent much of his man-power and gun-power. There had flowed up to his guns tides of shells, almost as great as flowed up to our guns in those later days of ammunition without stint. Throughout these months he never ceased, by day and night, to pour out hurricanes of fire over all these fields in the hope of smashing the British progress. A few days before, orders were issued to the German troops, given in the name of Hindenburg himself, that Passchendaele must be held at all costs, and if lost must be recaptured at all costs.

For several days the enemy had endeavored to thrust the British back from the positions held round Crest Farm and on the left beyond the Paddebeek, where all the ground was a morass. The Naval Brigade who had fought there

on the left in the last days of October, had a hard and
tragic experience; but it was their grim stoicism in holding
on to exposed out-posts—small groups of men under heavy
shell fire—which enabled the Canadians to attack from a
good position.

Great tribute is due to two companies of British infantry, who with Canadian guides, worked through a large
plantation, drove a wedge into the enemy territory, and held
it against all attempts to dislodge them.

Through the night the enemy, who was not taken by
surprise in what was happening, increased his fire, as though
he at least guessed his time was at hand and he must fight
with all the strength of desperation. All night long he
flung down barrages which were harrassing, rained shells
from his heavies and used gas shells to search and asphyxi-
ate our batteries. All night through he tried every devilish
thing in war to prevent the assembly of troops. Yet it was
done.

The Canadians assembled lying out in shell craters and
in the deep slime of the mud under all this fire. Though
these were anxious hours and a great strain upon officers
and men, and casualties happened here and there, the spirit
of the men was not broken, and in a wonderful way they
escaped losses.

The night had been soft and moist, with threatening
rain, but at daylight the sun shone in a clear sky. Below
the ridge our field guns were firing steadily and from away
behind them heavy guns were sending through the air
shells high overhead into the German lines. The forces
which made the attack were from Manitoba, Saskatchewan,
Alberta, and Eastern and Western Ontario. The enemy
had added to his defensive army a new division, brought
up the day before from Champagne.

All below the Passchendaele Ridge, the German monster
shells were flinging up masses of earth and water. Through
all this the Canadians burst upon the enemy. They
fought up to and around the crest village from which the
place takes its name. They fought up to and captured
blockhouses which were spitting streams of machine gun

fire. They fought in the cellars, in and around the village of Mosselmarkt and on the Goudberg spur. The Germans could not withstand the fury of the onslaught. Shot down, bayoneted and prisoners, they yielded, and the attacking forces passed on.

The bit of ridge so dearly held by the enemy was in the hands of the Canadians, and they had direct observation upon the enemy everywhere for miles around. How many were taken prisoner by the Canadians can never be known. Thousands of the stream which was sent back never reached our lines, being blown to pieces by their own barrage fire. It is known that the cost to the Germans was fully 100,000 men. The enemy simply swept all over the territory with his barrage fire when he knew he had lost. That is why so many of the German prisoners became German dead. Passchendaele was proudly added to the list of splendid engagements on the colors of Canada. The northern bastion of Flanders and a position of vital importance had been captured. The last of the chain of heights which the enemy had begun to fortify between the sea and Soissons at the end of 1914 had fallen. It had gone the way of the Albert, Vimy and Messines ridges.

Narrative by a German Soldier, in the Attack of November 6th. Published in Berlin

For weeks, day and night, the British kept our position under fire. Ever fiercer burned the glowing stream that poured crackling down upon us. Every day this fire grew hotter. Our artillery replied powerfully. The Army *communiqué* spoke of a concentration of enemy artillery fire on individual sectors. Even we cannot describe what that means. The history of the world has never seen anything more awful. All calibers were brought into action, and a crater of unprecedented extent opened beside the others, was excavated afresh, swallowed up the old ones, spread out beyond the lime trees, and threw up the hinterland. Nothing remained intact of all that nights of hard labor under the enemy's fire had created. The destroying fire did its work with depressing thoroughness, seeming to extinguish

all life, and now came the turn of the smoke shells. Thick
smoke lay before our eyes, so that we could see nothing,
and yet ever farther forward must we push our death-
defying posts. A real fog is mere patchwork compared
with this artificial fog which the British send out in order
to veil their dispositions. When this appeared inadequate
the enemy employed gas, and the evil mists came rolling
towards our lines and passed over them; only our gas-masks
prevented every living thing from being destroyed. The gas
had a singular effect on our weapons; all iron was covered
with thick rust. The English now judged that they had
done enough preparatory work, for suddenly drumfire
started with the most terrifying effect. Shells of the
heaviest caliber thundered across, with trench bombs, machine-gun volleys, and hand grenades all uniting in a blood-
curdling, hellish pandemonium such as even a Dante would
never be able to describe.

German nerves held out with the utmost resolution, constantly awaiting the moment when the hurricane of fire
would break loose. And the storm came. In the neighboring sector flame-throwers were turned on; against this
murderous engine no measures avail. There is nothing for
it but to get back into the rearward positions. And then
the enemy was on us. Tank after tank loomed forward.
These monsters appeared invincible, and if one of them was
hit by a heavy shell the guns and machine guns inside were
kept going unremittingly, until finally their iron hail reached
our lines. And behind the Tanks came Scots and Canadians. We see nothing but endless rows of enemies. At
last our reserves deliver a counter-attack. Murder breaks
out afresh. All the events of history are but small episodes
compared with this fury. Step by step the battle swayed
backwards and forwards till gradually the enemy pressed up
to the border of our old lines. The battle ebbed away, but no
rest came, no relief. We had to make fresh cover before
Tommy returned. Between us lay the ruins of Tanks and
dead enemies in masses on each other, among them many
brave comrades. The field of dead became once more a
battleground.

THE ITALIAN ATTACK ON THE ISONZO

THE STORMING OF MONTE SANTO

AUGUST 24TH

GIUSEPPE AGNINO   G. M. TREVELYAN

Of all the mountain fighting of the War, the most brilliant and spectacular feat was probably that of the Italians in storming Monte Santo. This precipitous peak had defied them for two whole years before they conquered it at last. Moreover, its capture marked the high-water mark of Italian advance into Austrian territory.

Ever since entering the War the Italians had been trying to fight their way out of the Isonzo River valley and over the mountains to the eastward so as to reach Trieste. But they had striven in vain. In 1916 they had won Gorizia, the capital of the Isonzo region. Now by a tremendous effort they captured Monte Santo. Two months later came the Caporetto breakdown. The story is here told by a most competent and sympathetic eye-witness, Dr. Trevelyan, head of the British Red Cross service in Italy during the campaign. In more vehement strain, we offer first the enthusiastic account of the well-known Italian author and patriot, Dottore Agnino.

BY GIUSEPPE AGNINO

THE spring of 1917 found the Italian army close against the wall of the Austrian defence, holding the positions in which it had been surprised by the winter. At one point of that wall the Italians had reached the threshold of the door which gave easiest access to the heart of the enemy's territory. This door was situated in the area that fronted the Italian occupation in Gorizia. Beyond it opened out the low-lying valley of Vippacco, the shortest road to Trieste, Adelsberg and Lubiana.

Two formidable pilasters supported this large door. One was the system Monte Santo, San Gabriele and San Daniele; the other the system of heights on the northern edge of the Carso. This second pilaster was wholly in the possession of the enemy. It was still far back in the rear

303

of their front. Any direct action against it was not to be thought of. On the other hand, the Italians were stationed at the base of the first pilaster. When this fell, the other would also fall automatically. For the enemy it was of the greatest possible importance to hold, at whatever cost, the pilaster of the *Tre Santi* [Three Saints]. For the Italians it was of the greatest possible importance to take it. Gorizia, occupied the year before, lay at the foot of this pilaster. A continual menace hung over it. For the Italians, the fall of the Tre Santi meant an immediate result—the security of Gorizia; and another eventual and more important result —the defeat of the enemy.

The conquest of the Tre Santi had to begin with the conquest of that height which the spring of 1917 had found the Italians already hanging on to, and which was like the vanguard of the other two—Monte Santo.

The epic period of the battle, which was called *La Battaglia del Monte Santo* from the place that symbolized it, began. The "epic period"—because the battle of Monte Santo did not begin then, in the spring of 1917. The first time the Italians attacked the system of the Tre Santi was three or four days after the taking of Gorizia (August 9th, 1916). At that time, the 43rd and 45th Divisions, already exhausted by a battle which had lasted since the 6th of August, and not supported by new and fresh reserves, broke their force against the rocky and precipitous spur of S. Caterina, which descends from S. Gabriele, as an advanced sentinel of the whole system, to the plain round Salcano. But, at that time Monte Santo had not gained that aureola of legend it gained in the spring of 1917, one which marked it for the Italians as the Battle of battles of the whole campaign.

Since August 1916 Monte Santo had been the torment of the Italian soldier. From there the enemy observed the Italian movements without being disturbed. From there he molested with unerring aim the Italian positions and the roads by which ammunition, water, food and reserves had to come up. In the sector of Salcano a continuous rain of artillery and machine-gun fire poured down from Monte Santo.

Little by little, not only in the army, but also in the whole country, a kind of legend had arisen about Monte Santo. It seemed to Italy that the whole war was centred in that name: "Monte Santo."

The battle of Monte Santo in May 1917 was an epopee of heroisms. It began on the 12th of May and continued until the 7th of June. On the morning of the 14th, the left wing of the 6th Corps attacked the precipitous western side of Monte Santo. The attack was exposed to the Austrian fire on both flanks, on the left from the Vodice and on the right from San Gabriele. In spite of their enormous losses the Italians advanced. A column climbed to the summit, bayoneting or capturing the defenders, and planted itself there amid a volume of smoke and heaps of shattered masonry.

All the Austrian defences reacted. A very intense artillery fire was concentrated upon the conquered position; from the reverse of the mountain men swarmed out of the caverns, where they and their machine-guns had remained safe during the bombardment, and launched a counter-attack. Those few heroic infantrymen resisted desperately, but all of them were killed or wounded. At last, as the position became untenable, the survivors were obliged to fall back from the summit.

Again other attempts were made and more than once the goal was bravely reached. But, once reached, again the enemy's reserves poured out of their caverns while their guns hammered the mountain-top. And again the Italians, in spite of their valor and their tremendous sacrifices, were driven back.

Besides the enormous losses, on account of the violence of the enemy fire the bringing up of reserves and food became impossible. So terrible was the fury of the battle and the alternate vicissitudes of advancing and recoiling that almost every day Italy believed Monte Santo was taken. This news was even brought to the assembled Parliament in Rome. But the Italians only succeeded in strongly entrenching themselves under the ruins of the convent; they could not wrench the summit from the Austrians. When, finally, the fierce fighting had died down, Monte Santo, now reduced to a vast waste of ruins and dead bodies, was still resisting. It resisted until August, a suspended menace above the head of the Italian soldier.

It is necessary to recall the troops whose names are indissolubly linked with the battle of May 1917: Florence Brigade (127th and 128th regiments), which lost 50 per cent. of its strength; Avellino Brigade (231st and 232nd regiments), which lost about 3,000 men out of 5,000 and more than 100 officers out of 140; Campobasso Brigade (23rd and 24th regiments).

The offensive of May was followed by another and worse period for the Italian soldiers hanging on under the summit of Monte Santo. Then began a long succession of humble and obscure sacrifices; a continual digging of trenches with rain soaking through the shelters, the bread and the clothes; a period of ignored and rapid deaths, of desperate counter-attacks. The enemy's firing never seemed to pause night or day. And, in the meantime, the Austrians tried another way of weakening the Italian resistance. Showers of pamphlets and posters with every kind of insinuating flattery poured like a stream of poison among that heroic handful of soldiers, but in vain. In spite of all, the Italian soldiers continued to dig trenches, set wire entanglements, and wait.

The Italian Commander-in-Chief, General Cadorna, convinced that it was almost impossible that the group of the Tre Santi would fall by a direct action, hoped it would fall by a lateral one, and he waited until August.

In August, after the fall of Monte Jelenik, pivot of the defence of the Bainsizza plateau (the broad upland between the Chiapovano valley and the Isonzo), the advance of the centre of the Second Army from the line of the Kuk-Vodice became easy. It moved forward with a conversion to the right and so facilitated, in its turn, the attack of the 6th Corps against Monte Santo, which then, finally, fell into the hands of the Italians (August 24th, 1917).

Monte Santo was thus conquered. But the battle which took its name from it still lasted. When Monte Santo felt itself in danger, it seemed to have consigned all its infernal power to San Gabriele—which already had so much of its own. As long as San Gabriele was able to resist, Monte Santo was not really conquered and from one moment to another could again take its place in battle against the Italians. The battle for the conquest of San Gabriele was but the second phase of that of the Santo.

At the same time in which Monte Santo fell, San Gabriele was furiously attacked. The early development of the battle followed very closely in its course the battle of May for the Santo.

First, a surprise attack succeeded. It was then that the Italian *reparti d'assalto* (storming troops) had their baptism of fire. These *reparti d'assalto* had, only shortly before, been. organized by the Commander of the Second Army, General Cappello; afterwards they became known as the *Arditi*. The infantry reached the summit of the mountain. All the defenders were taken prisoners. Without pausing, panting, like hounds in the chase, the Italians, after having reached the summit, passed beyond it and arrived on the slopes of Monte San Daniele. But, after waiting in vain for reinforcements, they were obliged to withdraw. The Austrians returned to the summit of San Gabriele.

In the meantime the general attack, which had advanced considerably into the Bainsizza plateau, having gained its objective, had stopped. The long battle-front now narrowed to one point: San Gabriele. General Cadorna gave the order that the entire weight of the Second Army, so increased as to constitute the most powerful concentration of artillery, should be directed against the amphitheatre of Gorizia for the conquest of San Gabriele. This was done; and the intensity of fire outdid all previous bombardments.

Still, the results obtained were meagre. The highest *quota* of San Gabriele (646 metres) was not occupied. Only a lower *quota*, the Veliki Hrib (526 metres), was held (August 30th). Also the *Sella di Dol*, the saddle which divides Monte Santo from San Gabriele, fell into the hands of the Italians. Thus, the legend of "invincibility" of the

Santo had passed intact to San Gabriele! The Italian valor was met by a superior force that repelled it.

Then, by the suggestion of the Commander of the Second Army, a fresh and different attempt was made. San Gabriele ought to be vanquished by an *assedio di fuoco* (siege of fire). *Assedio di fuoco* signified to hammer the mountain night and day, for a certain period, with such an avalanche of shells as to prevent the arrival of any reserves or provisions. The *assedio di fuoco* was initiated, but, as it became evident that the Austrians were preparing an offensive along the whole line from Tolmino to the Adriatic Sea, it lasted only three days and then stopped. And, thus, the highest *quota* of San Gabriele remained in possession of the enemy to dominate, until October, the old and new positions of defence and offence of the Italians.

The last general offensive of the Italians on the Isonzo front, that had lasted from the 18th of August until the middle of September, had concentrated its fiercest and most determined struggle in the area of Monte San Gabriele. For more than a fortnight the most tremendous fighting was confined (as has been already noted in England) to a space not much larger than Trafalgar Square, and into such a small furnace more than thirty Austrian battalions had been thrown.

San Gabriele—a mass of rocks covered with scanty red soil—was named "Inferno" by the Austrians, and they said that it had been lowered ten metres as the result of the cannonading. The Italians had remained, as before said, under the highest *quota*, at *quota* 552. Troops advanced meant, as before on the Santo, troops lost. Every night, from sunset to dawn, the Austrian fire harassed the Italian line and immediate rear. How often entire companies remained without food! How many men and mules were blown down into the swift-rushing Isonzo!

And, as before on the Santo, so now the Italian soldiers remained hanging on to San Gabriele in an almost untenable position. They remained there until the tragic October of the same year, 1917: Caporetto. When October came, San Gabriele had become a filthy *mêlée* of shattered rock and broken bodies, skulls, skeletons, pieces of clothing, helmets, boots, broken rifles and ammunition, viscid black slime and stench. To the living it gave a sense of utter desolation; the cold was intense, the clothing insufficient, the rain as incessant as the firing of the enemy.

The Austrian and Italian trenches were so close together that in moving only a few steps the direction could easily be lost. One night an Austrian postman arrived by mistake in the Italian line and brought the post of a whole battalion. Another time an Austrian, very innocently, brought to the enemy a much-appreciated gift—a barrel of rum. These Austrians had lost their way, or, more exactly, their direction. At the time of Vittorio Veneto, several tombs were found with only one cross, bearing words like these: "186 unknown Italians," "154 unknown Austrians."

And then came the retreat of Caporetto. At that time Monte Santo was held by the troops of the 8th Division. The 66th Division was holding San Gabriele. The connection between the two was on the north side of the Sella di Dol. Both these Divisions behaved magnificiently. The 66th Division, the last to defend San Gabriele, was formed with the Abruzzi Brigade (57th and 58th Regiments) and the Cuneo Brigade) 7th and 8th Regiments). The extreme right of the 8th Regiment, that was defending the spur of Santa Caterina, was joined with the left wing of the 24th Division.

When the gravity of the breach made by the enemy at Caporetto was realized, the troops of the Santo and San Gabriele were ordered to withdraw. Whoever witnessed the events of that time can never forget the magnificent behavior of these troops, who, not vanquished, were nevertheless obliged to give over to the enemy the places of their martyrdom and their glory. The days that preceded the total abandonment of the Tre Santi are the saddest in the whole long battle which took its name from them.

The enemy, emboldened by their success in the zone of Caporetto, immediately enlarged their attack along the whole sector of the Second Army and along the positions of the Third Army, the "Invincible," whose battle-front extended from Gorizia to the Adriatic Sea.

The main objective of the enemy was to conquer San Gabriele at one blow and then quickly invade the plain of Gorizia. If this manœuvre had succeeded, the enemy would have gained a shortcut to the unprotected flank of the Third Army, that was carrying out its retreat in good order, and would have reduced it to a desperate situation, with incalculable consequences for the whole development of the Italian campaign. But at that momentous time the soldiers of San Gabriele understood what their country demanded of them. From the 24th to the 28th of October the Austrians attacked San Gabriele with a fury increasing so much the more as the time necessary to cut off the retreat of the Second Army was diminishing.

Little is known of the events of those days—obscure days of obscure sacrifices and obscure heroisms. But one thing is known—the enemy could not break the resistance of the defenders of San Gabriele.

The attacks of the 24th, 25th, 26th, 27th were all victoriously repulsed, leaving prisoners in the hands of the Italians. Then, in order to protect the retreat a small body of troops remained behind. Little by little they were reduced to a battalion, then to a company, then to a platoon, and, finally, only a handful of heroes were left to throw bombs and stones at the advancing enemy.

BY G. M. TREVELYAN

In May, 1917, the long Isonzo gorge stretching from Tolmino to the Gorizia plain still divided the opposing armies, except for the Italian *tête-de-pont* at Plava and the Austrian *tête-de-pont* at Santa Lucia, farther north. The gorge was contained on the Italian side by one long, unbroken ridge, from two to three thousand feet in height, and largely clothed with oak woods. The ridge began at the southern end with Monte Sabotino, went on with Monte Planina and Monte Corada above the Plava bottom, turned sharply westward at the heights whence one looked down into the deserted streets of Tolmino, and finally dropped through steep forests into Caporetto. Before the summer

The Italian Disaster at Caporetto

The Italian troops, deceived by

The Italian Disaster at Caporetto

The Italian troops, deceived by enemy propaganda, desert their guns

Painting by the Hungarian artist Theo. Matejko

of 1917 the *genio* had completed a vast system of high-level roads from Sabotino to Caporetto along the top of this ridge and a whole network behind and athwart it. By means of these smooth and well-graded mountain roads hundreds of heavy cannon were placed along the ridge that summer, destined to blow the Austrians out of their positions beyond the Isonzo gorge, but too many doomed after that to be left behind in their mountain emplacements in the great Retreat.

Besides our work in Gorizia and Plava, our Unit had out-stations of ambulances on this ridge near Liga and Kambresko, as well as down in Caporetto itself. Driving that summer along that new high-level road with plain and sea and distant Western Alps in view on one side, and on the other the Isonzo gorge and the enemy heights beyond, on to which we were soon to cross, was the most exhilarating of all our customary routes. For not only was Nature seen in every direction in her most majestic aspects, whether of mountain, plain, or sea, but along the road itself one was in the very heart of preparations for a mighty effort of human skill and purpose, to which the keen upland air seemed to impart its own energy. Wooden *baracche* were rising tier above tier on the steepest parts of the mountain where the angle gave most protection from bombardment; here huts were being built out on platforms over the yawning chasm of a precipice round which the roadside curled; there yet another battery was being placed under a grove of chestnut trees.

The failure of the offensive from Plava in August, 1916, had been due partly to local conditions and partly to want of coördination with the plans for the most successful attack on Gorizia. In 1917 the forces of the Gorizia and Plava regions had been wisely united into one "Army of Gorizia," under General Capello. He and his Chief of Staff, General Badoglio, saw that the spell of chronic and now traditional failure of every effort to lift the Italians out of the hole that they were in at Plava on to the summit of Monte Kuk could be broken only by providing a second roadway down to the Plava bridgehead. On the existing exposed, one-way road from Verhovlje it was impossible to take down enough material for such an operation as the capture of Monte Kuk, still less of Monte Santo and the Bainsizza beyond. The new road was opened only a few days before the May offensive began.

Everything that could help to feed the great battle on Monte Kuk, and all the returning wreckage of that fierce strife, had to pass and repass by mule or portage over the string of boats swaying in the swift flood. In the lee of a shattered house just above the bridge the wounded were laid out by scores at a time on their stretchers, waiting for the cars to carry them up out of the valley of death. Beside them in the narrow space the war material brought down by the lorries was dumped in piles, picked up, and carried off over the pontoons. Above all this crush and confusion the enemy's shrapnel burst in periodic gusts of fury, striking the wounded where they lay, and rendering the unloading of the lorries and loading of the ambulances a task requiring the cool energy of the lieutenants and *aspiranti* (cadets) in charge of the operation.

Meanwhile, across the river the battle on Monte Kuk was speeding well. The sheer mountain side, unscalable for two years, was falling at last. The Italian preliminary bombardment, like that on Sabotino the year before, destroyed in a few hours the Austrian wire and trenches. Then the infantry, launched to the assault, climbed straight up the steepest part of the long slope; it was as though one should storm Bow Fell from Mickelden bottom in the face of machine guns and rifle fire of a determined enemy. Having reached the summit, they worked along the crest in a series of desperate engagements of attack and counter-attack. Every arm—infantry, *genio, artillery*—vied in their zeal. A few days after its capture I saw on the top of Monte Kuk some Italian "seventy-fives" that had been dragged up, Heaven knows how, by sheer strength of arm and will during the *mêlée* itself. By May 22nd, after ten days' fighting as fierce as any in the war, not only Monte Kuk but the greater part of Vodice and the lower slopes of Monte Santo had been captured,

Many began to see little chance of winning the war, as week after week during that summer and autumn more and more Austrian batteries and battalions gave evidence of their arrival from the Russian front. But in spite of all this, the finest effort of the Italian army was made in the last half of August and the first half of September, 1917. It was only after that magnificent and largely successful effort had proved inconclusive that the fruits of discouragement were reaped in late October.

The month of the most continuously fierce fighting in the whole Italian war opened on August 18, 1917, with a general bombardment from Tolmino to the sea. The guns massed along the Corada ridge searched the Austrian positions beyond the Isonzo. Next day, along the front from Plava northwards to Doblar, the infantry bridged and crossed the rapid river in face of the enemy, and began to ascend the eastern bank of the gorge. A more difficult operation, in face of machine-gun posts and a determined foe entrenched in ground of such vantage, has seldom been allotted to any force in the world war. Here and there a politically weak link in the enemy armor, like the Czechs on Monte Jelenik, rendered a general success just possible. Gradually, as day followed day of carnage, point after point was won. The high-lying hamlet of Vrh fell, and Hill 711, keys to a whole region. Near Plava, operations began with a false attack on Monte Santo to the south, while to the north the foot of the Rohot valley was seized.

But far to northward there was a serious setback. The attempt to turn from the south the positions of the enemy in the Santa Lucia and Tolmino region was held to be so important that General Badoglio himself had charge of that operation. But the Austrians could not be dislodged from their fastness round Lom protected by the steep banks of the Vogercek torrent. By this failure the strategic way was left open for the disaster of Caporetto.

The fall of Jelenik was followed on the 23rd and 24th of August by the decisive battle on Vodice and Kobilek, which opened out the Italian advance over the south of the Bainsizza plateau, as the victory on Jelenik had already opened it out over the part to the north. On the crest and flanks of Vodice both sides had been entrenched at close quarters ever since the battle in May. The hero of Vodice was the fine old soldier, General Prince Gonzaga. He combined a complete control of the operations of his Division with a boyish enjoyment of danger, a perpetual appearance on the top of the disputed mountain and a gayety which won the hearts of his soldiers and of all who came near him. On the 24th of August he and his troops had the reward of their long vigil; the whole system of Austrian trenches running from the farther part of Vodice round the head of the Rohot valley on to Kobilek itself, after being subjected to a destructive bombardment, was stormed in the grand style.

Once this obstacle was passed, the pursuit went raging over the Bainsizza plateau with the dash characteristic of the Italians whenever they are well led. Part of the enemy were driven steeply down into the Gargaro valley and chased along it to the northern foot of San Gabriele. Monte Santo was turned, surrounded, and forced to surrender; at long last the "red, white, and green" waved over the ruined convent on the summit, that Italian eyes had gazed on so enviously for two long years.

Farther to the north the conquerors of Kobilek, sweeping across the valley in which Ravne village lies, mounted the limestone crags of the heights beyond, which might have been easily defended, and had, indeed, been prepared for defense, but were carried in that first triumphant rush. On the afternoon of the 24th of August, standing on a line of trenches near Vodice in which the Austrians had been that morning, Baker and I saw a little string of men, black against the white limestone, struggling up those heights beyond Ravne, three miles away as the crow flies. At first we thought they were retreating Austrians, but presently, when the batteries on Ternovo began to shell them, we realized that they were the Italians who had a few hours before stormed the ground we stood on, and were now ranging over hill and valley like hounds on the trail. The string of men soon disappeared over the mountain top, where they and their comrades established on the far side the farthest line that Italy ever reached before the great Retreat.

ITALY'S BREAKDOWN AT CAPORETTO

GERMANY AND AUSTRIA SMASH THE ITALIAN FRONT

OCTOBER 21ST

GERMAN PROPAGANDA ORDER
GENERAL CADORNA   G. M. TREVELYAN
PERCEVAL GIBBON   GEORGES CLEMENCEAU
GENERAL VON CRAMON

The Caporetto disaster came perilously close to causing Italy's elimination from the War. The Teutons employed again the trick which had proved so successful against Russia. Indeed, it is Autocracy's obvious strength that it can and does compel any number of its subjects to take part in a campaign of deliberate falsehood. Democracy, since it moves openly, can only direct its people along paths of truth. Have the great masses of men reached such a degree of intelligence that they can recognize truth, cling to it, and win by means of it? That is really the one essential question which must settle whether Democracy can even now continue in the world. In Russia lies had conquered truth and Democracy was perishing. In Italy falsehood almost won—not quite.

We give here one of the Orders by which Germany set afoot her campaign of falsehood on the Italian front. Clever Teuton spies, posing as common soldiers, fraternized with the Italians in the front trenches and convinced them that Teuton soldiers and Italian soldiers could and would override their officers and make a peace together by the simple process of refusing to fight. Then a hundred thousand of Germany's best troops were placed in the front line opposite the deceived and trusting Italians at Caporetto, and attacked them suddenly.

The breakdown of the Italians was not wholly because of the pacifist propaganda. We give here the frank admission of defeat by the chief Italian Commander Cadorna, and the analysis of the situation from the French paper directed by M. Clemenceau, Prime Minister of France, which shows that in a military sense also Caporetto was a point of danger. Near it lay the great dams which the Italians had built to control the flow of the Isonzo River, and which made Caporetto of enormous value.

Of the actual disaster itself, by far the clearest picture is that drawn by the British Red Cross chief upon the spot, Mr. Trevelyan; and to this we add the glimpses of the panic behind the lines as caught by Perceval Gibbon, the noted newspaper correspondent. Finally the Teuton view is given by the chief German liaison officer with the Austrians, General von Cramon. Thus the tragic story is shown from every side.

315

BY THE GERMAN HEADQUARTERS STAFF

Secret German "Propaganda" order, captured on the Italian Front

TWO HUNDRED AND EIGHTY-FIRST DIVI-SION, First Section, No. 226.—Confidential.
Not to be communicated to troops in the first line.

First—Following the telephone order, Geroch No. 2,080, you are asked to intensify with efficacy the propaganda with the enemy army.

Second—The object of this propaganda is to disorganize the enemy army and to obtain information regarding it. The propaganda must be carried out in the following manner: (a) By throwing into the enemy's trenches newspapers and proclamations destined for the more intelligent elements; (b) by persuading the troops by oral propaganda. For that it will be necessary to utilize officers, under-officers, and soldiers who appear to be most adapted. The posts for making contacts with the enemy must be placed under the direction of the company commander, who must be in the first-line positions. These officers must ascertain the points where it will be the easiest to throw into the enemy trenches newspapers, proclamations, etc. At these points you must seek to gain contact with the enemy by means of our interpreters, and if the enemy consents then fix an hour for future conversations. You must then advise immediately by telephone the chief of the Information Bureau of the division of every contact with the enemy.

Only the chief of the Information Bureau will have the right to direct the conversations according to the instructions he has received. It is rigorously prohibited for any of our soldiers to enter into relation with the enemy except those who have received the mission to do so, for fear that the enemy may seek to profit by their ingenuousness. All letters and printed matter which the enemy may have on his person must be taken from him, and transmitted to the chief of the Information Bureau. Company commanders, above all, must seek to establish the points where the enemy's soldiers have received newspapers, the points where the newspapers were taken openly, and without precaution. There are posts of observation for the artillery, as it may happen that French officers or foreign army instructors are in these posts.

In these enterprises for obtaining contact with the enemy, success depends on the ability with which you operate. Good results can be obtained by calling in a friendly tone and indicating sentiments of comradeship or by reiterated promises not to fire and offers of tobacco. The tobacco for this purpose will be furnished by the company commanders.

Every evening, at 8 o'clock, the company commander must transmit directly to the information officer a report of the propaganda accomplished during the day. This report must contain the following indications: (a) Has the enemy picked up our newspapers and proclamations? (b) Have you endeavored to enter into relations with the enemy? (c) With whom have you had contact—officers, underofficers, soldiers? (d) Where and when were our newspapers and proclamations thrown into the enemy's trenches? (e) All other information of the enemy's conduct. At the same time, our interpreters will send to the chief of the Information Bureau a detailed report on all conversations they have had with the enemy. The enemy's positions where propaganda is under way must not be shelled by our artillery; they must indicate to the batteries the positions of these points to be spared. The enemy is perfidious and without honor, and it is necessary as a consequence to be careful that they neither take our propagandists prisoners nor kill them. Those of our soldiers who leave our lines for the purpose of carrying newspapers and pamphlets to the enemy must be advised. To protect them it will be necessary to constitute with care special detachments, who will mount guard in the trenches, and who will fire only on the order of the company commander who is directing relations with the enemy.—Signed, on behalf of the temporary commander of the division, the Major General commanding the 62nd Brigade.

BY GENERAL CADORNA

Official *Communiqué* of October 28th

A violent attack and the feeble resistance of detachments of the Second Army permitted Austro-German forces to pierce our left wing on the Julian front. The valiant efforts of other troops were not successful in preventing the enemy from penetrating to the sacred soil of our Fatherland.

The bravery displayed by our soldiers in so many memorable battles fought and won in the past two and a half years gives our Supreme Command a pledge that this time, too, the army to which the honor and safety of the country are entrusted will know how to fulfill its duty.

BY G. M. TREVELYAN

Now followed, as if from a blue sky, that tremendous cataclysm which almost ruined Italy and bade fair to ruin the cause of her Allies, but ended in giving to her a new national purpose and discipline, and to the Allies a closer unity. History, obedient to the popular instinct for the concentrated and the picturesque, has already decided to call the whole sequence of great events by the name of a little Alpine market-town. All the meanings now implied by the word "Caporetto"—the immense and complicated causes and effects of the disaster of which the military sweep over two provinces and the rally on the Piave were merely the symbols; the mentality and character of a race; the merits and defects of its political and educational system; the relations of the different classes and parties to the war; the enemy propaganda; the grievances of the soldiers at the front; the world-strategy of Ludendorff and the new German tactics; the actions of Cadorna and his subordinates; Rapallo and the coming of the Allies; and all the shifting fortunes of that wide-flung winter battlefield—these things will fill volumes, shelves, and libraries in the generations to come. And, regardless of all this massive learning and controversy, the people's own tradition, told by the peasant at his fireside, will burn itself, deep as the shame and pride of Cannæ and its sequel, into the memory of the oldest civilized race in the

world. Here I have only a few remarks to offer and a
few scenes to describe, which have no claim to notice beyond
the fact that I had lived long with the army most involved
in the disaster, and that I was one of the straws whirled on
that vast ebb-tide.

In order to understand the nature of the phenomenon,
before inquiring into its causes, it is necessary to realize
that there were three distinct categories of conduct among
the Italian troops. To confuse any one of these three categories with either of the other two is to misunderstand the
whole affair.

First, there were a few regiments who, in accordance
with a previously-formed intention, abandoned their duty,
and surrendered on purpose. This was "Caporetto" in the
narrower and more strictly accurate sense, for it was only
in that geographical zone that such betrayal occurred; but
unfortunately Caporetto was the key to the whole strategic
position. The phenomenon of voluntary surrender had been
so common in the Austrian army throughout the war, beginning with the early battles round Lemberg, that an elaborate system based on trustworthy machine gunners had been
devised to meet it; but it was so exceptional in the Italian
army that it took the authorities who might have prevented
it by surprise, and struck them with something akin to panic.

When, consequently, a general retreat had been ordered,
the second category of conduct was observable in a much
larger number of men. The army of Bainsizza, San Gabriele, and Gorizia, who had no thought of giving way when
the enemy offensive began in the last week of October, successfully resisted the attacks made on their positions, until
the order came from Cadorna to retreat beyond the Tagliamento. They carried out irreproachably the difficult retirement across the Isonzo gorge and out of the hills; but as
they proceeded over the plain, hustled by the victorious enemy pouring down on their flank from Cividale, they were
gradually infected by the sense that all was lost. Mainly
between Udine and the Tagliamento, they gave way at length
to the war-weariness which had so long been at strife with
their valor and patriotism, flung away their rifles wholesale,

and passed round the word, *"Andiamo a casa"* ("We're going home"). The last scenes of the Second Army were a sad falling from what the same men had shown themselves two months before.

The third and largest category of all consisted of the troops who did their duty throughout. Most of, though not quite all, the Third Army from the Carso, and the Fifth, First, and Fourth Armies on the Cadore and Trentino fronts, saved Italy by holding fast where required, and retreating in order where necessary, so that the shorter line was successfully established in the early days of November. Many heroic feats of individual companies, regiments, and divisions illumined the worst hours of the Retreat. And some of the finest of these were performed by units of the Second Army itself, both in the mountain region of Matajur above Caporetto, and in the plain of Udine.

I may be regarded as partial, but I believe that the Second Army, though it can scarcely complain if it has been made to bear the sins of the nation, was not really a worse army than any other, except for the untried and undesirable elements whom the authorities had carelessly thrust into Caporetto that autumn. The men at Plava and Gorizia had up till then performed the most brilliant and sustained feats of arms done by any part of the Italian forces, and if at last they gave way worse than the others, that was only in proportion to their geographical propinquity to the breakthrough on their flank and rear. Elements in the Third Army suffered the same disintegration for the same reason. The half-million men of whom the Second Army was composed must not be condemned in a mass, nor their previous achievements forgotten. None the less the now established tradition that the Duke of Aosta's Third Army saved the situation by its superior discipline in the retreat from the Carso and by turning to bay behind the Piave, represents an essential truth.

Such in the main were the phenomena; but their causes are a subject far more diffused and obscure, on which I can only aspire to throw some feeble lights from my personal experience and observation.

Of the positive treachery at Caporetto itself I can say little, because I was not there, and the cars of our Unit had been withdrawn from that zone before the regiments in fault were sent up. It is common knowledge that the ranks of these regiments were filled up with several thousands of the munition workers who had taken part in the recent Turin revolt. To concentrate these men at Caporetto as a punishment was not a very fortunate inspiration. I know from what I have been told by those who were in Caporetto in the last weeks before the disaster, that the soldiers made no secret of their intentions, and that many of their officers lived in fear of their own men, locking themselves up carefully at night. Indeed, certain of these troops refused to accept the usual gifts distributed by patriotic agencies among the men at the front, grounding their refusal on the fact that they regarded themselves as no longer in service. This refusal, as I know, gravely alarmed certain persons in Venice, and was, therefore, probably known in other quarters up and down Italy. But since there had been so little treachery in the Italian army heretofore, and since Caporetto was regarded as a quiet part of the line, the responsible authorities left matters alone. Possibly the too great isolation in which the Comando Supremo was said to live under General Cadorna's régime is partly responsible for the failure to scent the smoke before the fire. If so, that General, to whom Italy and the Allies owe so much, has dearly paid for the defects of his qualities.

With regard to the bulk of the Second Army, I can speak at first hand of the men who had hitherto borne the burden and heat of the day, but who, after the retreat had been ordered, were gradually infected by hills from Caporetto to Cividale, and if once the Austro-Germans could debouch on Cividale they had turned the flank and rear of all the armies on the Isonzo front. It was true that Monte Nero could not be taken by assault, but if low-lying Caporetto was captured behind it, the Alpini on the great mountain could be isolated and masked while the race to the plain went on. Caporetto could be attacked from Plezzo and from Tolmino, down and up the course of the Isonzo. The Monte

Nero positions were really too high up to protect the town at their feet. These operations were rendered the easier by the dangerously sharp angle here formed by the Italian line. This angle was threatened by the Austrians' bridgehead at Santa Lucia, which their successful defense of Lom in the last days of August had still left in their hands. And now they were in correspondence with the disaffected regiments sent up to guard these vital but little regarded positions. Everything pointed to this as the place for the attack by von Below's six German divisions, employing Ludendorff's new tactics of "infiltration," with which successful experiments had already been made on the Russian front in September.

On these lines the stroke was played on October 24, 1917, with complete success. The pace and course of the Austro-German advance after Cadorna had given the general order to retreat can be quickly traced. Not only did the debouchment into the plain at Cividale compel the rapid retirement of the Gorizia and Carso armies, but as the right wing of the victorious advance swept along the northern edge of the plain, closing up one valley's mouth after another, they dictated an ever-hastier evacuation of the Carnic, Cadore, and Feltre Alps by the Fourth Italian Army. Alpini officers have described to me their misery at having to abandon, through no fault of their own or of the men under them, not only their guns but all the marvelous positions in the highest Alps which it had been for two years past their pride to guard and perfect for Italy. Many of the retreating columns fought magnificent rearguard actions, attacking and thrusting back the enemy from points which imperiled the retreat of other units in the vast and difficult area of evacuation.

BY PERCEVAL GIBBON

The events of October 21st culminated in the enemy's occupation of Caporetto, a little village on the upper Isonzo, where a great series of dams had been constructed by which, if need were, Cadorna could have drained the Isonzo dry by nightfall. By October 26th his columns were driving northwest against Monte Stol and southwest along the Natison Valley and toward Tarcento.   Further east and south, along the Isonzo Valley, Italian troops were fighting desperately.   Guns which had been lost were being retaken by hand-to-hand fighting with the bayonet among batteries, and on Monte Nero the heroic Alpini, isolated from the rest of the army and hard pressed by the Germans, were holding out victoriously, sending messages by carrier pigeon announcing that they would continue to maintain their positions to the death.

I spoke to the Major commanding one of those superb battalions.   He had been wounded and had been rushed out on an ambulance under fire just before the roads were cut. He was desperate for nothing but an opportunity to get back to his battalion, but a breach in the line toward Caporetto made his heroism vain.   The Germans were already actually in the rear of certain sectors, and by October 27th the retreat had been begun.

The withdrawal from the front line was a maneuver of infinite difficulty, which a touch of panic would have converted into the ruin of the army.   The enemy maintained his terrific fire upon the Italian communications, so that the troops withdrew into the tornado of shells of every kind that makes a hell of war.   Gas shells loosed vapors that haunted the roads invisibly; acid shells set the men suddenly gasping and strangling; tear-producing shells half blinded them.   Nothing could have brought them help but the dozen rearguard actions roaring and flaming at their heels and superb and long-confirmed discipline.

While they withdrew, a force of those splendid desperadoes who volunteer for rearguard fighting smashed its way up to Liga and delivered attacks which cleared the army's feet on that sector.

Further south the Duke of Aosta's Third Army was giving proof of fine soldiership.   It answered the ponderous enemy attack upon Selo on the Carso by a counter-attack which actually carried its line forward to Stari Lokva and which under any other circumstances would have given it a permanent gain of ground; but its business now was to withdraw its retirement under unceasing pressure over the terrible ground of the Carso, made more terrible by the blinding rain which thrashed down throughout Saturday. With the Isonzo to cross and the infinitely delicate and perilous operation of the rearguard action to carry out, it was a feat which no defeated army could have attempted. It was one of the great achievements of the war. The British artillerymen, who bore a part in the action, saved all their guns.

During October 27th the civilians of the threatened districts of Udine and its adjoining villages began their flight westward. The little City of Udine poured itself along the great level highway which runs westward toward the cities of the plain, and by Sunday morning the poor little town with its shuttered shops and vacant streets, wherein one's footfall echoed forlornly through the deep arcades which shade its sidewalks, had taken on the air of a cemetery.

I walked to each of the city gates in turn. There were forgotten dogs sitting at the locked doors of abandoned houses, whining feebly. A terrified cat inside a window grating cowered and shivered in the station whence the last train had departed. A little group of walking wounded who had arrived too late were sitting on the platform waiting for some one to counsel them. Near the Aquileia Gate a row of great warehouses and factories belonging to the Department of Munitions had been set on fire and was burning with tremendous clear, red flames, which waved hundreds of feet high in the wet and rainy air.

Toward noon it was evidently time to leave. I think I was the last civilian to go. I took a last look around from the summit of Castle Hill. Rain squalls inhabited the wide landscape like a population. Roads seemed to crawl and writhe with their dense westward traffic, and from Cividale, where the army had set fire to military depots, there arose great spires of flame and smoke. In Udine no chimney smoked. The little Palazzo, the most dreamily beautiful thing in Northern Italy, showed no flag; only under its columned loggia the frescoes of Pordenone glowed in their immortal colors.

Warsaw, Vilna, Bucharest—I knew and loved them all;

and now little Udine, so meek, so comely in its surrender to the pest that infests Europe. My own way rearward was by the great road which runs through Codroipo, Pordenone, and Treviso. It was a river running bank-high with the population of the retreat—vehicles four abreast crawling at the pace of the slowest; guns and caissons, private motor cars and donkey carts, soldiers on foot, and all that infinitely pitiable débris of war, the weary women and crying children whom Germany has made homeless. It is these last who give to every retreat its air of tragedy and disaster.

BY GEORGES CLEMENCEAU

Let us consider the military aspect of the Italian situation. To begin with, the principal error of the Italian high command—alone sufficient to bring about the catastrophe—was the faulty disposition of its armies. The Second Army, after crossing the Isonzo, was drawn up facing northward on the high mountains of Mzli, Monte Nero, and Vrich, without having reached the crests, which were still in possession of the enemy. The Third Army, on the other hand, had conquered the crests and held Cucco, Monte Santo, and Vodice. It faced eastward and had advanced across the Bainsizza Plateau toward Laibach. But between these two armies the Austrians still held a whole sector which formed from Tolmino to Santa Lucia a kind of outpost separating the Italian forces.

Military critics had already drawn attention to the danger of this situation and pointed out that the strategic arrangements of both Italian armies might be thrown into confusion by the enemy if the latter, holding the intermediate high ground, should decide to attack on both sides with sufficient forces. That is precisely what happened when the Germans were able to transfer part of their troops from Russia to the Italian Alps.

The second error: Behind these armies, drawn up in so perilous a position, there were at least reserves ready in case of a surprise. In May, 1916, in the course of the Austrian offensive in the Trentino, General Cadorna had profited by a moment of respite to constitute the Fifth Army a reserve. It was the intervention of this force at the critical moment that forced the enemy to retreat. For reasons that we are unable to understand, this Fifth Army was dissolved one fine day: Not that man power was wanting; it was and still is plentiful in Italy. The reserves of man power were numerous enough to furnish other armies as well. But the Italian Generalissimo has always seemed unwilling to keep them near the front. So, when need came, they could not intervene, and thus the rout of the Second Army, followed by the beating up and precipitate retreat of the Third, carried everything away.

This error is connected with several others, all of which are to be explained by blind confidence in the solidity of the conquests made. Otherwise, what excuse is there for the mistake of massing all the main supply depots at so short a distance from the front, between Isonzo and the Tagliamento? To take the case of wheat alone: More than 300,-000 tons thus fell into the hands of the famished enemy.

How, too, are we to excuse the complete lack of entrenchments, in view of a possible retreat, and the fact that not a single road of retreat was prepared, or a single bridge—beyond five old ones—thrown across the Tagliamento? The congestion produced almost from the outset by the enormous mass of men and material on the river banks, all trying to cross at the same moment, cost the Italian Army almost as dearly as the sudden loss of all its supply sources which had to be left to the enemy.

BY GENERAL VON CRAMON

Renewed attacks of the Italians on the Isonzo front, although not crowned with a decisive success, had nevertheless weakened the defensive power of the Austrians and resulted in a not inconsiderable loss of ground on the Bainsizza plateau and in the direction of Kostanjevica. It became questionable whether Trieste could be held in the event of another Italian attack. At Austrian army headquarters an increasingly large number counselled an offensive as the most effective measure to be adopted. In the beginning of August, 1917, I made a report concerning the matter to the German high command and added that the resistance against the participation of German troops in this offensive had been abandoned even by the Emperor Charles, and that a combined attack for the rolling up of the Isonzo front from the north, after breaking through in the region of Tolmino, had been planned. Such an operation demanded a far smaller force than a frontal attack and promised great results if successful. The situation was not dissimilar to that at Gorlice.

Ludendorff was not at first very enthusiastic over a common offensive against Italy. He would have preferred to overthrow Rumania completely by an advance into Moldavia. He finally, however, gave his consent, Emperor William and Hindenburg also agreeing.

An understanding had been reached when a courier of Emperor Charles arrived in Kreuznach with a personal letter to Emperor William requesting him *not* to agree to the employment of German troops on the southwestern front. Emperor Charles, without the knowledge of his general staff, and probably under the influence of the Empress, had interfered quite arbitrarily and unmeaningly. General Arz was successful in neutralizing the incident by despatching General von Kaldstätten.

General Otto von Below was appointed to the chief command of the German 14th army, selected to operate on the Isonzo front. His chief of staff reconnoitered the ground on which the attack was to be made. In connection therewith all the details of the common undertaking were agreed upon at general headquarters in Kreuznach. Seven divisions were placed at disposal by the German high command. The 14th German Army, reinforced by Austro-Hungarian troops, was to deliver the main blow. Before the middle of October an offensive was not to be thought of, because the railroads would not permit of a more rapid assembling of troops.

The preparations were proceeding apace when the common offensive was again made questionable by another incident. The Reichstags deputy Haussmann had related to an officer of the general staff that Czernin had disclosed to one of the German deputies to the Reichstag that Austria had determined no longer to coöperate toward the realization of Germany's war aims; that it needed peace and did not think of starving or bleeding to death because of Germany's dreams of conquest, and that the deputy in question should use his influence in the Reichstag to the end that the Government, by reason of a refusal of further credits, would be compelled to begin negotiations for peace.

I was called to Kreuznach and commissioned by Emperor William to seek an audience with Emperor Charles, in which I was to state in unequivocal terms that, unless a satisfactory explanation were forthcoming, there could be no question of German military aid against Italy; that the granting of German troops would be conditional upon written guarantees.

This commission led to a long interview with Emperor Charles. He assured me that Czernin had not recently spoken with German deputies[1] and had not made the statements imputed to him; that there must have been a misunderstanding or deliberate mystification. True, Czernin had probably often discussed questions of peace and had promised to use his influence in Germany in behalf of peace, but never in the form here affirmed. The German Government ought not take steps which might result in the fall of Czernin, who, unquestionably, was pro-German and would be hard to replace. Emperor Charles went on to assure me of Austria's good faith as an ally, and that he had often rejected offhand many enticing offers on the part of the Entente. Germany should not make it too hard for her allies. The majority of the population of Austria-Hungary were opposed to the war and only the sentiment toward the monarchy kept them in line.

Toward the middle of October Emperor Charles repaired to Bozen. The journey and my participation in it were discussed in detail in the newspapers, in order to draw the attention of the Italians in a false direction. The object

---

[1] Count Czernin has since published his "Memories." In them he admits without reserve that he tried to influence the German Reichstag and endeavored to further the Resolution of July.

was attained: In Italy there was much talk now of impending military events on the Tyrolean front. In addition several German storming battalions were sent to Tyrol and participated ostentatiously in small enterprises, while a detachment of wireless operators was also despatched. These, from Bozen, gave all kinds of orders and instructions to German formations which, in reality, did not exist.

The offensive against Tolmino, originally planned for the 15th of October, had to be postponed until the 24th, because of the unfavorable weather conditions. This proved to be an advantage because of the fact that certain reports made to the Italians by Czechs who had gone over to them, although essentially true, were subsequently unverified: the Italians had fully prepared for battle, had expected our attack earlier, unnecessarily lost their composure and abandoned further waiting. The blow was in fact a surprise and broke through their front on both sides of Tolmino.

While the combat for the heights was raging, General Lequis, with the 12th Prussian infantry division, and favored by a misty, rainy day, marched to Karfreit, took the dominating Mount Matajur, and drove back the Italian reinforcements who had been hurriedly sent from Cividale. The conduct of the 12th division, both as regards leaders and men, is worthy of a place in the book of fame. The resolution required to march straight through the enemy's front, regardless of the exposure of one's flanks, is not readily appreciated by everyone. General v. Below had promised to recommend for the order *Pour le mérite* the officer who would capture Mount Matajur within 24 hours after the commencement of the offensive. Lieutenant Schnieber, of the 23d infantry regiment, succeeded in doing so before the expiration of the stipulated time.

The success at Tolmino quickly extended toward the north and the south. The whole northeastern circle of the Italian front collapsed. Parts of the 14th Army, proceeding southward from Cividale, forced the Italians, retreating from the Lower Isonzo, away from the Tagliamento, and brought in thousands of prisoners. Whoever did not see with his own eyes the avenues of retreat of the Italians east of the Tagliamento, can form no conception of the picture of wild, headlong flight which presented itself. Great quantities of war material and supplies fell into our hands.

The Tagliamento, which, according to the original plan, was to be the farthest goal of the offensive, was crossed on November 6th. The Italians retreated behind that part of the Piave, where the right bank as well as the region between the Piave and the Brenta, including Mount Grappa, had been well fortified.

Owing to the rapid forward march of our infantry, artillery and ammunition supplies could not follow, nor were the materials for bridge building immediately on the spot. A German division which wished to storm the commanding Mount Grappa, could not win through without the requisite artillery support. The continuation of the offensive would have required renewed preparation and reserve forces. Its success, in view of the formation of the ground, was questionable, more particularly as the Italians had been reënforced by English and French divisions. Therefore, a further attack was not undertaken.

General von Hoetzendorff had persistently urged the strengthening of the Tyrolean front also in such a way that it might take part in the offensive. The two operations could not, however, be carried out simultaneously because forces were lacking. When the Italian front on the Isonzo had been defeated, the Austro-Hungarian troops there could be dispensed with. Von Hoetzendorff did not relinquish his efforts toward this end; but for some time his words fell upon deaf ears. Neither Arz nor Waldstätten favored the proposition; they were of the opinion that the one operation had first to be completed. The German high command generally coincided with von Hoetzendorff, but did not hesitate to make use of its prerogative of "high command" because it did not desire to use up too great a part of its forces on the Austrian seat of war. When Austrian army headquarters toward the end of November decided to take up the recommendations of von Hoetzendorff it was too late; the bad conditions prevailing on the railroads made a rapid moving to and fro of troops impossible.

BOLSHEVISM TRIUMPHS IN RUSSIA

SOCIALISM OVERTHROWN BY ANARCHY AND MOB TYRANNY

NOVEMBER 7TH

ALEXANDER MOSLER NICOLAI LENINE
E. H. WILCOX

The name Nicolai Lenine is merely the pen-name of that remarkable man, Vladimir Ulianoff. A member of the Russian upper classes, Ulianoff first became known as a Socialistic writer and political leader. As early as 1903 he was the head of a strong proletarian party, known as Leninites or Maximalites, and later called Bolsheviks. He was urging violent revolution, the nationalizing of all property, and rule by the vote of the masses. Driven into exile in the days of the revolution of 1905, Ulianoff repaid class-hatred with class-hatred, and became an embittered foe of all aristocrats. In 1912 he began a most energetic Socialistic paper, *Pravda* (Truth), and thus even from exile carried his voice over all Russia.

When the new revolution began in March, 1917, Ulianoff gladly accepted German aid to help him back into power. His paper constantly urged that the revolution must go further, must overthrow all classes except the workers with their hands. He promised the masses anything and everything, peace, wealth, happiness, an immediate millennium, if only they would take this step.

In March the masses had demanded only food and an honest handling of the War, and had been content when they received that much from Prince Lvoff and the Democracy. But their hopes mounted with their freedom; and they turned to Socialism and to Kerensky, who promised them an impossible equality and freedom from all restraint. Kerensky's reckless casting aside of the law's restraint on ignorance resulted in the breakdown of the country in July. In November, amid that breakdown, Kerensky was outbid for the support of the masses by the still more impossible promises of Lenine.

There were good points in Lenine's teachings, of course. Even a madman must include some forms of truth amid his ravings. But as a practical method of reconstructing human society, or of creating a new civilization, Bolshevism was as bestial as it was hopeless, as awful as it was absurd. Its basic doctrine was that one class, the laborers, should destroy all other classes, and so remain sole rulers of the world. But, any real government by the distracted masses being impossible, Lenine had to begin with government by a single tyrant, himself, in a tyranny far more absolute and murderous than that of any monarch of the past. Moreover, while this first tyrant,

Lenine, may have been a well-meaning autocrat, he had to delegate his power in other places to a thousand other tyrants, most of them too ignorant to realize what they did, and many of them unspeakably vicious.

The veil of unwriting, unthinking obscurity, of wholesale massacre without record, of purposeless animal foulness, which descended like black night upon Bolshevik Russia, can never be wholly lifted. It wrapped her in a shroud, rent only by the shrieks of dying victims. The doings of the man called Lenine became a curse upon all mankind, as awful as the curse of William II. Yet they may both have been well-meaning men, unbalanced intellects upset by the gift of too much power.

Our description of the Bolshevist upheaval comes from three eyewitnesses, each of whom, however, viewed it from a wholly different attitude. Alexander Mosler was a German mercantile agent entangled in Russian affairs and watching all he saw with silent scorn. Nicolai Lenine speaks for himself and his party; and then a British philosopher, in spirit not unkindly to Lenine, sums up the whole.

C. F. H.

BY ALEXANDER MOSLER

A German Agent in Russia During the Revolution

FROM the balcony of the Swedish embassy one morning in July [1917], I saw warships and small boats filled with Kronstadt sailors and the Red Guard coming up the Neva. To the sound of the *"Marseillaise"* and the loud hurrahs of Petersburg Bolsheviki gathered on the bank, the sailors left the ships at double-quick. Their intention was to take the Kerensky cabinet by surprise. Some of the Bolsheviki were armed only with a policeman's sword; others had carbines or muskets of various design. Many wore red scarfs around their bodies or red cockades on their caps.

The embassy building was situated on the banks of the Neva, just below the first bridge over the river. Thus all ships coming from the Baltic or from Kronstadt which were too large to pass under the bridge had to anchor in front of the embassy.

Many angry looks were directed up at me from the crowd, who, seeing me on the balcony of a palatial house, took me for a hated bourgeois. A sailor called up to me, "We'll pay a visit to you this evening to find where you keep your money and whether you have any brandy in your cellars." However, the red-scarfed heroes came neither on that nor on the next evening.

They left the ships at double-quick; they came back spent, ragged, and dirty—singly or in twos and threes. Without caps and without weapons they came looking for their ships. Some carried their muskets concealed under their coats and only brought them out when the proximity of the boats made them feel safe from their pursuers. Many had fallen during the adventure; a good third must have been taken prisoner; the survivors hastily weighed anchor and went silently down stream in the falling darkness.

While at the embassy I saw Kerensky and heard him speak. After the sailors' deputation with the ultimatum from Kronstadt had been arrested, he went on board a ship held by the mutineers. I could observe him closely as he came down the street accompanied by his adjutant and some staff officers. He wore a black Russian blouse fastened high at the neck and hanging over his trousers and a black tasseled girdle around his hips. Officers and soldiers he greeted with a brief handshake; I heard plainly his curt "Good morning, comrades." On board ship he spoke to the assembled sailors so impressively and convincingly that their mood changed completely. His last words were greeted with cheers; the black flag of anarchy which the ship was flying was hauled down, and in its place was raised the red flag of the Revolution. Ten minutes later the cruiser with Kerensky on board left its anchorage for Kronstadt.

Had Kerensky concluded peace earlier, had he in midsummer 1917 not given the order for a last attack upon the German lines, he would probably still sit upon the "golden chair." It was the military breakdown that caused his overthrow. During the fall of 1917, the situation slipped rapidly out of his control. I could draw a thousand pictures of the increasing anarchy; let a few such suffice.

On the street railways hubbub and license ruled. The cars were literally stuffed with soldiers, who of course paid no fare and whose behavior was so insolent and speech so filthy that no respectable woman could think of riding with them. At any moment a quarrel was likely to break out. When this occurred, the passengers instantly ranged themselves into two hostile camps, declaiming and arguing as in a popular mass meeting. From their talk I learned how embittered against the Bolsheviki were the greater part of the people of Petersburg. Only the peasant soldiers, who had no conception of the meaning of Socialism, and the ragged, uneducated proletariat belonged to the Bolsheviki. The organized factory workers lined up with the Social Revolutionists. Non-commissioned officers and clerks also were opposed to the Bolsheviki, and the master craftsmen, the educated classes, and members of the Conservative and Liberal parties positively foamed with rage if one mentioned the Bolsheviki to them. As the peasant soldiers, however, possessed rifles and machine guns, the helpless majority had to nurse their rage in silence.

Among the passengers once standing in a car, I saw an officer of the Women's Battalion of Death. With a white fur cap saucily perched on her head, her hair combed high under it, and spurs on her boots, she was a sturdy and pleasing figure. Standing in front of her was a slovenly looking sailor, the band of his cap so loosely fastened that it hung almost over one eye. On it I read the name of his ship, the *Pamjat Asowa*, "In Memory of Asow"—Asow, the revolutionist. Soon the sailor began a conversation with the "lady soldier." "Well, my officer in petticoats, whom do you want to make war against now?" Receiving no answer, he broke out with "The devil take the wench" and other remarks unfit to print. The girl turned first red, then white; but the fellow kept up his stream of vile talk until she left the car. Not one of the onlookers took her part.

That happened in November. In the vicinity of the Winter Palace, where I got out, signs of the shooting which took place there at the time of Kerensky's fall were plainly visible. Thousands of rifle and machine gun bullets were lodged in the walls. The windows were almost all shattered and had paper stuck over the holes.

There were plenty of people on the street, but few among them that were well dressed. People in possession of good clothes had, indeed, good reason to stay inside their own four walls. In one of the cross streets of the Nevski Prospect, that is, in the very heart of the city, I myself saw three soldiers stop a lady and in spite of her tears and appeals for mercy take her shoes off her feet. The poor creature, still moaning, had to go home through the deep snow in her stocking feet, while the "comrades" sold their booty on the next street corner for two hundred roubles.

At about this time the contents of strong boxes in the banks were confiscated. Anxious throngs of people gathered before the doors of the banks, but no one was allowed to enter. Owners of buildings might not deposit their rents, but must turn them over to the Commissariat. Nor could a house owner keep more rooms for himself than there were members in his family. Many days there was no electric light at all in dwellings or on the streets; or the lights went out at five o'clock in the afternoon.

Every court, every establishment, every community, was a little republic by itself. There was no general law or standard to which all men must conform. In the Petersburg district, for example, the head of the precinct decreed that government employees should receive a salary of three hundred roubles a month. This applied to everybody, from the man who checked overcoats and rubbers at the door to his own exalted self; not the productivity but the person was rewarded. In other public departments other regulations were laid down, each chief acting as he saw fit.

Among the soldiery, especially, turbulence and anarchy prevailed. All officers, from the commander of the regiment to the youngest lieutenant, were chosen by the soldiers. The men of a regiment met together, debated the matter excitedly, and then took a vote. Whoever received the most votes became the commander, whether or not he had the necessary education or ability for such a responsible post. The candidate who received the second largest number of votes became the second in command, and so on down. Former officers if not reëlected were reduced to the rank and pay of private soldiers. No account was taken of their age or the families they might have dependent on them. So to escape starvation many ex-colonels, captains, and lieutenants took any work they could find to do. Officers of the Guard were to be seen acting as baggage men in the railway stations or as dock hands along the water front.

The soldiers passed their time playing cards and carrying on a small trade in cigarettes, spirits, and old clothing. Or they formed into bands and with fixed bayonets, "in the name of the law," entered and searched the houses of prosperous citizens. Everything which was not fastened down they carried off. At the slightest show of resistance they threatened the inmates with death. Men were killed like cattle on these occasions.

A lady told me later how these beasts in soldiers' uniforms had slowly tortured her husband to death before her own and her children's eyes. After chopping off his fingers one by one and putting out his eyes, they dragged him half conscious down the stairs and clubbed and bayoneted him to death. Then four soldiers stuck the bleeding corpse on their bayonets and carried it overhead as a panoply through the streets of Petersburg to the river. There they scraped the body off on the bridge railing and pitched it into the water.

I saw this family two days after the murder. The mother lay in bed out of her mind. The son, a university student, answered every question with the words, "They spitted him and threw him into the river." The seventeen-year-old daughter sat in a corner of the room on the floor weeping steadily, oblivious of what went on about her. Only the little sister, three years old, sat under the table and played with her doll.

BY NICOLAI LENINE
Appeals issued in the Bolshevist organ, urging revolt.

November 1st.

Facts prove to us most plainly that after the July days the majority of the population began rapidly to join the ranks of the Bolshevists. This is proved by the elections at Petrograd on September 2nd, before the Korniloff affair, when the Bolshevist votes rose from 20 per cent. to 33 per cent., as also by the September elections of the district dumas in Moscow, when the percentage of Bolshevist votes rose from 11 per cent. to 49 per cent. This was also proved by the fact that the bulk of the Peasants' Soviets, contrary to the advice of their "Avksentieff's" Central Soviet, declared against a coalition; for to be against a coalition is, in reality, to go with the Bolshevists. Further, communications from the front with increasing frequency and definiteness show that the mass of the soldiery, in spite of malicious libels and attacks by the leaders of the Menshevists, the officers, deputies, etc., etc., more and more decisively came over to the side of the Bolshevists. Finally, the most important fact in the present juncture is the Peasants' Rising. These are the object lessons which prove the passing of the population to the side of the Bolshevists. The movement of the peasants in the Tamboff Government was a revolution, both in a physical and political sense, which gave such important political results as, in the first place, the consent to transfer the land to the peasants. Not without cause does the whole of the riff-raff Press, up to the *Delo Naroda,* now wail of the need to hand over the land to the peasants. Here you have the proof of the soundness of Bolshevism and of its success. Another splendid political and revolutionary consequence of the Peasants' Rising is the arrival of grain at the railway stations in the Tamboff Government. Here, perplexed comrades, is another argument in favor of a rising as the only means of saving the country from famine, which is already knocking at the door, and from a crisis of unheard-of proportions. Whilst the Menshevist traitors to the people growl, threaten, write resolutions, and hold out the empty convocation of the Constituent Assembly, the people will proceed by Bolshevist tactics with the settlement of the food question by a rising against the landed proprietors, capitalists, and middlemen. No, to doubt now that the bulk of the people is going, and will continue to go, with the Bolshevists is shamefully to hesitate and tantamount to throwing over all principles of proletarian revolutionism and totally to repudiate Bolshevism.

We have no right to wait until the *bourgeoisie* has smothered the Revolution. The famine does not wait. The Peasant Rising did not wait. The war does not wait. History does not repeat itself, but, if we turn our backs on it, what will happen? We must wait for a miracle.

November 3rd.

There is no doubt that the revolution in Russia has reached its turning point. In a country of peasants, under a revolutionary Republican Government, supported by the parties of the Revolutionary Socialists and the Menshevists, parties which until recently had the majority of the *bourgeoisie* behind them, there is rising to-day a peasants' rebellion. This fact has not surprised us—the Bolshevists. We have always maintained that the policy of the famous "Coalition" with *bourgeoisie* was a policy of an imperialist war, a policy of protecting capitalism and Junkerdom from the people. There exists in Russia, thanks to the treason of the Revolutionary Socialists and Menshevists, at the same time as the Government of the Soviets, a Government of capitalists and Junkers. Why should we be surprised that in Russia, with all the wretchedness brought by the continuation of the imperialist war upon the nation, a peasants' rebellion should break out and spread?

Not only has the policy of the followers of Prince Lvoff broken down; but also the Revolutionary Socialists, who suffer a Kerensky in their midst, have sunk to the level of a party hostile to the people, hostile to the peasants, to the level of a counter-revolutionary party. The Russian Revolution has reached a turning-point. A peasants' rebellion in a country of peasants against the Government of the Revolutionary Socialist Kerensky, against the Menshevists Nikitin and Gvozdeff, against the other Ministers—representatives of Capital and Junkerdom!—that is the situation. The crushing of this rebellion by military force at the command of the Republican Government—that is the consequence of this situation! In the face of these facts, is it possible for an honest adherent of the peasants' cause to deny, with indifference, that the crisis has come to a head, and that the victory of the Government over the peasants is the death-knell of the Revolution, and the triumph of the counter-revolution?

Yes, the leaders of the Central Executive Committee are practicing a regular policy of protecting the *bourgeoisie* and the Junkers. And there is no doubt that the Bolshevists who were to let themselves be caught in the snare of constitutional illusions, of "belief" in the elections to the Constituent Assembly, of the "expectation" of the Congress of all the Soviets, and so forth, that such Bolshevists would be nothing less than miserable traitors to the cause of the proletariat.

The crushing of a peasants' rebellion by a Government, which is compared even by the *Delo Naroda* to Stolypin, means the destruction of the Revolution. They drivel about anarchy, about the indifference of the masses: the masses cannot be indifferent in the elections if the peasantry is obliged to rebel, and if the revolutionary democracy suffers that rebellion to be quelled. To allow the rebellion to be crushed at this hour means to allow the elections for the Constituent Assembly to be tampered with, and this would be done more barefacedly than was the case of the elections for the Democratic Conference, and for the Preliminary Parliament. The crisis is approaching its final stage. The whole future of the Russian Revolution is at stake. The whole future of the International Proletarian Socialistic Revolution is at stake. The final stage of the crisis is at hand.

Proclamation of Nicolai Lenine Summoning His Followers to Assume Power, November 6th

The Councils of Workers', Soldiers' and Peasants' Delegates must at once take every practicable and feasible step for the realization of the Socialist program.

The Bolsheviki demand a republic of the Councils of Workers', Soldiers' and Peasants' Delegates; abolition of the standing army and the police, substituting for them an armed people; officials to be not only elected but also subject to recall and their pay not to exceed that of a good worker.

Sole authority must be in the hands of the Councils of

Workers', Soldiers' and Peasants' Delegates. There must be no dual authority.

No support should be given to the Provisional Government. The whole of the people must be prepared for the complete and sole authority of the Councils of the Workers', Soldiers' and Peasants' Delegates.

A constituent assembly should be called as soon as possible, but it is necessary to increase the members and strengthen the power of the Councils of Workers', Soldiers' and Peasants' Delegates by organizing and arming the masses.

A police force of the conventional type and a standing army are absolutely unnecessary. Immediately and unconditionally a universal army of the people should be introduced, so that they and the militia and the army shall be an integral whole. Capitalists must pay the workers for their days of service in the militia.

Officers must not only be elected, but every step of every officer and General must be subject to control by special soldiers' committees.

The arbitrary removal by the soldiers of their superior officers is in every respect indispensable. The soldiers will obey only the powers of their own choice; they can respect no others.

The Bolsheviki are absolutely opposed to all imperialist wars and to all bourgeois Governments which make them, among them our own Provisional Government. The Bolsheviki are absolutely opposed to "revolutionary defense" in Russia.

The Bolsheviki are against the predatory international treaties concluded between the Czar and England, France, etc., for the strangling of Persia, the division of China, Turkey, Austria, etc.

The Bolsheviki are against annexations. Any promise of a capitalist Government to renounce annexations is a huge fraud. To expose it is very simple, by demanding that each nation be freed from the yoke of its own capitalists.

The Bolsheviki are opposed to the (Russian) Liberty Loan, because the war remains imperialistic, being waged by capitalists in alliance with capitalists, and in the interests of capitalists.

The Bolsheviki refuse to leave to capitalist Governments the task of expressing the desire of the nations for peace.

All monarchies must be abolished. Revolutions do not proceed in fixed order. Only genuine revolutionaries may be trusted.

The peasants must at once take all the land from the landholders. Order must be strictly maintained by the Councils of Peasants' Delegates. The production of bread and meat must be increased and the soldiers better fed. Destruction of cattle, of tools, etc., is not permissible.

It will be impossible to rely upon the general Councils of Peasants' Delegates, for the wealthy peasants are of the same capitalist class that is always inclined to injure or deceive the farmhands, day laborers, and the poorer peasants. We must at once form special organizations of these latter classes of the village population both within the Councils of Peasants' Delegates and in the form of special Councils of Delegates of the Farmers' Workers.

We must at once prepare the Councils of Workers' Delegates, the Councils of Delegates of Banking Employees, and others for the taking of all such steps as are feasible and completely realizable toward the union of all banks in one single national bank, and then toward a control of the Councils of Workers' Delegates over the banks and syndicates, and then toward their nationalization, that is, their passing over into the possession of the whole people.

The only Socialist International, establishing and realizing a brotherly union of all the workers in all countries, which is now desirable for the nations, is one which consists of the really revolutionary workers, who are capable of putting an end to the awful and criminal slaughter of nations, capable of delivering humanity from the yoke of capitalism. Only such people (groups, parties, etc.) as the German Socialist, Karl Liebknecht, now in a German jail, only people who will tirelessly struggle with their own Government and their own *bourgeoisie,* and their own social-patriots, and their own "centrists," can and must immediately establish that international which is necessary to the nations.

The fraternization between soldiers of the warring countries, at the front, must be encouraged; it is good and indispensable.

Proclamation of November 7th

We have deposed the Government of Kerensky, which rose against the revolution and the people. The change which resulted in the deposition of the Provisional Government was accomplished without bloodshed.

The Petrograd Council of Workmen's and Soldiers' Delegates solemnly welcomes the accomplished change and proclaims the authority of the Military Revolutionary Committee until the creation of a Government by the Workmen's and Soldiers' Delegates.

Announcing this to the army at the front, the Revolutionary Committee calls upon the revolutionary soldiers to watch closely the conduct of the men in command. Officers who do not join the accomplished revolution immediately and openly must be arrested at once as enemies.

The Petrograd Council of Workmen's and Soldiers' Delegates considers this to be the program of the new authority:

First—The offer of an immediate democratic peace.

Second—The immediate handing over of large proprietarial lands to the peasants.

Third—The transmission of all authority to the Council of Workmen's and Soldiers' Delegates.

Fourth—The honest convocation of a Constitutional Assembly.

The national revolutionary army must not permit uncertain military detachments to leave the front for Petrograd. They should use persuasion, but where this fails they must oppose any such action on the part of these detachments by force without mercy.

The present order must be read immediately to all military detachments in all arms. The suppression of this order from the rank and file by army organizations is equivalent to a great crime against the revolution and will be punished by all the strength of the revolutionary law.

Soldiers! For peace, for bread, for land, and for the power of the people!

(Signed) THE MILITARY REVOLUTIONARY COMMITTEE.

Proclamations of November 8th

(FIRST)

To All Provincial Councils of Workmen's and Soldiers' and Peasants' Delegates:

All power lies in the Workmen's and Soldiers' Delegates. Government commissaries are relieved of their functions. Presidents of the Workmen's and Soldiers' Delegates are to communicate direct with the Revolutionary Government. All members of agricultural committees who have been arrested are to be set at liberty immediately and the commissioners who arrested them are in turn to be arrested.

(SECOND)

The death penalty reëstablished at the front by Premier Kerensky is abolished and complete freedom for political propaganda has been established at the front. All revolutionary soldiers and officers who have been arrested for complicity in so-called political crimes are to be set at liberty immediately.

(THIRD)

Former Ministers Konovaloff, Kishkin, Terestchenko, Malyanovitch, Nikitin, and others have been arrested by the Revolutionary Committee.

M. Kerensky has taken flight and all military bodies have been empowered to take all possible measures to arrest Kerensky and bring him back to Petrograd. All complicity with Kerensky will be dealt with as high treason.

RESOLUTIONS PASSED BY "THE WORKMEN'S AND SOLDIERS' CONGRESS" ON NOVEMBER IOTH

The Government considers a peace to be democratic and equitable, which is aspired to by a majority of the working classes of all the belligerent countries, worn out and ruined by war—the peace which the Russian workmen called for on the fall of the monarchy. It should be an immediate peace, without annexation (that is to say, without usurpation of foreign territory and without violent conquest of nationalities) and without indemnities.

The Russian Government proposes to all belligerents to make this peace immediately, declaring themselves ready without delay to carry out all the conditions of this peace through plenipotentiaries of all countries and nations.

By annexation or usurpation of territory the Government means, in accordance with the sense of justice of democracy in general and of the working classes in particular, any annexation to a great and powerful State of a weak nationality without the consent of that nationality and independently of its degree of civilization and its geographical situation in Europe or across the ocean.

If any population be kept by force under the control of any State, and if, contrary to its will, expressed in the press or in national assembly, or to decisions of parties, or in opposition to rebellions and uprisings against an oppressor, the population is refused the right of universal suffrage, of driving out an army of occupation and organizing its own political régime, such a state of things is annexation or violent usurpation. The Government considers that the active carrying on of the war in order to share weak nationalities which have been conquered between rich and powerful nations is a great crime against humanity.

Accordingly, the Government solemnly proclaims its decision to sign peace terms which will bring this war to an end on the conditions mentioned above, which are equitable for all the nationalities.

BY E. H. WILCOX

When the Revolution broke out in Russia, Lenine felt that the chance of his life had come, and he fretted to get back to Petrograd. He applied for leave to travel through France and England, but the Allied Governments regarded him with only too well-founded suspicion, and placed obstacles in his way. As things turned out, this was unfortunate, though Lenine was probably not a man to be biassed by personal chagrins, as Trotsky appears to have been by his detention at Halifax while on his way back to Russia from the United States. Lenine was in a hurry, for he had started with a heavy handicap, and it was essential for his purposes that he should be in Russia before the process of reconstruction could begin in earnest. He appealed to the Swiss Socialist Robert Grimm, the Editor of the *Berner Togwacht*, who had presided over the Kiental Conference, and together they concocted the plan of traveling back through Germany. Some say the idea originated with the one, some with the other, but the point is negligible. For Lenine there were no conscientious objections to it: there were only tactical objections. To him, international frontiers, whether in peace or war, were artificial and conventional barriers, with no realities to correspond to them in the nature of things. In his eyes, there were no nations, but only two classes, into which all mankind was divided; the "bourgeoisie" in all countries formed the one class, and the proletariat of all countries the other. These two classes, so he argued, were natural and eternal enemies to one another, and the War was merely a predatory feud, in which the bourgeoisie of one group of countries was making use of its "enslaved proletarians" to raid the ill-gotten possessions of the bourgeoisie of another group. In Russia a state of things had arisen, in which it might be possible for the proletariat to throw off its yoke; and if that could be done in one country, the example would soon be followed in others, perhaps in all others. If the German Government, in the mistaken idea that it was promoting its own ends, was foolish enough to help him to carry out his plan, why should be refuse its assistance? The "Imperialists" in Berlin would soon learn that they had been mistaken, and had, in reality, forged a weapon for use against themselves. On the other hand, Lenine doubtless recognized, that if he traveled through Germany, he would excite against himself a prejudice which would seriously hamper his agitation in Russia. But, after weighing the pros and cons, he decided that a prompt arrival in Russia would more than counter-balance the drawbacks which would result from "traffic with the enemy." Unhappily, the sequel proved that he was right.

Naturally, the Berlin Government welcomed the proposal that the most potent agent of dissolution should be let loose on the already deliquescent mass of Russian society, and on April 9, 1917, Lenine, Zinovieff, and thirty other political refugees crossed the Swiss frontier on to German territory in "sealed" railway carriages. The party was not exclusively composed of Bolsheviks, as it had been stipulated by the Russians that political refugees of all shades should be allowed to take advantage of the opportunity. It was accompanied by the Swiss pacifist Fritz Platten, who had acted as intermediary between the refugees and the German authorities; and it was under the surveillance of three German officers. The travelers seem to have pledged themselves to do their utmost to secure the release of the civilian German and Austrian prisoners of war in Russia. Any other obligations which they may have entered into have been kept secret. They were not allowed to leave the train during the three days of their passage across German soil.

When Lenine reached Petrograd, he found the conditions anything but favorable for his agitation. The archives of the Ohrana had been opened, and prominent Bolsheviks had been exposed as police spies in nearly every big town in Russia. Among these "Provokatory," as has been seen, were the leader of the Bolshevik Party in the Duma, and a prominent member of the editorial staff of the Bolshevik paper, *Pravda*. To a plain mind, it might well have seemed that the whole Bolshevik Party was so tainted with treachery that no confidence could be placed in it. The circumstances of Lenine's journey also produced a very unfavorable impression when they became known. At the beginning of the Revolution, at any rate, the popular feeling was still bitterly anti-German, and for many months the "sealed carriages" haunted the Russian newspapers. Moreover, Lenine had to suffer under a further handicap. When the Revolution came, nearly all his ablest lieutenants were either in Siberia or abroad; and before they could be assembled in

Petrograd from all the ends of the earth, the Social-Revolutionaries and Mensheviks had had time to consolidate their power over the masses. As a set-off to this was the icy fanaticism, the inexhaustible energy, and the indomitable will of the Bolshevik leader, who in force of character towers above all the other men brought to the surface by the Revolution.

In an atmosphere which was certainly rather hostile than friendly, Lenine set vigorously to work. The handsome villa of the ballerina Kshesinskaya, on the fashionable Kameno-ostrovski Prospect, opposite the Peter and Paul Fortress, and within view of the windows of the British Embassy, had been abandoned by its owner in the first days of the revolutionary tumult, and was now "requisitioned" as the Bolshevik headquarters. From a kiosk in the garden, inflammatory harangues were delivered daily to open-mouthed crowds of workmen and soldiers in the street on the other side of the palings. Money Lenine had in abundance, and the smartest motor-cars in Petrograd carried his army of orators into the remote working-class districts on the rim of the city. Where the funds came from, it is as easy to guess as it is difficult to prove. "From a rich lady in Zurich, who is interested in the cause," said the Bolsheviks themselves; but there were many others "interested in the cause," from ulterior motives, who were both able and willing to lend it substantial financial aid—on one side all those who had to gain from a restoration of the Old Régime, on the other, the Germans, so far the chief beneficiaries from Lenine's labors. The aims of the Russian reactionaries and the German Imperialists were, up to a point, identical with those of Lenine. Like him, they desired the failure of the Revolution in its existing form, and, as a feature of that failure, the destruction of the Russian Army. It was only when the first Revolution had collapsed that their roads parted; and from that point, the wishes of no two of the three were coincident.

The Bolsheviks have always been cynically frank as to their readiness to accept assistance from any source whatsoever. When they were taxed with taking money from the Germans, they replied that they would take it willingly from any one who chose to give it, and whatever his motive in giving it might be. To them there was only one standard and one sanction—the cause. Whatever helped the cause was good, whatever hindered it was bad. Bolshevism was not only their political platform, but also their religious creed and the basis of their moral code. It is this which has made it so difficult for people with other religious creeds and moral codes to understand their actions.

In the direct appeal to the masses, Lenine himself had a comparatively small share. He has always been the veiled oracle rather than the popular demagogue of the movement. His strength is not the fiery oratory which moves mobs, but the conviction, will and knowledge that control counsels. In this he is the very antithesis of Kerensky, who needs the inspiration of the crowd in order to inspire it in his turn. Critical auditors often found it hard to explain the enthusiasm which Lenine's speeches aroused in uneducated audiences. Neither his physical nor his mental equipment is of a sort to appeal to the crowd. He is a little man of commonplace figure, with no other outward mark of distinction than the high bald dome of his forehead. His slovenliness is merely that of indifference, and has none of the calculated picturesqueness which excites curiosity and rivets attention. His gesture as he speaks is casual and spasmodic. His speech is swift and fluent, simple in its form and free from ornament, but crowded with facts. He frequently introduces political and economic conceptions which can hardly be intelligible to untrained minds. What he says is, in fact, better suited to the lecture-room than to the party platform—his opponents have often said of him that his whole being is academic rather than political, and that both his mistakes and his atrocities would have been fewer, if he had spent more of his time with men and less with books. That, in spite of the aridity and abstraction of his thought, he should have his almost unexampled sway over the multitude, is probably due to his authority as undisputed head of the movement. To the masses, he is what the Czar once was—the source of all power and authority, the man from whom the Trotskys, Zinovieffs, and Lunacharskis hold their commissions, and of whose ideas and orders they are but the executive agents. The monarchical principle has been rejected by the minds of the Russian proletariat, but it still lingers in their souls. In their eyes, every big movement must be incorporated in a single man, and to them Lenine is the embodiment of Bolshevism.

In identifying Lenine with Bolshevism, the masses are undoubtedly right. As one of the "bourgeois" Petrograd papers put it, he has better grounds to boast "I am Bolshevism" than had Louis XIV. to declare *"L'état c'est moi."* Fourteen years ago, Rosa Luxemburg, the German Spartacus leader, flung at him the reproach that he really despised the rights and power of the laboring classes, and that what he aimed at was to rule alone. She was justified by subsequent developments, for Lenine had been the autocrat of Bolshevism long before he became "Nicholas III.," and ruled all that was left of Russia with a much more absolute sway than Nicholas II. had ever actually exercised. Her taunt was published shortly after the split at the 1903 Conference, in the *Iskra,* which had then become the organ of the Mensheviki. To them, Lenine was already "the iron fist," and ever since his chief characteristics have always been defined by the same metallic term. Both friends and foes speak of his "iron will" and his "iron nerve"; and it is these qualities, coupled with the rather mechanical smoothness and precision of his mental processes, which have made him the unchallenged chief over the associates of his work. At the same time, with all his ruthlessness and determination in what he regarded as essentials, he retained in intimate relationships a great deal of the amenity and "sweet reasonableness" for which the Russians are famous. P. Orlovski, a Bolshevik writer, says of him: "No one is so ready as he to follow the advice of others, if the advice is good; no one so amiably suffers his manuscripts to be revised and modified; no one so gladly submits to the opinion of the majority. True, only when he is not convinced that in that way the interests of the Party and of the laboring class would come to harm. Then he is firm in his demands, even if they may mean a breach with his best friends." An English merchant who, in order to extricate his family from a critical situation, had to seek Lenine's personal aid, was astonished to find the "blood-thirsty tyrant" a mild-mannered man, courteous and sympathetic in bearing, and almost eager to afford all the assistance in his power. Many Entente officials, both military and civilian, who have been brought into personal contact with Lenine have been greatly impressed by the force of his personality and his intellectual powers.

The principles of the agitation by which Lenine destroyed Russia's military power, and thus probably postponed the day of reckoning with Germany for a full year, were peculiar neither to himself nor to Bolshevism. They had long formed an intrinsic part of Marxian doctrine. Experience, so it was taught, had shown that the fruits of revolutions were reaped at once or not at all. It had also shown that political revolutions merely transferred authority from one section of the bourgeoisie to another, and left the position of the proletariat substantially unchanged. Therefore, if the Russian Revolution was to be of real benefit to the laboring classes, it must upset the social and economic as well as the political structure of the country. That, however, could be effected only by a "dictatorship of the proletariat." But before that dictatorship could be firmly established, all organs of the old order which contained in themselves forces of resistance and possibilities of reaction must be abolished. The chief of these organs was the Army, which had been recruited on a monarchical basis, sworn in to a monarch, and imbued with monarchical traditions. As long as the old Army existed, it might at any time become a reactionary instrument in the hands of a popular royalist general. Therefore the Army must be destroyed. If peace could be secured before the destruction of the Army was complete, so much the better. If not, the process of world regeneration would only be postponed—for Lenine was convinced, as Marx and Engels had been in 1848, that Europe was ripe for universal revolution, and that if one country would but set the example, the others would hasten to follow it. He did not ignore the risks to Russia involved in this experiment, but what did Russia matter? His province was the world. He thought in continents, not in parishes. After the very first speech which he made in the Petrograd Soviet, he was asked whether the trial of his ideas might not be dangerous for a backward agricultural country like Russia, and he replied: "Let it be so. Let her perish; but we will kindle social revolution throughout the world, and, if necessary, hand on its banner to other nations."

The Bolshevik propaganda in the Russian Army was greatly aided by the ambiguity of the Allies as to their war aims. If they had been in a position to state clearly and categorically that they were fighting solely for the rights of the smaller nationalities, and were determined not to retain for themselves one square inch of enemy soil, it is possible that the Russian Army would have continued to fight, and that the War would have been finished a year sooner and in a much more satisfactory manner than was actually the case. The Russians are a generous-hearted people, and respond very warmly to disinterested ideals. The proposal to fight for the restoration of Poland, the independence of the Czecho-Slovaks, and the union of the Southern Slavs, would have made a strong appeal to them. Till they went to pieces, they were quite sound on the question of Belgium, Serbia, Montenegro, Rumania and even Alsace-Lorraine.

The Allies were not, however, in a position to give the assurances mentioned, and by their silence they remained burdened with all the evil inheritance of their connection with the former Russian Government. The proposition that the Czardom was fighting for the freedom of any one or anything, was a contradiction in terms. The Czarist "liberation of Poland" merely meant the reunion of all that country under the scepter of the Romanoffs. To the Russians, Slav ideals in the Balkans really did mean something, but to their Government these ideals were merely a political weapon. At the time of the Revolution, Russia had dropped virtuous pretenses everywhere except in official documents, and was frankly fighting for Constantinople. Even so liberal and enlightened a politician as Milyukof admitted that for him this was the only "war aim" that really mattered. The Russians knew these facts about their own country, and not unnaturally inferred that the professions of the Allies were as hollow as those of their own dethroned Government had been. They themselves disclaimed all desire for "annexations," and they expected a like disclaimer from their partners.

The Bolshevik argument to the Russian soldiers took the following form: "Why should you go on fighting? You have renounced all annexations, and the enemy is willing to make peace with you to-morrow on the condition of the *status quo*, which is all you ask. And yet you are told that you must further risk life and limb. Why? We will tell you. It is because the English want the German Colonies, Mesopotamia, and Palestine. You must shed your blood and give your lives in order that the English Imperialists and capitalists may increase their already excessive colonial empire. And the reason why you must do this is that Russia is bound by secret treaties to continue the War till those aims have been attained."

This argument was all the more seductive because it contained elements of truth. It is almost certain that, at the beginning of the Revolution, Germany would have been very glad to make peace with Russia on the basis of the *status quo*, in order to have her hands free in the West. We have learnt from Count Czernin that, in April, 1917, Austria was already anxious to throw up the sponge, and was only prevented from doing so by German threats. It was also true that there were secret treaties of a rather compromising character between the Allies though they did not include the stipulations attributed to them by Lenine, who actually asserted that Great Britain, France and Russia had contracted to divide up China among themselves. Of course, it was also true that the War had originally been Russia's special affair; that the Revolution had begun and was being continued behind the shield of her Allies; that if Germany had not been held by the throat in the West, Russia would have had either to stop talking and fight, or to submit to conditions beside which the Brest-Litovsk treaties would have been positive benevolence; that, in short, all the bombastic rhetoric about "revolutionary achievements" and the "rights and power of free men," whether it came from Kerensky or from Lenine, was only possible because Great Britain and France were fighting, though Russia, to succor whom they had entered the conflict, was not. The airy dialectics of Trotsky at Brest-Litovsk were, indeed, only the conduct of the street urchin who has been murderously attacked, and, seeing a policeman engaged in a death-grapple with his assailant, hurls abuse at both of them indifferently. All this was true, but as it apparently did not strike the men who were at the head of revolutionary Russia, it could hardly be expected to occur to the ignorant soldier, artisan and peasant.

While the Army was learning that it was being called upon to sacrifice itself for the "imperialistic" purposes of Great Britain and France, the masses as a whole were being plied with another seduction just as persuasive. The other parties emulated one another in the prodigality of their promises, but at the same time they counseled patience till peace could be concluded, and the Constituent Assembly convened. The peasants were assured that their traditional claim to the land should be duly satisfied, in one way or another, if they would but wait a little longer; and all sorts of dazzling prospects in an indefinite future were opened up to the artisan. But the Bolsheviks not only promised much more than any one else—they promised it immediately. "If you will but trust us," they said, "you shall have peace at once and food at once; while as for the land and the means of production in the factories, you must seize them for yourselves without a moment's hesitation, for if you don't, you will probably never get them at all."

Unhappily, this seductive agitation was never understood by the Allies, and consequently was not met in the right way. Quite naturally, the man in the street could only interpret Bolshevism as a particularly insidious form of German machination. Lenine had traveled through Germany on his way back to Russia. He had almost certainly received money, directly or indirectly, from Germany. The Germans had given him every possible assistance, and they alone had received any material benefit from his activities. Indeed, Lenine accomplished a work which had been too much for all the Hindenburgs, Ludendorffs, and Mackensens, for he destroyed the Russian Army. What other explanation of such a man could there be than that he was a hireling of William II.? But those whose business it is to instruct and guide the public should have known better. Seventy years had passed since the publication of the Communist Manifesto by Marx and Engels, and the whole Bolshevik policy was summed up in the culminating passage of that document: "The proletarians have nothing to lose but their chains: they have a world to win. Proletarians of all lands, unite!" The Internationale was not a secret society, and its theories and objects were accessible to all. The purpose of the Zimmerwald and Kiental conferences was perfectly well known. Lenine had for years before the War preached in the Press the doctrines which he promulgated on his return to Russia, and he has done nothing grossly inconsistent with his previous thirty years' political work.

If you wish to beat an opponent, whether in sport, politics, or war, the first thing is to understand his game. Instead of doing this in their struggle against Lenine, the Allies jumped to hasty conclusions. Any stick was good enough to beat him with, except the only one which could really hurt him. It was said that he was a Jew, and that his name was Zederbaum. Actually, he is almost the only prominent Bolshevik leader who is not racially a Jew, and Zederbaum is the real family name of his most immediate opponent, the Menshevik leader, Martoff. It was even sought to discredit the Bolshevik leader by the wild assertion that the real Lenine was no more, and that the man who passed under his name was an impostor, who had got hold of his identification papers. But the ultimate general line of attack against him was that he was a "German agent," that is to say, a hired instrument, whose activity deliberately aimed at the advantage of the Imperialists of the Central Empires.

Everything is possible to human nature, and Lenine may be a second Faust who has sold himself to the devil for the selfish pleasures of life. Men do sometimes undergo a process of complete conversion or perversion. But when such a change is very sudden and very complete, we rightly demand convincing evidence that it has actually taken place. Lenine is unquestionably a man of no average ability, who could have made a comfortable position for himself in any human society. Nevertheless, he devoted the earlier years of his adult career to a vocation which, at that time, involved greater risks and smaller chances of personal advantage than almost any other—the vocation of a Russian revolutionary. What it actually brought him was what it brought most of those who adopted it with energy and fervor—jail, Siberia and exile. The ponderous works which he has published could have been produced only after laborious poring over what most people regard as one of the most arid of all subjects. Like the original prophet whose mantle he aspired to wear, Karl Marx, he was never happier than when exploring the treasures of the British Museum. This institution, one of his friends has told us, he regarded with enthusiastic admiration. "His eyes always shone," when he spoke of it, and "it was his fondest dream to live near it." It was here that he found his "favorite recreation." Clearly, evidence of a very convincing nature is required to prove that a man with such a record and such pursuits has sold himself to a cause like that of which William II. was the representative figure.

Evidence was demanded, and naturally it was forthcoming. Some of it was produced at the time of the unsuccessful Leninite *coup de main,* in July, 1917, and it contributed to the failure of that first Bolshevik clutch at power. It was not particularly plausible and has since been generally repudiated as forged. But the great effort to prove Lenine's complicity with the Governments of the Central Empires was the series of documents collected by the American Committee on Public Information, and published by that body as a pamphlet with the title "The German-Bolshevik Conspiracy." This pamphlet will always remain a monument of that paralysis of the critical faculties which seems inseparable from a state of war. In the introduction, the documents are said to show "that the present Bolshevik Government is not a Russian Government at all, but a German Government, acting solely in the interests of Germany and betraying the Russian people, as it betrays Russia's natural Allies, for the benefit of the Imperial Government alone." Unfortunately, they show nothing of the kind. Indeed, the only thing they show quite plainly is the incapacity of those who collected them for the mission with which they were entrusted. The detailed examination of these documents is impossible here, but one illustration will suffice to characterize them. The pamphlet includes some fifteen or sixteen facsimiles by way of corroboration. One of these facsimiles purports to be a circular sent out on November 28, 1914, by the "General Staff" of the German High Sea Fleet. Now, such a body as a "General Staff" does not exist in the German Navy. What corresponds in the Navy to the General Staff of the Army is the "Admiral Staff." The circular itself consists of eighteen lines. In these eighteen lines are two mistakes in grammar, seven mistakes in spelling and seven mistakes in phrasing. An expert on the German language has given the following opinion: "This circular was most certainly not written by a German. It would appear to be a very poor attempt to copy German official language." That, it is true, is only one of the documents; but its inclusion in the pamphlet undoubtedly shows a failure so gross to apply the most rudimentary tests, that in itself it throws grave doubts on the authenticity of the whole collection.

It has been left to Russian anti-Bolsheviks to speak manly common sense on this pamphlet. The new school of refugees from Russia in London—those who have fled from Bolshevik tyranny—have banded themselves together in an association which issues a little paper called *The Russian Commonwealth*. In the opinion of this paper, "the documents in question say nothing, because they produce an uneasy impression of forgery." The most important of them "appear too 'proving,' too 'conclusive' to be authentic. They leave a comic impression that the German General Staff was very anxious to divulge, in every trivial order, the most important State secrets. On the other hand, all these people, Lenine, Trotsky, Chicherin, and others, are too anxious to supply us in every document with an ineffaceable trace of their treachery in the form of annotations, signatures, and so on. . . . By such evidence, open to sound criticism, we only help these men to pose as the victims of calumny. We give them the opportunity to say: 'Our enemies must have resort to forgery in order to denounce us.' Let us hate, despise and fight the Bolsheviks without mercy, but let us keep our hands clean. Our reckoning with them is a blood feud—not a mud feud."

The fact is that, if we start from the standards of right and wrong universally acknowledged by all white men who are not Bolsheviks, complicity in the designs of William II. and Ludendorff is about the only form of wickedness with which Lenine and his chief assistants cannot fairly be charged. It would not be difficult to convict them, under common human laws, of every kind of murder, atrocity, robbery, fraud and forgery. In duplicity and mendacity they have probably surpassed all political parties in history. At the same time, it is a mistake to attribute to all of them the ordinary motives of crime. Lenine himself is reported to have said, that for every genuine, convinced Bolshevik, there are thirty-nine scoundrels and sixty fools. That is probably a very fair estimate. Bolshevism has drawn to itself every kind of folly and rascality, because its doctrines are alluring to empty minds and its tactics are profitable to rogues. But the real danger of the thing lies in "the one just man." To him, Bolshevism is a religion, for which he is prepared to die himself and to make others die—in thousands, in hundreds of thousands, if need be. It is his sincere and self-sacrificing fanaticism which gives Bolshevism its firmest grip on the masses and holds them in the belief that all the blood and tears, that so far have been its most noticeable results, will some day be redeemed by the Millennium. No man is so dangerous as the fanatic of a false idea, and the only way to disarm him is to treat him as what he is. The Allies hastily jumped to the conclusion that the fanatic Lenine was what he was not—"a German agent"—and by doing so they lost their opportunity of meeting his agitation with the only weapon to which it was vulnerable.

By the part he played in the Korniloff affair,[1] Kerensky destroyed the last barrier between Russia and anarchy—his own personal hold on the masses. The Bolsheviks, who throughout the Revolution had been the only party to make for a definite goal with unfaltering energy and determination—for the simple reason that they alone had no interest in the War, and consequently were not hampered by the necessity for compromise—lost no time in exploiting the advantage Kerensky had given them, and the "counter-revolutionary" action of the Minister-President became the chief weapon of their agitation. It proved a most effective one, and a fortnight after the Korniloff affair was first made known to the world, the Bolsheviks secured a majority in the Petrograd Soviet for a resolution embodying their party cry, "All power to the Soviets." The immediate consequence was that the Menshevik Chairman, Cheidze, and the other members of the "Presidium"—who were all either his fellow-partisans or Social-Revolutionaries—resigned in a body, and their places were taken by Bolsheviks and other supporters of the All-power-to-the-Soviets policy. Kerensky, who had been one of the Vice-Presidents of the Petrograd Soviet, had resigned that position somewhat earlier. The full significance of the change was clearly expressed by one fact: Cheidze was replaced by Trotsky. Lenine, for whose arrest a warrant had been out since his unsuccessful attempt against the Government in July, had not yet ventured from his hiding-place, where he was preparing to convert the world by pamphlets. Naturally, he continued to be the chief driving and directing force of his Party. He had controlled it from Paris and Cracow under the Old Régime, and it was not difficult for him to do so now from Kronstadt or some small village across the Finnish frontier.

At first sight, the appearance of a Bolshevik majority in the Petrograd Soviet suggests an exceedingly sudden and violent swing of the electorate in consequence of the Korniloff

[1] Kerensky lent some support to General Korniloff in an effort to restore military authority over the disorganized army. Korniloff moved troops toward Petrograd. Then the two leaders disagreed, and Kerensky had Korniloff dismissed as a traitor seeking to overturn the Revolution.

affair.   Municipal elections—on the basis of universal suffrage for both sexes—had taken place during the first week
of September; and though the Bolsheviks had nearly doubled
their number of seats, they nevertheless obtained only sixty-
seven out of a total of two hundred. It must be remembered,
however, that it was the artisans and soldiers alone who
elected the Soviet, and that the large classes outside these
two categories had nothing whatever to do with it.   Moreover, as the Soviet elections were carried out in whatever way
any particular group of constituents preferred—the general
rule seems to have been a simple show of hands—they naturally lent themselves admirably to the employment of im-
pudence and intimidation, in both of which the Bolsheviks
were infinitely superior to any of their opponents.   There
were, further, no fixed terms of election.   If the inmates
of a workshop or a company of soldiers took it into their
heads that their delegate was not representing them properly,
they simply cancelled his mandate out of hand, and chose
some one else in his place.   Thus the rank and file of the
Soviet was a constantly fluctuating body, and the transfor-
mation of a majority into a minority was effected not so much
by the conversion of members as by their replacement.

Amid the welter of more dramatic and exciting doings,
the capture of the Petrograd Soviet by the Bolsheviks passed
almost unnoticed at the time, but it was probably the most
decisive event that had occurred since the March outbreak,
for it really sealed the fate of what we may call the "Coalition Revolution."   Control over the Soviet meant control
over the Petrograd garrison; control over the Petrograd garrison meant control over the Government; and control over
the Government, when that Government was entirely identified with the Soviets, meant control over the greater part
of the country and over the front.   If Lenine had cared to
run any risks, he could, in all likelihood, have had the whole
game in his hands three days after his followers came to
the top in the Petrograd Soviet.   But he was wise enough
to wait till all danger of serious opposition had passed; and
when he did strike his blow, on November 7th, he gained an
immediate, complete and almost bloodless victory.   Among

the whole of the Petrograd garrison, Kerensky had no firm
supporters but the Women's Battalion, and the gallant youths
of the officers' training schools, who had to pay a heavy
price for their loyalty to the Government.

After the Bolsheviks got the machinery of government
into their hands, only one faint hope was left. That hope
lay in the Constituent Assembly. Ever since there had been
a revolutionary organization in Russia, the convocation of
this body had been its chief immediate demand. The necessity of convening a Constituent Assembly had been the one
point on which all parties had been absolutely agreed at the
time of the March Revolution, and none of them had insisted
on it more emphatically than the Bolsheviks. From that
time forward, there had never been on the surface of Russian public life any indication of an organized movement to
prevent the Constituent Assembly from meeting or to give it
other than a thoroughly democratic character. It was precisely because the entire nation looked to the Constituent Assembly to solve all outstanding problems and clear away all
difficulties, that the Bolsheviks systematically accused their
opponents of opposition to it. Lenine's main justification
of his *coup de main* was the contention that only Bolshevik
control could insure the safety of the Assembly; and the issue
of a decree to that effect was one of his first acts as President
of the Council of People's Commissaries. There seemed,
therefore, reason to hope that, before he and his disciples
could have time to destroy the Russian Army and do irreparable damage, the Constituent Assembly would meet, and
impose its veto with an authority recognized by the whole
of Russia.

The elections had been timed to take place on November
25th, and the Assembly was to meet on December 13th. These
dates had been finally decided on in the middle of October,
after several postponements. The delay had been in the
nature of things, and there is no ground whatever for supposing that either the Lvoff or the Kerensky Government
in any way retarded the preparations. On the contrary, they
must have realized at a very early date that until the Assembly met there could be no political stability in Russia.

Thus what Lenine and his disciples could do, by fair means or foul, to bring a majority of the electorate over to their side, they did with all their might; but, in the time at their disposal, they could not uproot the tradition established among the peasantry by the Social-Revolutionaries, and the first election returns made it practically certain that this Party would have an absolute majority in the Assembly. Even in their own particular stronghold, Petrograd, the town that had made the "November Revolution," the Bolsheviks were in an absolute minority, though their list received a much larger number of votes than that of any other party—424,000, as compared with 246,000 given for the Cadets, and 152,000 for the Social-Revolutionaries. And it may be noted in passing, that the Mensheviks, whose leaders, Cheidze, Skobeleff, and Tseretelli, had been so prominent and influential in the early stages of the Revolution, now practically disappeared from the scene, in Petrograd at any rate, while the veteran Plehanoff, the founder of the Social-Democratic Party, induced only 1,823 electors to vote for that "unity" or "concord" aimed at by the very designation of his new group. One thing was certain, that if the Constituent Assembly was to assume the rôle in national affairs which every one, including the Bolsheviks themselves, had attributed to it, there would be a speedy end to the supremacy of Lenine and his particular type of "proletarian dictatorship."

It was in this dilemma that Lenine invented the soviet form of government, or rather decided that the system by which the soviets had asserted their domination should be perpetuated as the permanent sovereignty of Russia. This was another example of the unhesitating opportunism which has marked every step of Lenine's progress. He had already stolen the Social-Revolutionaries' agrarian program; he now stole an idea which, in the past, had been another of the distinguishing features of their doctrine. For the soviet system undoubtedly has the same theoretical basis as anarcho-communism, which was one of the evolutionary steps of Social-Revolutionary Socialism. Marxian socialism, which Lenine had all along professed, had, on the other hand, always been understood as a highly-centralized system, that could only be put into force after the control of industry had been concentrated in a small number of hands.

The only real case against the Constituent Assembly was that it meant an end to the power of Lenine, but some presentable justification for this change of view was necessary. It was found in the principle of the "dictatorship of the proletariat," which was one of the fundamental ideas of Marx. Lenine's interpretation of this principle against the Constituent was not original. In his analysis of socialism, which was first published many years ago, Professor Sombart speaks of "the dictatorship of the proletariat, that is the idea that the transition from the capitalistic to the socialisic state must be effected by the proletariat seizing political power and decreeing the necessary laws."

The elections to the Constituent were all to have taken place on November 25th; but, owing to local difficulties of various kinds, there were many postponements. In the first days of December, however, the newly-elected members began to trickle into Petrograd by twos and threes, and the impending opening of the Assembly became the chief object of public interest. The feeling of the population was evidently on the side of the Constituent, and the Bolsheviks began to take precautionary measures to safeguard their interests. All arrangements for the convocation of the Constituent had been placed in the hands of a Special Commission, appointed by the Provisional Government. The members of this Commission were now arrested, and Ouritski, one of the many leading Bolsheviks of Hebrew race, was installed in its place as "Commissary for the Constituent Assembly," with practically autocratic powers of control over its membership. He began by issuing an order that no deputies would be allowed to take part in the sittings till they had satisfied him of the authenticity of their mandates and received from him a ticket of authorization. A merciless campaign was also set on foot against the Cadets. Three of their leaders, Kokoshkin, Shingareoff and Prince Dolgoroukoff, were imprisoned, and orders were given to arrest all the Cadet leaders.

The decisive act in the tragedy of the Constituent Assembly opened on December 11th, in the Tauride Palace, which had been the home of the Imperial Duma. From an early hour, the Commissary Ouritski sat in his office in a posture of expectancy, waiting for deputies to present themselves for authorization; but no one came. All the members with the exception of the Bolsheviks had agreed to ignore Ouritski and the Government he represented. About 1 o'clock, the members of the Commission of the Constituent, who had now been released, gathered in one of the committee rooms to transact their business; but hardly had they commenced their deliberations when Ouritski appeared on the scene, with the announcement that the Commission could sit only in his presence. The Commission, however, refused either to do this or to leave the building till it had finished its day's business. Ouritski then gave orders that the commissioners should be removed from the Palace; and a detachment of armed soldiers entered the room. However, no attempt at expulsion was made. The soldiers merely stood on guard at the doors for two or three hours, while the commissioners completed their business.

Meanwhile, after a preliminary "private meeting" in another committee room, some fifty or sixty delegates gathered in the Session Hall of the Palace. In spite of their disregard for the claims of Ouritski, they were left to say their say without molestation. The practical business of the sitting was summed up in a resolution to the effect that those present did not yet constitute a quorum, but that they would meet every day till they considered themselves qualified in that respect, and, in the meantime, would do all in their power to expedite the arrival of further delegates in Petrograd.

The most stirring events of the day, however, took place not inside but outside the Tauride Palace. Here throughout the afternoon, endless processions trudged along, bearing banners with inscriptions in honor of the Constituent Assembly. The manifestants included people from all classes and callings. There were deputations from the Municipal Council, the State Bank, and the Ministries. Large contingents were supplied by the political parties. The great Obouhoff Ordnance Factory, where the heavy naval guns were made, and other big industrial concerns sent many thousands of workmen. University students, soldiers, railway servants, employees of the postal and telegraphic services came in organized bodies. A friendly estimate, which no doubt would not minimize, put the total of the manifestants at 200,000. They were nearly all of one mind, for the Bolshevik leaders had mercifully ordered their followers to hold aloof from the manifestations. But for this decree, the opening of the Constituent Assembly would undoubtedly have been the cause of another day of bloodshed in the streets of Petrograd. Each procession made a halt outside the Palace, and one or other of the members of the Assembly came out and spoke a few words to the demonstrators.

The opening day of the Assembly had been marked by many discouraging omens, but it still left some room for hope. There had been ambiguities and hesitancies, which seemed to indicate that Lenine was still a little uncertain as to the course to pursue. On the morrow, however, all hopes were dispersed, and the iron grip of Bolshevism closed firmly on the Assembly. When the deputies arrived at the Tauride Palace, they found the building and its environment crowded with soldiers, like an armed camp. Pickets had been posted at intervals along the neighboring streets. The courtyard of the Palace was filled with armed men, and the ramp leading up to the main entrance bristled with machine guns. Inside the Palace, soldiers and sailors were everywhere. In the Session Hall and all the adjoining rooms, they lay about on the floor, and even on the tables. It was characteristic that half of them were from the Lettish and Lithuanian regiments, which were to remain the Pretorian Guard of Bolshevism. The Machine-gun Regiment, which had distinguished itself by insubordination and debauchery from the very beginning of the Revolution, had also furnished a detachment. Many of the "guards" had been brought in from Helsingfors, Abo, and other places outside Petrograd; for the feeling in the metropolitan garrison towards the Constituent was still rather uncertain. That was the end of democracy in Russia. The Constituent Assembly never really held a meeting. Lenine ruled instead.

ITALY'S GREAT RALLY ON THE PIAVE

THE HEROIC STAND WHICH SAVED THE NATION

NOVEMBER 18TH

JOHN BUCHAN
NARRATIVES OF ITALIAN PARTICIPANTS AND EYE-
WITNESSES

When we speak of the breakdown of the Italians at Caporetto, let
us always speak and think in the same breath of their wonderful rally
on the Piave. No nation has ever fought better, more persistently,
more gallantly, with absolute devotion to a cause. Italy stands honored among the nations, because of her great recovery in 1917.

When on October 21st the line broke at Caporetto the Italian
armies were wholly on Austrian territory. When on the 23rd they
began their military withdrawal, they had first to fight rearguard
actions along the Isonzo River and then along their own frontier.
On October 28th Cividale, the first Italian town was taken by the
enemy; and on the 30th Udine, the Italian frontier city which had been
the military headquarters for over two years, was abandoned to the
Teutons.

Always there existed the danger that Teuton forces would outflank
the Italians by means of the Alpine passes in the north, and so get
behind the retreating armies and capture them all. General Cadorna
had therefore to watch and guard these heights while falling back
from one Italian river valley to the next. He fought rearguard actions
at the Tagliamento River and again at the Livenza, losing confused
and straggling bodies of troops at each withdrawal, but delaying the
Teuton advance while a stronger defense was built behind. At the
Tagliamento the German official report claimed a total of nearly 200,000
prisoners. At the Livenza 50,000 more. But on the Piave the Italian
line held firm. General Cadorna had now been replaced by General
Diaz. There was fighting from the mouth of the river to its source.
At the mouth the Italians opened the dams and flooded the lowlands
as a barrier. Gradually the fight shifted higher up the river and into
the Alps. In December the last assaults were delivered far to the
north and westward among the higher Alps.

The Piave battle lasted for three weeks in full fury and then gradually died down as the Teutons saw that it was hopeless, that the
Italians had at last become as strong and well-posted as before.
Marshal von Hoetzendorff, the Austrian leader, received word from
von Ludendorff, the German Chief of Staff and real directing head
of the attack, that the assault was to be given over. The Allied world,
terrified by Russia's anarchistic breakdown, could resume hope, confident that Italy was not to be destroyed in similar fashion.

BY JOHN BUCHAN

THE situation was the gravest that Italy had met since she entered the war—the gravest, save for the tremendous days of the Marne and the crisis of First Ypres, which the Allies had yet witnessed on the West. Capello's command had been broken in pieces, and was no longer an army. Streaming back in wild disorder to the Friulian plain, it uncovered the Duke of Aosta's flank, and seemed to imprison him between the invaders and the Adriatic. The suspicion that treachery had in some degree contributed to the disaster was like to make the retreat more difficult, for such news spreads like a fever among troops and saps their resolution. The undoubted fact that the enemy was pursuing new tactics, as yet not understood and therefore unanswered, nullified the plans of the High Command. The huge salient had broken at the apex, and every mile of retirement on the east meant a complex withdrawal on the north. Upon forces wearied with a long campaign descended in a black accumulation every element of peril which had threatened Cadorna since Italy first drew the sword.

The spirit of the nation rose gallantly to the call of danger. The grim *communiqué* of the 28th brought down many a politician's castle of cards. On the 27th of October the king had arrived in Rome, and on the 1st of November the new Ministry was announced, with Orlando as Premier, Sonnino at the Foreign Office, the young Neapolitan Nitti at the Treasury, and Alfieri as Minister of War. More important than Cabinet changes was the unanimity of the people. All—almost all—sections of the nation and the Press faced the crisis with a splendid fortitude. Party quarrels were forgotten, there was little recrimination for past blunders, and the resolution of a united Italy was braced to meet the storm. Only the extreme Socialists, to whom the disaster was not unwelcome, stood aloof, and their organ, the *Avanti*, continued to preach the arid platitudes of the class war.

The strain was increased by ignorance as to what forces were sweeping down on the northern plain from the Isonzo hills. Rumor spoke of twenty, thirty, forty German divisions under von Mackensen marching through the gap, and the legend grew with every lip that uttered it. Even the High Command was in perplexity, and put the enemy at a far higher figure than the facts warranted. But it was the new tactics, and not weight of numbers, that had broken the line. Otto von Below had but his six German divisions, and could not hope for reënforcements yet a while. It was Italy's salvation that the enemy was as much surprised as herself. He had made an experiment which he hoped would return to Austria her old western boundaries; it had in fact opened the way to Milan, but he was not prepared for such a miracle of fortune. Had he been ready to strike from the Trentino against the Italian First Army, and from Carnia against the Fourth, while von Below and Boroevitch pressed in the Second and Third, he might have annihilated the military power of Italy. Broken at the point of her salient, she could not in these terrible days have resisted even a moderate offensive on her northern flank, and the line of the Adige might have been turned before Cadorna's rearguards reached the Tagliamento. But Ludendorff had not made the plan for so wholesale a conquest; that came later, but when it came the golden opportunity had gone.

On Saturday, October 27th, von Below was in Cividale; the Third Army, after a fine rearguard action in the Vallone, had retired from the Carso, and Boroevitch was in Gorizia. Next day von Below was on the edge of Udine, the little city with its cathedral-crowned height and its narrow, arcaded streets which mounts guard over the Friulian plain. The gravest problem was the position of the Third Army. When it began to fall back from the Carso, it was no nearer the Tagliamento than the spearhead of the enemy, and the Tagliamento was the first halting-place for Cadorna's retreat. The Second Army had gone, and by Sunday the enemy had 100,000 prisoners from it, and 700 of its guns. For a moment it seemed certain that the Duke of Aosta would share the fate of Capello. A million of men were retreating along the western highways, encumbered with batteries and hospitals and transport, while by every choked route peasants and townsmen fled for refuge from the Austrian cavalry.

Units lost discipline, orders miscarried, roads were blocked for hours, and all the while down from the north came the menace of von Below, swooping southward to cut off all retreat. There had been nothing like it before in the campaign, not even in the Russian *débâcle* of 1915, for then there had been great open spaces to move in. In the gut of Friulia, between the foothills and the sea, a mass of humanity was struggling westward, soldiers and civilians mingled inextricably. Under leaden skies and pouring rain they pressed feverishly on, for it was a race against time if they were not to find the Tagliamento held by the enemy. And from the country they were leaving, now lit up with the glow of bursting shells and blazing villages, came horrible tales, only too true, of rapine and outrage by the Austrian vanguards. If ever panic was to be forgiven it was on those nightmare miles where troops were set a task too high for human valor.

But to its eternal glory the Third Army did not fail. With heavy losses, and by the narrowest margin, it won the race. There were two roads of retreat, each attended by a railway—that from Udine to Pordenone, which crosses the Tagliamento by the long bridge of Codroipo first built by Napoleon, and that from Monfalcone to Portogruaro, with a bridge at Latisana. There were many byroads and lesser bridges, but these were the only highways for heavy traffic. For three days—from October 28th to October 30th—a curtain of darkness seemed to descend on the Italian stage. There were no claims from the enemy, no clear news from Cadorna. On the 28th the Austrians were in Cormons; on the 29th the Germans were in Udine. On the 30th remnants of the Second Army were crossing the river at Codroipo, and a kind of defensive flank had been established facing north to cover the vital crossing of Latisana. Next day the bulk of the Third Army crossed, sacrificing its rear divisions and 500 guns; and on the first day of November the Duke of Aosta was in position on the western bank, with the river roaring in flood between him and his pursuers. For a moment there was a pause, while the enemy, who had outstripped his heavy batteries, waited on their arrival. The race had been won, but it was a shattered remnant of Cadorna's armies which drew breath after their week of torment. The enemy claimed 200,000 prisoners and 1,800 guns, and his claim was not far from the truth. He seemed on the eve of a decisive victory.

The Duke of Aosta's retreat was one of those performances in war which succeed against crazy odds, and which, consequently, we call inexplicable. It made an Italian stand possible, and deprived the enemy of the crowning triumph which he almost held in his hands. How desperate was the struggle may be judged from what we know of the retirement of the naval batteries on the coast flank. There were such batteries at Monfalcone, at Punta Sdobba, and at the point of Grado; and when, on the 28th, the Third Army's retirement began, there seemed nothing to prevent the Austrian fleet from issuing from Pola and landing on the Venetian shore in rear of the retreat. For only light naval forces watched the coast, and the main Allied Navy was at Taranto, 600 miles away. The rain fell in sheets, and a wind from the sea drove up the tide so that the canals overflowed and flooded the marshes. After thirty-six hours of heavy toil the guns were got out of Monfalcone, but not before the rearguard of Italian marines was exchanging rifle shots with the Austrian van. The guns were dragged through the swamps, or placed on rafts and poled through the shallows amid the rising storm. Grado was reached and presently evacuated, and with the enemy pressing on their heels, the marines succeeded in making their way through the labyrinth of the coastal lagoons till they reached the Piave mouth, and became the pillar of the right wing of the new front.

The Tagliamento was clearly no line to abide on. In seasons of flood it was in places a mile wide, but for most of the year it was a tangle of shallow channels flowing among wastes of pebbles. The bed of the stream, silted up with gravel brought down from the hills, was a score of feet above the level of the surrounding country. At the moment it was in flood, but by November 1st the rain had stopped and the stream was falling, so it opposed but a slender obstacle to the enemy. Moreover, it could be easily turned on the north, and in the main railway through the Pontebba pass the Austrians had the means for such an operation to their hand. Cadorna could halt for a day or two to re-form, but he dare not linger.

If the Tagliamento were given up, there was no good line till the Adige was reached, some sixty miles to the west. But to retire to the Adige would be to uncover Venice. The importance of that famous city was more than sentimental. It was the key to the Adriatic, the key to the whole of Italy's defense. With Venice in the enemy's hands, the Italian war-ships would have been compelled to fall back four or five hundred miles to a base at Brindisi. Austria would have controlled the Northern Adriatic, and her fleet could no longer be shut up in Pola and inside the Dalmatian islands. She would be able to send her submarines in large numbers out into the Mediterranean and dislocate the Allied naval commerce with the East. She would have a free hand to harry the coasts of Italy. With Venice gone, Italy's right flank was unprotected, for in truth her front did not stop short with the shore line. The Adige was therefore out of the question, and by hook or by crook a halting-place must be found which kept Venice inside her country's battle line. To this problem there could be only one answer. The stand must be on the Piave.

It was not a front which a general would select had he any choice. The river rises among the fantastic Dolomite peaks, and flows south in a narrow mountain vale till at Belluno it turns to the southwest and emerges from the hills. In the forty miles of its mountain course it is no serious ob-stacle to any enemy. At Belluno it has become a consider-able stream, and, after a wide bend through the leaf-shaped hollow towards Feltre, the foothills close in on it at the pass of Quero. It has now something of the character of the Tagliamento, a broad bed where many branches strain through gravel, between embankments to keep the floods from the lower levels of the surrounding country. It then bends to the southeast, past the bridge of Vidor, where Napoleon and Massena crossed in 1797, and flows through the gap between the Asolo hills and the wooded Montello. From Nervesa for the remaining twenty-five miles to the sea it is a better defense—short, straight, and protected by the Montello on one flank, and the sea marshes on the other. The Piave was a strong line only towards its mouth, a weak and difficult line in the center, and no line at all in its upper glens. Carnia and Cadore must be relinquished, and the Fourth Army brought back from those peaks and gorges, which it had won with such boldness and resolution through two arduous years, to hold a front from the Montello by the *massif* of Monte Grappa and across the Val Sugana to link up with the First Army in its old position on the Asiago plateau. While, therefore, the Duke of Aosta was struggling westward from the Tagliamento, de Robilant had fallen back from Cadore, and was moving with all haste towards the Middle Piave.

On Saturday, November 3rd, a German and a Hungarian division from von Below's army forced the passage of the Tagliamento at Pinzano, where the river leaves the foothills, thereby cutting off the Italian troops and guns on the line between Tolmezzo and Gemona. Cadorna still held on to the middle and lower river, and on the 4th repulsed an enemy attempt to cross near San Vito. But von Below's vanguards were already moving west along the edge of the hills, and on Tuesday, the 7th, the Tagliamento line was abandoned. The next stage was the Livenza, a small stream running in a single channel, which carried little water save in flood-time. The pursuit was close and persistent, and already on the 6th the enemy cavalry were in action at Sacile, where the Treviso-Udine railway crosses the Upper Livenza. The Italian line was now bent back heavily on its left, and, while the main force was still on the Livenza, the left wing was back on the Upper Monticano, which enters the Livenza at Motta. The Motta crossing was held long enough to get the guns of the center away, and on the 8th the Livenza was abandoned. On the 10th Cadorna was everywhere back on the Piave, and the retreat had ended.

It had been conducted wholly by Italian troops, and the credit was Italy's alone. But the first news of the break at Caporetto had brought her Allies to her aid. Before the end of October French divisions were crossing the frontier, and a French force, the 12th Corps, under General Fayolle, was preparing to take its place on the Italian front. A British contingent, the 14th Corps, under Sir Herbert Plumer, the commander of the Second Army, had come into being by November 10th. In the first days of November Mr. Lloyd George left London for Italy, with General Smuts, Sir William Robertson, and Sir Henry Wilson. They were joined in Paris by the Premier, M. Painlevé, and General Foch; and on Monday, November 5th, at the village of Rapallo, sixteen miles from Genoa, they met Orlando, Sonnino, and Alfieri. That conference was one of the most fruitful of the war. Out of it sprang the Allied Council at Versailles, which we shall consider later, and, indeed, the whole movement for a unified Western command. It settled the assistance which France and Britain were to give to their hard-pressed neighbor, and it resulted in vital changes in the Italian High Command. Cadorna was transferred to Versailles, and his place as Commander-in-Chief taken by the Neapolitan General Diaz, who had led with brilliant success the 23rd Corps in the Carso battles. General Badoglio became his Chief of the General Staff.

The critical part of the Piave was the Montello height, which was, so to speak, a hinge between the northern front facing the hills and the river front covering Venice. If the Montello went, the bridge which carried the Treviso-Udine railway would go, and so would the crossing at the Vidor gap to the north. But the crucial point on the whole front was the mass of Monte Grappa between the Piave and the Brenta. If it were carried, the enemy could debouch from the Brenta valley and turn the flank of the Piave defense. It was the threat from the north which occupied the mind of the new Commander-in-Chief, for the most gallant stand on the river line would be futile if the enemy broke down from the northern hills to the low country around Bassano. He had already begun to move in this direction. On the 9th, when the last of the Duke of Aosta's rearguards were fording the Piave, and when de Robilant's Fourth Army was hastening through Belluno, pressure began in the Val Sugana and on the Asiago plateau, and the remains of the village of Asiago fell once again into Austrian hands.

On the 11th de Robilant was in position from the Montello to the Brenta, and the Austrians, pushing down the Upper Piave past Feltre, had linked hands with their troops in the Val Sugana. The rain had begun again, and the soldiers on the Piave looking northward saw the high hills white with snow. It was a spectacle to cheer the soul of the High Command, for it lessened the risk of that break out from the mountains which was their worst peril. The forces were now set for the culminating struggle—Pecori-Giraldo's First Army facing Scheuchensteuel's Eleventh Austrian Army on the Asiago plateau, de Robilant's Fourth Army facing Krobatin's Tenth Austrian Army and part of von Below's Fourteenth Army from the Brenta to the Montello, the Duke of Aosta from the Montello to the sea opposed by von Below and Boroevitch. Clearly de Robilant had far too long a front for a single army, and to hold it boys of seventeen and eighteen were brought up from the depots and the garrisons, often after only a month's training. How valiantly they acquitted themselves this record will show. In the moment of their country's agony they flung themselves into the most desperate breach, and d'Annunzio's burning words have made their prowess immortal. Such were the dispositions during November. It was not till December 4th that Plumer and Fayolle took over the Montello sector facing von Below, and so allowed de Robilant to concentrate on the Grappa area.

The points of danger, as we have said, were the northern flank, between Asiago and the Piave, and the gate of the Montello; but from some cause or other the enemy did not concentrate all his efforts there. The lure of Venice made him strike also direct against the Lower Piave, where the Italian defenses were by nature the strongest. One reason for this may be found in the character of his communications. In the plains they were excellent, but in the hills he had but the one railway down the Upper Adige valley, and the roads he had built for the 1916 attack were now deep in snow. Nevertheless, the attempt offered superb strategic prospects. The wall of the Alps above the plain of Bassano is cut clean as with a knife. It runs in a scarp at an average height of some 5,000 feet, broken only by the trough of the Brenta. Behind it rises a second tier, which, west of the Brenta, forms the rim of the Asiago plateau. To understand the position it is necessary to keep this formation in mind. The Italian front occupied the edge of the second tier east and west of the Brenta, with the Grappa *massif* and Monte Tomba well inside their lines. If the enemy could force his way to the edge of the first tier, he commanded the plains and had turned the Piave.

On the night of Sunday, the 11th, the Austrians attacked Monte Longaro, northeast of Asiago, but were held by the Alpini. Next day, after a heavy barrage, Boroevitch's forces succeeded in crossing the Piave at the Zenson bend, eighteen miles from the sea—the first bridgehead on the western bank secured by the enemy. On the 13th Longaro had fallen, and the fighting was at Monte Sisemol, a peak east of Asiago, on the very edge of the second tier. That day, too, no less than four attempts were made to cross the Lower Piave, at Quero, Fenere, St. Dona, and Intestadura, while Hungarian battalions crossed the canalized stream at Grisolera, and made their way through the marshes to the old channel, the Vecchia Piave. On Wednesday, the 14th, the Italian left was firm on the edge of the second tier, across the peak of Castelgomberto to Cismon, in the Brenta valley, but east it was forced by the loss of Monte Tomatico to descend to the first tier just above the Piave. Next day the pressure in the hills became stronger, and Cismon was lost.

On Friday, the 16th, Boroevitch made a vigorous attempt to cross the Piave. He tried at two points, Folina and Fogare, north of where the Treviso line crosses the river at the Ponte di Piave, failing conspicuously at the first, but winning a bridgehead at the second. That same day he had a success in the hills, carrying Monte Prassolan, east of the Brenta. He had greatly strengthened his troops in this area, and on Sunday, the 18th, had won Quero, on the Piave, and forced part of the Italian front off the second tier of upland on to the first. They were now on Monte Tomba, on the very edge of the plains. The position was that on the Lower Piave the enemy held two bridgeheads, but had not elbow-room to develop them; while in the hills he was held on the second tier west of the Brenta, but had fought his way to the front tier at one point between that stream and the Piave. For the moment this little section of twelve miles was the critical part of the battle.

The rest of November saw a desperate struggle from Asiago to the Piave, especially in the Monte Grappa quarter. Elsewhere little happened, for the natural difficulty of the Lower Piave line, the stout resistance of the Italian marines in the marshes, and the constant shelling from monitors off the coast, made a crossing in force a forlorn enterprise for the enemy. But it was otherwise in the mountains, where, in spite of the snow, he made a resolute effort to reach the last rim of upland which would give him a decisive success. The struggle was carried on mainly by Austrian mountain troops and Hungarian divisions, and von Below's Germans played small part in it. Blow after blow was delivered, alternately east and west of the Brenta, blows which were gallantly parried, though the weary Italian lines had slowly to give ground. In the first week of December it was clear that a great effort was maturing on the Asiago plateau, where, against a front of less than twelve miles, some 2,000 guns of all calibers were concentrated.

The attack was launched, after a furious bombardment, on December 6th, two Austrian forces moving from the northwest and the northeast against the salient at Asiago, which had its apex at Castelgomberto. It succeeded in driving Pecori-Giraldo altogether off the second tier of hills back to the first tier; but he still held Valstagna in the Brenta valley, and all but the top of the little Val Frenzela, which descends to it from the west. The enemy claimed 15,000 prisoners, for gallant companies of Alpini had held out on the lost peaks of Castelgomberto and Sisemol long after the line had retired. A week later, after a still greater massing of artillery, Krobatin attacked between the Brenta and the Piave. His aim was to win the debouchment of the Brenta valley by carrying the hills on the eastern side, and especially the passes of Caprile and Barretta, and the peak called Asolone, south of the latter. He struck on the 11th, and for four days the battle lasted; but by Saturday, the 15th, he had achieved little beyond reaching the summit of the Caprile pass. This did, indeed, give him a certain advantage by facilitating his movement of troops in the Brenta valley. On the 18th he succeeded in securing most of Monte Asolone, and farther east he held the lower of the two summits of Monte Tomba. This gave him positions outflanking Monte Grappa, and the possession of Asolone further endangered Valstagna on the Brenta. He was endeavoring to advance down the Val Sugana by taking forward steps alternately on each side of it.

On December 22nd the Italians counter-attacked at Monte Asolone, and recovered all its south slopes. On the 23rd they had to face another dangerous thrust south of Asiago to the left of the Frenzela glen, where the enemy took Monte di Val Bella, the Col del Rosso, and Monte Melago, which brought him nearer to the rim of the heights. A counter-attack recovered the last point, but on Christmas Day the position was still anxious. On both sides of the Brenta the enemy was getting terribly near the plains. Before the close of the year, however, an event happened which eased the situation. The French left had been moved west of the Piave to assist de Robilant in the Grappa region, and on December 30th, supported by British batteries, it attacked the eastern shoulder of Monte Tomba, and won it, together with 1,392 prisoners.

With the New Year the prospect steadily brightened. The wild weather in the hills handicapped the enemy effort, and gradually the German divisions were removed, since, in the view of Ludendorff, a decision could no longer be hoped for and he had need of them elsewhere. The long front of the Piave was quiet, with a swollen stream running fourteen knots before it. In the British section there were many adventurous raids, and in the first days of January the Duke of Aosta cleared the Austrians from the bridgehead at Zenson. On January 14th de Robilant made a successful attack on Monte Asolone, and before the end of the month Plumer had extended his right so as to ease the Third Army in its task. On January 28th Pecori-Giraldo attacked the Col del Rosso and Monte di Val Bella, and took 2,500 prisoners.

With this episode the campaign which began at Caporetto may be said to have reached its close. It had taken heavy toll of Italy's strength, but it had failed to show that decisive victory which for some weeks had seemed inevitable. The German High Command had turned its mind from Austria and her troubles to a far greater plan in a more vital field, and Conrad von Hoetzendorff and the Archduke Eugene were left once more to their own devices.

BY ITALIAN PARTICIPANTS
Narrative of an Eye-witness at the Inundated Mouth of the Piave

The water effectively holds the enemy at most exposed points and for fifteen miles on the west bank of the Piave. The flooded area is about seventy square miles, and the water is a foot to five feet deep and twelve miles in width at some points, making the district impossible of occupation or movement by enemy troops. The enemy clings to the west bank at Zenson, but is crowded into a small U-shaped position and relying on batteries across the river to keep the Italians back. Austro-German efforts to bring over large forces by pontoons have not succeeded, according to latest reports, either at Zenson or at points further north, where the invaders are feeling their way in an effort to get across.

The lower floors of the houses in such villages as Piave Vecchia are under water, and the campanili stick up from the mud-hued level of the flood like strange immense water plants; and here in the silence of the floods the enemy is moving in boats and squelching over mud islands. Peasants, awaiting rescue from the inundation, see him arrive with feelings much like those of shipwrecked people who hail a passing sail and find it is a pirate craft.

Everywhere the enemy had been thrown back, except at the brink of the river at Zenson, where a few men were huddled in the bushes, unable to go backward or forward, and were being slowly cut to pieces. At Fagare, Follina, and the Sega Mill the rout of the enemy was complete, having been accomplished in fearful hand-to-hand fighting on November 16th and 17th.

On the cemetery road, where the Austrians advanced and set up their line of quick-firers, a fearful scene was spread before the party. The road was littered as though a tornado had passed by. Dead horses lay all about in contorted shapes. The highway was strewn with enemy helmets, blood-stained clothing, cartridge belts, and all kinds of accouterments. The trees on either side were cut in two, and the lines of bushes were leveled like grain before a storm.

Just ahead on the road was Sega Mill, where the bloodiest fighting was centered. The mill wheel was still running, and the water was flowing peacefully, but all about were evidences of fearful carnage. The soldiers who held the mill stood unconcernedly at the door, while all over the ground were tatters left by the Austrians as they were driven on the mill and thrown into the river.

Passing on to the bank of the river, just back of the mill, a horrible sight opened just under the eyes of the visitors. Over there on the sand bar in midstream lay corpses in heaps, as far as the eye could see, the uniforms showing plainly that they were Austrians. Some lay on the bank, and some floated in the water. The Italians had just buried the bodies of 300 Austrians, but those other hundreds could not be brought back for decent burial, as the Austrian guns cut down stretcher bearers every time they went off toward the sand bar. An officer's dead horse, with saddle and rich saddle cloth, lay among the bodies.

The grewsome line of bodies extended far down the river. The Austrians had been cut down by machine-gun fire as though by a scythe. All the men in the line pitched forward on their faces and lay there, as though on dress parade, but prostrate.

Going on to Zenson, the little town could be seen to have been retaken by the Italians after the enemy had obtained a brief lodgment in it. Behind the town on the river edge are bushes. Here were huddled what remained of the first enemy storming party which crossed the river. The whole place was swept by fire, and one realized the fearful furnace these men were in.

As our party passed the inundated region the tops of cornstalks could be seen above the long stretches of water, indicating that it was about five feet deep. Similar traces of vineyards could be seen above the flood. Soldiers of the Engineer Corps were along the banks of the canal. They had opened the sluices wide, and the water was up to the sills. The harvest had been gathered, but there can be no planting or sowing there next spring.

Narrative of an eye-witness where the Piave Flows down from the Alps

For three days the Italians on the west bank at Cornuda, at Vidon Bridge, and along the banks had seen the distant roads on the other side crowded with the enemy—a whole army moving in plain sight against the background of autumn hills and flowing down to threaten the river. Such gunfire as only a month ago the Italians could have developed on the Isonzo would have shut the roads in a hundred places, but that is not possible now, and the great machine of death and destruction came down to its place. Ahead of it the big motor guns flung their fire curtain among the villages that so recently were new to war, and at about 8 o'clock in the evening of Saturday (November 17th), as soon as it was definitely dark, came the first attempt to cross.

Von Below wasted no time in attempts to bridge the river. He had a flotilla of those large, high-nosed boats which are used on the rivers of the plain, and several companies occupying about forty of these craft came suddenly poling and rowing into the glare of the searchlights in an attempt to get across and gain a footing by mere swiftness and suddenness of maneuver.

The Piave at Fener has two channels separated by a long island of shingle, and the boats came shooting around the head of this island into a strange blaze of illumination— searchlights converging, rockets ascending and descending in showers of blinding white magnesium flame, and gun flashes flickering afar like wildfire. The Italian machine guns and those deadly Fiat machine pistols, which fire faster than any known weapon, started to life with a single rending roar. The boats, which had been rowed with desperate energy, and were crammed to the gunwales with men, stopped as though they had run aground, flogged to a standstill by the frenzy of fire. Some went drifting down stream, full of dead and dying Germans. Two were overturned, and from yet others there were seen men leaping overboard to take the chance of saving themselves by swimming. Others got back around the nose of the island and reached the eastern bank again, but, save for the swimmers who surrendered and the wounded who came ashore lower down, not a man of them reached the Italian side.

But another attack was already in preparation opposite the village of Fener itself, and already the German guns were shelling the ruins of the little place and the positions around it, and at 1 o'clock Sunday morning a large body of them managed to pass the water in the darkness and to secure a footing on the western bank. Supported by intense shellfire from their guns across the river, they pushed on and occupied the village, while the Italians fell back with their machine guns.

The enemy's organization was as good as always. Hardly were his first men in the village when his pontoons were swinging down the river into position, and from above, on Monfenera, searchlights showed the methodical bustle of activity as the Germans and Austrians brought their forces forward for the next prompt step in the unending battle.

There was no rest. Before noon on Tuesday the big Prussians were thrusting at the slopes at Monfenera, and by night they were aloft on the steep sides of the river. Their fire was truly infernal at this time. They moved behind a walking wall of shells converging from the eastern roads, where their motor guns were massed in large numbers.

Yesterday morning an Italian counter-attack was launched. It is the Italian Fourth Army which fights on

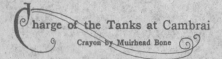

Charge of the Tanks at Cambrai
Crayon by Muirhead Bone

this sector, and its chosen brigades, such as the Brigata and the Como, are as sound as ever they were. They charged with the bayonet again and again, turning the fight into a hand-to-hand struggle at a dozen points. From the very start the enemy began to yield ground, and when night fell he had been thrown back for more than half the distance to the river. He tried more than once to return to the attack, but failed to achieve anything.

The gorge of the Brenta became a spout of shells, aimed at the Italian machine-gun positions, and the Grappa front, where Monte Pertica flanks it on the north and Col del Orso and Monte Solarolo on the northeast, were searched from end to end with exhaustive fire by great masses of medium caliber artillery, in which the enemy is especially rich.

The Italian guns here were mostly mountain artillery, little guns which fire more rapidly than any I have ever seen, but so light and small that I witnessed a gunner lift the barrel off its carriage and carry it away. The answering fire was, therefore, negligible. It was only when big attacks showed themselves that the Italians were able to get some of their own back.

It was a country as little favorable as can be imagined for the German method of trampling down the defense by the mass and momentum of large bodies of attacking troops, as Prussians, who followed their shells down the Brenta gorge, went forward easily enough till they reached a point where the valley suddenly widens. There they met a blast of machine guns and were stopped as though at a dead wall.

Three times they withdrew to shelter, while their guns searched afresh for the Italian emplacements, and three times went forward again, always with the same result. A number of them, led by a Lieutenant, who managed to crawl beyond the dead line of machine-gun fire along the stones that litter the river side, were observed and forced to take to the water by riflemen above the road. There the waters of Brenta took charge of them and hustled them down, drenched and frozen, into captivity.

It was a clear repulse for the enemy, and his next attack

was upon another point of the Grappa front, where the Col della Berreta lifts over the Brenta valley east and a little south of San Marino. The fine flower of Austrian mountain troops was brought up, the famous Edelweiss, who wear their badge, a specimen of that depressing flower. The bombardment was varied by truly a frightful fire, directed beyond the defenders' lines, a curtain of shells designed to shut them in with the slaughterers and shut reënforcements out.

Then up came the Edelweiss, a whole division of it, to the attack. There was a moment when the situation was grave for the Italians. The Alpini and infantry, who held the line, were terribly outnumbered, and from the first moment their communications with the rear were broken, the telephone wires cut into short lengths by shells, the signalers shot down as they tried to speak with flags, and runners who started were never heard of again.

There were also a certain number of gas shells beginning to flavor the incessant bombardment, sending up a dense, acrid smoke that drifted toward the defenders and blinded them as to what was taking place beyond the smoke. Out of that darkness the Edelweiss came pressing up, taking their positions for a final rush in parties of one platoon at a time, getting their machine guns into position among the rocks and finally attacking with the usual bombing parties.

The leading Italian infantry and Alpini fought desperately in their trenches and out of them; there was never a moment at which they were not snowed under by weight of numbers. Yet they fought on, and here and there even succeeded in clearing their front for a short time and attempting local counter-attacks. But it was a pretty hopeless business, and in the minds of the commanders there was always dawning the knowledge that the question of retreating must be faced.

The curtain fire was still roaring in their rear when from the right of the line the uproar of the fight took a new note, and among that battered front there ran news that reënforcements were coming up and that some were already there and counter-attacking. It was true. They had come through the curtain of death, paying a toll of losses, half a dozen battalions of them, and not feeling any the kindlier to the Edelweiss for the trouble they had in getting there. They went into the fight with a dash which Italian troops seem able to command at any moment, and the Edelweiss never had another chance. The newcomers simply rushed them down the hill to the woods and fought them there in the smoke and over the charred wood underfoot, killing lavishly with the long sword bayonets which infantrymen are prone to slip from their rifles and use as daggers.

There can be no question as to the gravity of the enemy losses. The slopes above the wood and fringes of the burning wood itself were full of his dead, and he had not gained an inch of ground. Edelweiss badges can be bought very cheaply in the Italian lines to-day.

Narrative of the last great Teuton attack from the mountains, December 3rd

It was upon the uplands of Sette Comuni that the last great hope of Germany in Italy was frustrated by something more than heroism. A wind drove into the faces of the Italians, the iron Bersaglieri, the glorious infantry, the red hot Alpini, and they saw beyond the slope in the moving mists the mass of their foe. Nothing but that vision and the memory of Italy's subjection and humiliation could have furnished and nourished that feverish fire of battle which has raged over the plateau of the seven communes during the four days and halted General Conrad von Hoetzendorff in sight of the goal of his life's ambition.

It was gunnery and nothing else which carried the Austrians around Badenecche on the south to the Pit of Vorlara and across its northern saddle between its main height and that of Tondarecar upon the evening of the 5th. After a day of grim fighting the Bersaglieri, baptized with their own blood, stopped dead attack after attack and saw a barricade of Austrian corpses build itself in front of their machine-gun positions.

To realize what was then happening, you need a vision of death striding those misty valleys like a proprietor walk-

ing in his own fields. The hill of the Bersaglieri was held
by front men who had fought since the offensive in August
on the Bainsizza Plateau. They fought till fighting availed
no longer, and then fell back, fighting still and attacking
at every opportunity with the bayonet.

That night with the enemy moving in columns behind
his first line of mountain barrier and his men exhausted and
reduced by long days of intermittent fighting, the General
gave the order for retirement to the line of Mont Spil, Monte
Miela, and Lazzaretti village.

When next morning General von Hoetzendorff turned
up before the final line, he was stopped dead. The great
battle was over. It has been a strange business at ghastly
cost, which none but the Austrians who paid it can reckon
fully. The sum is told in the mounds and litters of dead
among the snow patches of the mountain desolations.

*Eye-witness narrative of the fighting around Venice in
December*

Since November 13th, when the Austrians in crossing the
lower Piave in their headlong rush to Venice were suddenly
checked by the Italian lagoon defenses, the entire Gulf of
Venice, with its endless canals and marshes, with islands
disappearing and reappearing with the tide, has been the
scene of a continuous battle. The fighting is absolutely without precedent.

The Teutons are desperately trying to turn the Italian
right wing by working their way around the northern limits
of the Venetian Gulf. The Italians inundated the region and
sealed all the entrances into the gulf by mine fields. The gulf,
therefore, was converted into an isolated sea. Over this inland waterway the conflict is raging bitterly. The Italians
have a "lagoon fleet" ranging from the swiftest of motor
boats, armed with machine guns, small cannon, and torpedo
tubes, to huge, cumbersome, flat-bottomed British monitors,
mounting the biggest guns.

The Italian vessels navigate secret channels dug in the
bottom of the shallow lagoons. Only the Italian war pilots
know these courses. Even gondolas straying out of the chan

nels are instantly and hopelessly stranded. Not only this, but since the muddy flats and marshy islands do not permit of artillery emplacements, the Italians have developed an immense fleet of floating batteries. The guns range from three-inch fieldpieces to great fifteen-inch monsters Each is camouflaged to represent a tiny island, a garden patch, or a houseboat. Floating on the glass-like surface of the lagoons, the guns fire a few shots and then change position—making it utterly impossible for the enemy to locate them. The entire auxiliary service of supplying this floating army has been adapted to meet the lagoon warfare. Munition dumps are on boats, constantly moved about to prevent the enemy spotting them. Gondolas and motor boats replace the automobile supply lorries customary in land warfare. Instead of motor ambulances, motor boats carry off dead and wounded. Hydroaëroplanes replace ordinary fighting aircraft.

Along the northern limit of the Venetian Gulf, where the Austrians, having filtered into the Piave Delta, now seek to cross both the Sile and the Piave, the enemy each night hooks up pontoons. At daybreak every morning one end of a huge pontoon structure is anchored to the east bank of the Piave and the other flung out to the strong current, which soon stretches the makeshift bridge across.

The moment this happens the enemy infantry madly dashes across. Simultaneously the Italian floating batteries open a terrific fire. Every morning so far the Austrians have tried the trick, and every morning they have failed, with heavy losses, to effect a crossing.

The flooding of the delta maroons thousands of Italian families on island-like patches, and likewise cuts off some Austrian troops. The latter stick stubbornly to their strongholds, supplied by Austrian boats. Day after day these patches of land are the scenes of fierce hand-to-hand fighting, when small detachments of either side try to drive the others off.

THE SURPRISE ATTACK AT CAMBRAI

BYNG LEADS THE BRITISH TO VICTORY AND A REPULSE

NOVEMBER 19TH

SIR A. CONAN DOYLE   MARSHAL HINDENBURG

The Cambrai battle was a sudden, unexpected stroke delivered by
the British near the southern extremity of their line in France. For
months they had been fighting their great Flanders battle around
Ypres. Now, hoping that the rest of the line against them might be
weakly held, they rushed it suddenly and at first successfully.

The element of surprise in this battle prevented them from preparing for it by a tremendous cannonade, so General Byng—whose
name lent itself so readily to the universal pun in describing the
attack—gathered over four hundred tanks, and used these to smash
the German lines. His infantry rushed forward after the tanks.
This was the largest tank battle of the War.

Protected by the tanks, the British pushed forward several miles,
breaking the first Hindenburg line, and almost reaching Cambrai. The
Germans were, however, prompt with vigorous counter-attacks. The
advance was thus held up at Bourlon woods, scarce four miles from
Cambrai. Here there was desperate fighting for several days. Then
on November 30th a huge German attack swept the British back
from almost all the ground they had won. There was much recrimination in Britain because General Byng had not been supported with
sufficient strength, and thus this final battle of the year had been but
another costly effort without adequate result.

The German bewilderment over this new form of attack, as well as
the German courage in meeting it, are clearly seen in Marshal Hindenburg's account.

BY CONAN DOYLE

WE shall now descend the British battle line to the section which extends from Bullecourt in the north to
Villers-Ghislain in the south, opposite to the important town
of Cambrai, some seven miles behind the Hindenburg Line.
It was here that Field-Marshal Haig had determined to
strike his surprise blow, an enterprise which he has described
in so lucid and detailed a dispatch that the weary chronicler
has the rare experience of finding history adequately re-
corded by the same brain which planned it. The plan was a
very daring one, for the spot attacked was barred by the
full unbroken strength of the Hindenburg main and support lines, a work so huge and solid that it seems to take
us back from these superficial days to the era of the Cyclopean builder or the founder of the great monuments of an-

tiquity. These enormous excavations of prodigious length, depth, and finish are object lessons both of the strength of the Germans, the skill of their engineers, and the ruthlessness with which they exploited the slave and captive labor with which so much of it was built.

Besides this terrific barricade there was the further difficulty that the whole method of attack was experimental, and that to advance without artillery fire against such a position would appear to be a most desperate venture. On the other hand it was known that the German line was thin and that their man-power had been attracted northwards by the long epic of the Passchendaele attack. There was a well-founded belief that the tanks would prove equal to the task of breaking the front, and sufficient infantry had been assembled to take advantage of any opening which might be made. The prize, too, was worth a risk, for apart from the possibility of capturing the important center of Cambrai, the possession of the high ground at Bourlon would be of great strategic value. The enterprise was placed in the hands of General Byng, the famous leader of the Third Cavalry Division and afterwards of the Canadian Corps, who had taken Allenby's place at the head of the Third Army. Under him were some of the most seasoned fighting material in the army. The troops were brought up stealthily by night, and the tanks which were crawling from every direction towards the trysting-place were carefully camouflaged. The French had been apprised of the attack, and had made arrangements by which, if there were an opening made to the south, some of their divisions should be available to take advantage of it.

The tanks were about four hundred in number and were under the separate command of General Ellis, a dashing soldier who inspired the utmost enthusiasm in his command. It had always been the contention of the tank designers in England that their special weapon needed, what it had never yet found, virgin ground which was neither a morass nor a wilderness of shell-holes. The leading lines of tanks had been furnished with enormous fagots of wood which they carried across their bows and which would be released so as to fall forward into any ditch or trench and to form a rude bridge. These ready-made weight-bearers were found to act admirably.

One difficulty with which the operations were confronted was that it was impossible for the guns to register properly without arousing suspicion. It was left to the gunners, therefore, to pick up their range as best they might after the action began, and this they did with a speed and accuracy which showed their high technical efficiency.

North of the main battle the Fifty-sixth Division kept up a spirited Chinese attack all day. The real advance was upon a frontage of six miles which covered the front from Hermies in the north to Gonnelieu in the south. Every company of the advancing units had been instructed to fall in behind its own marked tank. At 6.20, just after dawn, in a favoring haze, General Ellis gave the signal, his iron-clad fleet flowed forward, the field of wire went down with a long splintering rending crash, the huge fagots were rolled forward into the gaping ditches, and the eager infantry crowded forward down the clear swathes which the monsters had cut. At the same moment the guns roared out, and an effective smoke-barrage screened the whole strange spectacle from the German observers.

The long line of tanks magnified to monstrous size in the dim light of early dawn, the columns of infantry with fixed bayonets who followed them, all advancing in silent order, formed a spectacle which none who took part in it could ever forget. Everything went without a hitch, and in a few minutes the whole Hindenburg Line with its amazed occupants was in the hands of the assailants. Still following their iron guides, they pushed on to their further objectives.

They made a fine advance, but were held up by the strongly organized village of Flesquières. The approach to it was a long slope swept by machine-gun fire, and the co-operation of the tanks was made difficult by a number of advanced field-guns which destroyed the slow-moving machines as they approached up the hill. If the passage of the Hindenburg Line showed the strength of these machines the check at Flesquières showed their weakness, for in their present state of development they were helpless before a well-served field-gun, and a shell striking them meant the destruction of the tank, and often the death of the crew. It is said that a single Prussian artillery officer, who stood by his gun to the death and is chivalrously immortalized in the British bulletin, destroyed no less than sixteen tanks by direct hits. At the same time the long and solid wall of the château formed an obstacle to the infantry, as did the tangle of wire which surrounded the village. The fighting was very severe and the losses considerable, but before evening the Highlanders had secured the ground round the village and were close up to the village itself.

The delay had, however, a sinister effect upon the British plans, as the defiant village, spitting out flames and lead from every cranny and window, swept the ground around and created a broad zone on either side, across which progress was difficult and dangerous. It was the resistance of this village, and the subsequent breaking of the bridges upon the canal which prevented the cavalry from fulfilling their full rôle upon this first day of battle. None the less as dismounted units they did sterling work, and one small mounted body of Canadian Cavalry, the Fort Garry Horse from Winnipeg, particularly distinguished itself, getting over every obstacle, taking a German battery, dispersing a considerable body of infantry, and returning after a day of desperate adventure without their horses, but with a sample of the forces which they had encountered. It was a splendid deed of arms, for which Lieutenant Henry Strachan, who led the charge after the early fall of the squadron leader, received the coveted cross.

At Marcoing the bridge was captured intact, the leading tank shooting down the party who were engaged in its demolition. At Mesnières, which is the more important point, the advancing troops were less fortunate, as the bridge had already been injured and an attempt by a tank to cross it led to both bridge and tank crashing down into the canal. This proved to be a serious misfortune, and coupled with the hold-up at Flesquières, was the one untoward event in a grand day's work. Both the tanks and the cavalry were stopped by the broken bridge, and though the infantry still pushed on their advance was slower, as it was necessary to clear that part of the village which lay north of the canal and then to go forward without support over open country. Thus the Germans had time to organize resistance upon the low hills from Rumilly to Crevecœur and to prevent the advance reaching its full limits.

BY MARSHAL HINDENBURG

While we were delivering the final blows against Russia and bringing Italy to the very brink of military collapse, England and France were continuing their attacks on the Western front. There lay the greatest danger of the whole year's campaign for us.

From the point of view, not of scale, but of the obstinacy which the English displayed and the difficulties of the ground for the defenders, the battles which now raged in Flanders put all our battles on the Somme in 1916 completely in the shade. The fighting was over the marshes and mud of Flanders instead of the hard chalk of the Artois. These actions, too, developed into one of the long-drawn-out battles with which we were already so familiar, and in their general character represented an intensification of the sombre scenes peculiar to such battles. It is obvious that these actions kept us in great and continual anxiety. In fact, I may say that with such a cloud hanging over our heads we were seldom able to rejoice wholeheartedly over victories in Russia and Italy.

It was with a feeling of absolute longing that we waited for the beginning of the wet season. As previous experience had taught us, great stretches of the Flemish flats would then become impassable, and even in firmer places the new shell-holes would fill so quickly with ground water that men seeking shelter in them would find themselves faced with the alternative: "Shall we drown or get out of this hole?" This battle, too, must finally stick in the mud, even though English stubbornness kept it up longer than otherwise.

The flames of battle did not die down until December. As on the Somme, neither of the two adversaries could raise the shout of victory in Flanders.

As the Flanders battle was drawing to a close, a fierce conflict unexpectedly blazed up at a part of the line which had hitherto been relatively inactive. On November 20th we were suddenly surprised by the English near Cambrai. The attack at this point was against a portion of the Sieg-fried Line which was certainly very strong from the point of view of technical construction, but was held by few troops and those exhausted in previous battles. With the help of their tanks, the enemy broke through our series of obstacles and positions which had been entirely undamaged. English cavalry appeared on the outskirts of Cambrai. At the end of the year, therefore, a breach in our line appeared to be a certainty. At this point a catastrophe was averted by German divisions which had arrived from the East, and were more or less worn out by fighting and the long journey. Moreover, after a murderous defensive action lasting several days we succeeded in quickly bringing up compara-tively fresh troops, taking the enemy's salient in flank by a counter-attack, and almost completely restoring the orig-inal situation at very heavy cost to the enemy. Not only the Army Headquarters Staff on the spot, but the troops themselves and our railways had performed one of the most brilliant feats of the war.

The first considerable attack on our side in the West since the conduct of operations was entrusted to me had come to a victorious conclusion. Its effect on me personally was as strong and invigorating as on our troops and their leaders. I felt it as a release from a burden which our defensive strategy on the Western Front had placed upon my shoulders. For us, however, the success of our counter-attack involved far more than mere satisfaction. The ele-ment of surprise which had led to our success contained a lesson for the future.

With the Battle of Cambrai the English High Command had departed from what I might call the routine methods which hitherto they had always followed. Higher strategy seemed to have come into its own on this occasion. The pinning down of our main forces in Flanders and on the French front was to be used to facilitate a great surprise blow at Cambrai. It must be admitted that the subordinate commanders on the English side had not been equal to the demands and possibilities of the situation. By neglecting to exploit a brilliant initial success they had let victory be snatched from them, and indeed by troops which were far inferior to their own, both in numbers and quality. From this point of view our foe at Cambrai deserved his thorough defeat. Moreover, his High Command seemed to have failed to concentrate the resources required to secure the execution of their plans and their exploitation in case of success. Strong bodies of cavalry assembled behind the triumphant leading infantry divisions failed, even on this occasion, to overcome the last line of resistance, weak though it was, which barred the way to the flanks and rear of their opponents. The English cavalry squadrons were not able to conquer the German defence, even with the help of their tanks, and proved unequal to decorating their standards with that victory for which they had striven so honorably and so often.

The English attack at Cambrai for the first time revealed the possibilities of a great surprise attack with tanks. We had had previous experience of this weapon in the spring offensive, when it had not made any particular impression. However, the fact that the tanks had now been raised to s ich a pitch of technical perfection that they could cross our undamaged trenches and obstacles did not fail to have a marked effect on our troops. The physical effects of fire from machine-guns and light ordnance with which the steel Colossus was provided were far less destructive than the moral effect of its comparative invulnerability. The infantryman felt that he could do practically nothing against its armored sides. As soon as the machine broke through our trench-lines, the defender felt himself threatened in the rear and left his post. I had no doubt, however, that our men would soon get on level terms even with this new hostile weapon.

BOLSHEVIK RUSSIA ACCEPTS AN ARMISTICE

RUSSIAN DISMEMBERMENT BEGUN AT BREST-LITOVSK

DECEMBER 1ST

DR. RICHARD VON KUEHLMANN   LEON TROTSKY
OFFICIAL RUSSIAN AND GERMAN REPORTS

The right hand man of Lenine, or Ulianoff, through all his struggle for power, was Leber Braunstein, who, like his chief, became generally known by his pen-name, Leon Trotsky. Braunstein was a Jew born in southern Russia, he himself says of wealthy parents. He early joined the extremist party of Lenine and was exiled from Russia. For a time he lived and studied in New York. Now he became Lenine's Minister of Foreign Affairs. As such he had to match his brains against the trained diplomats of the Teuton Powers.

What Germany thought of the unexpected triumph which had come to her through the ascendancy of the Bolshevik leaders can be easily read in the eager speech that follows. Germany's unlucky Foreign Minister Zimmermann had been crowded out of office after his blundering entanglement with the United States and had been succeeded by Dr. von Kuehlmann. The latter on November 30th assured the Reichstag that Germany would devour Russia in the kindliest possible manner, and would then crush western Europe.

Trotsky had already announced openly to his people that he would make peace with the Teutons. It was part of the Bolshevik theory that the War was everywhere being carried on by upper-class governments in defiance of the wishes of the masses, and that therefore the moment Russia insisted on peace, the Teuton masses would do the same, and would compel their Governments at Berlin and Vienna to grant Russia an "equal" peace. To encourage this idea Germany announced a temporary armistice on December 1st; and her army chiefs at Brest-Litovsk welcomed the Bolshevist delegates who came to arrange to make the armistice mutual. A preliminary mutual armistice was promptly agreed to on December 5th, and then after much dispute a more permanent one was signed on December 16th, with arrangements for a peace parley to meet in the new year.

It was in these armistice proceedings that the emptiness of the Bolshevist dreams was first made manifest. Trotsky, who conducted the negotiations for Russia, found himself that most unhappy thing, a talker and theorist who finds some mighty opportunity to apply his theories and learns that they shrivel and crack at every point and are utterly impractical. The German leaders fed him with fine words, stripped Russia of the last shreds of military power, and meanwhile held their own people absolutely obedient and their military machine in perfect order. In vain did the Bolshevists try to delay the negotiations so as to let their speeches reach the German masses. Germany, as a whole, vastly preferred devouring Trotsky to embracing him.

Yet Trotsky had to have an armistice; he had promised one to his people. Therefore he took what the Germans chose to give him; and then proceeded by the method common to every demagogue before and since. He told his ignorant people that he had secured for them exactly what they needed; he made a wordy victory of his defeat.

C. F. H.

BY RICHARD VON KUEHLMANN

An Address to the Reichstag on November 30th

OUR eyes at the present moment are turned toward the east. Russia has set the world ablaze. The gang of bureaucrats and sycophants, rotten to the core, overruling the weak and misguided though probably well-meaning autocrat, surreptitiously brought about the mobilization of that country, which was the actual and immediate cause of the gigantic catastrophe which befell the world.

Now, however, Russia has swept aside the culprits, and she is laboring to find through an armistice and peace an opportunity for her internal reconstruction. I need not supplement the clear words in which the Chancellor yesterday stated the attitude of the German Government toward these aims. Here again our policy will adhere to the principle of firm but moderate statesmanship based upon facts.

The principles hitherto announced to the world by the present rulers in Petrograd appear to be entirely acceptable as a basis for reorganization of affairs in the east—a reorganization which, while fully taking into account the right of nations to determine their own destinies, is calculated permanently to safeguard the essential interests of the two great neighboring nations, Germany and Russia.

I am profoundly satisfied that we shall be able to pursue this course in full agreement with our allies and, I take it, also with the almost unanimous moral support of the representatives of the German people here assembled—a fact which will give our action necessary weight.

In Germany the great words spoken by the Emperor at the outset of the war have during the war borne fruit, and have developed relations between the people and the Crown which have on the basis of the most sincere and mutual confidence forever more been rendered freer and more active, and, therefore, stronger.

In Germany the Government is carrying out the program laid down by the Chancellor yesterday, not giving way under party pressure, but rather proceeding with clear perception of historical necessity. The development has been actually opposite that of England and France, where freedom of thought and freedom of speech have been suppressed, partly by violent and brutal measures. In these countries, which had been democracies, things are tending more and more toward absolute dictatorship.

If our adversaries are anxious to know what our aims are, this matter is very simple indeed. There is a sufficient number of ways at their disposal. History has not furnished a single example of any great diplomatic assembly purporting to settle international affairs ever having been convened without previously having informed itself as to the intentions of the parties concerned.

Germany welcomes the clearing of the situation as regards the western powers, under pressure of our recent successes.

Those in favor of war to the extreme have come out into the open, demanding victory and nothing but victory. How they intend to use this victory is shown by the secret documents published by the Russian Government. To-day it is certain that the Pope's message is receiving no response from the western powers, and that France and England are resolved to rely only on violence. Therefore the German people will stand up and be prepared to beat force with force until the dawn of the better and more humane understanding which is beginning to appear in the eastern sky shall arise in the nations of the west, which are as yet filled with greed for money and power.

BY LEON TROTSKY

Announcement of Foreign Policy, Issued November 20th

By order of the All-Russian Workmen's and Soldiers' Congress, the Council of The People's Commissaries assumed power, with obligation to offer all the peoples and their respective Governments an immediate armistice on all fronts, with the purpose of opening pourparlers immediately for the conclusion of a democratic peace.

When the power of the council is firmly established throughout the country, the council will, without delay, make a formal offer of an armistice to all the belligerents, enemy and ally. A draft message to this effect has been sent to all the Peoples' Commissaries for foreign affairs and to all the plenipotentiaries and representatives of allied nations in Petrograd.

The council also has sent orders to the citizen Commander in Chief that, after receiving the present message, he shall approach the commanding authorities of the enemy armies with an offer of a cessation of all hostile activities for the purpose of opening peace pourparlers, and that he shall, first, keep the council constantly informed by direct wire of pourparlers with the enemy armies, and, second, that he shall sign the preliminary act only after approval by the Commissaries Council.

Report by Delegate Kameneff of the First Conference, held December 1st

We crossed the line, preceded by a trumpeter carrying a white flag. Three hundred yards from the German entanglements we were met by German officers. At 5 o'clock, our eyes blindfolded, we were conducted to a battalion staff of the German Army, where we handed over our written authorization from the National Commissaries to two officers of the German General Staff, who had been sent for the purpose.

The negotiations were conducted in the French language. Our proposal to carry on negotiations for an armistice on all the fronts of belligerent countries, in order later to make peace, was immediately handed over to the staff of the division, whence it was sent by direct wire to the staff commander of the eastern front and to the chief commander of the German armies.

At 6.20 o'clock we were taken in a motor car to the

Minister's house on the road from Dvinsk to Ponevyezh, where we were received by Divisional General von Hoffmeister, who informed us that our proposal had been handed to the highest commander, and that a reply probably would be received in twenty-four hours. But at 7.30 o'clock the first answer from the chief of the general command already had been received, announcing agreement to our proposals, and leaving the details of the next meeting to General von Hoffmeister and the Parliamentarians. After an exchange of opinion and further communication by wire from the chief of the general command, at midnight a written answer to our proposal was given to us by von Hoffmeister. In view of the fact that ours was written in Russian, the answer was given in German. The reply was:

"The chief of the German eastern front is prepared to enter into negotiations with the Russian chief command. The chief of the German eastern front is authorized by the German Commander in Chief to carry on negotiations for an armistice. The chief of the Russian armies is requested to appoint a commission with written authority to be sent to the headquarters of the commander of the German eastern front. On his side, the German commander likewise will name a commission with special authorization.

"The day and hour of the meeting are to be fixed by the Russian Commander in Chief. It is demanded that the German commander be warned in due time to prepare a special train for the purpose. Notice must be given at which part it is intended to cross the front. The commander of the German eastern front will place at the disposition of the Russian commission the necessary apparatus, so that it may keep in communication with its chief command.

(Signed) "VON HOFFMEISTER."

The Russian Parliamentarians decided to appoint as the place the junction of the Dvinsk-Vilna line, whence the Russian representatives will be conducted to the Brest-Litovsk headquarters of the German commander. The time appointed is midday of November 19th (Russian calendar, or December 2nd, new calendar). At the same time we were informed that no firing would occur unless prompted, and that enemy fraternization would be stopped. We were blindfolded again and conducted to our lines.

Report by Secretary Trotsky of the Conference held December 5th

The conference opened in the presence of representatives of Germany, Austria-Hungary, Turkey, and Bulgaria. Field-Marshal von Hindenburg and Field-Marshal von Hoetzendorff charged Prince Leopold of Bavaria with the negotiations, and he in his turn nominated his Chief of Staff, General Hoffmann. Other delegates received similar authority from their highest Commander in Chief. The enemy delegation was exclusively military.

Our delegates opened the conference with a declaration of our peace aims, in view of which an armistice was proposed. The enemy delegates replied that that was a question to be solved by politicians. They said they were soldiers, having powers only to negotiate conditions of an armistice, and could add nothing to the declaration of Foreign Ministers Czernin and von Kuehlmann.

Our delegates, taking due note of this evasive declaration, proposed that they should immediately address all the countries involved in the war, including Germany and her allies, and all States not represented at the conference, with a proposal to take part in drawing up an armistice on all fronts.

The enemy delegates again replied evasively that they did not possess such powers. Our delegation then proposed that they ask their Government for such authority. This proposal was accepted, but no reply had been communicated to the Russian delegation up to 2 o'clock, December 5th.

Our representatives submitted a project for an armistice on all fronts, elaborated by our military experts. The principal points of this project were: First, an interdiction against sending forces on our fronts to the fronts of our allies, and, second, the retirement of German detachments from the islands around Moon Sound.

The enemy delegation submitted a project for an armistice on the front from the Baltic to the Black Sea. This proposal is now being examined by our military experts. Negotiations will be continued to-morrow morning.

The enemy delegation declared that our conditions for an armistice were unacceptable and expressed the opinion that such demands could be addressed only to a conquered country.

GERMAN OFFICIAL REPORT OF THE CONFERENCE OF DECEMBER 5TH

Yesterday the authorized representatives of the chief army administrations of Germany, Austria-Hungary, Turkey, and Bulgaria concluded in writing with the authorized representatives of the Russian chief army administration a suspension of hostilities for ten days for the whole of the mutual fronts. The commencement is fixed for Friday noon. The ten days' period will be utilized for bringing to a conclusion negotiations for an armistice. For the purpose of reporting verbally regarding the present results, a portion of the members of the Russian deputation has returned home. The sittings of the commission continue.

ARMISTICE AS SIGNED ON DECEMBER 16TH

Between the representatives of the higher command of Russia on the one hand and of Bulgaria, Germany, Austria-Hungary, and Turkey on the other hand, for the purpose of achieving a lasting and honorable peace between both parties, the following armistice is concluded:

The armistice shall begin on December 17th at 2 o'clock in the afternoon and continue until January 14th. The contracting parties have the right to break the armistice by giving seven days' notice. Unless notice is given the armistice automatically continues.

The armistice embraces the land and aërial forces on the front from the Baltic to the Black Sea and also the Russo-Turkish front in Asia Mnior. During the armistice the parties concerned obligate themselves not to increase the number of troops on the above fronts or on the islands in Moon Sound, or to make a regrouping of forces.

Neither side is to make operative any transfers of units

from the Baltic-Black Sea front until January 14th, excepting those begun before the agreement was signed. They obligate themselves not to concentrate troops on parts of the Black Sea or Baltic Sea east of the fifteenth degree of longitude east of Greenwich.

The line of demarkation on the European front is the first line of defense. The space between will be neutral. The navigable rivers will be neutral, their navigation being forbidden except for necessary purposes of commercial transport or on sections where the positions are at a great distance. On the Russo-Turkish front the line of demarkation will be arranged by the mutual consent of the chief commanders.

Intercourse will be allowed from sunrise to sunset, no more than twenty-five persons participating at a time. The participants may exchange papers, magazines, unsealed mail, and also may carry on trade in the exchange of articles of prime necessity.

The question of release of troops freed from service who are beyond the line of demarkation will be solved during the peace negotiations. This applies also to Polish troops.

Naval Fronts—The armistice embraces all the Black Sea and Baltic Sea east of the meridian 15 degrees east of Greenwich, applying to all naval and aërial forces. In regard to extension of the armistice to the White Sea and the Arctic Russian coast a special agreement will be made. Attacks upon war and commercial vessels must cease in the above regions, and attacks in other seas must be avoided.

With the purpose of facilitating the conduct of peace negotiations and the speedy healing of the wounds caused by the war, the contracting parties take measures for reestablishment of cultural and economic relations among the signatories. Within such limits as the armistice permits, postal commercial relations, the mailing of books and papers, will be permitted, the details to be worked out by a mixed commission, representing all the interested parties, at Petrograd.

THE CONQUEST OF JERUSALEM

BRITISH TROOPS WIN THE HOLY CITY

DECEMBER 11TH

GASTON BODART   E. W. MASTERMAN
GENERAL SIR EDMUND ALLENBY

From almost the beginning of the War there had been a Palestine-Egypt campaign, a struggle where Turkey and Britain clashed along the line of the Suez Canal. At first Britain had been on the defensive; but gradually she brought troops from Australia and from Britain to Egypt and built up an army strong enough to assume the offensive. In February, 1917, this army established itself firmly on the southern border of Palestine, having made secure its difficult lines of transport across the Sinai desert. Gaza, that ancient stronghold of the Philistines against which Samson fought, was besieged in February but not finally captured until November 6th.

The defeat of the Turks at Gaza proved really the breaking of their forces. In quick succession the Britons now fought their way from one old Bible spot to another, until on December 8th they fought the Turks immediately in front of Jerusalem and put them to flight. The city itself was formally entered by the British troops in solemn procession on December 11th. General Allenby, commander of the expedition, tells briefly here of its closing battle; and a more general account of the campaign is given by the Teuton authority, Dr. Bodart and by Mr. Masterman, Secretary of the British Palestine Society.

During the campaign the Turks had been guided by German generals. Toward the close they were even honored with the leadership of General von Falkenhayn, who had been Chief-of-Staff for all the German High Headquarters until superseded by von Ludendorff in 1916. But even von Falkenhayn could no longer check the disintegration of the semi-barbaric Turkish army. Everywhere now the feebler peoples were breaking under the prolonged strain of the War.

BY GASTON BODART

ENGLISH diplomacy and English gold probably succeeded in burdening the Porte with another adversary. The Grand Sherif of Mecca, the highest ecclesiastical dignitary of the holy city, received from England the title of "King of Arabia," because, as an inveterate enemy of the Young Turks, he had denied to the Caliphate in Constantinople the right of declaring a "Holy War" against the Entente and had proclaimed Arabia as a state independent of

401

the Porte. The Arab tribes now unfurled the "Green Flag of the Prophet" to fight against, not for, Constantinople. This dangerous flanking movement, which now threatened from the East, induced Djemal Pasha to refrain from a second invasion of Egypt.

After the completion of a field railroad on the Syrian Caravan road, already used by Napoleon in 1799, General Murray, the new British commander-in-chief, in December, 1916, began his advance to the Egyptian-Turkish border. The army which he commanded was excellently equipped and constantly remained in touch with a squadron of war and merchant ships. The British operations began with the occupation of El Arish and the capture of Rafa. By March, 1917, the English had reached Gaza without any serious struggle.

An attempt on the part of General Dobell to take Gaza by a coup-de-main failed, the English suffering heavy losses. An attack made by the Turks on the following day against the English position (first battle of Gaza, March 27th and 28th, 1917) likewise met with no success. In a second battle for the historically celebrated place (April 17th), the British, although not successful in breaking through, secured to themselves positions from which the trench war against the powerful Turkish line Gaza-Beersheba could be conducted with greater hope of success.

After the opponents had remained for seven months in these positions, the new commander-in-chief, General Allenby, began the operations on October 31st, 1917, by capturing the strategically highly important point, Beersheba, the former chief halting-place of the Turks on their advance to Egypt, and now the chief station for the protection of Palestine. The position at Gaza, in consequence of this victory, now became untenable. An immediate attack with his left wing and center brought Allenby in possession of the entire Turkish line extending from the coast to Beersheba by way of Gaza. The latter city was entered by the British on November 7th. The energetic pursuit which followed soon led to the capture of Ascalon, on the coast and to a nearer approach to the railroad between Jaffa and Jerusalem. The British general finally succeeded in surrounding Jerusalem, and on December 9th, 1917, the city was captured with the coöperation of French and Italian contingents. The moral significance of this event was even greater than its military importance.

BY E. W. MASTERMAN

On October 26, 1917, the final preparations for the advance commenced. The railway was pushed forward from Shellal, fourteen miles south of Gaza on the Wady Ghuzzeh, towards Karm in the direction of Beersheba. Another branch was run to another point on the Beersheba road, El Baggar, and arrangements for watering the troops were made at Wady Asluj, sixteen miles southeast of Gaza. These movements were not unperceived by the Turks, who made a great attack with two regiments of cavalry and some two battalions of infantry against Karm, but were beaten off with great gallantry by our London Yeomanry Brigade. The same day a fierce bombardment of the Gaza defenses was commenced from the sea.

On the night of October 30th, mounted troops were got into position on the northeast of Beersheba, while infantry in the early dawn of the 31st were marched to positions on the southwest. The attack was commenced at an early hour, and before evening, after fierce fighting, the position was captured. Among the outlying fortified posts was Tell es Saba, the before-mentioned site of Beersheba or Sheba of the Canaanite time. A number of German machine gunners had to be cleared off this site. On November 1st, the infantry moved nine miles to the north of Beersheba, and mounted troops pushed forward to within four miles of Dhaheriyeh. Meanwhile some of our infantry moved into a position northwest of Beersheba in the neighborhood of Abu Irgeig. Thus the capture of the eastern end of the long fortified line of the Turkish defense was now complete.

At the western end on the morning of November 2nd, British infantry advanced and captured a hill nicknamed "Umbrella Hill," some 500 yards west of the Dir el-Belah-Gaza road and proceeded to take the whole of the Gaza first line defenses between there and the sea. In this attack they were assisted by the "Tanks."

On November 6th, our infantry north of Beersheba at Ain Kohle advanced two miles to the Turkish position at Khuwelifeh, while dismounted Yeomanry and Irish and London infantry, advancing from the neighborhood of Abu Irgeig, captured the whole of the Turkish lines up to Abu Hareira. By nightfall a general retreat of the Turks had commenced, the British infantry and mounted troops pursuing them towards Jemmameh and Huj. The eastern line having now completely given way, the attack on Gaza was renewed at midnight on the 6th, and the city was captured without much opposition; the British left wing—Scottish infantry—pushing forward through the heavy sand dunes with great energy the same night towards the mouth of Wady Hesy: they at once attacked the Turks entrenched on the north bank, although it was then dark, and captured the position by midnight. Other battalions advancing along the high road further east met with most determined opposition at Deir Sincid, further east on the banks of the same wady, the enemy counter-attacking four times before being driven out. Still further to the east mounted troops, Anzacs and others, pushed northwards from Sheria, and took Tell es Sheria the next morning at 4.30.

Meanwhile at Attawiney, some seven miles from Gaza on the Beersheba road, the Turks still made a show of resistance, but by the 8th they retired, and thus the whole line of original defense passed into our hands.

The advance now became rapid. During November 8th mounted troops—the Warwickshire and Worcestershire Yeomanry—reached the middle course of the Wady Hesy passing Tell-el-Hesy. They captured Huj in a brilliant action, in which they took twelve guns, three machine guns, and 100 prisoners, the accumulated stores in the town having been set on fire by the retreating Turks. After a brilliant action by the Indian Imperial Service Cavalry in Beit Hanun, the terminus of the Gaza branch of the railway was captured, with large stores of heavy gun ammunition, the retreating troops being harassed by the Royal Flying Corps with machine guns and bombs.

On the 9th mounted troops moved forward rapidly, through Askelon and El Mejdel successively, and by night reached Esdud (Ashdod) further inland; at Et Tineh, where the retreating Turks set fire to enormous stores at the railway junction, the Australians were in time to save and capture a vast booty.

On the 11th, although the mounted troops had proceeded a good deal further north, our infantry had to clear a strong body of Turks out of the village of Beit Duras, a little on the southern edge of the Wady Sukreir, along which ravine 13,000 Turks had been frantically entrenching themselves to resist our advance. The retreat by now had become in many parts precipitate. A correspondent wrote at this time:

"I have been over many miles of battlefield, and saw everywhere many wagons and an enormous amount of un-destroyed gun ammunition, in places piles of field and heavy gun shells in boxes and wicker crates. I hear that a number of exploded dumps are to be found all over the country."— (W. T. Massey, in *The Daily Telegraph*.)

The next day, after a desperate fight at Burkah, where the Turks had to be driven out of a strongly fortified post with two lines of trenches, the enemy occupied the general line from the mouth of the Wady Sukereir, twelve miles north of Askelon, running southeast to Beit-Jabrin, the line being considerably more advanced near the coast than further east. Still further east our troops in the mountains had captured Dhaheriyeh.

The next day, November 13th, was a day of fierce fighting, the Turks making a brave and obstinate resistance to our advance along their chosen line. El Mesmiyeh, Katrah and Mughar were each taken after heavy fighting. Here the Berkshire, Buckinghamshire and Dorsetshire Yeomanry greatly distinguished themselves, and by coming to the assistance of the Scottish infantry captured 1,500 prisoners, twenty machine guns and four guns, and 400 Turks were buried after the action. Our line was thus advanced from Et Tineh through Katrah, to Yebnah in the west.

By the 14th our troops occupied the Wady Rubin, with its narrow flowing stream, and due east of this seized the railway in the vicinity of Naameh and El Mansurah, including the junction with the central railway from the north.

The next day, the 15th, our troops after slight resistance occupied the line Ramleh and Ludd and reached some three miles south of Jaffa. At Abu Shusheh (Gezer) the Yeomanry captured this historic site.

On the 17th, Australian and New Zealand troops captured at Ludd (Lydda) 300 prisoners and four machine guns, and later occupied Jaffa without opposition. The area now reached was fairly thickly populated, as numbers of the fellahin had been removed there from the neighborhood of Gaza by the Turks.

The picture of the welcome received by the troops is very delightful:

"The people turned out by the Turks from Gaza and the surrounding country were trekking back with all their worldly goods and chattels packed on overloaded camels and donkeys, the women bearing astonishingly heavy loads on their heads, while the patriarchs of families rode, or were carried on the shoulders of the younger men. The agriculturists are beginning to turn out to plow and till the fields, now they have the security of British protection. Our troops receive the liveliest welcome in passing the villages, and in this unchanging part of the world the women sit and gossip during the process of drawing water from the well, just as they did in Biblical days, unhindered by the war's progress, though not heedless of it. There is peace and safety for them all.

"This end to extortion, oppression, and pillage under the name of requisitions has, in the short space of a week, wrought a wondrous change in the happiness and contentment of the people.

"The German propaganda has failed miserably here.

"British ideals of freedom are thoroughly known, and the exemplary behavior of our troops has confirmed all previous knowledge of the work done by Great Britain for civilization.

"To say that this country, which a fortnight ago was under the Turkish scourge and war, has suddenly become normal for the civil population, is not to use words of exaggeration. In Ramleh people are practicing the arts of peace and the bazaars are busy. Our Yeomanry are buying Jaffa oranges, vegetables, and fresh bread, a welcome change from the diet of a fortnight's strenuous times, at fair rates, the traders receiving payment in cash, an alteration from the depreciated Turkish note to which they are accustomed."
—W. T. MASSEY, in *The Daily Telegraph*.

Ramleh, Lydda and Jaffa and the villages around being now secured, an advance was made towards Jerusalem itself. The historic pass through the Vale of Ajalon was followed by our cavalry, who reached Beit-Ur-el-Tahta (lower Beth-Horon) on November 18th, and worked their way in contact with the enemy four miles west of Beria; after reaching Beitunia, which commands the Northern road, they had again to fall back to Beit-Ur-el-Foka (Beth-Horon the Upper). Meanwhile, by the 19th, infantry had with heavy fighting advanced to Kuryet-el-Enab, six miles west of Jerusalem, and Beit Likia, on the road from the Vale of Ajalon towards El Kukeibeh (Emmaus), and by the 21st the lofty dominating mountain of Nebi Samuel, the site of the traditional tomb of the Prophet Samuel, was stormed. In trying to drive out the British, the Mosque over the tomb seems to have been destroyed, which is not remarkable, as its lofty position would have given the British a unique point of vantage.

The campaign takes on a new aspect when it turns from the occupation of the maritime plain to the investment of Jerusalem.

Jerusalem lies high up, some 2,450 feet above the Mediterranean, in the plateau of central Judea. In the days of ancient warfare its military strength lay largely in the deep valleys almost surrounding its site, and the powerful walls rising from these valley slopes made the city almost impregnable from all sides but the north, where the absence of a valley was, in Roman times, compensated for by a triple wall.

The line of defense of Jerusalem now lies far out from the city. From the south, in past history, the desert and the almost waterless Negeb have been such a defense that directly from this direction the inhabitants of Jerusalem might well think themselves secure. "No army of invasion, knowing that opposition awaited them on the Judean frontier, would venture across those steep and haggard ridges. . . . Hence we find Judea almost never invaded from the south."—(G. A. Smith.) But this present war has entirely altered the conditions. In earlier invasions the army had behind them but a waterless desert; now, thanks partly to the Turks themselves, the British Army has an excellent road from Beersheba northwards, and railway tracks connect this town southwards with El Auja, and eastwards with Gaza and the maritime plain. As the British Army advanced very early to Dhaheriyeh they had before them a straight high road to the vine-clad valleys of Hebron. From Hebron to the neighborhood of Bethlehem the road traverses the ridge of the water shed, and is by no means difficult; there are no deep gorges or precipitous gulleys, and in many places the valleys open out into small plateaus.

With respect to the western approach, Judea always had natural defenses of considerable strength. The northernmost of the passes that start in the Vale of Ajalon is the one which, all through history, has been associated with great battles. Passing from the level plains around Gezer, Wady Selman, or the Valley of Ajalon, runs northeastward into the mountains, and from the most eastern end of the wide valley three paths ascend into the hills. Of these the most famous is that by the two Beth-Horons, along which historic battles have been waged of great importance. Here Joshua fought the Canaanites and drove them in headlong slaughter to the plains. By this route the first Crusaders reached Jerusalem in two days. It was the great high road into the heart of the land from the earliest times to three or four centuries ago, and history repeats itself as we read that the British troops reach Beit-Ur-el-Tahta and Beit-Ur-el-Foka, the two Beth-Horons.

South of this pass is Wady Ali. The road where it runs

between high steep hills, would be quite impassable if any adequate defense was put up, and report says that it was strongly fortified. There are, however, at points (besides the one mentioned above) narrow paths which ascend the hills and reach the high road after it leaves this valley either at Saris or a little further east at Kuriet-el-Enab. From these places to Jerusalem the road, though rising and falling several times, is by no means impassable for an army. After crossing the deep valley at Kulonyeh, situated in the deep northern arm of the Wady el-Suras, two routes are possible, one to the south by the old road (now much out of repair), another to the north of the main more modern road, and both converge just before the first houses of Jerusalem begin. The third pass, Wady es Surar, has already been described, and it may be said at once that this deep winding gorge would be quite impossible as a route of military approach unless the hills on each side were first seized, and it is certain that great resistance will be offered to the Army obtaining possession to so vital a thing as the railway. The fourth pass is the Wady es Sunt, known of old as the Vale of Elah; the higher reaches of this valley, known as the Wady es Sur, run due north and then east, reaching the hill country near Beit Sur, the ancient Beth-Zur (Josh. xv. 58; Neh. iii. 16). This route has been used several times by armies, the most famous invasion being that of Antiochus III., who with Lysias as his general, led the Syrian Army, accompanied by elephants, up this route and defeated Judas Maccabeus at Beth Zacharya, near the Wady el-Arrub (1 Macc. vi. 32f.). Richard, King of England, in the third Crusade, attempted this route after failing to reach Jerusalem through the Vale of Ajalon. An attack on Jerusalem after the plateau is reached is one from the south, as contrasted with that through the Vale of Ajalon approaches from the north.

After the first rush up the plains and the rapid seizure of the western approaches to Jerusalem a necessary pause occurred while supplies were brought up and the lines of communication were improved. It was necessary to improvise some roads into the mountains to bring up the artillery. All this took time, while the onset of the heavy winter's rains increased the difficulties of transport. Meanwhile the British Army held a long line running from the mouth of the river Aujeh the west—westwards and southwestwards into the hill country. Here, the center and most actively attacking force held the line of the Beth-Horon pass from el Burj— the site of an old crusading fort, erected by Richard Cœur de Lion, to protect this very road—past the two Beth-Horons, southwards past the great mountain of Nebi Samuel—which dominates all the country round—to Ain Kairem and Bettir. Both these two last sites have the best springs of water in the whole district. Ain Kairem is a beautiful little town, by tradition the birthplace of John the Baptist, and here there is a charming settlement of Russian nuns built amid groves of cypresses and other trees. From Ain Kairem to Jerusalem there is a good carriage road. Bettir is important as the last station on the railway as Jerusalem is approached. It was the site of a great Jewish tragedy when (A.D. 135) the last remaining followers of the false Messiah Bar Cochba, who had raised rebellion against Rome, were besieged and finally massacred so that, it is said, the place ran with torrents of blood. The ancient site is known as Khirbet el Yahud, the Jews' ruin.

The extreme right of the Army meanwhile occupied edh Dhaheriyeh, ancient Debir, and an extended line held the western passes between.

The western (left) end of the attacking force continued to be held back by the Nahr Aujeh—probably they only intended to protect what had been gained. This river is the largest and southernmost of the short low-lying streams, with marshy banks liable after rain to overflow, which traverse the Plain of Sharon from east to west. It has formed a military barrier before, as when Alexander Jannæus tried in vain to fortify this line to resist the advance of Antiochus. Several skirmishes occurred here, and on one occasion Australian mounted troops captured at Birket el Jamus, "the pool of the Buffaloes," a number of Turks.

The central attacking force was heavily engaged for several days. At El Burj, on a ridge overlooking the pass, the Turkish forces, to the number of 600, at one time reached the thinly guarded British trenches, but were counter-attacked and almost annihilated.

Beit ur et Foka changed hands several times and eventually proved to be a place impossible to hold on either side as long as the heights around were held by opposing parties. The lofty mountain of Nebi Samuel—the site of the traditional tomb of Samuel and by many considered that of Mizpah—dominates the country round for miles. British troops early captured the site and entrenched themselves against the most determined attacks, the opposing forces being in places on the steep hillsides but forty yards apart. The recently rebuilt shrine crowning the hill, which had been occupied as a place of refuge by the Mohammedans of the neighboring village, was entirely destroyed by Turkish gunfire. It might have been more "pious" to leave it, but it would hardly have been war, as it affords the finest lookout of all.

While the Turks were heavily engaged from the west the right wing commenced to fold in from the south. This seemed from the first to present the most favorable approach—under modern conditions. Hebron was occupied on December 8th. This ancient city, sacred to Moslems, Jews and Christians as the site of the Cave of Machpelah where were buried Abraham, Isaac and Jacob and their wives, lies in the Wady el Khulil amid wide spreading vineyards, fertile fields and abundant springs. It lies high-over 3,000 feet above sea level, and is surrounded by still loftier hills. From Hebron to Jerusalem, though there are many "ups and downs," the road—an excellent carriage road—is mainly a descent.

The Army rapidly advanced—probably the Turks were too much occupied on their extended front to concentrate great forces on this new attack. Bethlehem and Beit Jala, with their great forests of olive-trees, were passed and from here the approaches to the city, both from the south and—by detaching troops eastwards—from the Jordan Valley in the east, were cut. Meanwhile the central forces had reached the northern Jerusalem-Nablus road, and the city being thus isolated it surrendered to General Allenby. The following day he, accompanied by French, Italian and Mohammedan representatives, entered the Holy City in triumph.

NARRATIVE OF AN EYE-WITNESS WITHIN JERUSALEM

It was whispered in Jerusalem on November 9th that the British were at Huj, behind the center of the Gaza-Beersheba line, and that Tel-el-Sheria and Gaza had fallen. The Germans and Austrians were even now preparing to evacuate the Holy City. Rumor for once was true. During the next few days lame or exhausted Turks, wounded and stragglers, whom the German motor-lorry drivers refused to pick up, and Turkish officers shaken into truthfulness by the extent of their defeat, brought news of the victory. Turkish officials at once began to leave the city with their families. The German depots were hurriedly emptied of unessential supplies, such as sugar, which were sold for a song. Munitions and essential stores were then sent north to Shechem, or east to Jericho. From the high towers of the city and from the Mount of Olives one could see a great double wall of dust along every road each day, and on a clear day one could see lorries, carts, and pack animals streaming up and down. Owners of the few horse carriages left asked for and obtained £10 a seat from fugitives who were making for Shechem.

The great commanders hastened to Jerusalem. Enver, who had hurried from the imperial headquarters at Constantinople to harangue his defeated Generals, departed as suddenly and silently as he had come. Falkenhayn came from the city of Aleppo to reorganize the beaten army. Meanwhile the British troops had pushed up the passes into the highlands of Judea. Their guns were faintly heard at Jerusalem as they fought their way up the valley of Sorek, and thenceforward the sound of battle grew louder day by day.

Falkenhayn himself departed for Shechem on November 16th, and on the 19th Latin, Greek, Armenian, and Coptic patriarchs, with the principal ecclesiastics from the churches, left for the same place; so also went certain Jewish notables suspected of Zionism.

Then came a sudden change in the temper of the Turks; the British were held up at Neby Samwil, in sight of Shechem, by reason of difficulties of transport. The Turks had received the command to stand from their German masters, who had preached the uselessness of attempting to hold Jerusalem once the Gaza line had gone, but their pride forbade them to surrender one of the holiest cities of the Turkish Caliphate without a struggle.

Falkenhayn having gone, the control of policy reverted to Turkish hands, and Ali Fuad Pasha, commander of the Turkish forces in Jerusalem, issued two proclamations to the people of the city. He first warned all civilians that street fighting was to be expected, and when it began they were to keep indoors and assist the troops in the impending house-to-house conflict under pain of severe penalties. The second proclamation stated that the Turks had held Jerusalem for 1,300 years (an exaggeration of only nine centuries) and would not abandon it. The inhabitants were ordered to have complete confidence in the good behavior of the troops detailed to defend the city to the last. Dismayed by threats and informed by Turkish officers that the British advance had spent itself, and that a new period of trench warfare was at hand, the people despaired. Arrests and confiscations multiplied, and the innate spitefulness of the Young Turk official manifested itself in many ways.

On December 6th and 7th the fighting on the hills west of Jerusalem and the rapid advance of a British force from Hebron began to revive the hope of a decision. On the morning of December 8th large numbers of the inhabitants, with the remaining religious chiefs, were personally warned by the police to be ready to leave at once. The extent to which the Turks were prepared to clear the city is shown by the fact that out of the Armenian community of 1,400 souls 300 received this notice. The tyrannical Djemal Pasha, when warned that vehicles were unavailable for the transport of the unhappy exiles to Shechem or Jericho, telegraphed curtly that they and theirs must walk. The fate of countless Armenians and many Greeks has shown that a population of all ages suddenly turned out to walk indefinite distances under Turkish escort is exposed to outrage and hardship which prove fatal to most of them; but the delay in telegraphing had saved the population, and the sun had risen for the last time on the Ottoman domination of Jerusalem, and the Turks' power to destroy faded with the day.

Toward dusk the British troops were reported to have passed Lifta, and to be within sight of the city. On this news being received, a sudden panic fell on the Turks west and southwest of the town, and at 5 in the afternoon civilians were surprised to see a Turkish transport column galloping furiously cityward along the Jaffa road. In passing they alarmed all units within sight or hearing, and the wearied infantry arose and fled, bootless and without rifles, never pausing to think or to fight. Some were flogged from behind by officers and were compelled to pick up their arms; others staggered on through the mud, augmenting the confusion of the retreat.

After four centuries of conquest the Turk was ridding the land of his presence in the bitterness of defeat, and a great enthusiasm arose among the Jews. There was a running to and fro; daughters called to their fathers and brothers concealed in outhouses, cellars, and attics from the police, who sought them for arrest and deportation. "The Turks are running," they called; "the day of deliverance is come." The nightmare was fast passing away, but the Turk still lingered. In the evening he fired his guns continuously, perhaps comforting himself with the loud noise that heartens the soul of a barbarian, perhaps to cover the sound of his own retreat. Whatever the intention was, the roar of the gunfire persuaded most citizens to remain indoors, and there were few to witness the last act of Osmanli authority.

BY GENERAL SIR EDMUND ALLENBY

The date for the attack on Jerusalem was fixed as December 8th. Welsh troops, with a cavalry regiment attached, had advanced from their positions north of Beersheba up the Hebron-Jerusalem road on the 4th. No opposition was met, and by the evening of the 6th the head of this column was ten miles north of Hebron. The infantry were directed to reach the Bethlehem-Beit Jala area by the 7th, and the line Surbahir-Sherafat (about three miles south of Jerusalem) by dawn on the 8th, and no troops were to enter Jerusalem during this operation.

It was recognized that the troops on the extreme right might be delayed on the 7th and fail to reach the positions assigned to them by dawn on the 8th. Arrangements were therefore made to protect the right flank west of Jerusalem, in case such delay occurred.

On the 7th the weather broke, and for three days rain was almost continuous. The hills were covered with mist at frequent intervals, rendering observation from the air and visual signaling impossible. A more serious effect of the rain was to jeopardize the supply arrangements by rendering the roads almost impassable—quite impassable, indeed, for mechanical transport and camels in many places.

The troops moved into positions of assembly by night, and, assaulting at dawn on the 8th, soon carried their first objectives. They then pressed steadily forward. The mere physical difficulty of climbing the steep and rocky hillsides and crossing the deep valleys would have sufficed to render progress slow, and the opposition encountered was considerable. Artillery support was soon difficult, owing to the length of the advance and the difficulty of moving guns forward. But by about noon London troops had already advanced over two miles, and were swinging northeast to gain the Nablus-Jerusalem road, while the yeomanry had captured the Beit Iksa spur, and were preparing for a further advance.

As the right column had been delayed and was still some distance south of Jerusalem, it was necessary for the London troops to throw back their right and form a defensive flank facing east toward Jerusalem, from the western outskirts of which considerable rifle and artillery fire was being experienced. This delayed the advance, and early in the afternoon it was decided to consolidate the line gained and resume the advance next day, when the right column would be in a position to exert its pressure. By nightfall our line ran from Neby Samwil to the east of Beit Iksa, through Lifta to a point about one and a half miles west of Jerusalem, whence it was thrown back facing east. All the enemy's prepared defenses west and northwest of Jerusalem had been captured, and our troops were within a short distance of the Nablus-Jerusalem road.

The London troops and yeomanry had displayed great endurance in difficult conditions. The London troops especially, after a night march in heavy rain to reach their positions of deployment, had made an advance of three to four miles in difficult hills in the face of stubborn opposition.

During the day about 300 prisoners were taken and many Turks killed. Our own casualties were light.

Next morning the advance was resumed. The Turks had withdrawn during the night, and the London troops and yeomanry, driving back rearguards, occupied a line across the Nablus-Jerusalem road four miles north of Jerusalem, while Welsh troops occupied a position east of Jerusalem across the Jericho road. These operations isolated Jerusalem, and at about noon the enemy sent out a *parlementaire* and surrendered the city.

In the operations from October 31st to December 9th over 12,000 prisoners were taken. The total captures of material have not yet been fully counted, owing to the large area covered by these operations; but are known to include about 100 guns of various calibers, many machine guns, more than 20,000,000 rounds of rifle ammunition, and 250,-000 rounds of gun ammunition. More than twenty airplanes were destroyed by our airmen or burned by the enemy to avoid capture.

I entered the city officially at noon, December 11th, with a few of my staff, the commanders of the French and Italian detachments, the heads of the political missions, and the Military Attachés of France, Italy, and America.

The procession was all afoot, and at Jaffa gate I was received by the guards representing England, Scotland, Ireland, Wales, Australia, New Zealand, India, France, and Italy. The population received me well.

Guards have been placed over the holy places. My Military Governor is in contact with the acting custodians and the Latin and Greek representatives. The Governor has detailed an officer to supervise the holy places. The Mosque of Omar and the area around it have been placed under Moslem control, and a military cordon of Mohammedan officers and soldiers has been established around the mosque. Orders have been issued that no non-Moslem is to pass within the cordon without permission of the Military Governor and the Moslem in charge.

PROCLAMATION OF GENERAL ALLENBY

To the Inhabitants of Jerusalem the Blessed and the People Dwelling in Its Vicinity:

The defeat inflicted upon the Turks by the troops under my command has resulted in the occupation of your city by my forces. I, therefore, here now proclaim it to be under martial law, under which form ot administration it will remain so long as military considerations make necessary.

However, lest any of you be alarmed by reason of your experience at the hands of the enemy who has retired, I hereby inform you that it is my desire that every person pursue his lawful business without fear of interruption.

Furthermore, since your city is regarded with affection by the adherents of three of the great religions of mankind and its soil has been consecrated by the prayers and pilgrimages of multitudes of devout people of these three religions for many centuries, therefore, do I make it known to you that every sacred building, monument, holy spot, shrine, traditional site, endowment, pious bequest, or customary place of prayer of whatsoever form of the three religions will be maintained and protected according to the existing customs and beliefs of those to whose faith they are sacred.

Guardians have been established at Bethlehem and on Rachel's Tomb. The tomb at Hebron has been placed under exclusive Moslem control.

The hereditary custodians at the gates of the Holy Sepulcher have been requested to take up their accustomed duties in remembrance of the magnanimous act of the Caliph Omar, who protected that church.

THE VAST REORGANIZATION OF AMERICA FOR WAR

THE ENTIRE NATION PREPARES FOR LABOR AT HOME AND BATTLE IN FRANCE

APRIL–DECEMBER

D. F. HOUSTON   DANIEL WILLARD
GENERAL JOHN PERSHING

On the day that the United States entered the Great War, its army numbered 190,000 men; on the day of the armistice a year and a half later, that army numbered 3,665,000, of whom over 2,000,000 were actually in France fighting or ready to fight. This army cost the United States in direct appropriations over twenty billion dollars, that is over five thousand dollars per soldier. Yet back of this great military preparation there was necessarily an industrial preparation, incalculable in exact figures, but many times more vast. It was this stupendous industrial effort, and this alone, that made the huge American army possible. Every patriotic citizen contributed as he could in service or in money; and the readiness and steadiness of this self-sacrifice amazed the world and profoundly altered its opinion of Americans.

Some outline of what this united effort of the people accomplished is here attempted by Secretary Houston, head of the government's Department of Agriculture; and the special problem of railroad transportation is explained by Mr. Willard, who acted as president of the Railroads' War Board. To give the detailed effort of every "board" would be a matter of many volumes.

BY D. F. HOUSTON [1]

THE first great step toward winning this war was taken when the President of the United States, on April 2nd, in advising Congress to declare the existence of a state of war with Germany, pointed out what war would involve and demand. The striking thing about that historic address was not so much the advice it contained, momentous as that was, but rather the clear perception it revealed of the magnitude of the task before the nation.

[1] Reprinted from "The Proceedings of the Academy of Political Science," Volume 7, Entitled "The Foreign Relations of the United States."

The response of Congress was prompt and adequate. It authorized and directed the President to employ the entire military and naval forces of the Union and pledged to the government all the resources of the nation to bring the conflict to a successful termination. The task of making good this pledge was entered upon and discharged in such manner as to startle many at home and to amaze even foreigners who had become habituated to prodigious operations. I well remember some characteristic remarks of Lord Northcliffe during his visit to Washington. Suddenly stopping and turning to me, he said, "Am I dreaming?" I asserted that he did not look like a dreamer. He continued: "I am told that Congress declared war on the sixth of April, authorized the Secretary of the Treasury to borrow approximately eleven and a half billion dollars, enacted a new tax law designed to raise two and a half billions in addition to ordinary revenues, appropriated or authorized nine billions for the army and navy, over a billion for ships, with a maximum authorization of nearly two billions, six hundred and forty millions for aëroplanes, credits to the Allies of seven billions, a total of actual appropriations and authorizations of twenty-one billions, gave power to commandeer plants, ships and materials, provided for conscription, which England had not fully resorted to and Canada had not then adopted, that there had been registered or enlisted nearly ten and a half million men, that Pershing was in France and naval vessels were in Europe, that the food-production and food-control measures had been passed, and that authority had been given for the control of exports and imports and of priorities." He repeated: "Am I dreaming or is it true?" I replied that unless I was dreaming it was true. He said: "I can't believe it." I told him I could believe it but that I could not comprehend it. It is difficult now to do so. The figures even for particular items are beyond comprehension. Think of them. For ships an authorization of a billion nine hundred millions, nearly double our former federal budget; for aviation, six hundred and forty millions; for torpedo-boat destroyers, three hundred and fifty millions; for army subsistence and regular quartermaster supplies, eight hundred and sixty millions; for clothing and camp and garrison equipment, five hundred and eighty-one millions; for transportation, five hundred and ninety-seven millions; for medicine, one hundred millions; for mobile artillery, one hundred and fifty-eight millions; for ordnance stores and supplies, seven hundred and seventeen millions; for heavy guns, eight hundred and fifty millions; and for ammunition for the same, one billion eight hundred and seven millions.

Clearly Congress for the time being had taken the necessary steps to make good its pledge of placing the resources of the country at the disposal of the government. At the same time, it created or authorized the creation of essential administrative agencies. In respect to administrative agencies important developments had already taken place. Most striking and significant of all was the enactment of the federal reserve law and the creation of the reserve board and banks. This action obviously was taken without suspicion that the world was on the verge of war and that we should soon be involved. It was taken to insure better banking conditions in time of peace, and especially to enable us to weather financial storms. Before the reserve act was passed the nation, as you well know, had no adequate banking system. Its financial arrangements had never been able to withstand strain either in peace or in war. In each of our considerable struggles we had promptly suspended specie payments, with all the attendant disabilities and burdens. But now, after four years of world financial strain such as no financier dreamed it possible for the world to bear—I might say six years, because there was a world-wide financial chill for at least two years before 1914, due to apprehension of war and to the undoubted financial preparations made by the Central Powers—after this long strain and the shock of the last six months, our finances are sound and we are proceeding in orderly fashion. For this reason and because of our obligation to extend liberal credits, it is not extravagant to say that no greater contribution to the winning of this war has been or will be made than through the passage of the Federal Reserve Act in 1913 and the successful establishment of the system well in advance of trouble.

Steps toward preparedness in respect to other highly essential interests were taken much before war was declared. Their significance was not grasped by the public at the time. For the most part they have been overlooked. Pursuant to an Act of Congress of March 3, 1915, two years before the war, the President appointed the National Advisory Committee for Aëronautics, composed of the most eminent students of the subject. In connection with the work of this committee and in part through its labors has been developed our enormous aviation program and expansion. Likewise, during the summer of 1915, the secretary of the navy organized the admirable Naval Consulting Board with Edison as chairman and two representatives elected by each of eleven great engineering and scientific societies. Furthermore, on September 7, 1916, after a long and unfortunate delay caused by unintelligent opposition, the Shipping Act was passed, creating a board with large powers, and appropriating fifty million dollars for the construction, purchase, charter, and operation of merchant vessels suitable for naval auxiliaries in time of war. This was the beginning of the present huge shipbuilding program whose speedy execution is of paramount importance.

But that is not all in the way of early preparedness. On August 29, 1916, the Council of National Defense, consisting of six heads of departments and an advisory commission of seven, nominated by the council and appointed by the President, was created. The council was charged with the duty of mobilizing military and naval resources, studying the location, utilization and coördination of railroads, waterways and highways, increase of domestic production for civil and military purposes, the furnishing of requisite information to manufacturers, and the creation of relations which would render possible the immediate concentration of national resources.

The creation of the Council of National Defense was not the result of sudden inspiration. It was directly suggested by the activities of two very important groups of individuals. In March, 1916, a committee from the five great medical and surgical associations, having an aggregate membership of from 70,000 to 100,000, was formed. It met in Chicago on April 14, 1916, and tendered to the President the services of the medical men of the nation. In March, also, representatives of five engineering organizations with a membership of 35,000 met in New York and formulated a plan to make an inventory of the country's production and manufacturing resources. The thought and purposes of these two bodies were brought to the attention of the President, and their consideration resulted in recommendations for the creation of the Council of National Defense.

Thus, a number of months before war was declared, agencies had been created covering at least in outline many of the essential new activities. Seven of these of peculiar importance had begun to find themselves and to chart their course. I refer to the shipping board, the aviation, the medical, the manufacturing, the transportation, the munitions, and the labor committees. When war came these bodies greatly speeded up their work. Others were created—among them, the Food Administration, the Fuel Administration, the War Trade Council, the War Trade Board, and the War Industries Board.

The last is of unique importance, and yet its work is little understood. Its members are the direct representatives of the government and of the public interest. The tasks of the board are stupendous. It acts as a clearing-house for the needs of the government, determines the most effective ways of meeting them, the best means of increasing production (including the creation of new facilities), the priority of public needs and also of transportation. It considers price factors, the labor aspects of industrial operations, and large purchases of commodities where market values are greatly affected, and makes appropriate recommendations to the secretaries of war and the navy. Judge Lovett is in immediate charge of priorities, Mr. Baruch of raw materials, and Mr. Brookings of finished products. These three constitute a commission for the approval of purchases by the Allies in this country from credits made through the secretary of the treasury. I need only remind you of the items of the appropriations for supplies, ordnance and other things, to impress you with the magnitude of the board's task. Its machinery is not yet perfect but it is working, and I am sure that no step will be omitted to make it as nearly adequate as possible. If a better scheme can be devised, it should be promptly adopted. It is obviously of the highest importance that the resources of the nation, made available by Congress, should be administered with the utmost skill and effectiveness.

No machinery is of great value unless it is properly manned. The right sort of men is the first requisite of any kind of successful enterprise. I believe this requisite has been satisfied and that the nation is mobilizing for this emergency additional men of as high character and fine talent as it possesses. Where so many are involved special mention is invidious, and I cite the names of the following merely as samples: Willard, Gompers, Baruch, Rosenwald, Coffin, Martin, and Godfrey; Hoover, Garfield, Vanderlip, Davison, Vauclain; McCormick, Thos. D. Jones, Lovett, Brookings, and Frayne; Dr. Anna Shaw, Mrs. Phillip Moore, Mrs. Cowles, Mrs. Catt, Miss Wetmore, Mrs. Lamar, Mrs. Funk, Mrs. McCormick, and Miss Nestor; and Drs. Simpson, Crile, Janeway, Flexner, Vaughn, Mayo, and Welch—all fine types of American citizenship, only a few of the hundreds working in their respective spheres in the nation and in the states, having no selfish end to serve, working with an eye single to the public interest and to the winning of this war, giving freely their services in as fine spirit as the nation ever witnessed, revealing the real strength of democracy.

So much, and perhaps more than enough, as to the congressional pledge of resources and the creation of machinery. Let us turn to other matters which I am sure you have in mind. I know you are asking what is being accomplished. What are the results? Obviously, some of them it would be inadvisable to indicate. Others I can only hint at. For the most part they have been detailed to the public through one agency or another from time to time. I shall try to summarize.

The nation has to-day in all branches of its military services under arms and in training over 1,800,000 men, some in France, some on the ocean, and others in camps or at their posts of duty at home. Approximately ten and a half millions of men have been enlisted in the regular army, incorporated in the national guard, or registered under the draft act. Those registered but not yet called out are being classified on the basis of national need. Rapid headway has been made in training subordinate officers, and the gigantic undertaking of providing suitable quarters or camps for the men in training has practically been finished. The nation now has thirty-five army cantonments, sixteen for the National Army, sixteen for the National Guard, two at points of embarkation and one for the quartermaster's training school, all complete in respect to buildings or tents, lighting, sanitary arrangements, and temporary roads. The National Army cantonments were completed within the time set by the General Staff. What this involved can not easily be set forth. It entailed the selection of sites, the planning of buildings, the securing of responsible contractors, the mobilization of labor, the assembling of materials, and the construction of modern hospitals and roads. These camps alone cover 150,000 acres and called for the use of 75,000 carloads of materials, including 500,000,000 feet of lumber. Their cost was approximately one hundred and twenty-eight millions of dollars. The work was begun June 15th and the finishing touches were put on by December 1st. In addition sixteen canvas camps for the National Guard were completed at a cost of approximately forty-eight millions of dollars. Thus local habitations were quickly provided for the new army, superior in respect to ventilation and conveniences to the best practice of Europe.

Five instrumentalities or factors highly necessary for victory, it may be asserted without hesitation, are destroyers, the enemies of the submarine, airplanes, ships, medical service, and food. What of these?

Of the first, the torpedo-boat destroyers, all I may say is that the construction program of the navy contemplates 787 ships of all types at an estimated cost of $1,150,000,000, including additional destroyers costing $350,000,000. The

latter are to be of uniform standard model, large and fast.
Some are to be built within nine months, and all within
eighteen months. This vast and urgent undertaking required
a great extension of building facilities, and, as private capital was unable or unwilling to make the extensions, the government had to do so. When completed these plants belong
to the nation. I may add that these destroyers will require
thousands of men to man them. The men are being trained
and when the vessels are completed the crews will be ready.

The work for the control of the air grows apace. Of the
great aviation training fields, seventeen in number, two are
old, one is rebuilding, seven were practically completed by
September 1st, and seven others will be finished within two
weeks. In addition, there are in operation to-day at leading
universities ten ground schools giving preparatory instruction in flying. Finishing courses are being given to our
students in most of the Allied countries and more than thirty
experienced foreign air veterans have been loaned to us for
duty in Washington and elsewhere. The building program
calls for twenty thousand machines. It will be expedited
by reason of a great and interesting achievement, that of
a standardized engine, something which no European nation
has developed even after three and a half years of war. This
accomplishment is in line with the best American traditions,
and was made with unique speed. What standardization of
the engine and of its parts means in respect to speed and
quantitative production, in repairs and economy of materials,
need not be dwelt upon. It has been estimated that the service
when in full strength will require a full force of 110,000
officers and enlisted men, an army greater than our regular
military force of a few months ago.

All agree that the enemy submarine must be destroyed.
In the meantime shipping sunk by them must be replaced.
England must not be starved. Supplies to all the Allies must
go forward without interruption. Our own troops must be
transported and provided with everything essential for effectiveness and comfort, and domestic transportation of men
and commodities must be maintained and greatly increased.
Furthermore, commodities must be brought here from many

distant places. Therefore we must have ships, more ships, at once. Nothing more urgent! How is this matter proceeding? In the first place, the Shipping Board on August 3rd commandeered 426 vessels either in course of construction for domestic or foreign account or contracted for, with a tonnage of over 3,000,000. Thirty-three of these ships, with a tonnage of 257,000, have been completed and released. German and Austrian ships with a capacity of 750,-000 tons have been taken over for government use. The Fleet Corporation has contracted for 948 vessels with a total tonnage of 5,056,000, of which 375, with a tonnage of one and a third million, are wooden; 58, with a tonnage of 270,000, are composite; and 515, with a capacity of 3,500,-000, are steel. All these ships have an aggregate tonnage of 8,835,000, or nearly a million and a half tons more than the regular merchant marine of the nation in 1916. Contracts for 610,000 tons additional are pending. The total building program calls for over 10,000,000 tons, and it is proposed that a considerable part of it shall be executed by the end of 1918. The nature of this task may be more easily appreciated when it is remembered that the construction in the United States for 1916 did not exceed 400,000 tons and that the average for the five years preceding was 350,000 tons. At present there are one hundred yards building ships, exclusive of twenty building the commandeered vessels, and of these one hundred, seventy are new. The policy of standardization has been pursued and five classes of ships have been adopted.

I have already referred to the preliminary steps toward medical organization. Further action was promptly taken. An inventory was made of the medical resources of the nation, of doctors, nurses, and others who could be called by the surgeon general, and of hospitals and supplies. Courses in modern military medicine and surgery for third and fourth-year students were formulated and adopted by seventy-five of the ninety-five medical schools in January, 1917. It was known that eighty per cent. of the instruments used in this country were made in Germany. It was necessary to develop their production here, and to facilitate this the

first essential step was to introduce standardization, to resort to staple articles. More liberal standards were authorized and the variety of types was greatly reduced. Instead
of scores of kinds of scissors a dozen were agreed upon.
Instead of many sorts of needles, forceps and retractors,
two, three, or four types were adopted. Manufacturers
were given priority of materials and consequently full military orders will be delivered in less than eight months. It
is illuminating that one concern, taking its chances, had
manufactured according to specifications, by the time it was
awarded a contract, enough material to require ten carloads
of lumber for packing. This was the result of the efforts of
seventy-five of the most eminent medical specialists of the
nation, working with the military staff in contact with two
hundred and fifty leading manufacturers.

The peace strength of the medical forces of the army
was 531 and of the navy 480. Now the surgeon general
of the army has in his regular force and in the new enrollment of physicians actually accepting commissions 16,432, a
number sufficient for an army of two and one-third millions,
and a dental force of 3,441, adequate for an army of 3,400,-
000. The navy now has 1,795 medical officers, a number
in excess of present needs. The Red Cross has enrolled
15,000 trained nurses, organized forty-eight base hospitals
with 9,600 doctors, nurses and enlisted men, sixteen hospital
units with smaller staffs to supplement the work of the base
hospitals, is furnishing supplies to thirty-five hospitals of all
sorts in France, and since May has raised over $100,000,000.

What shall I say about the organization of agriculture
for the production of food, clothing and other materials?
It is unnecessary to dwell upon the need of an adequate supply of food for the civilians and soldiers of this nation and
also for those of the nations with whom we are associated.
When we entered the war, this country was and had been
facing an unsatisfactory situation in respect to its supply
of foods and feedstuffs. The production in 1916 of the leading cereals was comparatively low, aggregating 4.8 billions
of bushels as against 6 for 1915, 5 for 1914, and 4.9 for the
five-year average. The wheat crop had been strikingly small,

and it was certain that on account of adverse weather conditions the output for 1917 would be greatly curtailed. The situation was no better in respect to other conspicuously important commodities such as potatoes and meats. The need of action was urgent and the appeal for direction insistent. The nation looked for guidance primarily to the federal department and to the state agencies which it had so liberally supported for many years. It was a matter of great good fortune that the nation had had the foresight, generations before, in another time of national stress, in 1862, to lay soundly the foundations of agriculture. In respect to agencies working for the improvement of rural life the nation was prepared. In point of efficiency, personnel and support, it had establishments excelling those of any other three nations combined, and a great body of alert farmers who were capable of producing two or three times as much per unit of labor and capital as the farmers of Europe.

Steps were quickly taken to speed up production. In a two-day session at St. Louis, the trained agricultural officers of the country conceived and devised a program of legislation and organization, the essential features of which have not been successfully questioned, and the substantial part of which has been enacted into law and set in operation. Initiative was not wanting in any section of the Union. Effective organizations quickly sprang up in all the states, and the services of experts everywhere immediately were made available. The response of the farmers was prompt and energetic. Weather conditions for the spring season were favorable and the results are that crop yields have been large and that the nation is able not only to feed itself but in considerable measure to supply the needs of those with whom we are coöperating.

It is no time for any class to hug to its bosom the delusion that it possesses a monopoly of patriotism. Human nature is pretty evenly distributed, and no little selfishness manifests itself in every direction. Unfortunately there are self-seekers in every group. I have heard manufacturers solemnly assert that, if the government wished them to speed up their operations, to extend their plants, or to take additional trouble in any direction, it must guarantee to them an abnormally large profit in addition to the requisite allowance for amortization. One of them recently suggested to me that he was getting weary of the burdens he had assumed and that, if the government wished him to continue or to undertake new tasks, it would have to induce him to do so by permitting him greatly to increase his profits. What would he or others say of a soldier, of a man drafted into the army, who protested that for so much he would go to the seaboard, but, if the government wished him to go abroad, it must stimulate him with a twenty-five-per cent. increase in his pay, or, if he went to the front trenches, with fifty per cent.? In the words of the President:

"Patriotism has nothing to do with profits in a case like this. Patriotism and profits ought never in the present circumstances to be mentioned together. It is perfectly proper to discuss profits as a matter of business . . . but it would be absurd to discuss them as a motive for helping to serve and save our country. In these days of our supreme trial, when we are sending hundreds of thousands of our young men across the seas to serve a great cause, no true man who stays behind to work for them and sustain them by his labor will ask himself what he is personally going to make out of that labor. No true patriot will permit himself to take toll of their heroism in money or seek to grow rich by the shedding of their blood."

BY DANIEL WILLARD

The voluntary act of the 693 railroads of this country in merging their competitive activities for the period of the war and uniting in one continental system has not only made the transportation problem presented by the war less cumbersome to handle, but surer of satisfactory solution.

In addition to welding into one loyal army each and every one of the 1,750,000 persons employed by the railroads, the coördination of the nation's carriers has made possible the most intensive use of every locomotive, every freight car, every mile of track, and every piece of railroad equipment in the country. It has also facilitated the securing of invaluable coöperation from the shippers and the general public.

Skilled and experienced railroad men have been sent to every cantonment to assist the constructing Quartermaster there in the movement of all supplies necessary to the erection and maintenance of these military cities. A trained executive has also been stationed in the Washington Headquarters of the Supervising Constructing Quartermaster, so that every car needed in the transportation of Government supplies might be made available when needed. As a result of these coöperative activities, the movement of thousands of carloads of lumber and other supplies has been accomplished practically without a hitch.

In addition, at the request of the Government, plans have been perfected whereby 1,000,000 men will be moved from nearly 5,000 different points to the thirty-two training camps for the National Army and National Guard by October 20th.

Among some of the things accomplished by the board in the first four months of its existence have been the organizing of special equipment for hospital and troop train service, the standardization of settlements between the Government and the railroads, eliminating a large volume of correspondence and red tape, and the creation of a special committee on express transportation, to coördinate the work of the companies with the general problem of transportation.

Car shortage has been reduced 70 per cent. On April 30th the so-called car shortage amounted to 148,627; on June 30th these figures had been cut to 77,144; on August 1st the excess of unfilled car requisitions over idle cars amounted to only 33,776.

In May freight transportation service rendered by about 75 per cent. of Class 1 roads—earnings of $1,000,000 or more—was 16.1 per cent. in excess of the service rendered in 1916. In that year, which was one of unusual activity, the freight service rendered by the carriers was 24 per cent. in excess of that rendered in 1915.

Approximately 20,000,000 miles of train service a year has been saved by the elimination of all passenger trains not essential to the most pressing needs of the country. Freight congestion at many important points has been averted by promptly moving empty cars from one railroad to another, irrespective of ownership. Through the pooling of lake coal and lake ore a saving of 52,000 cars in moving these commodities alone has been achieved. A further saving of 133,-000 cars has been made possible by the pooling of tidewater coal.

By regulating the movement of grain for export, the number of cars ordinarily required for this service has been reduced, despite an abnormal export increase this year, 75,-682,028 bushels of wheat, corn, barley, and oats being shipped to the Allies from May 1st to July 14th. Commercial bodies and individual shippers in all parts of the country are giving hearty coöperation to the railroads' campaign to make one car do the work of two.

BY GENERAL JOHN PERSHING

Official Report of September 1, 1919, by the Commander-in-Chief of the American Expeditionary Force

Period of Organization

I assumed the duties of this office on May 26, 1917, and, accompanied by a small staff, departed for Europe on board the S.S. *Baltic,* May 28th. We arrived at London on June 9th and, after spending some days in consultation with the British authorities, reached Paris on June 13th.

Following the rather earnest appeals of the Allies for American troops, it was decided to send to France, at once, one complete division and nine newly organized regiments of Engineers. The division was formed of regular regiments, necessary transfers of officers and men were made, and recruits were assigned to increase these units to the required strength.

The offer by the Navy Department of one regiment of Marines to be reorganized as Infantry was accepted by the Secretary of War, and it became temporarily a part of the First Division.

Prior to our entrance into the war, the regiments of our small army were very much scattered, and we had no organized units, even approximating a division, that could be sent overseas prepared to take the field. To meet the new conditions of warfare an entirely new organization was adopted in which our Infantry divisions were to consist of 4 regiments of Infantry of about treble their original size, 3 regiments of Artillery, 14 machine-gun companies, 1 Engineer regiment, 1 Signal battalion, 1 troop of Cavalry, and other auxiliary units, making a total strength of about 28,000 men.

The relatively low strength of the German forces on the Western front led the Allies with much confidence to attempt a decision on this front; but the losses were very heavy and the effort signally failed. The failure caused a serious reaction especially on French morale, both in the army and throughout the country, and attempts to carry out extensive or combined operations were indefinitely suspended.

In the five months ending June 30th, German submarines had accomplished the destruction of more than three and one-quarter million tons of Allied shipping. During three years Germany had seen practically all her offensives except Verdun crowned with success. Her battle lines were held on foreign soil and she had withstood every Allied attack since the Marne. The German general staff could now foresee the complete elimination of Russia, the possibility of defeating Italy before the end of the year and, finally, the campaign of 1918 against the French and British on the Western front which might terminate the war.

It can not be said that German hopes of final victory were extravagant, either as viewed at that time or as viewed in the light of history. Financial problems of the Allies were difficult, supplies were becoming exhausted and their armies had suffered tremendous losses. Discouragement existed not only among the civil population but throughout the armies as well. Such was the Allied morale that, although their superiority on the Western front during the last half of 1916 and during 1917 amounted to 20 per cent., only local attacks could be undertaken and their effect proved wholly insufficient against the German defense. Allied resources in man power at home were low and there was little prospect of materially increasing their armed strength, even in the face of the probability of having practically the whole military strength of the Central Powers against them in the spring of 1918.

This was the state of affairs that existed when we entered the war. While our action gave the Allies much encouragement, yet this was temporary, and a review of conditions made it apparent that America must make a supreme material effort as soon as possible. After duly considering the tonnage possibilities I cabled the following to Washington on July 6, 1917: "Plans should contemplate sending over at least 1,000,000 men by next May."

Organization Projects

A general organization project, covering as far as possible the personnel of all combat, staff, and administrative units, was forwarded to Washington on July 11th. This was prepared by the Operations Section of my staff and adopted in joint conference with the War Department Committee then in France. It embodied my conclusions on the military organization and effort required of America after a careful study of French and British experience. In forwarding this project I stated: "It is evident that a force of about 1,000,000 is the smallest unit which in modern war will be a complete, well-balanced, and independent fighting organization. However, it must be equally clear that the adoption of this size force as a basis of study should not be construed as representing the maximum force which should be sent to or which will be needed in France. It is taken as the force which may be expected to reach France in time for an offensive in 1918, and as a unit and basis of organization. Plans for the future should be based, especially in reference to the manufacture of artillery, aviation, and other material, on three times this force, i.e., at least 3,000,000 men."

The original project for organized combat units remained our guide until the end.

While this general organization project provided certain Services of Supply troops, which were an integral part of the larger combat units, it did not include the great body of troops and services required to maintain an army over-seas. To disembark 2,000,000 men, move them to their training areas, shelter them, handle and store the quantities of supplies and equipment they required called for an extraordinary and immediate effort in construction. To provide the organization for this purpose, a project for engineer services of the rear, including railways, was cabled to Washington August 5, 1917, followed on September 18, 1917, by a complete service of the rear project, which listed item by item the troops considered necessary for the Services of Supply.

American Front and Line of Communications

Before developing plans for a line of communications it was necessary to decide upon the probable sector of the front for the eventual employment of a distinctive American force. Our mission was offensive and it was essential to make plans for striking the enemy where a definite military decision could be gained. While the Allied armies had endeavored to maintain the offensive, the British, in order to guard the Channel ports, were committed to operations in Flanders and the French to the portion of the front protecting Paris. Both lacked troops to operate elsewhere on a large scale.

To the east the great fortified district east of Verdun and around Metz menaced central France, protected the most exposed portion of the German line of communications, that between Metz and Sedan, and covered the Briey iron region, from which the enemy obtained the greater part of the iron required for munitions and material. The coal fields east of Metz were also covered by these same defenses. A deep advance east of Metz, or the capture of the Briey region, by threatening the invasion of rich German territory in the Moselle Valley and the Saar Basin, thus curtailing her supply of coal or iron, would have a decisive effect in forcing a withdrawal of German troops from northern France. The military and economic situation of the enemy, therefore, indicated Lorraine as the field promising the most fruitful results for the employment of our armies.

The complexity of trench life had enormously increased the tonnage of supplies required by troops. Not only was it a question of providing food but enormous quantities of munitions and material were needed. Upon the railroads of France fell the burden of meeting the heavy demands of the three and one-half million Allied combatants then engaged.

The British were crowding the Channel ports and the French were exploiting the manufacturing center of Paris, so that the railroads of northern France were already much overtaxed. Even though the Channel ports might be used to a limited extent for shipments through England, the railroads leading eastward would have to cross British and French zones of operation, thus making the introduction of a line of communications based on ports and railways in that region quite impracticable. If the American Army was to have an independent and flexible system it could not use the lines behind the British-Belgium front nor those in rear of the French front covering Paris.

The problem confronting the American Expeditionary Forces was then to superimpose its rail communications on those of France where there would be the least possible disturbance to the arteries of supply of the two great Allied armies already in the field. This would require the utmost use of those lines of the existing French railroad system that could bear an added burden. Double-track railroad lines from the ports of the Loire and the Gironde Rivers unite at Bourges, running thence via Nevers, Dijon, and Neufchâteau, with lines radiating therefrom toward the right wing of the Allied front. It was estimated that these with the collateral lines available, after considerable improvement, could handle an additional 50,000 tons per day, required for an army of 2,000,000 men. The lines selected, therefore, were those leading from the comparatively unused south-Atlantic ports of France to the northeast where it was believed the American Armies could be employed to the best advantage.

In the location of our main depots of supply, while it was important that they should be easily accessible, yet they must also be at a safe distance, as we were to meet an aggressive enemy capable of taking the offensive in any one of several directions. The area embracing Tours, Orleans, Montargis, Nevers, and Chateauroux was chosen, as it was centrally located with regard to all points on the arc of the Western front.

The ports of St. Nazaire, La Pallice, and Bassens were designated for permanent use, while Nantes, Bordeaux, and Pauillac were for emergency use. Several smaller ports, such as St. Malo, Sables-d'Olonne, and Bayonne, were available chiefly for the importation of coal from England. From time to time, certain trans-Atlantic ships were sent to Le Havre and Cherbourg. In anticipation of a large increase in the amount of tonnage that might be required later, arrangements were made during the German offensive of 1918 to utilize the ports of Marseilles and Toulon as well as other smaller ports on the Mediterranean.

For all practical purposes the American Expeditionary Forces were based on the American Continent. Three thousand miles of ocean to cross with the growing submarine menace confronting us, the quantity of ship tonnage that would be available then unknown and a line of communications by land 400 miles long from French ports to our probable front presented difficulties that seemed almost insurmountable as compared with those of our Allies.

Training

Soon after our arrival in Europe careful study was made of the methods followed by our Allies in training combat troops. Both the French and British maintained continuously a great system of schools and training centers, which provided for both theoretical and practical instruction of inexperienced officers and noncommissioned officers. These centers were required not only to train new troops, but to prepare officers and soldiers for advancement by giving them a short course in the duties of their new grades. These school systems made it possible to spread rapidly a knowledge of the latest methods developed by experience and at the same time counteract false notions.

A similar scheme was adopted in August, 1917, for our Armies in which the importance of teaching throughout our forces a sound fighting doctrine of our own was emphasized. It provided for troop training in all units up to include divisions. Corps centers of instruction for non-commissioned officers and unit commanders of all arms were established. These centers also provided special training for the instructors needed at corps schools. Base training centers for replacement troops and special classes of soldiers, such as cooks and mechanics, were designated. The army and corps schools were retained under the direct supervision of the Training Section, General Staff. The schools mentioned graduated 21,330 noncommissioned officers and 13,916 officers.

Particular care was taken to search the ranks for the most promising soldiers, in order to develop leaders for the command of platoons and companies. There were graduated from these candidate schools in France 10,976 soldiers.

Every advantage was taken of the experience of our Allies in training officers. It was early recommended to the War Department that French and British officers be asked for to assist in the instruction of troops in the United States. Pending the organization and development of our own schools, a large number of our officers were sent to centers of instruction of the Allied armies.

The long period of trench warfare had so impressed itself upon the French and British that they had almost entirely dispensed with training for open warfare. It was to avoid this result in our Army and to encourage the offensive spirit that the following was published in October, 1917:

"(a) The above methods to be employed must remain or become distinctly our own.

"(b) All instruction must contemplate the assumption of a vigorous offensive. This purpose will be emphasized in every phase of training until it becomes a settled habit of thought.

"(c) The general principles governing combat remain unchanged in their essence. This war has developed special features which involve special phases of training, but the fundamental ideas enunciated in our Drill Regulations, Small Arms Firing Manual, Field Service Regulations, and other service manuals remain the guide for both officers and soldiers and constitute the standard by which their efficiency is to be measured, except as modified in detail by instructions from these headquarters.

"(*d*) The rifle and the bayonet are the principal weapons of the infantry soldier. *He will be trained to a high degree of skill as a marksman, both on the target range and in field firing. An aggressive spirit must be developed until the soldier feels himself, as a bayonet fighter, invincible in battle.*

"(*e*) All officers and soldiers should realize that at no time in our history has discipline been so important; therefore, discipline of the highest order must be exacted at all times. The standards for the American Army will be those of West Point. The rigid attention, upright bearing, attention to detail, uncomplaining obedience to instructions required of the cadet will be required of every officer and soldier of our armies in France."

The system of training profoundly influenced the combat efficiency of our troops by its determined insistence upon an offensive doctrine and upon training in warfare of movement.

Summer of 1917 to Spring of 1918

In order to hinder the enemy's conquest of Russia and, if possible, prevent a German attack on Italy, or in the near east, the Allies sought to maintain the offensive on the Western front as far as their diminished strength and morale would permit. On June 7, 1917, the British took Messines, while a succession of operations known as the Third Battle of Ypres began on July 31st and terminated with the capture of the Passchendaele Ridge, November 6th-10th. The British attack at Cambrai is of special interest, since it was here that American troops (Eleventh Engineers) first participated in active fighting.

The French successfully attacked on a limited front near Verdun, capturing *Mort Homme* on August 20th and advancing their lines to La Forge Brook. In another offensive, begun on October 23rd, they gained considerable ground on *Chemin des Dames* Ridge. These French attacks were characterized by most careful preparation to insure success in order to improve the morale of their troops.

Notwithstanding these Allied attacks on the Western front, the immense gains by the German armies in the east, culminating at Riga on September 3rd, precipitated the collapse of Russia. The following month, the Austrians with German assistance surprised the Italians and broke through the lines at Caporetto, driving the Italian armies back to the Piave River, inflicting a loss of 300,000 men, 600,000 rifles, 3,000 guns, and enormous stores. This serious crisis compelled the withdrawal of 10 French and British divisions from the Western front to Italy. The German situation on all other theaters was so favorable that as early as November they began the movement of divisions toward the Western front.

A review of the situation showed that with Russia out of the war the Central Powers would be able to release a large number of divisions for service elsewhere, and that during the spring and summer of 1918, without interfering with the *status quo* at Salonika, they could concentrate on the Western front a force much stronger than that of the Allies. In view of this, it was represented to the War Department in December as of the utmost importance that the Allied preparations be expedited.

On December 31, 1917, there were 176,665 American troops in France and but one division had appeared on the front. Disappointment at the delay of the American effort soon began to develop. French and British authorities suggested the more rapid entry of our troops into the line and urged the amalgamation of our troops with their own, even insisting upon the curtailment of training to conform to the strict minimum of trench requirements they considered necessary.

My conclusion was that, although the morale of the German people and of the armies was better than it had been for two years, only an untoward combination of circumstances could give the enemy a decisive victory before American support as recommended could be made effective, provided the Allies secured unity of action. However, a situation might arise which would necessitate the temporary use of all American troops in the units of our Allies for the defensive, but nothing in the situation justified the relinquishment of our firm purpose to form our own Army under our own flag.

While the Germans were practicing for open warfare and concentrating their most aggressive personnel in shock divisions, *the training of the Allies was still limited to trench warfare. As our troops were being trained for open warfare, there was every reason why we could not allow them to be scattered among our Allies,* even by divisions, much less as replacements, except by pressure of sheer necessity. Any sort of permanent amalgamation would irrevocably commit America's fortunes to the hands of the Allies. Moreover, it was obvious that the lack of homogeneity would render these mixed divisions difficult to maneuver and almost certain to break up under stress of defeat, with the consequent mutual recrimination. Again, there was no doubt that the realization by the German people that independent American divisions, corps, or armies were in the field with determined purpose would be a severe blow to German morale and prestige.

It was also certain that an early appearance of the larger American units on the front would be most beneficial to the morale of the Allies themselves. Accordingly, the First Division, on January 19, 1918, took over a sector north of Toul; the Twenty-sixth Division went to the Soissons front early in February; the Forty-second Division entered the line near Luneville, February 21st, and the Second Division near Verdun, March 18th. Meanwhile, the First Army Corps Headquarters, Maj. Gen. Hunter Liggett, commanding, was organized at Neufchateau on January 20th, and the plan to create an independent American sector on the Lorraine front was taking shape.

This was the situation when the great German offensive was launched in 1918.